ART ONE

NO SCORE, GODAI!

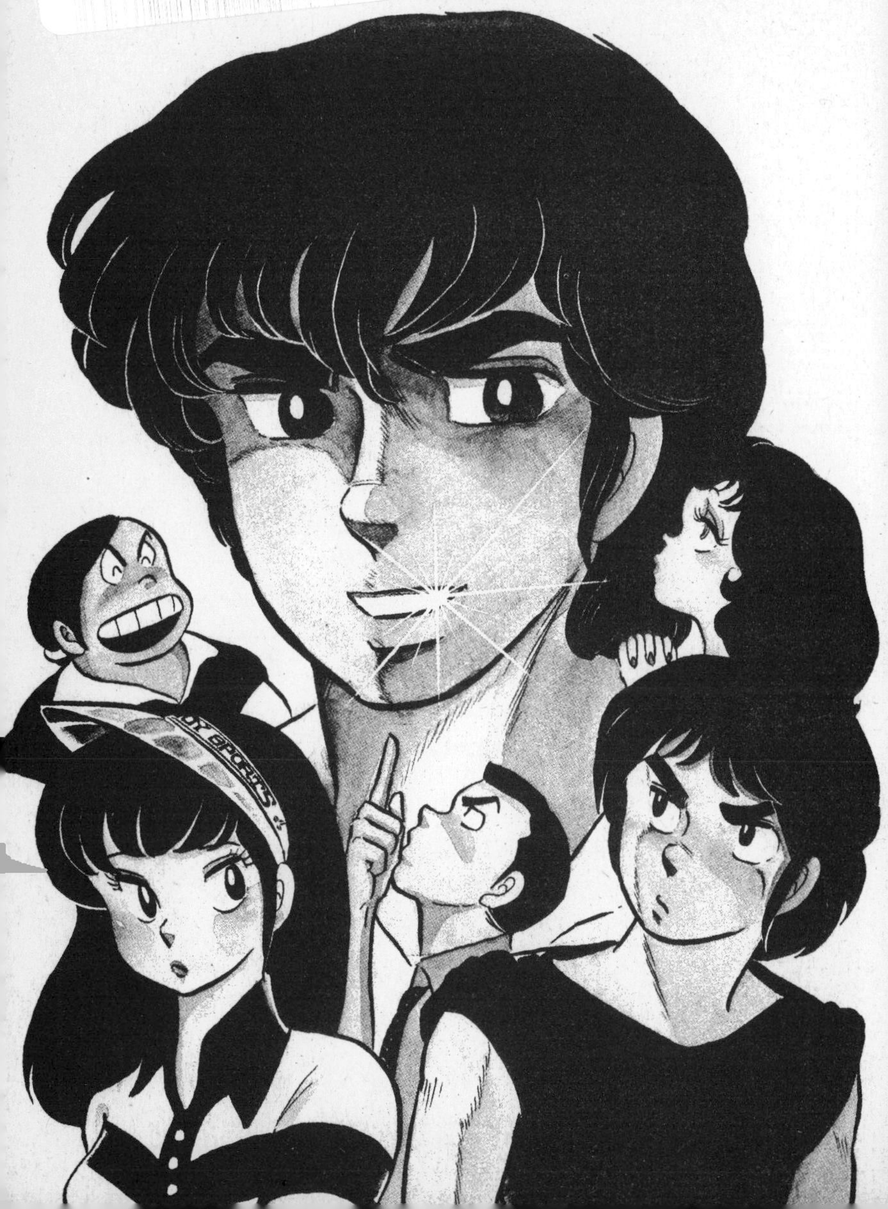

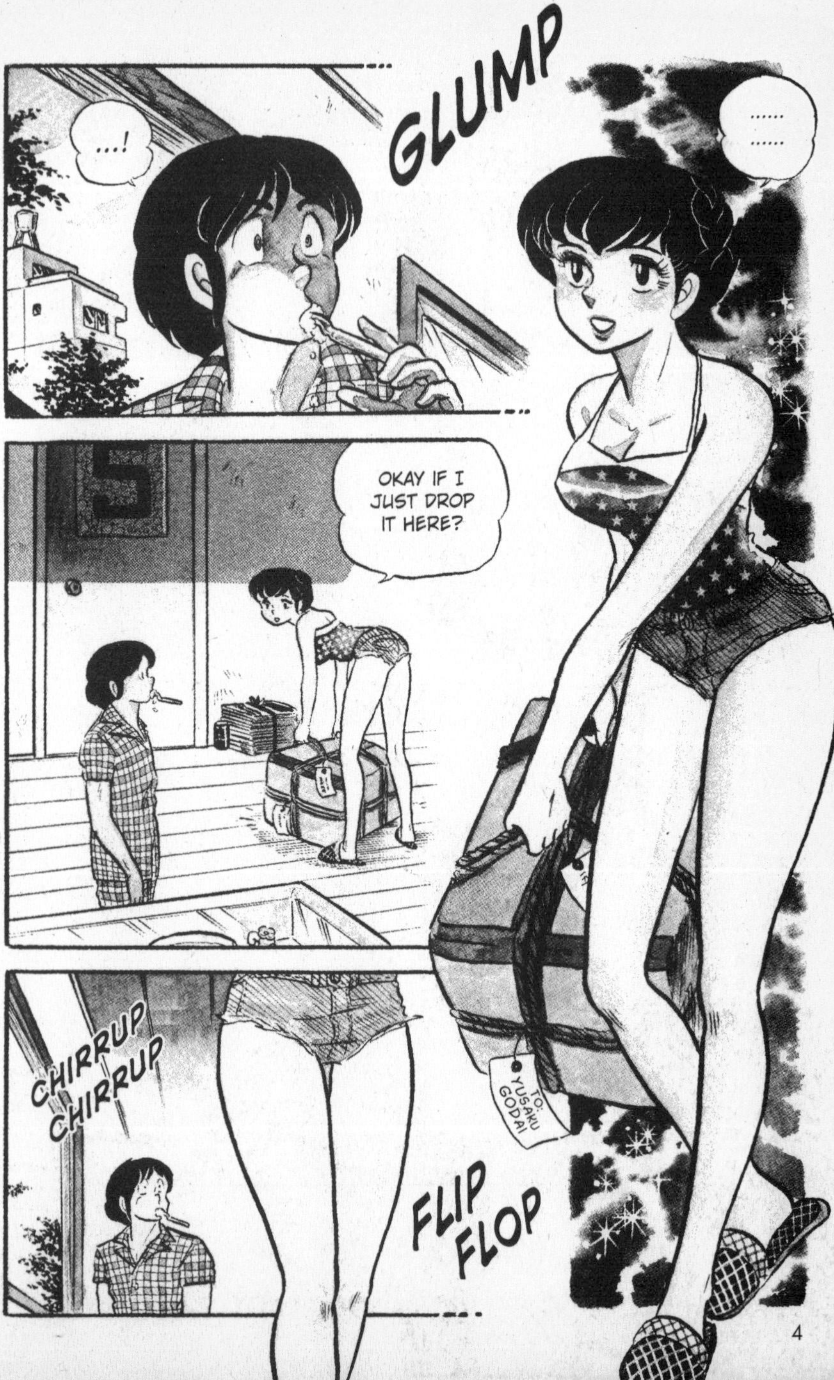
GLUMP
……
……
TO: YUSAKU GODAI
FLIP FLOP
...!
OKAY IF I JUST DROP IT HERE?
CHIRRUP CHIRRUP

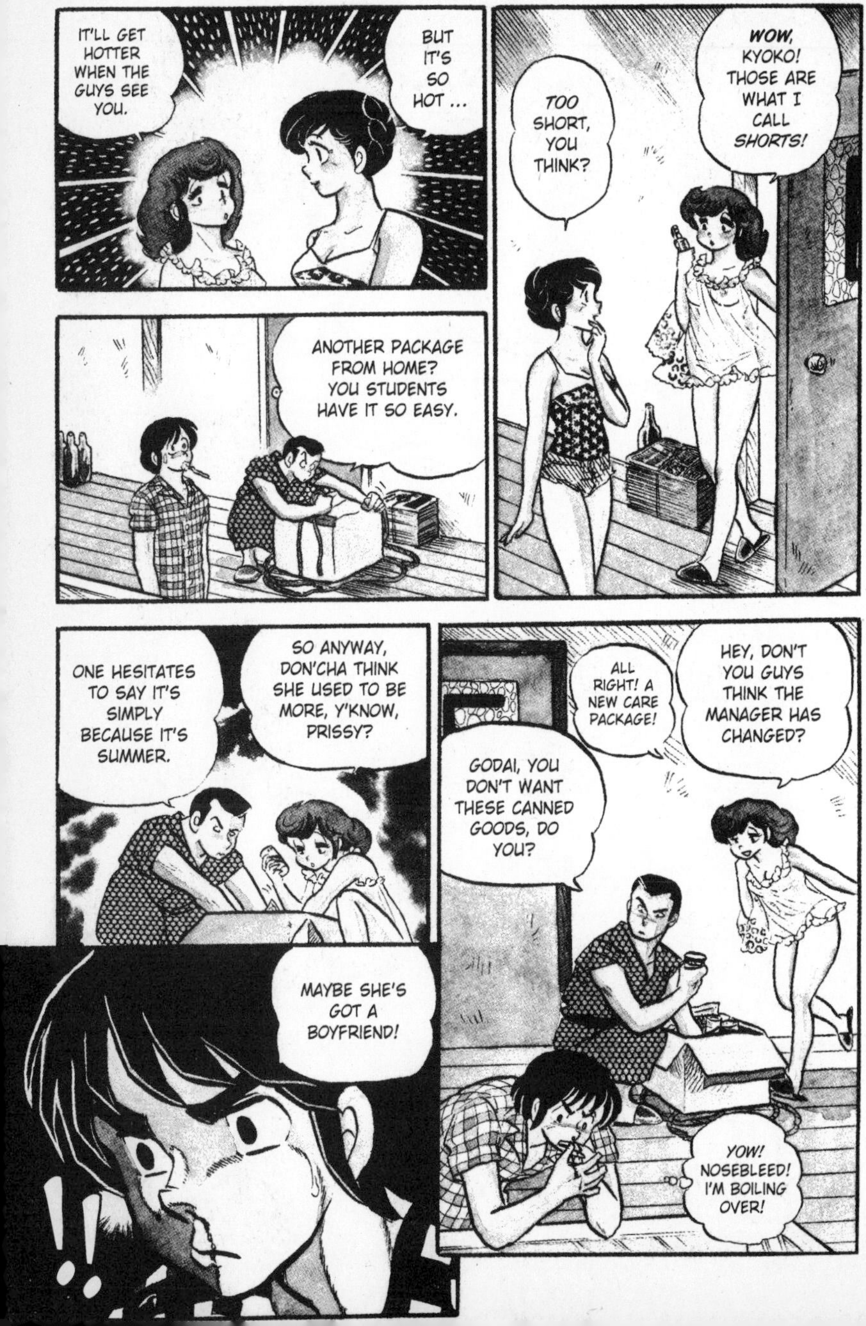
WOW, KYOKO! THOSE ARE WHAT I CALL SHORTS!
TOO SHORT, YOU THINK?
BUT IT'S SO HOT ...
IT'LL GET HOTTER WHEN THE GUYS SEE YOU.
ANOTHER PACKAGE FROM HOME? YOU STUDENTS HAVE IT SO EASY.
HEY, DON'T YOU GUYS THINK THE MANAGER HAS CHANGED?
ALL RIGHT! A NEW CARE PACKAGE!
GODAI, YOU DON'T WANT THESE CANNED GOODS, DO YOU?
YOW! NOSEBLEED! I'M BOILING OVER!
SO ANYWAY, DON'CHA THINK SHE USED TO BE MORE, Y'KNOW, PRISSY?
ONE HESITATES TO SAY IT'S SIMPLY BECAUSE IT'S SUMMER.
MAYBE SHE'S GOT A BOYFRIEND!
!!

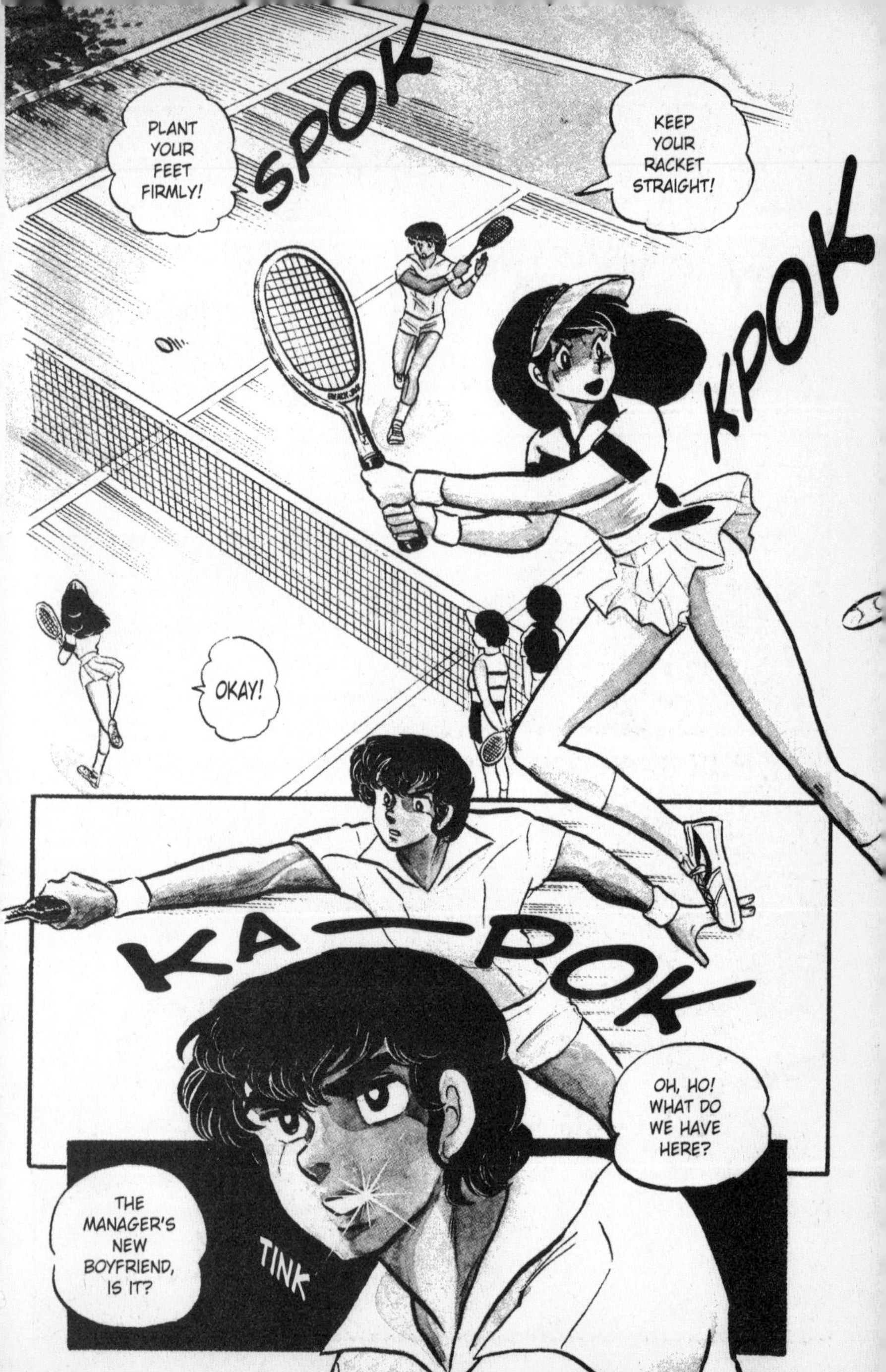
KPOK
KEEP YOUR RACKET STRAIGHT!
SPOK
PLANT YOUR FEET FIRMLY!
OKAY!
KA—POK
OH, HO! WHAT DO WE HAVE HERE?
THE MANAGER'S NEW BOYFRIEND, IS IT?
TINK

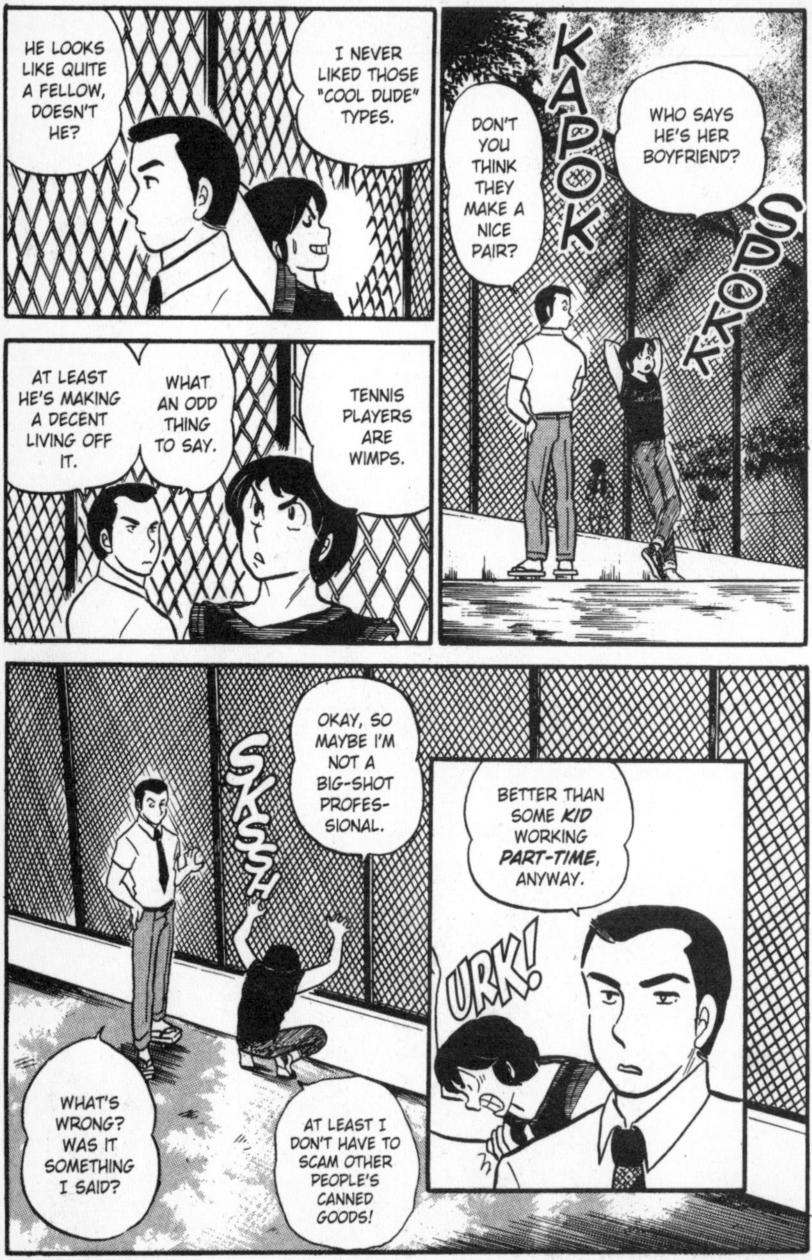
WHO SAYS HE'S HER BOYFRIEND?
KAPOK
DON'T YOU THINK THEY MAKE A NICE PAIR?
SPOKK
I NEVER LIKED THOSE "COOL DUDE" TYPES.
HE LOOKS LIKE QUITE A FELLOW, DOESN'T HE?
TENNIS PLAYERS ARE WIMPS.
WHAT AN ODD THING TO SAY.
AT LEAST HE'S MAKING A DECENT LIVING OFF IT.
BETTER THAN SOME *KID* WORKING ***PART-TIME***, ANYWAY.
URK!
OKAY, SO MAYBE I'M NOT A BIG-SHOT PROFES-SIONAL.
SKSSH
AT LEAST I DON'T HAVE TO SCAM OTHER PEOPLE'S CANNED GOODS!
WHAT'S WRONG? WAS IT SOMETHING I SAID?

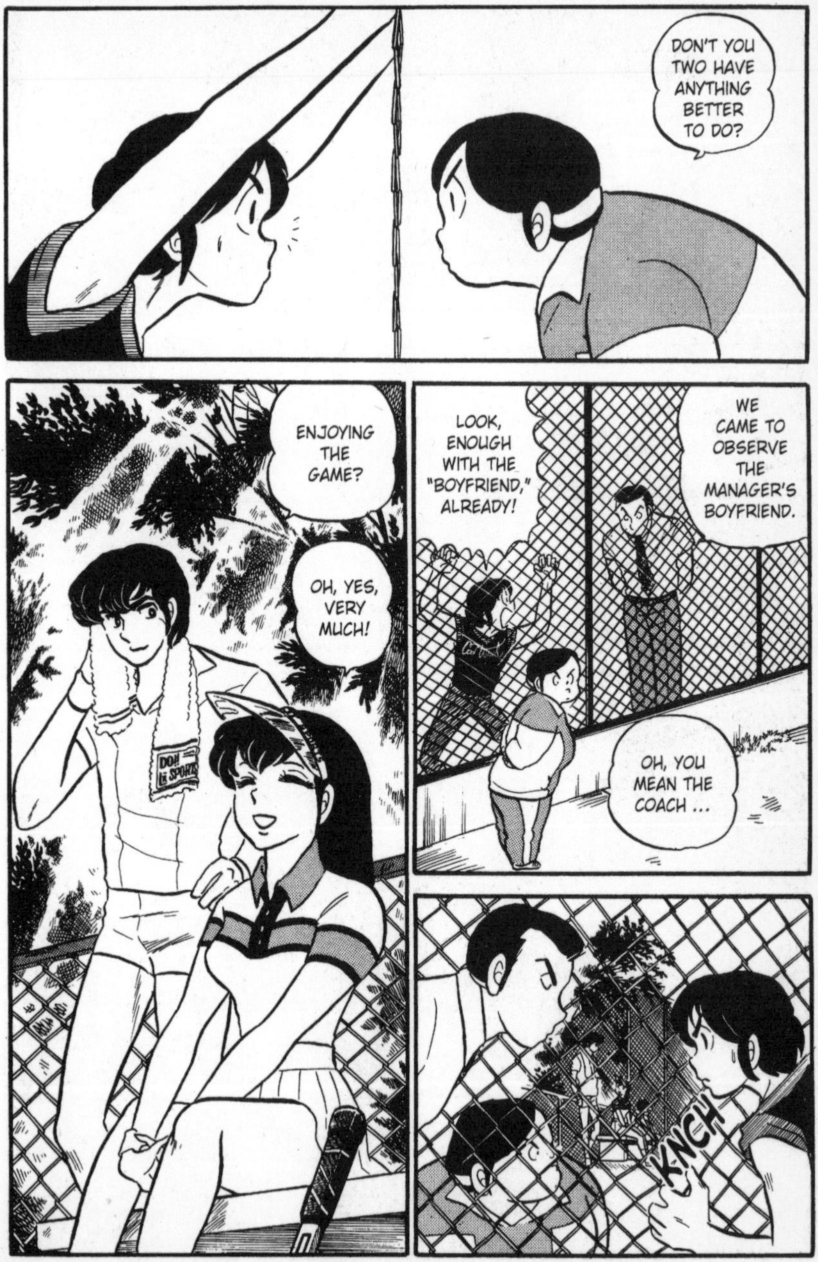
DON'T YOU TWO HAVE ANYTHING BETTER TO DO?
WE CAME TO OBSERVE THE MANAGER'S BOYFRIEND.
LOOK, ENOUGH WITH THE "BOYFRIEND," ALREADY!
OH, YOU MEAN THE COACH ...
K-NCH
ENJOYING THE GAME?
OH, YES, VERY MUCH!

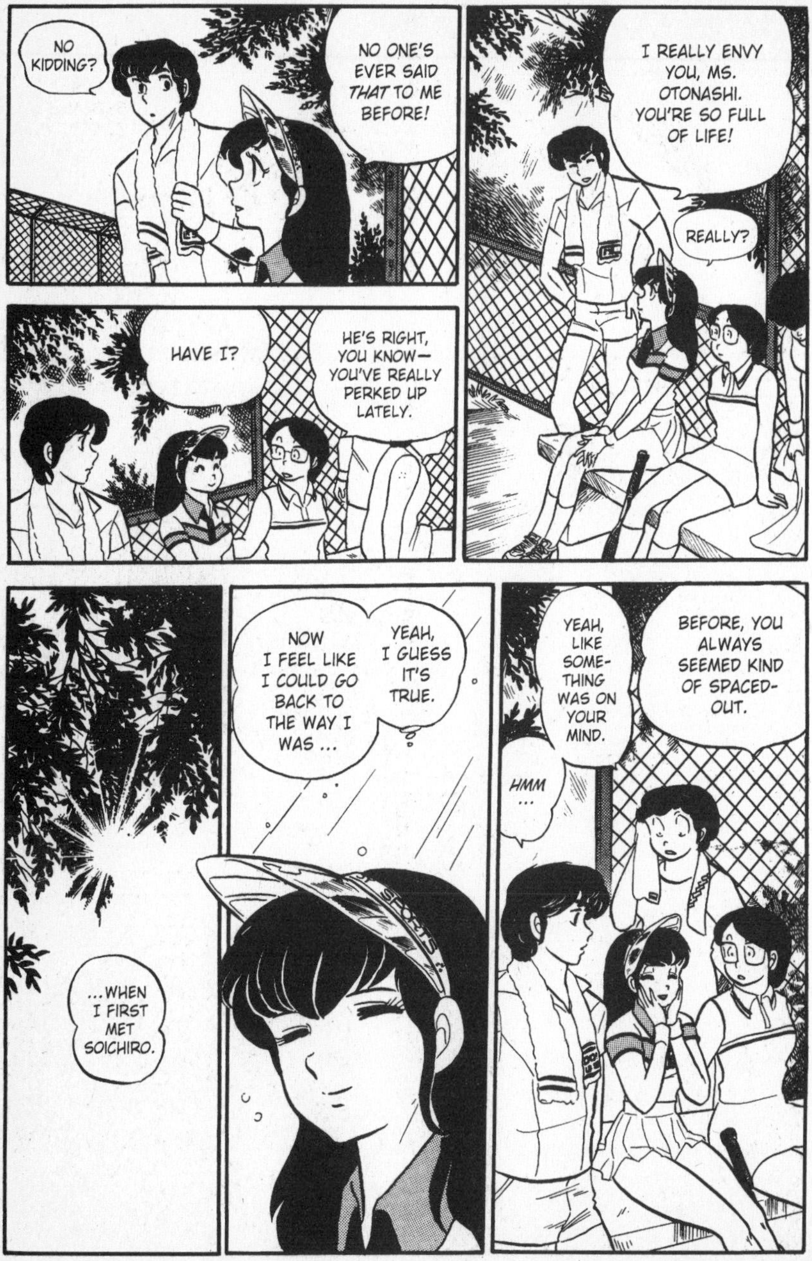
I REALLY ENVY YOU, MS. OTONASHI. YOU'RE SO FULL OF LIFE!
REALLY?
NO ONE'S EVER SAID *THAT* TO ME BEFORE!
NO KIDDING?
HE'S RIGHT, YOU KNOW— YOU'VE REALLY PERKED UP LATELY.
HAVE I?
BEFORE, YOU ALWAYS SEEMED KIND OF SPACED-OUT.
YEAH, LIKE SOME-THING WAS ON YOUR MIND.
HMM ...
YEAH, I GUESS IT'S TRUE.
NOW I FEEL LIKE I COULD GO BACK TO THE WAY I WAS ...
...WHEN I FIRST MET SOICHIRO.

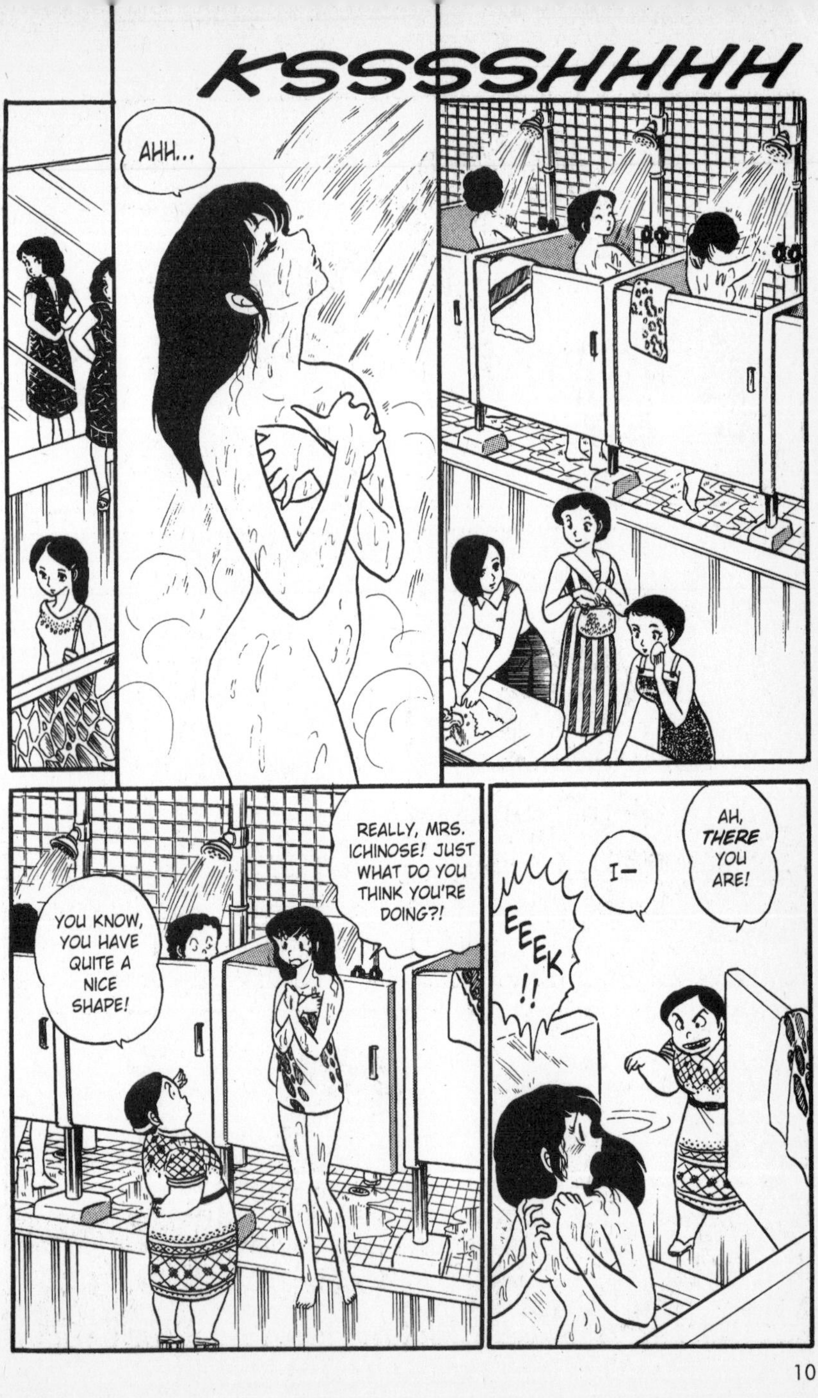
KSSSSHHHH
AHH...
AH, THERE YOU ARE!
I—
EEEK!!
REALLY, MRS. ICHINOSE! JUST WHAT DO YOU THINK YOU'RE DOING?!
YOU KNOW, YOU HAVE QUITE A NICE SHAPE!

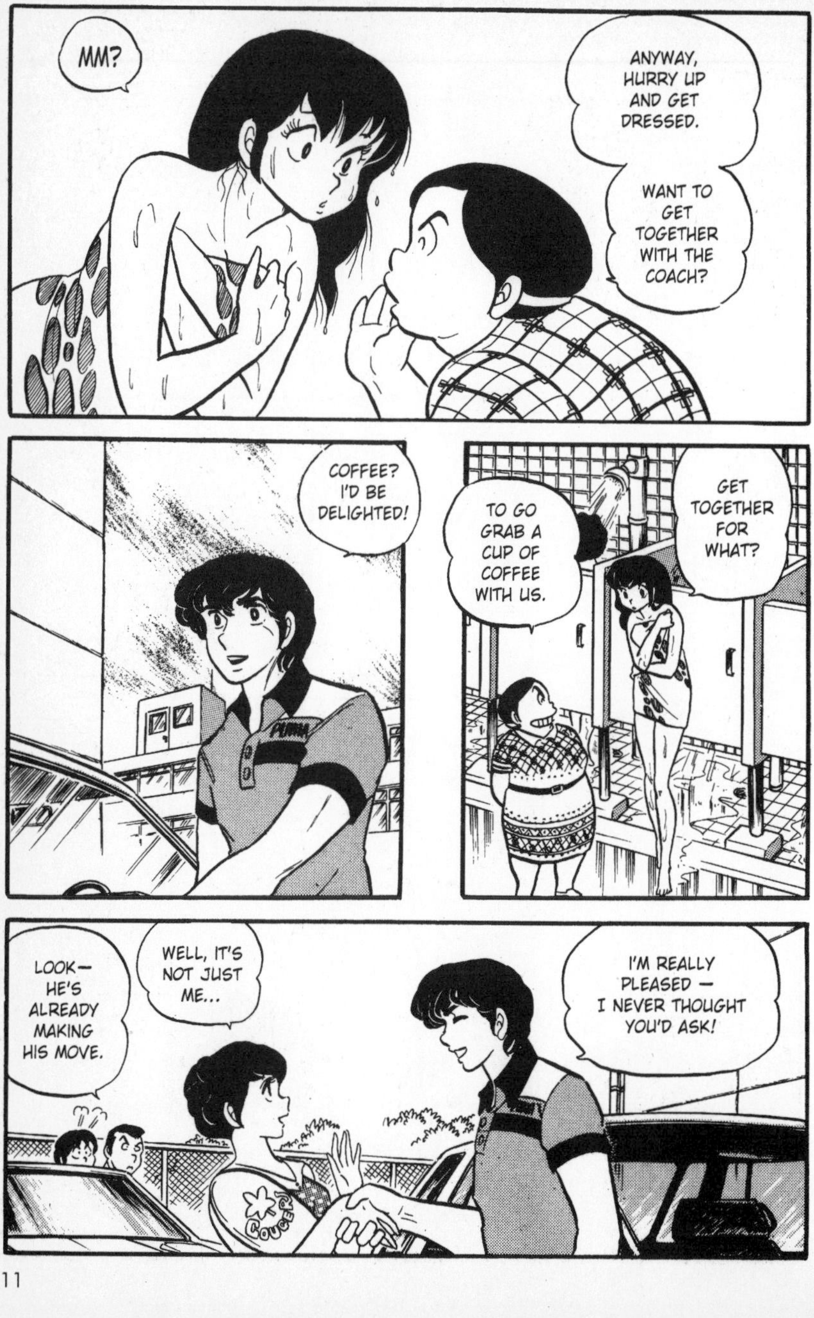
ANYWAY, HURRY UP AND GET DRESSED.
WANT TO GET TOGETHER WITH THE COACH?
MM?
GET TOGETHER FOR WHAT?
TO GO GRAB A CUP OF COFFEE WITH US.
COFFEE? I'D BE DELIGHTED!
I'M REALLY PLEASED — I NEVER THOUGHT YOU'D ASK!
WELL, IT'S NOT JUST ME...
LOOK— HE'S ALREADY MAKING HIS MOVE.

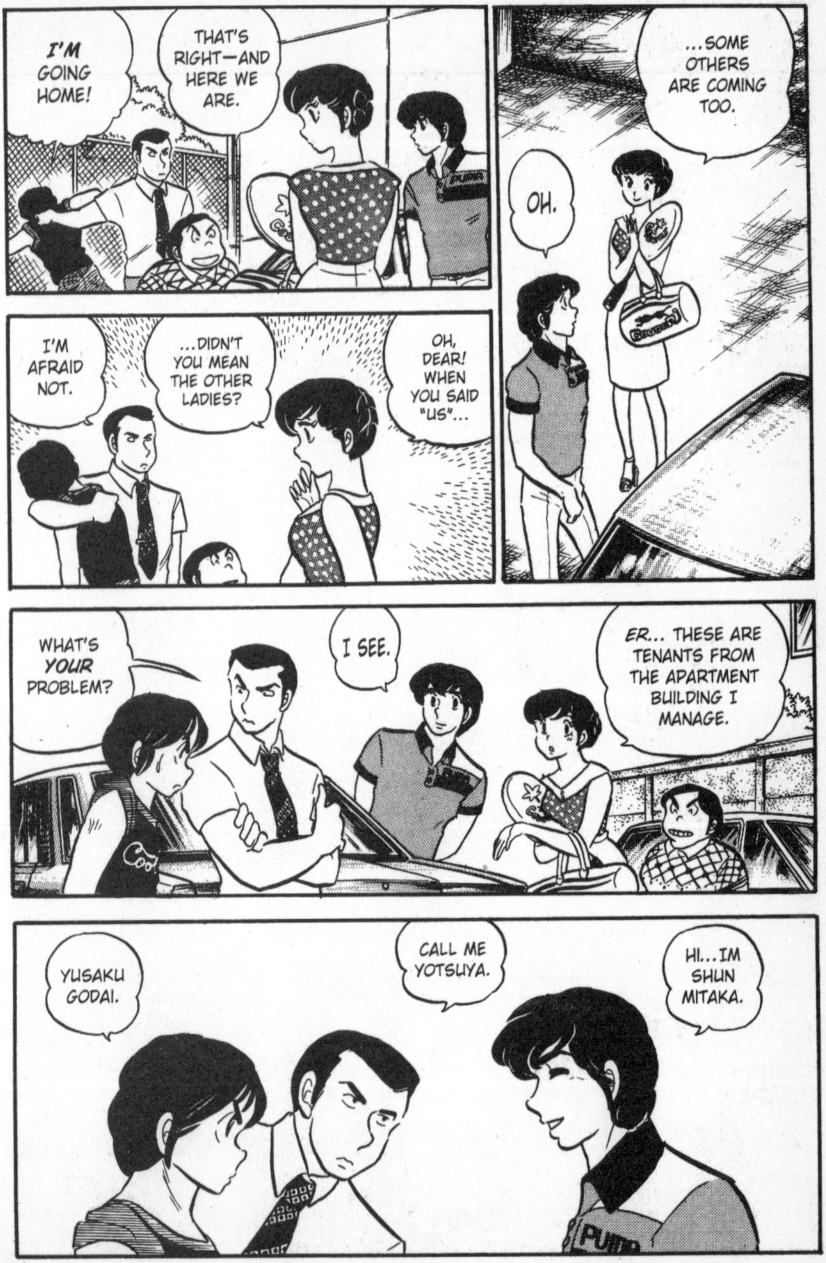
...SOME OTHERS ARE COMING TOO.
OH.
THAT'S RIGHT—AND HERE WE ARE.
I'M GOING HOME!
OH, DEAR! WHEN YOU SAID "US"...
...DIDN'T YOU MEAN THE OTHER LADIES?
I'M AFRAID NOT.
ER... THESE ARE TENANTS FROM THE APARTMENT BUILDING I MANAGE.
I SEE.
WHAT'S *YOUR* PROBLEM?
HI...IM SHUN MITAKA.
CALL ME YOTSUYA.
YUSAKU GODAI.

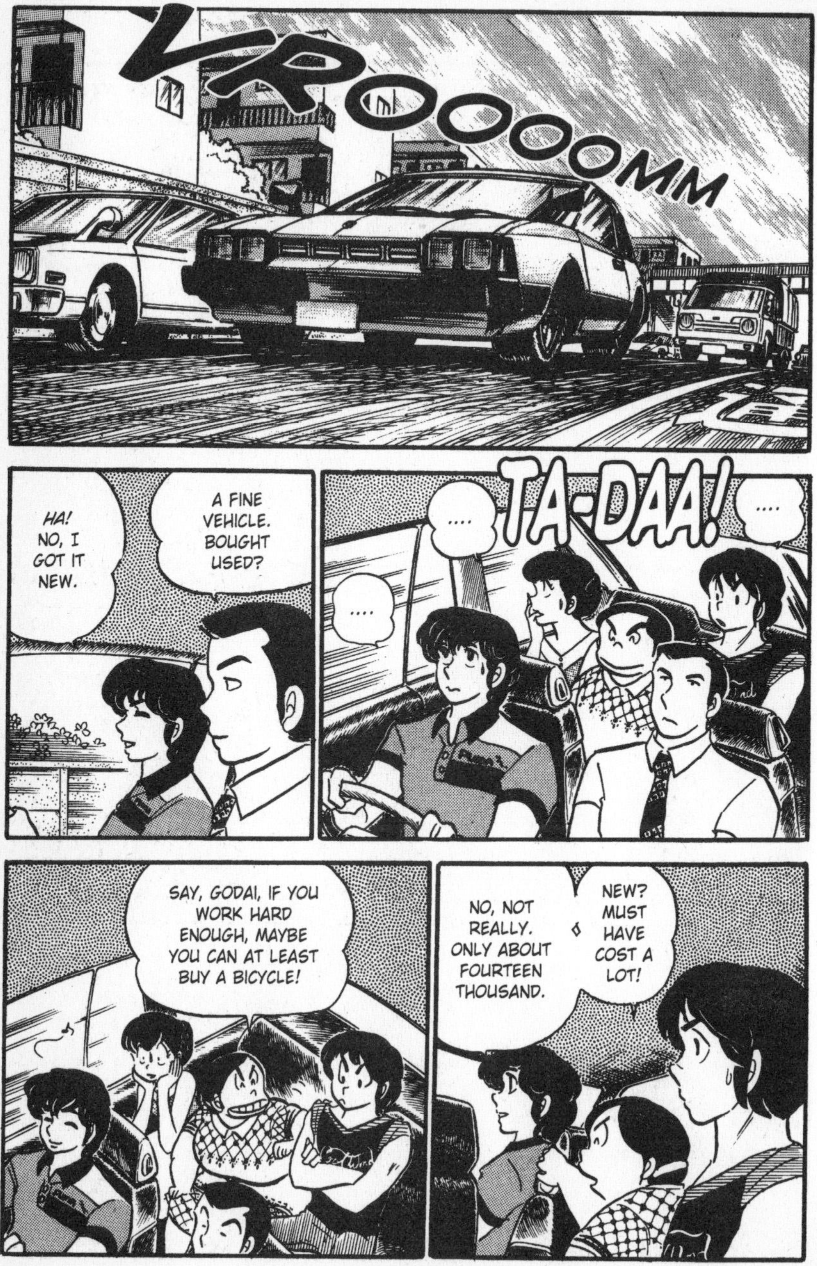
VROOOOOMM
....
TA-DAA!
....
....
A FINE VEHICLE. BOUGHT USED?
HA! NO, I GOT IT NEW.
NEW? MUST HAVE COST A LOT!
NO, NOT REALLY. ONLY ABOUT FOURTEEN THOUSAND.
SAY, GODAI, IF YOU WORK HARD ENOUGH, MAYBE YOU CAN AT LEAST BUY A BICYCLE!

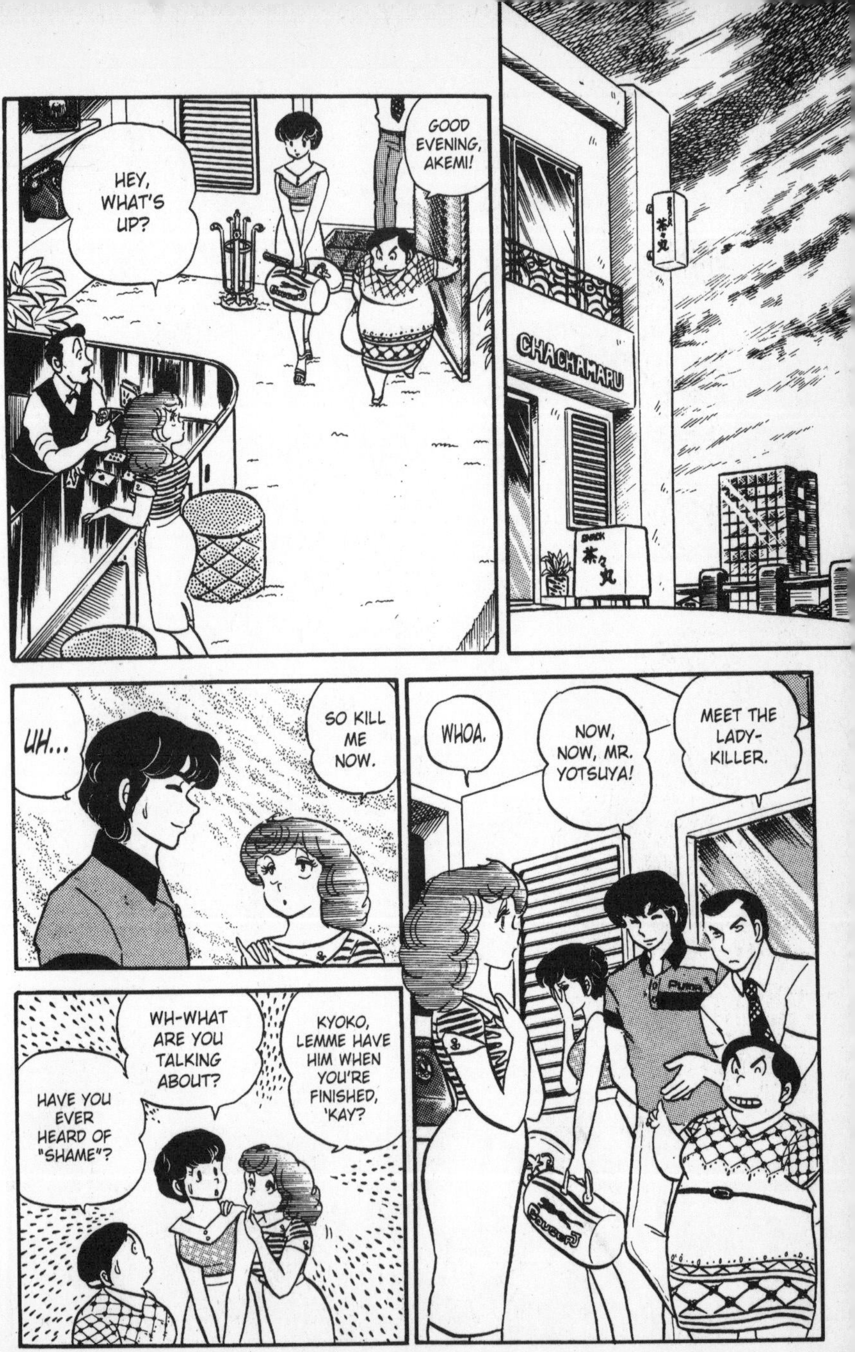
CHACHAMARU
GOOD EVENING, AKEMI!
HEY, WHAT'S UP?
MEET THE LADY-KILLER.
NOW, NOW, MR. YOTSUYA!
WHOA.
SO KILL ME NOW.
UH...
KYOKO, LEMME HAVE HIM WHEN YOU'RE FINISHED, 'KAY?
WH-WHAT ARE YOU TALKING ABOUT?
HAVE YOU EVER HEARD OF "SHAME"?

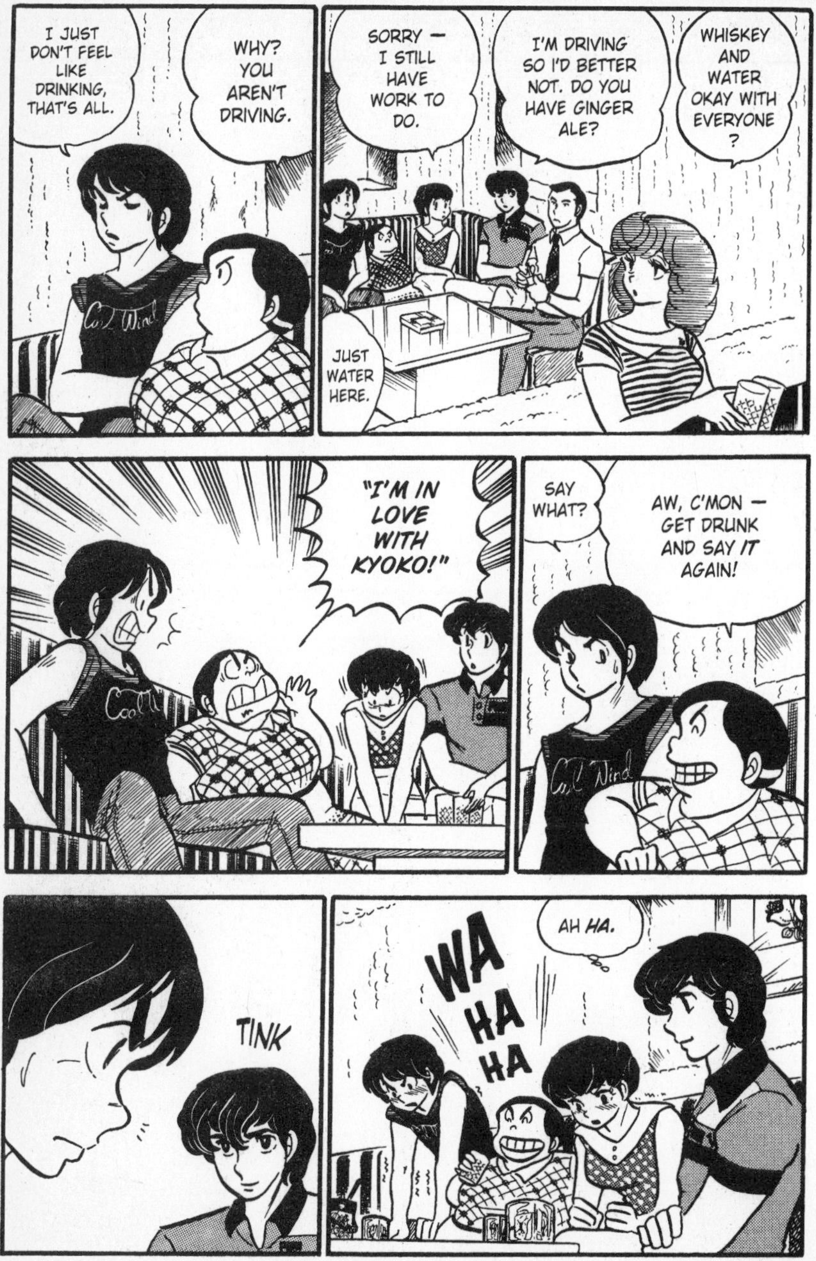
WHISKEY AND WATER OKAY WITH EVERYONE ?
I'M DRIVING SO I'D BETTER NOT. DO YOU HAVE GINGER ALE?
SORRY — I STILL HAVE WORK TO DO.
JUST WATER HERE.
WHY? YOU AREN'T DRIVING.
I JUST DON'T FEEL LIKE DRINKING, THAT'S ALL.
AW, C'MON — GET DRUNK AND SAY IT AGAIN!
SAY WHAT?
"I'M IN LOVE WITH KYOKO!"
AH HA.
WA HA HA
TINK

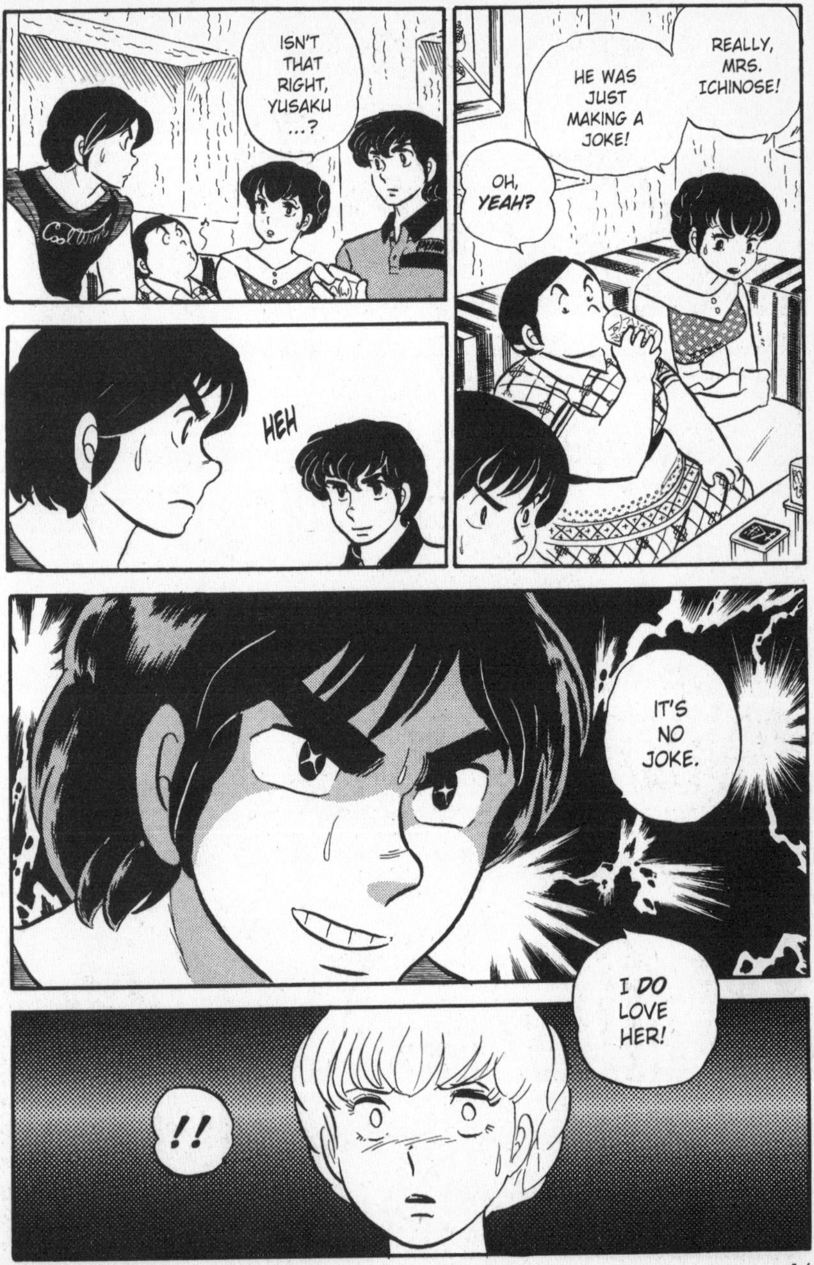
REALLY, MRS. ICHINOSE!
HE WAS JUST MAKING A JOKE!
OH, YEAH?
ISN'T THAT RIGHT, YUSAKU ...?
HEH
IT'S NO JOKE.
I DO LOVE HER!
!!

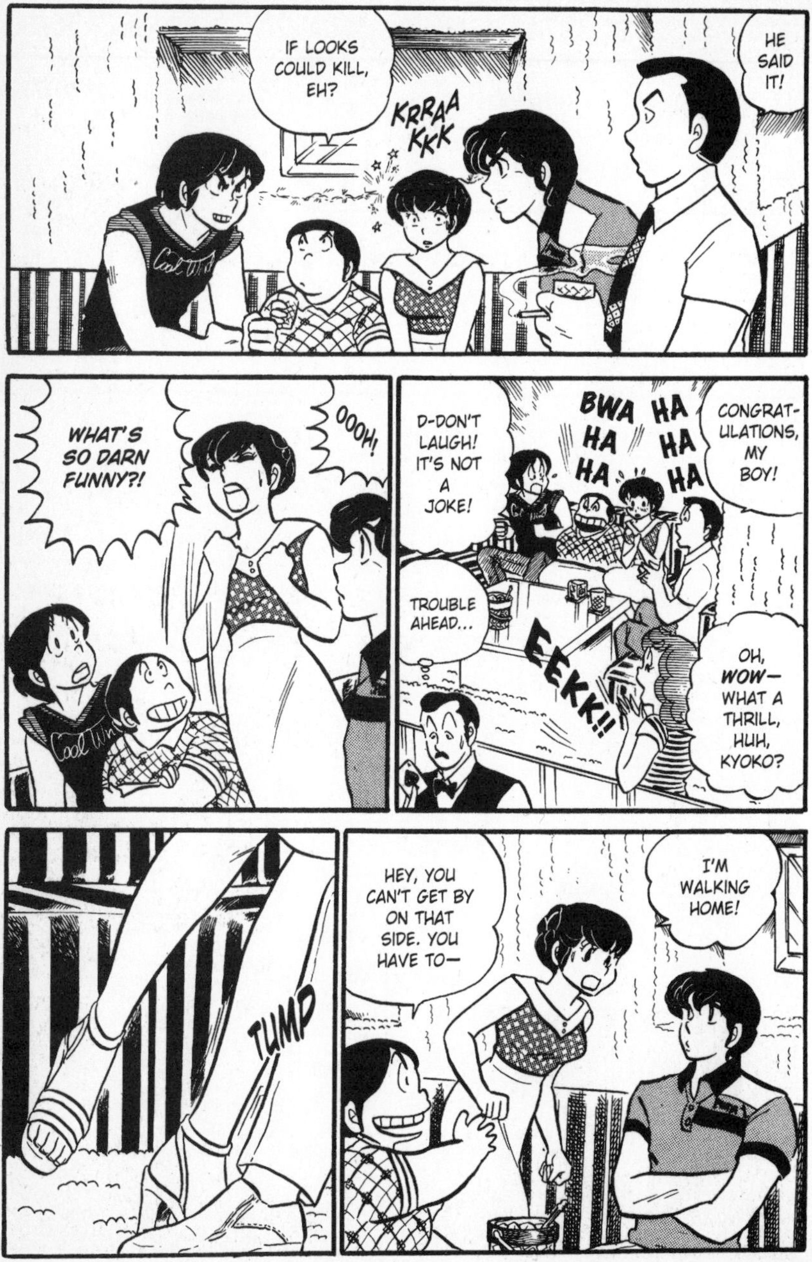
HE SAID IT!
IF LOOKS COULD KILL, EH?
KRRAAKKK
CONGRATULATIONS, MY BOY!
BWA HA HA HA HA HA HA
D-DON'T LAUGH! IT'S NOT A JOKE!
OH, *WOW*—WHAT A THRILL, HUH, KYOKO?
TROUBLE AHEAD...
EEKK!!
OOOH!
WHAT'S SO DARN FUNNY?!
I'M WALKING HOME!
HEY, YOU CAN'T GET BY ON THAT SIDE. YOU HAVE TO—
TUMP

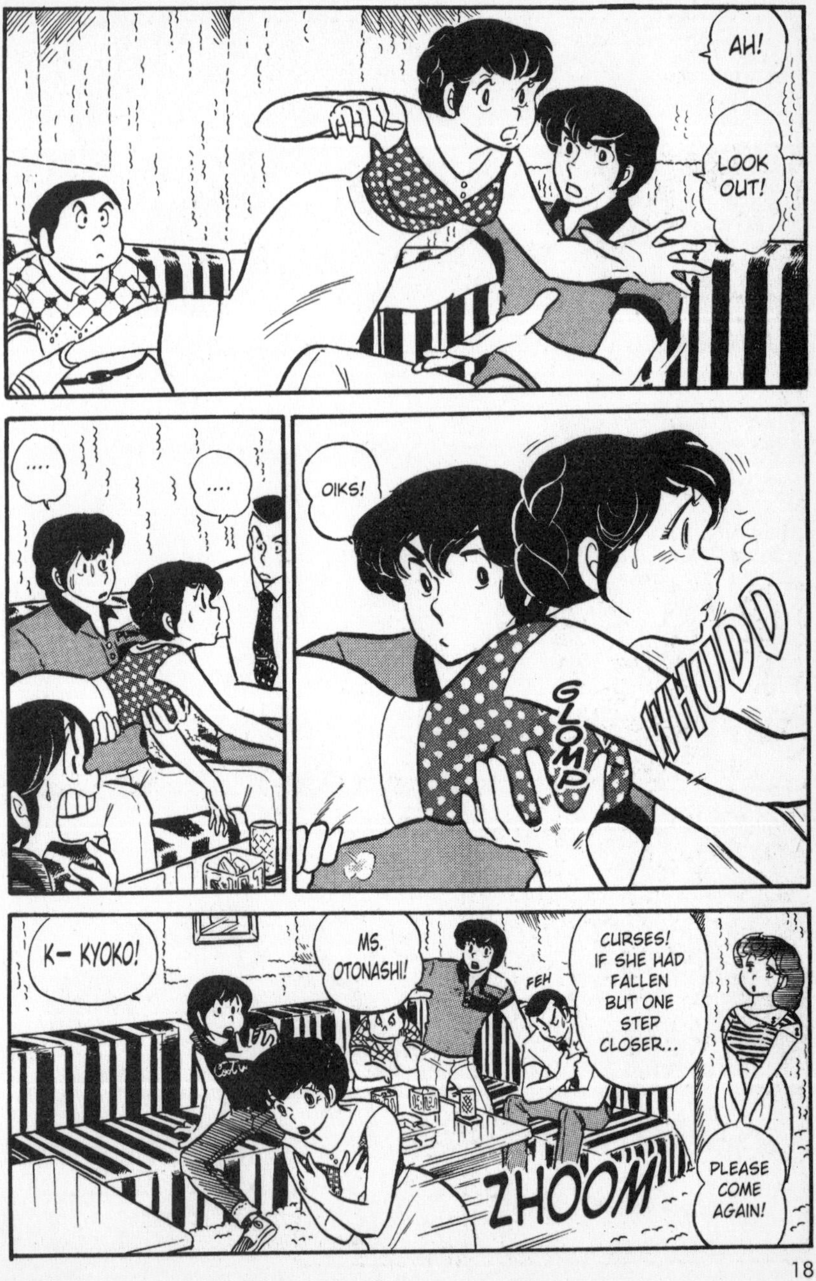
AH!
LOOK OUT!
OIKS!
WHUDD
GLOMP
....
....
CURSES! IF SHE HAD FALLEN BUT ONE STEP CLOSER...
PLEASE COME AGAIN!
FEH
MS. OTONASHI!
K- KYOKO!
ZHOOM

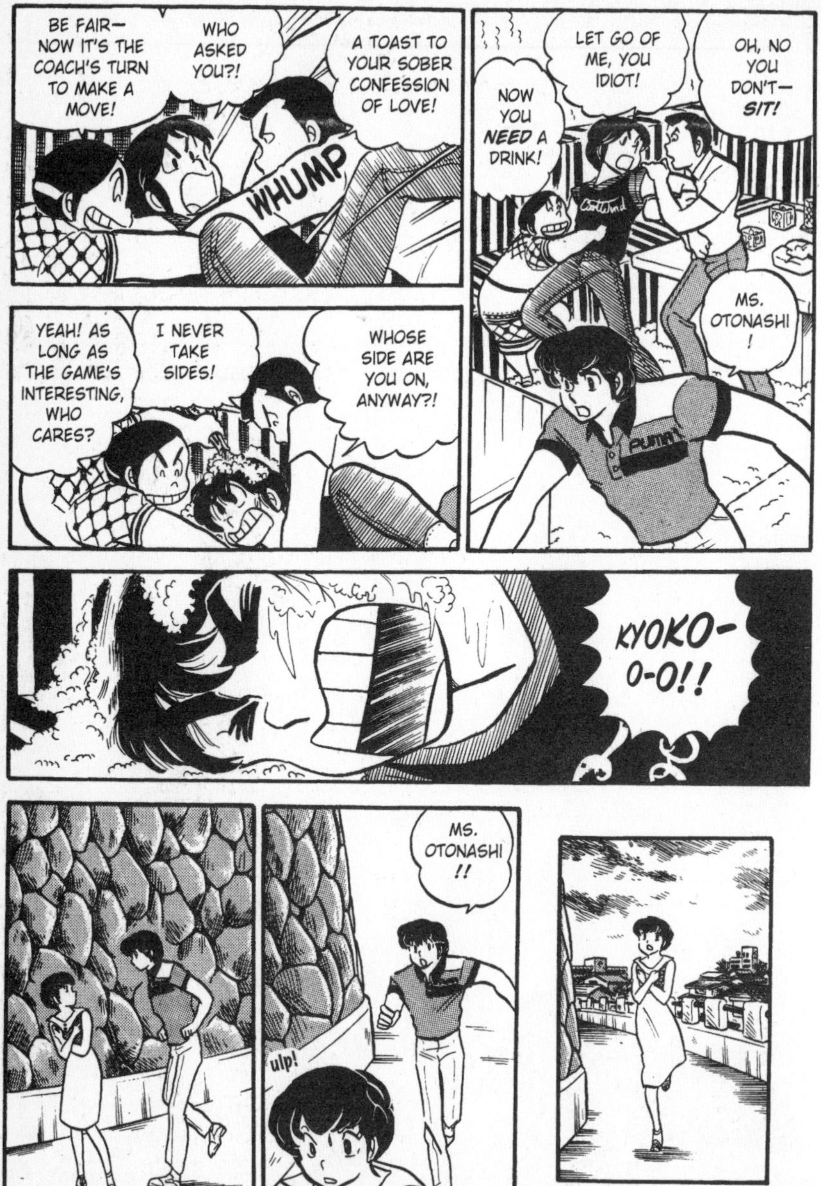
OH, NO YOU DON'T— *SIT!*
LET GO OF ME, YOU IDIOT!
NOW YOU *NEED* A DRINK!
MS. OTONASHI!
A TOAST TO YOUR SOBER CONFESSION OF LOVE!
WHO ASKED YOU?!
BE FAIR— NOW IT'S THE COACH'S TURN TO MAKE A MOVE!
WHUMP
WHOSE SIDE ARE YOU ON, ANYWAY?!
I NEVER TAKE SIDES!
YEAH! AS LONG AS THE GAME'S INTERESTING, WHO CARES?
KYOKO-O-O!!
MS. OTONASHI!!
ulp!

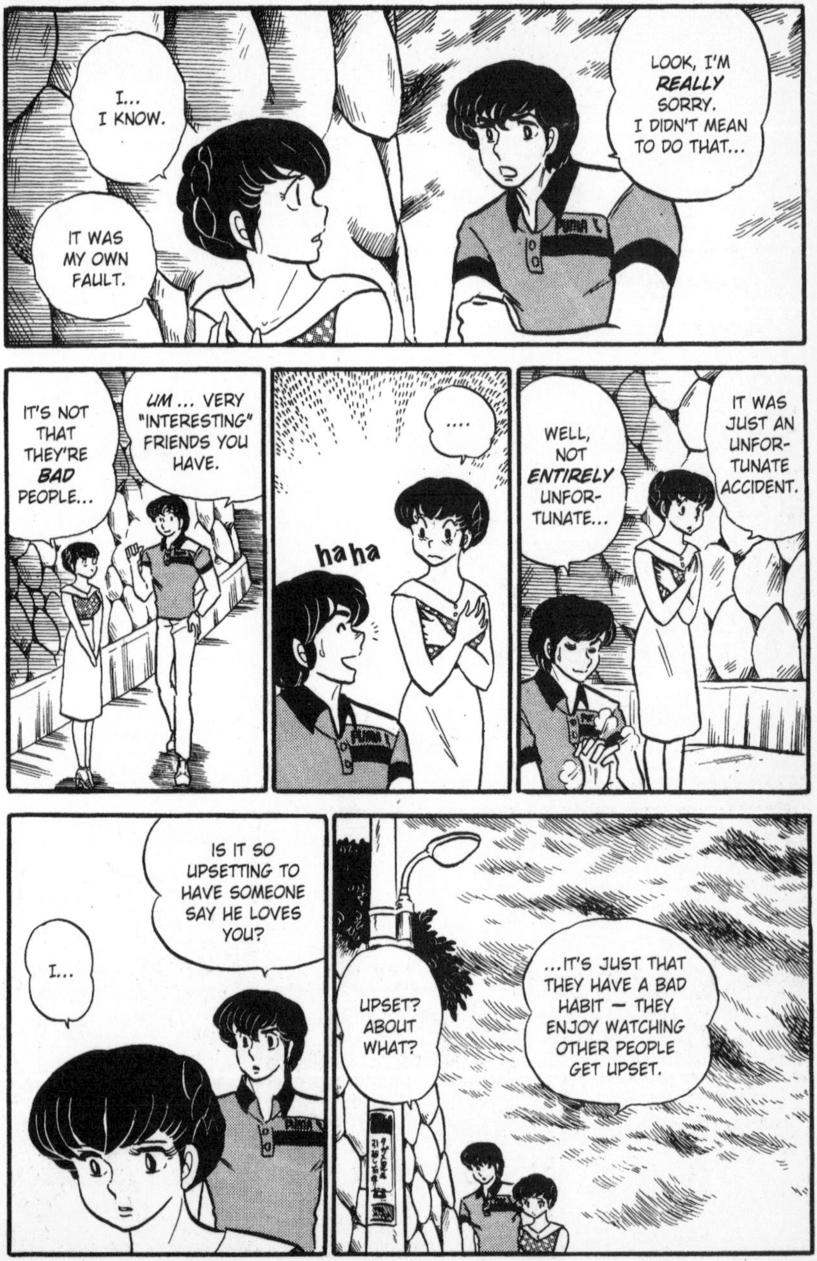
LOOK, I'M REALLY SORRY. I DIDN'T MEAN TO DO THAT...
I... I KNOW.
IT WAS MY OWN FAULT.
IT WAS JUST AN UNFORTUNATE ACCIDENT.
WELL, NOT ENTIRELY UNFORTUNATE...
....
haha
UM... VERY "INTERESTING" FRIENDS YOU HAVE.
IT'S NOT THAT THEY'RE BAD PEOPLE...
...IT'S JUST THAT THEY HAVE A BAD HABIT — THEY ENJOY WATCHING OTHER PEOPLE GET UPSET.
UPSET? ABOUT WHAT?
IS IT SO UPSETTING TO HAVE SOMEONE SAY HE LOVES YOU?
I...

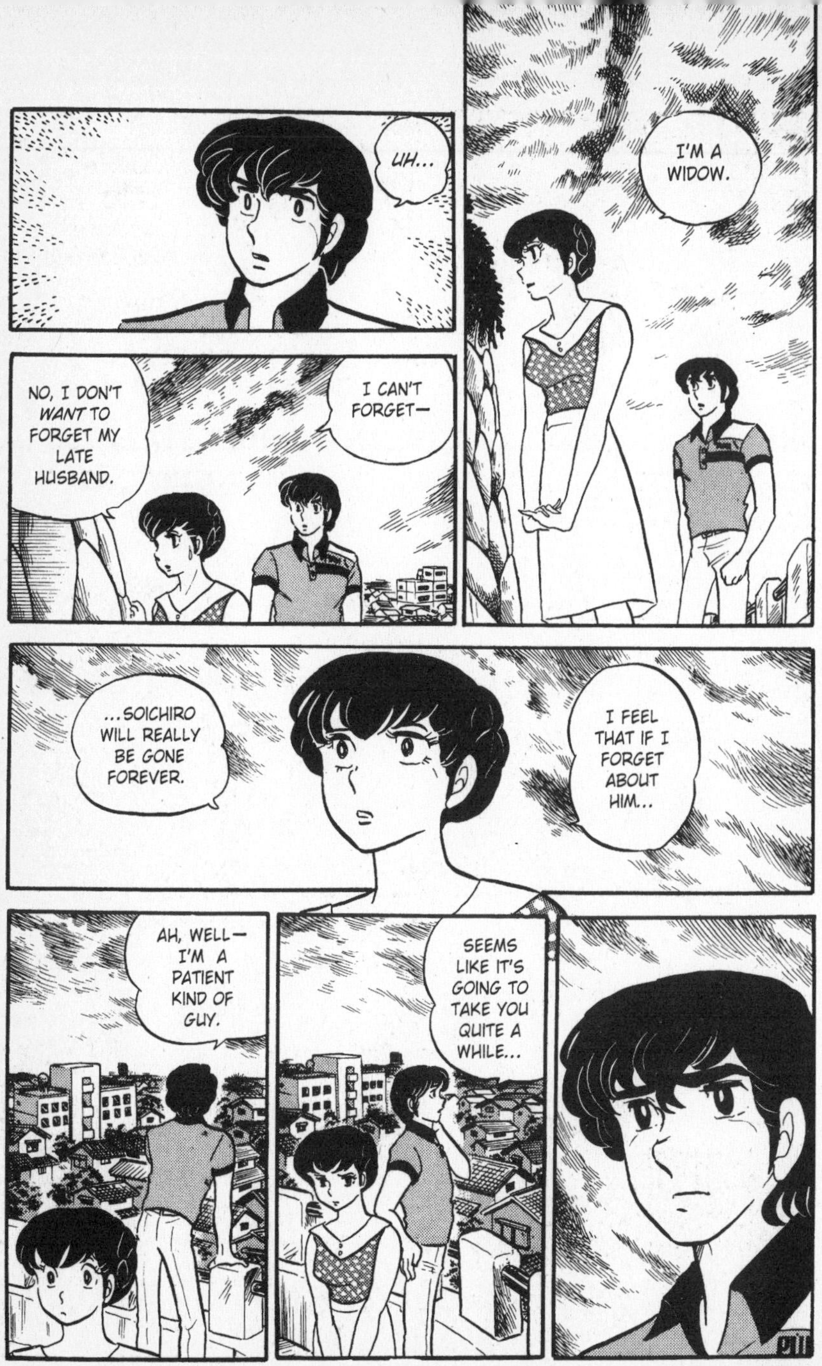
I'M A WIDOW.
UH...
I CAN'T FORGET—
NO, I DON'T *WANT* TO FORGET MY LATE HUSBAND.
I FEEL THAT IF I FORGET ABOUT HIM...
...SOICHIRO WILL REALLY BE GONE FOREVER.
SEEMS LIKE IT'S GOING TO TAKE YOU QUITE A WHILE...
AH, WELL— I'M A PATIENT KIND OF GUY.

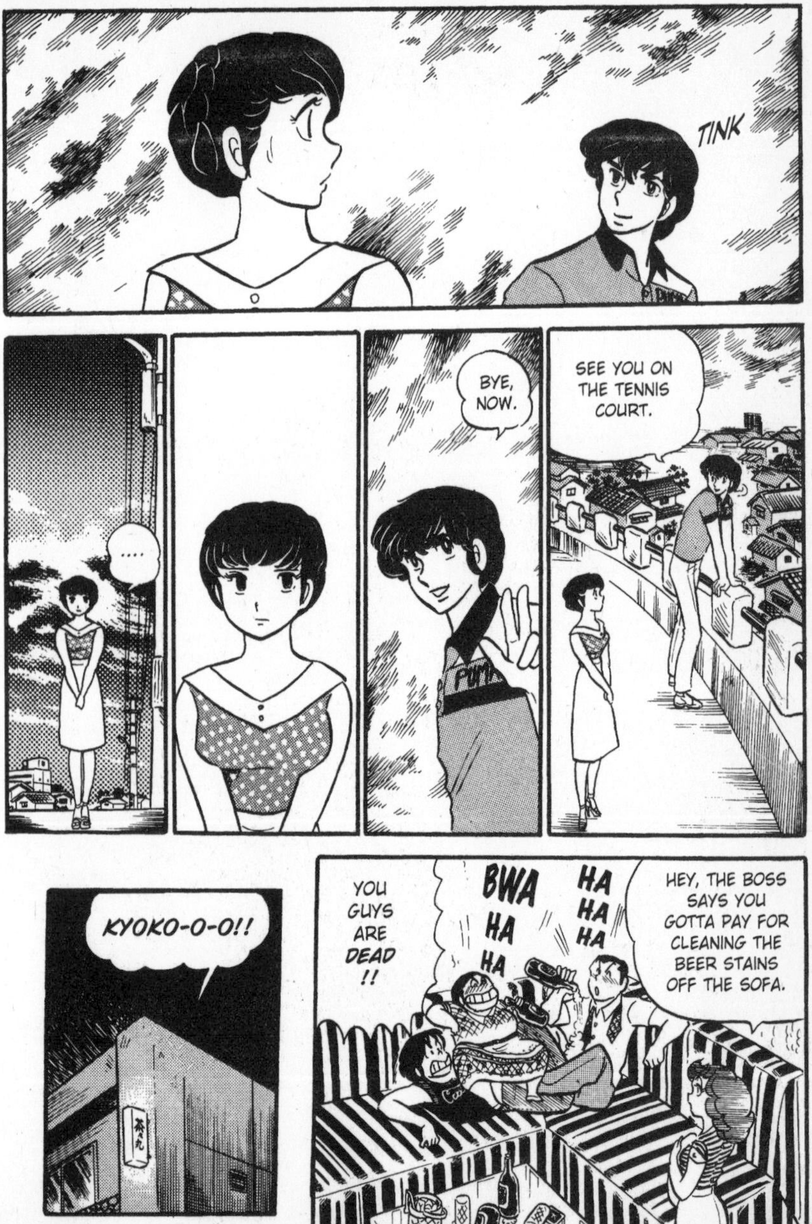
TINK
SEE YOU ON THE TENNIS COURT.
BYE, NOW.
.....
HEY, THE BOSS SAYS YOU GOTTA PAY FOR CLEANING THE BEER STAINS OFF THE SOFA.
HA HA HA
BWA HA HA
YOU GUYS ARE DEAD !!
KYOKO-O-O!!

PART TWO

DOG DAZE

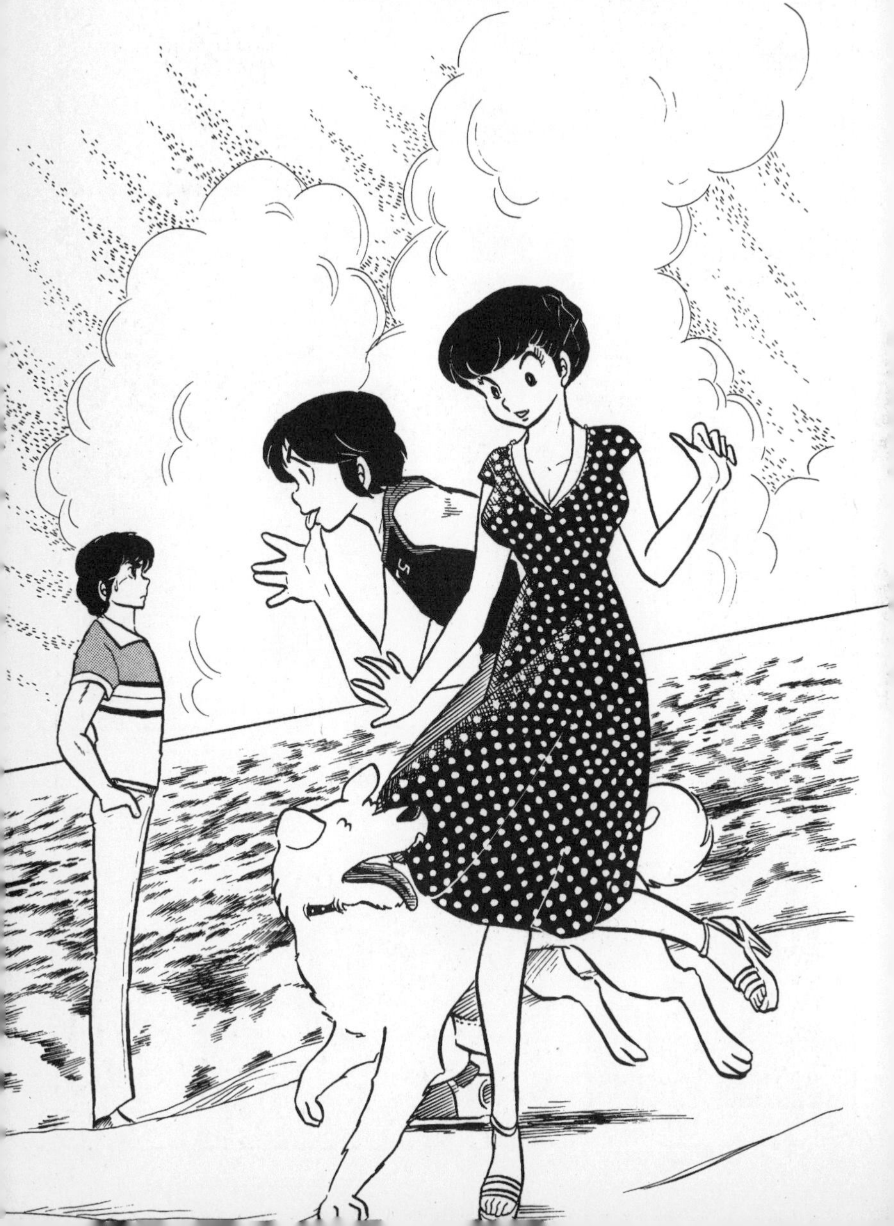

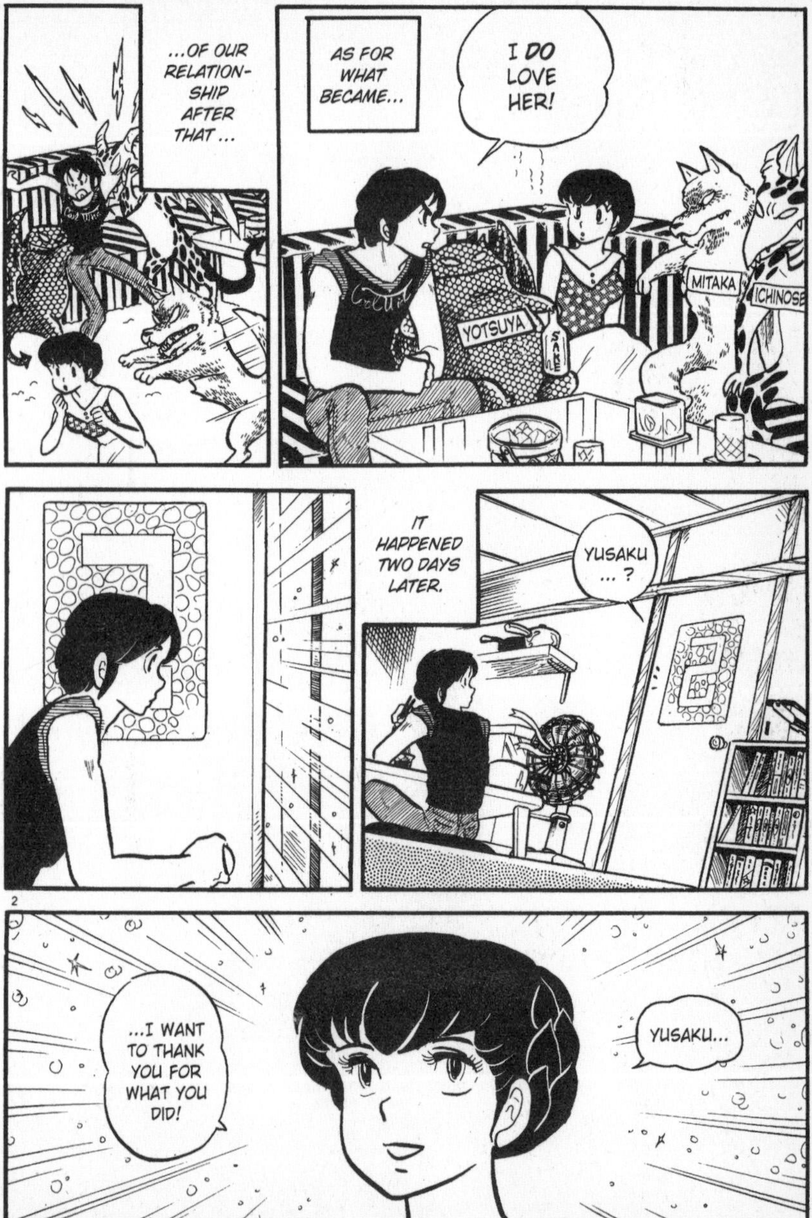
AS FOR WHAT BECAME...
I DO LOVE HER!
YOTSUYA
SAKE
MITAKA
ICHINOSE
...OF OUR RELATION-SHIP AFTER THAT...
IT HAPPENED TWO DAYS LATER.
YUSAKU ...?
YUSAKU...
...I WANT TO THANK YOU FOR WHAT YOU DID!

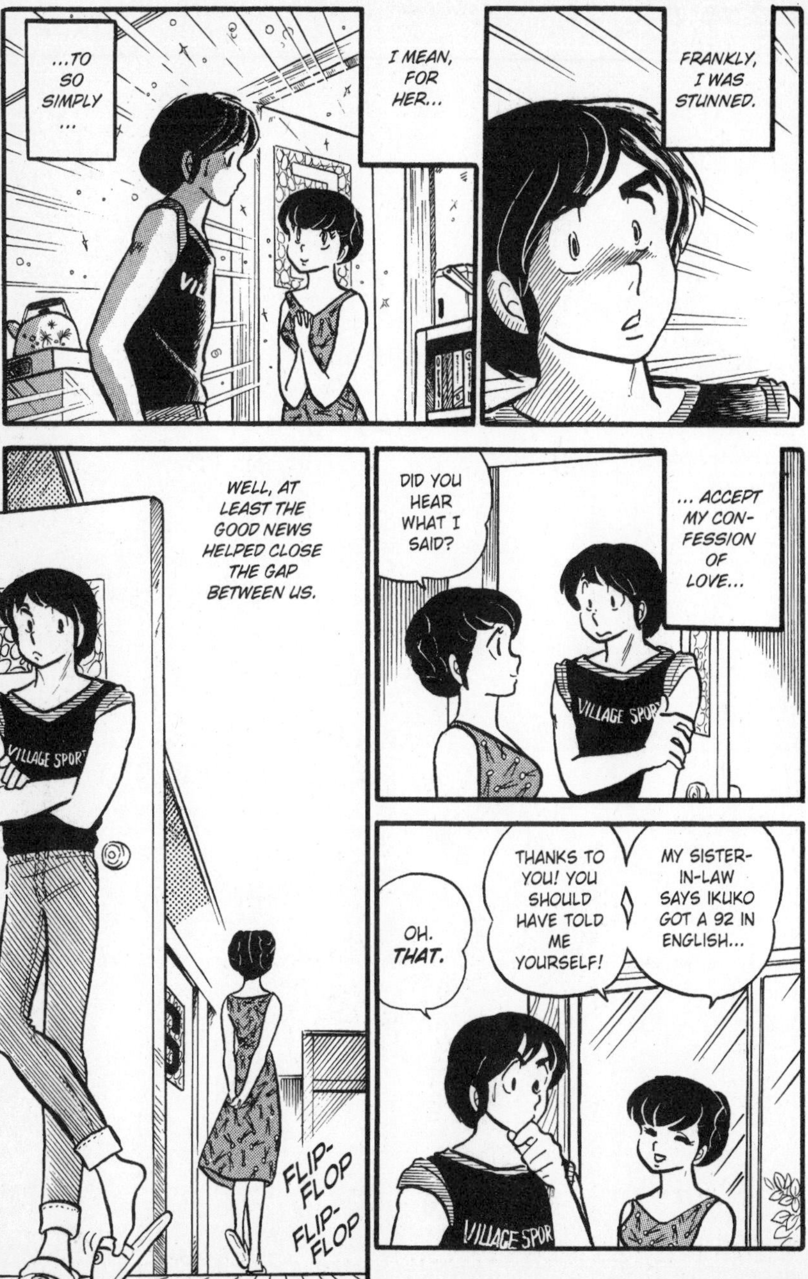
FRANKLY, I WAS STUNNED.
I MEAN, FOR HER...
...TO SO SIMPLY ...
... ACCEPT MY CON-FESSION OF LOVE...
DID YOU HEAR WHAT I SAID?
MY SISTER-IN-LAW SAYS IKUKO GOT A 92 IN ENGLISH...
THANKS TO YOU! YOU SHOULD HAVE TOLD ME YOURSELF!
OH. THAT.
WELL, AT LEAST THE GOOD NEWS HELPED CLOSE THE GAP BETWEEN US.
FLIP-FLOP
FLIP-FLOP

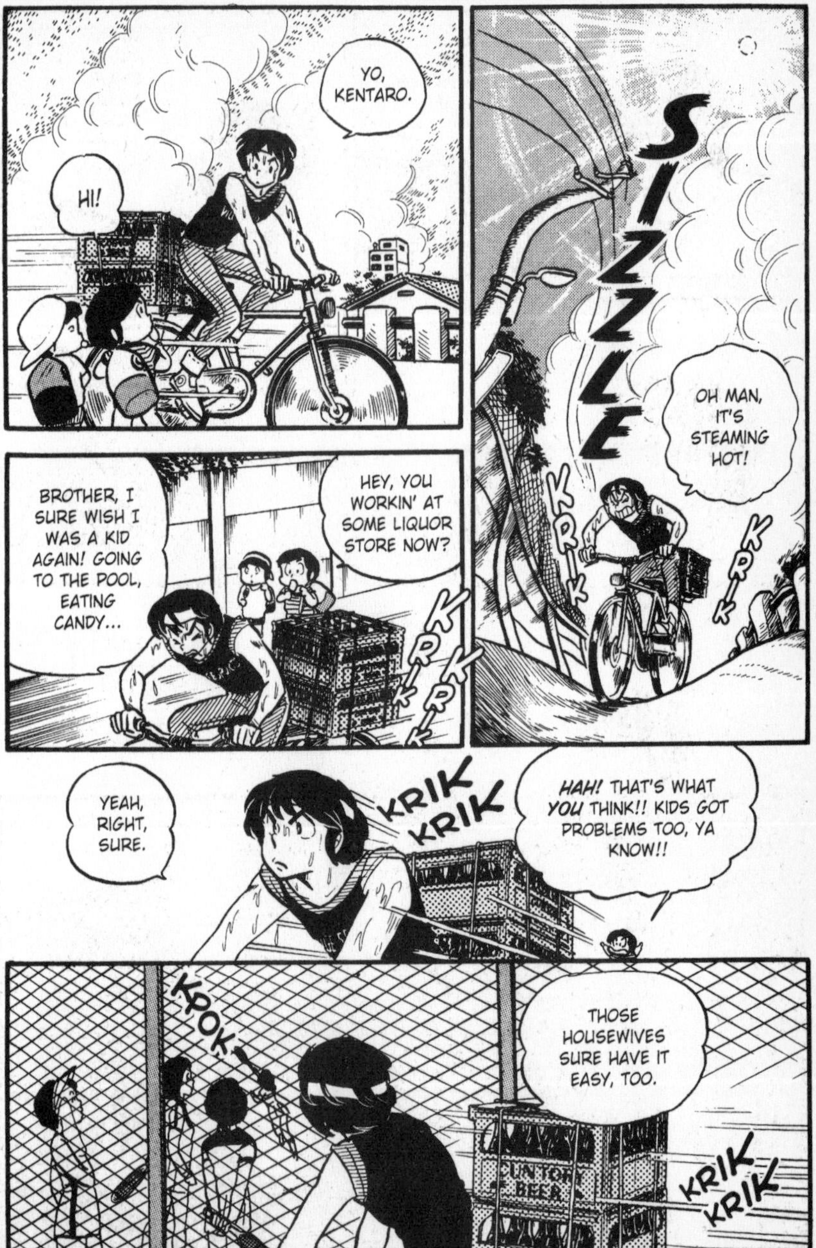
SIZZLE
OH MAN, IT'S STEAMING HOT!
KRIK
KRIK
YO, KENTARO.
HI!
HEY, YOU WORKIN' AT SOME LIQUOR STORE NOW?
BROTHER, I SURE WISH I WAS A KID AGAIN! GOING TO THE POOL, EATING CANDY...
KRIK KRIK
KRIK
HAH! THAT'S WHAT *YOU* THINK!! KIDS GOT PROBLEMS TOO, YA KNOW!!
KRIK KRIK
YEAH, RIGHT, SURE.
THOSE HOUSEWIVES SURE HAVE IT EASY, TOO.
KPOK
SUNTORY BEER
KRIK KRIK

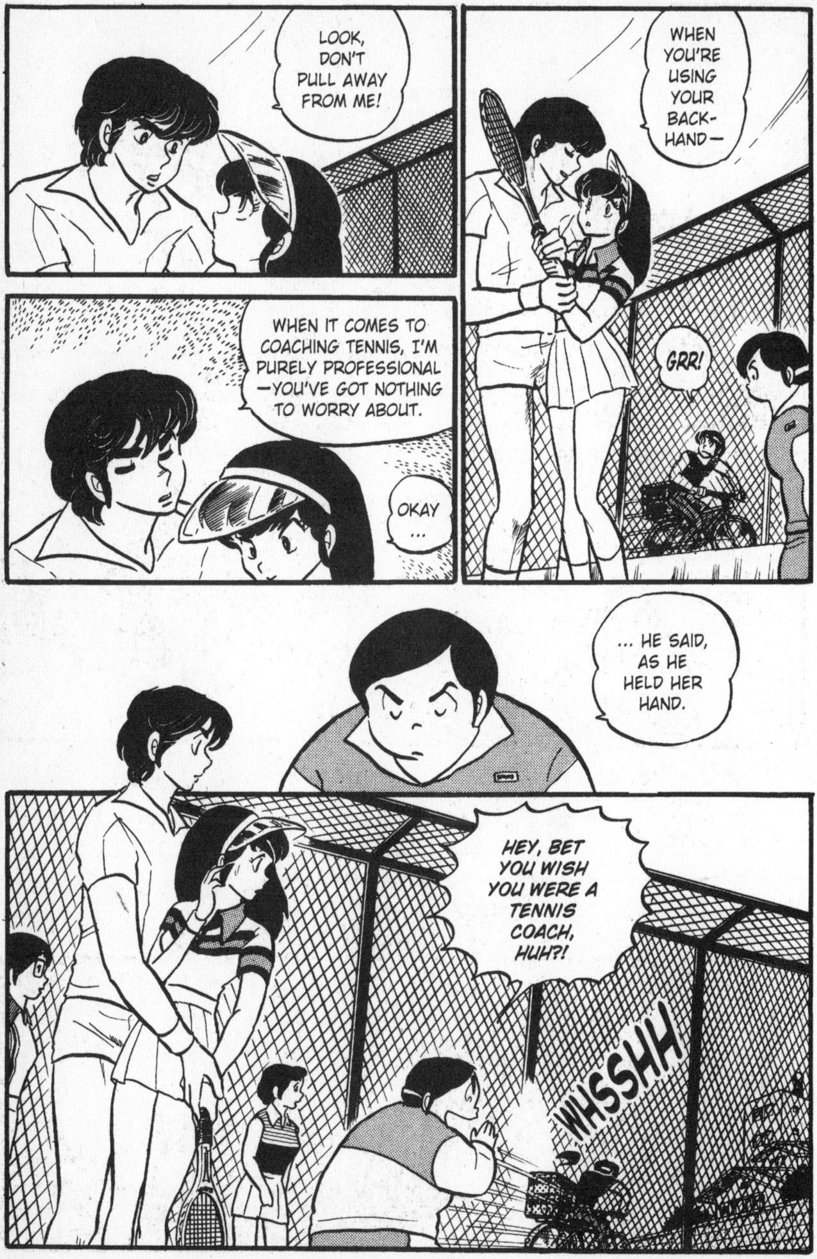
WHEN YOU'RE USING YOUR BACK-HAND—
GRR!
LOOK, DON'T PULL AWAY FROM ME!
WHEN IT COMES TO COACHING TENNIS, I'M PURELY PROFESSIONAL —YOU'VE GOT NOTHING TO WORRY ABOUT.
OKAY ...
... HE SAID, AS HE HELD HER HAND.
HEY, BET YOU WISH YOU WERE A TENNIS COACH, HUH?!
WHSSHH

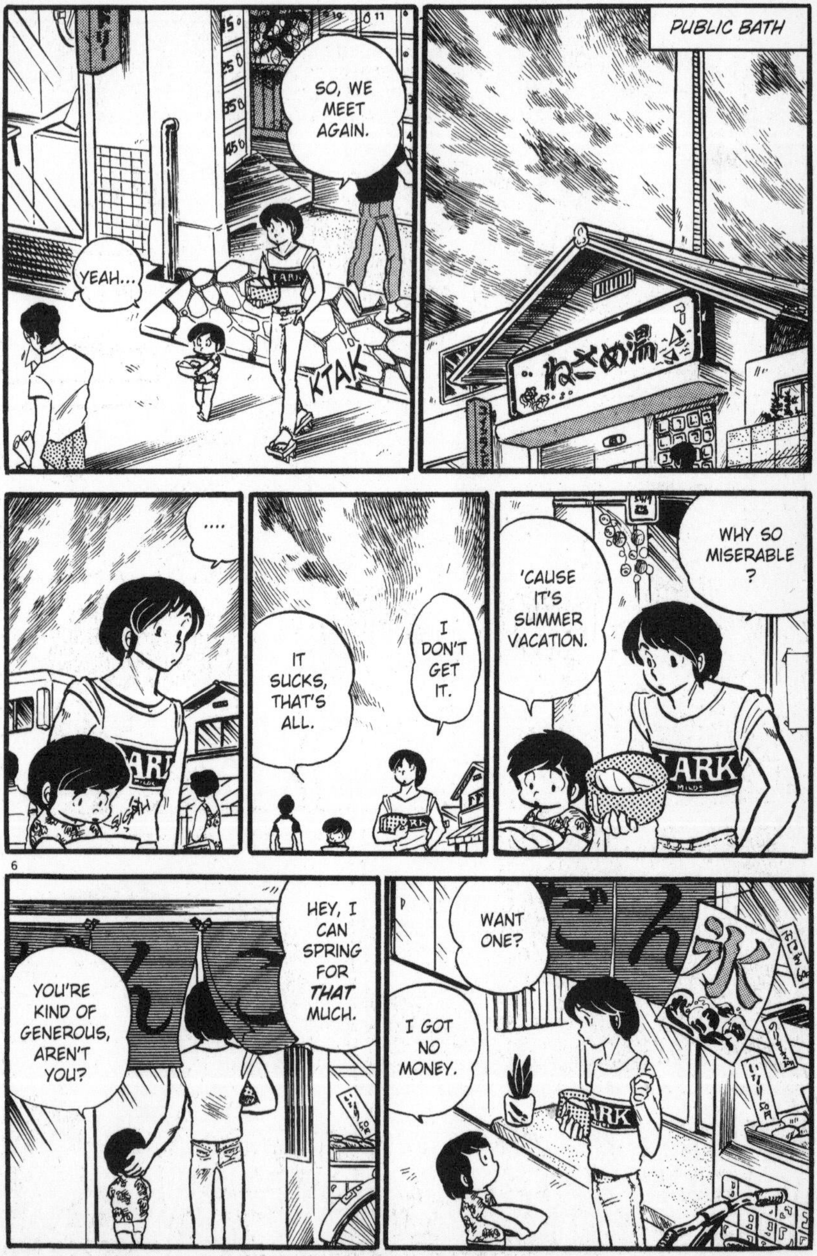
PUBLIC BATH
SO, WE MEET AGAIN.
YEAH...
KTAK
WHY SO MISERABLE ?
'CAUSE IT'S SUMMER VACATION.
I DON'T GET IT.
IT SUCKS, THAT'S ALL.
....
WANT ONE?
I GOT NO MONEY.
HEY, I CAN SPRING FOR *THAT* MUCH.
YOU'RE KIND OF GENEROUS, AREN'T YOU?

6

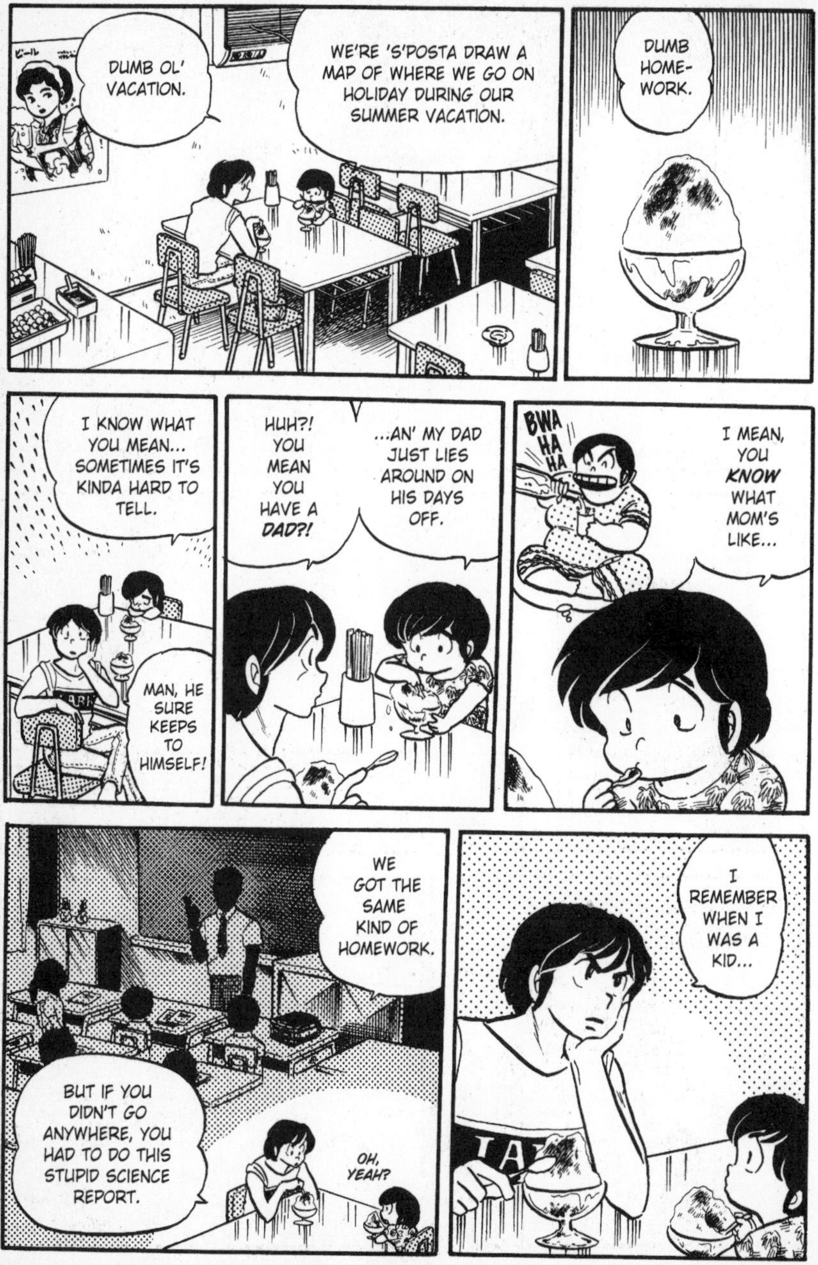
DUMB HOMEWORK.
WE'RE 'S'POSTA DRAW A MAP OF WHERE WE GO ON HOLIDAY DURING OUR SUMMER VACATION.
DUMB OL' VACATION.
I MEAN, YOU *KNOW* WHAT MOM'S LIKE...
BWA HA HA
...AN' MY DAD JUST LIES AROUND ON HIS DAYS OFF.
HUH?! YOU MEAN YOU HAVE A *DAD?!*
I KNOW WHAT YOU MEAN... SOMETIMES IT'S KINDA HARD TO TELL.
MAN, HE SURE KEEPS TO HIMSELF!
I REMEMBER WHEN I WAS A KID...
WE GOT THE SAME KIND OF HOMEWORK.
BUT IF YOU DIDN'T GO ANYWHERE, YOU HAD TO DO THIS STUPID SCIENCE REPORT.
OH, YEAH?

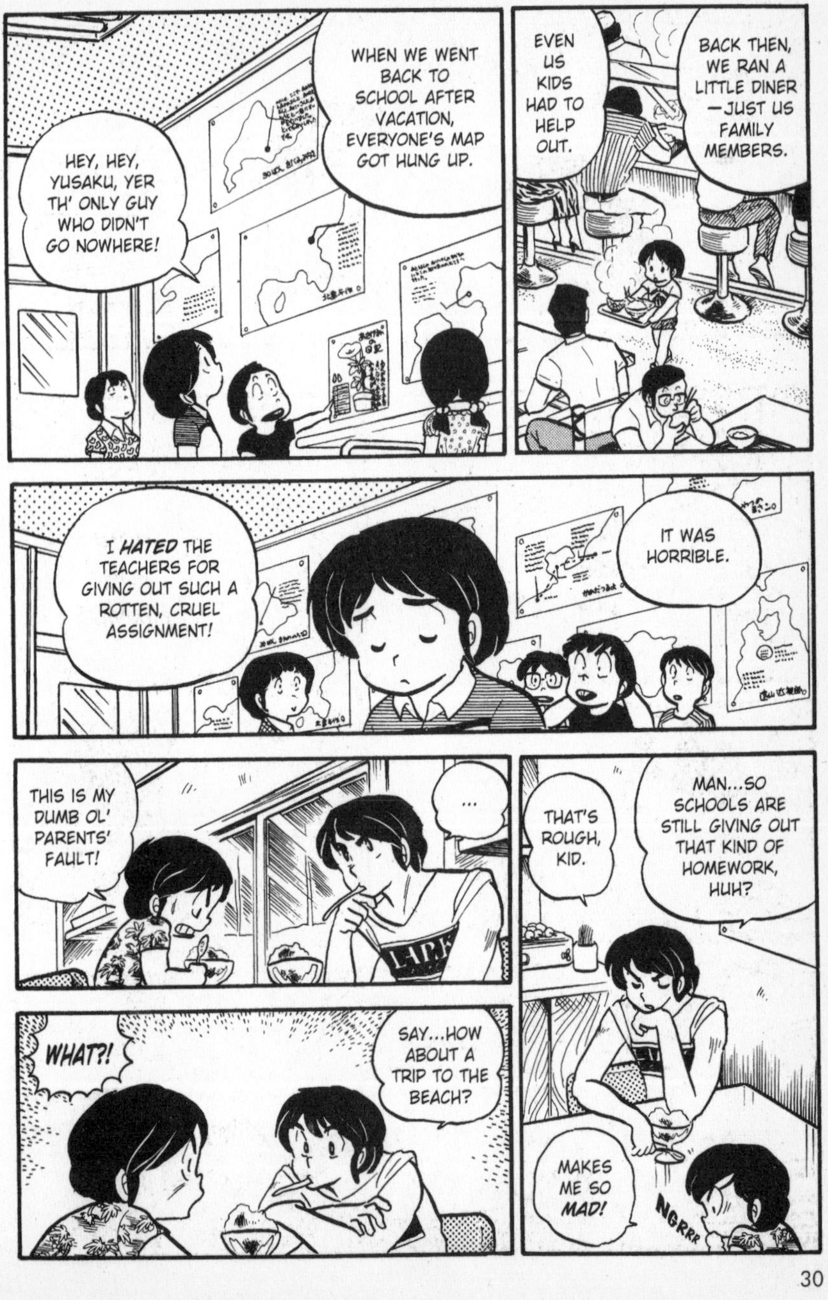
BACK THEN, WE RAN A LITTLE DINER—JUST US FAMILY MEMBERS.
EVEN US KIDS HAD TO HELP OUT.
WHEN WE WENT BACK TO SCHOOL AFTER VACATION, EVERYONE'S MAP GOT HUNG UP.
HEY, HEY, YUSAKU, YER TH' ONLY GUY WHO DIDN'T GO NOWHERE!
IT WAS HORRIBLE.
I *HATED* THE TEACHERS FOR GIVING OUT SUCH A ROTTEN, CRUEL ASSIGNMENT!
MAN...SO SCHOOLS ARE STILL GIVING OUT THAT KIND OF HOMEWORK, HUH?
THAT'S ROUGH, KID.
MAKES ME SO *MAD!*
NGRRR
...
THIS IS MY DUMB OL' PARENTS' FAULT!
SAY...HOW ABOUT A TRIP TO THE BEACH?
WHAT?!

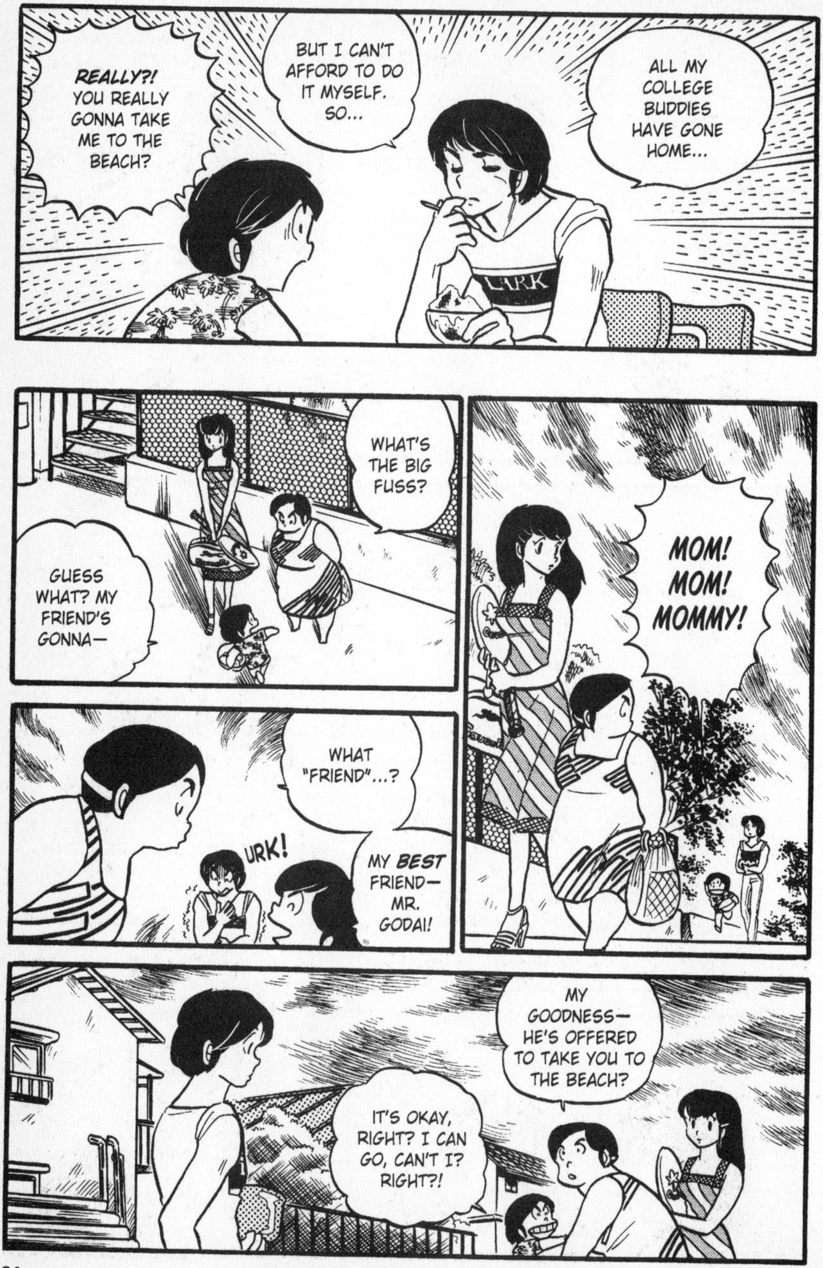
ALL MY COLLEGE BUDDIES HAVE GONE HOME...
BUT I CAN'T AFFORD TO DO IT MYSELF. SO...
REALLY?! YOU REALLY GONNA TAKE ME TO THE BEACH?
MOM! MOM! MOMMY!
WHAT'S THE BIG FUSS?
GUESS WHAT? MY FRIEND'S GONNA—
WHAT "FRIEND"...?
MY *BEST* FRIEND— MR. GODAI!
URK!
MY GOODNESS— HE'S OFFERED TO TAKE YOU TO THE BEACH?
IT'S OKAY, RIGHT? I CAN GO, CAN'T I? RIGHT?!

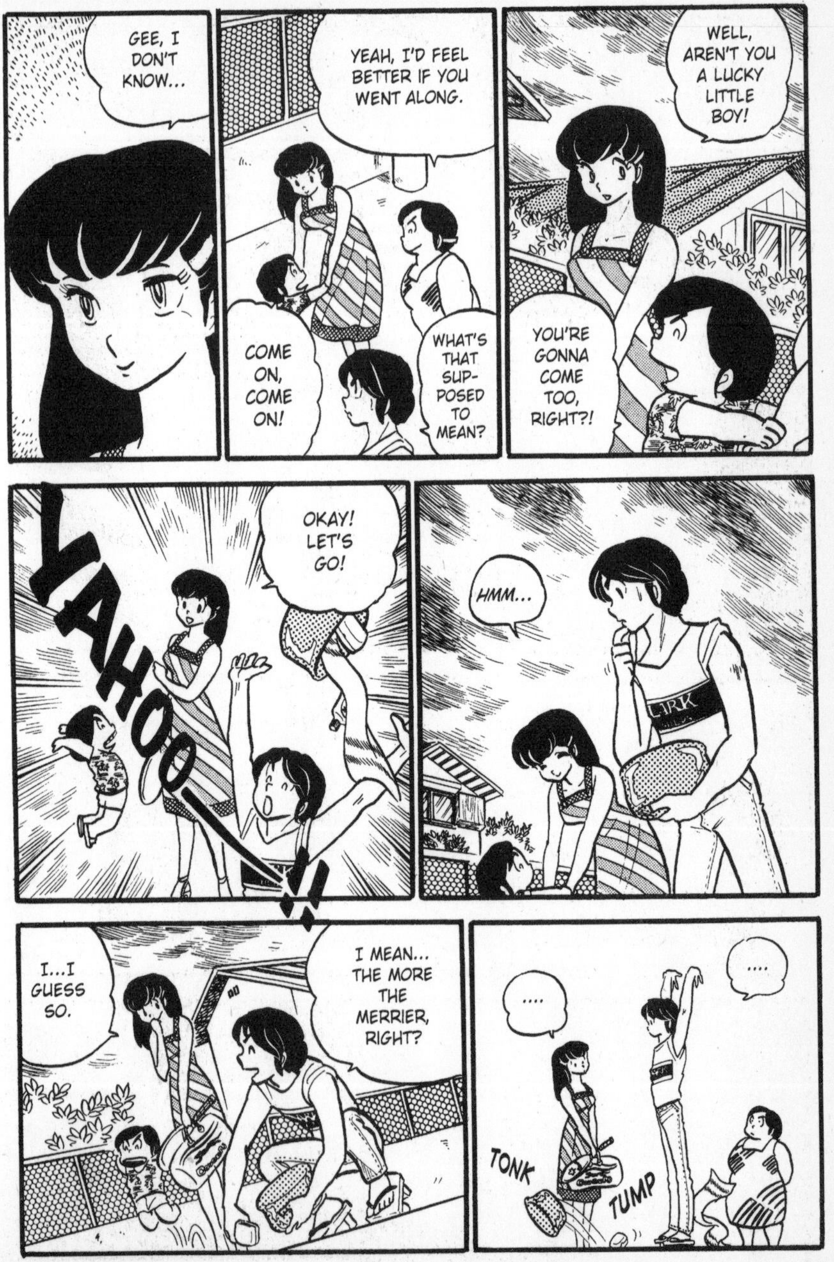
WELL, AREN'T YOU A LUCKY LITTLE BOY!
YOU'RE GONNA COME TOO, RIGHT?!
YEAH, I'D FEEL BETTER IF YOU WENT ALONG.
WHAT'S THAT SUP-POSED TO MEAN?
COME ON, COME ON!
GEE, I DON'T KNOW...
HMM...
OKAY! LET'S GO!
YAHOO!!
....
....
TONK
TUMP
I MEAN... THE MORE THE MERRIER, RIGHT?
I...I GUESS SO.

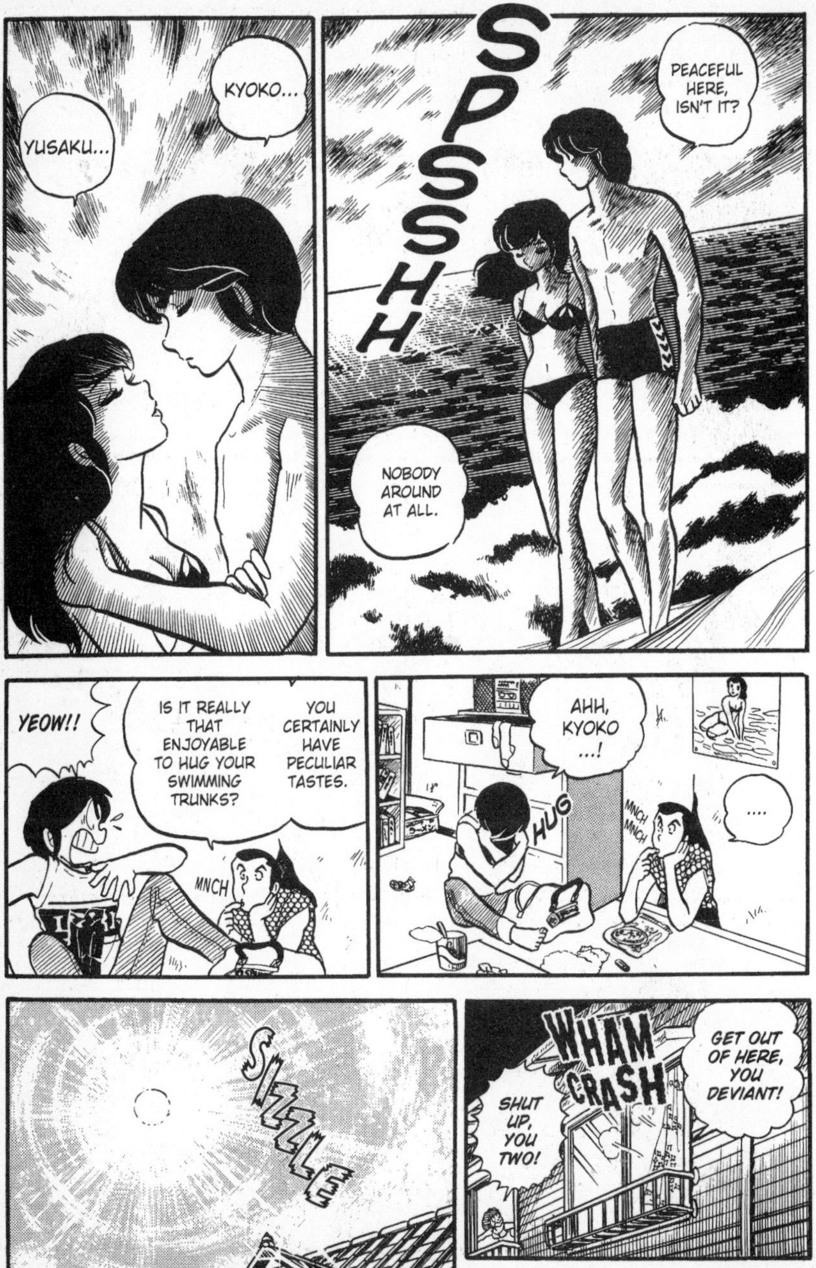
SPSSHH
PEACEFUL HERE, ISN'T IT?
NOBODY AROUND AT ALL.
KYOKO...
YUSAKU...
AHH, KYOKO ...!
HUG
MNCH MNCH
....
YOU CERTAINLY HAVE PECULIAR TASTES.
IS IT REALLY THAT ENJOYABLE TO HUG YOUR SWIMMING TRUNKS?
MNCH
YEOW!!
GET OUT OF HERE, YOU DEVIANT!
WHAM
CRASH
SHUT UP, YOU TWO!
SIZZLE

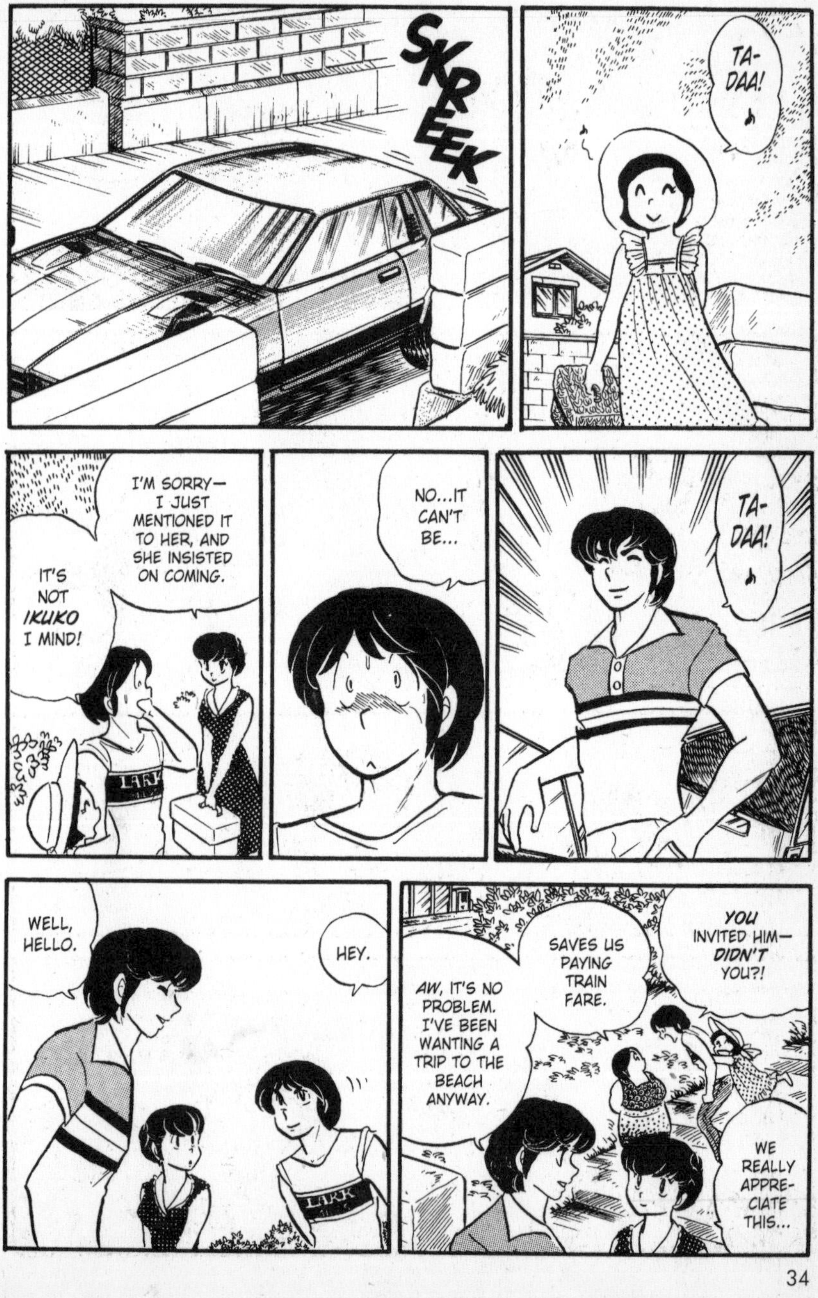
TA-DAA! ♪
SKREEEK
TA-DAA! ♪
NO...IT CAN'T BE...
I'M SORRY—I JUST MENTIONED IT TO HER, AND SHE INSISTED ON COMING.
IT'S NOT *IKUKO* I MIND!
LARK
YOU INVITED HIM—*DIDN'T* YOU?!
SAVES US PAYING TRAIN FARE.
AW, IT'S NO PROBLEM. I'VE BEEN WANTING A TRIP TO THE BEACH ANYWAY.
WE REALLY APPRECIATE THIS...
HEY.
WELL, HELLO.
LARK

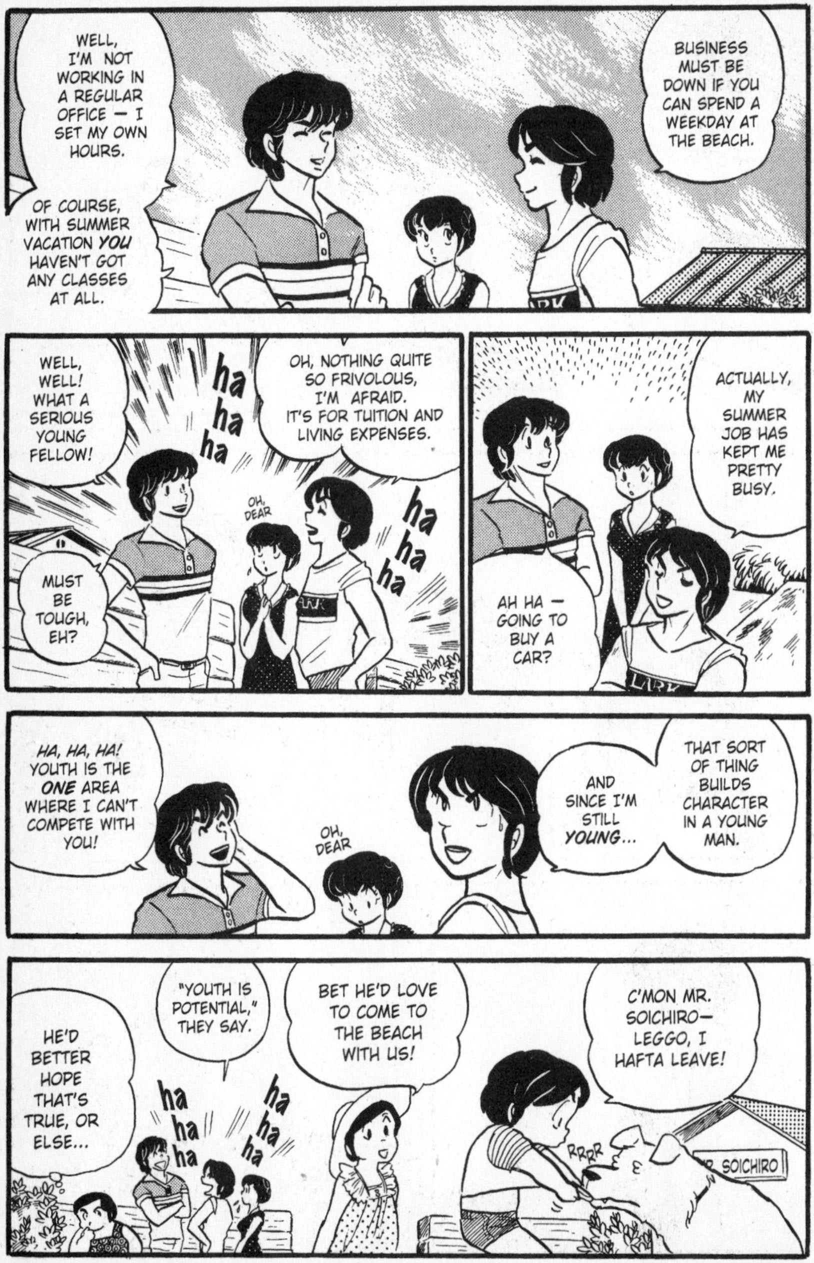
BUSINESS MUST BE DOWN IF YOU CAN SPEND A WEEKDAY AT THE BEACH.
WELL, I'M NOT WORKING IN A REGULAR OFFICE — I SET MY OWN HOURS.
OF COURSE, WITH SUMMER VACATION *YOU* HAVEN'T GOT ANY CLASSES AT ALL.
ACTUALLY, MY SUMMER JOB HAS KEPT ME PRETTY BUSY.
AH HA — GOING TO BUY A CAR?
OH, NOTHING QUITE SO FRIVOLOUS, I'M AFRAID. IT'S FOR TUITION AND LIVING EXPENSES.
ha ha ha
WELL, WELL! WHAT A SERIOUS YOUNG FELLOW!
ha ha ha
OH, DEAR
MUST BE TOUGH, EH?
THAT SORT OF THING BUILDS CHARACTER IN A YOUNG MAN.
AND SINCE I'M STILL *YOUNG*...
OH, DEAR
HA, HA, HA! YOUTH IS THE *ONE* AREA WHERE I CAN'T COMPETE WITH YOU!
C'MON MR. SOICHIRO— LEGGO, I HAFTA LEAVE!
RRRR
SOICHIRO
BET HE'D LOVE TO COME TO THE BEACH WITH US!
ha ha ha
"YOUTH IS POTENTIAL," THEY SAY.
ha ha ha
HE'D BETTER HOPE THAT'S TRUE, OR ELSE...

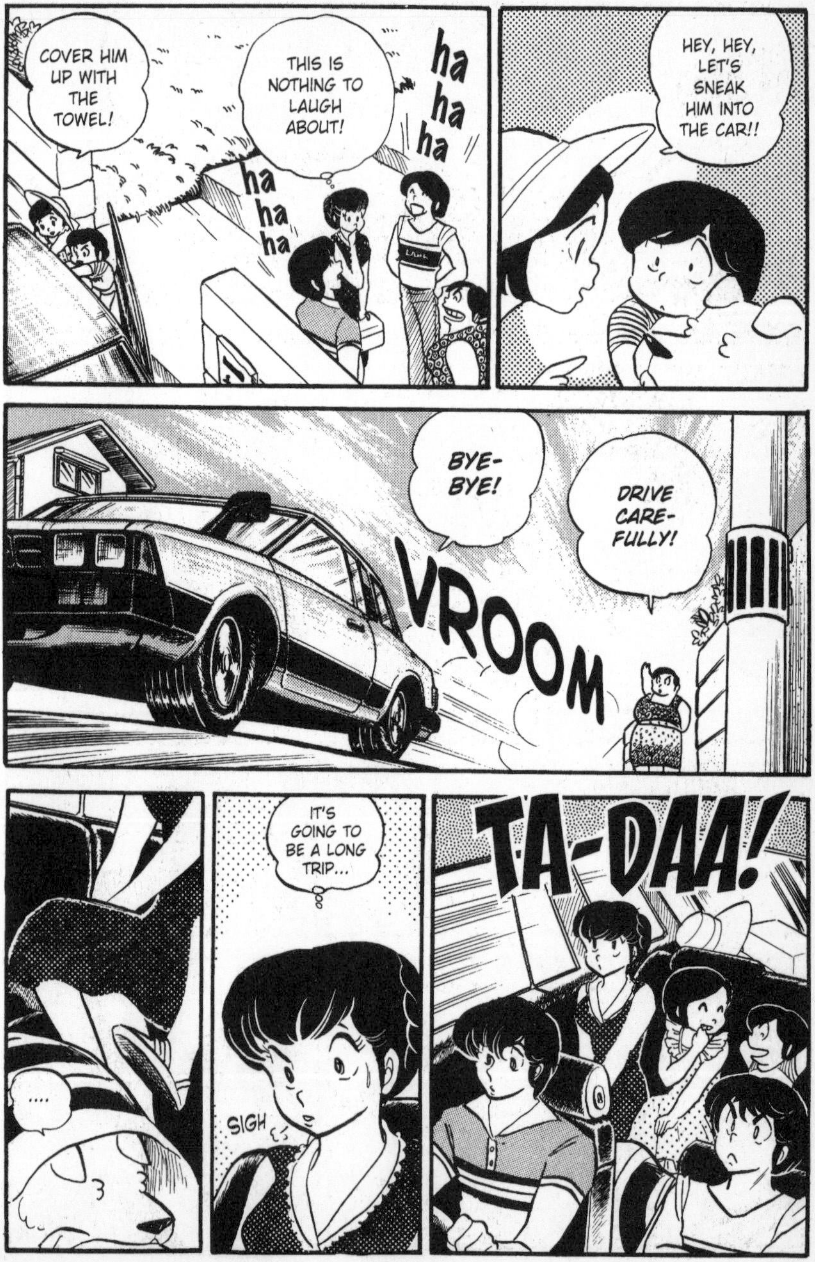
HEY, HEY, LET'S SNEAK HIM INTO THE CAR!!
ha ha ha
THIS IS NOTHING TO LAUGH ABOUT!
COVER HIM UP WITH THE TOWEL!
ha ha ha
DRIVE CARE-FULLY!
BYE-BYE!
VROOM
TA-DAA!
IT'S GOING TO BE A LONG TRIP...
SIGH
....

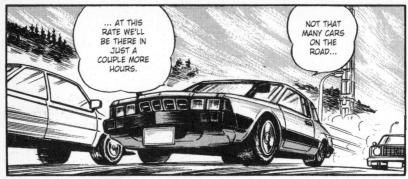

NOT THAT MANY CARS ON THE ROAD...
... AT THIS RATE WE'LL BE THERE IN JUST A COUPLE MORE HOURS.
snf snf
NO, AUNTIE! DON'T LOOK!
WHAT IN THE WORLD—
WHA-?!
Wuh Wuh
MR. SOICHIRO !!
BOWF !
URK!
SKREEEEK
EEK!
EEK!
YOW!

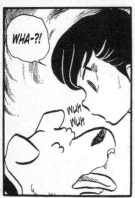

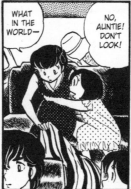

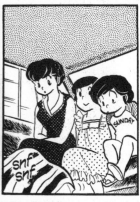

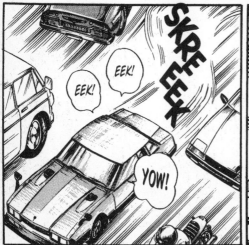

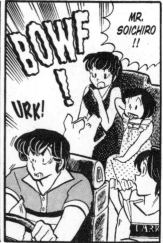

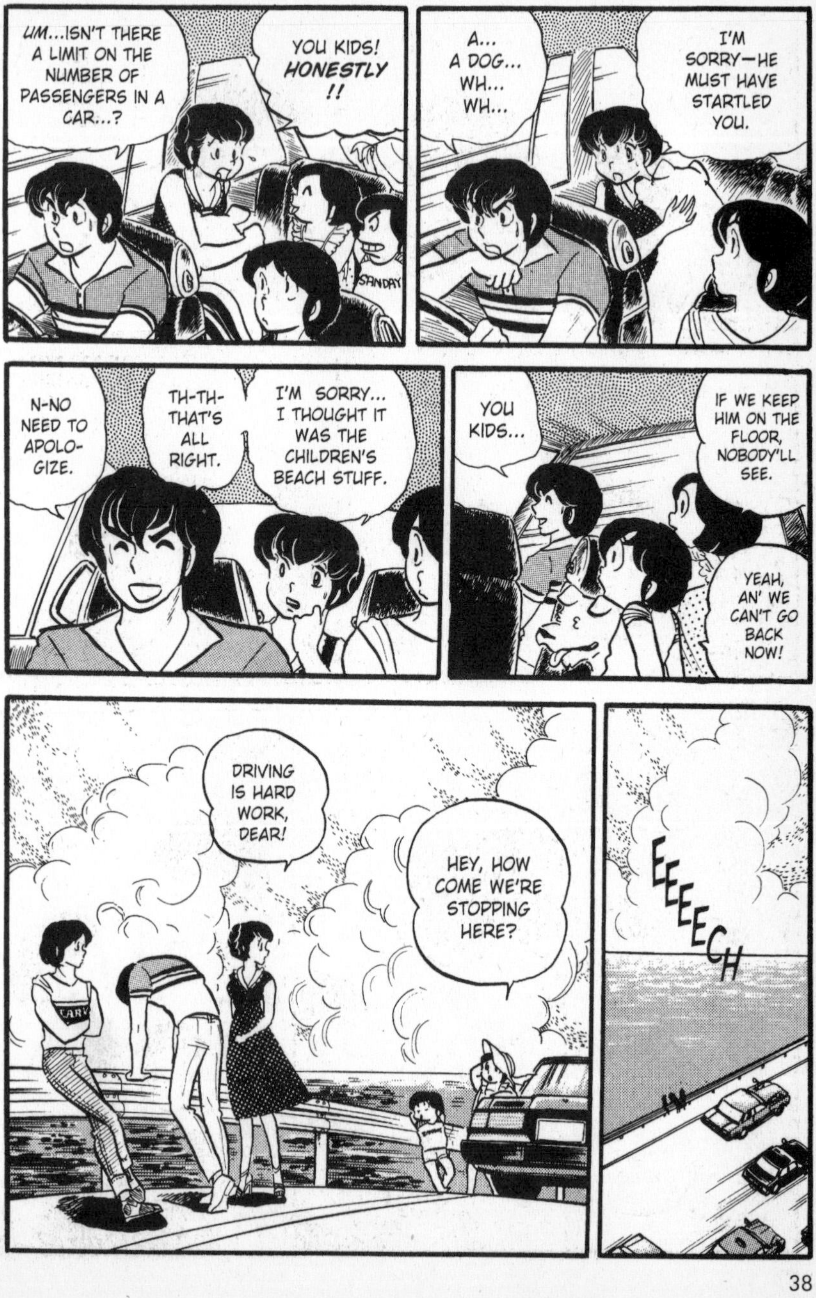
I'M SORRY—HE MUST HAVE STARTLED YOU.
A... A DOG... WH... WH...
YOU KIDS! HONESTLY!!
UM...ISN'T THERE A LIMIT ON THE NUMBER OF PASSENGERS IN A CAR...?
SANDAY
IF WE KEEP HIM ON THE FLOOR, NOBODY'LL SEE.
YOU KIDS...
YEAH, AN' WE CAN'T GO BACK NOW!
I'M SORRY... I THOUGHT IT WAS THE CHILDREN'S BEACH STUFF.
TH-TH-THAT'S ALL RIGHT.
N-NO NEED TO APOLOGIZE.
EEEEECH
HEY, HOW COME WE'RE STOPPING HERE?
DRIVING IS HARD WORK, DEAR!

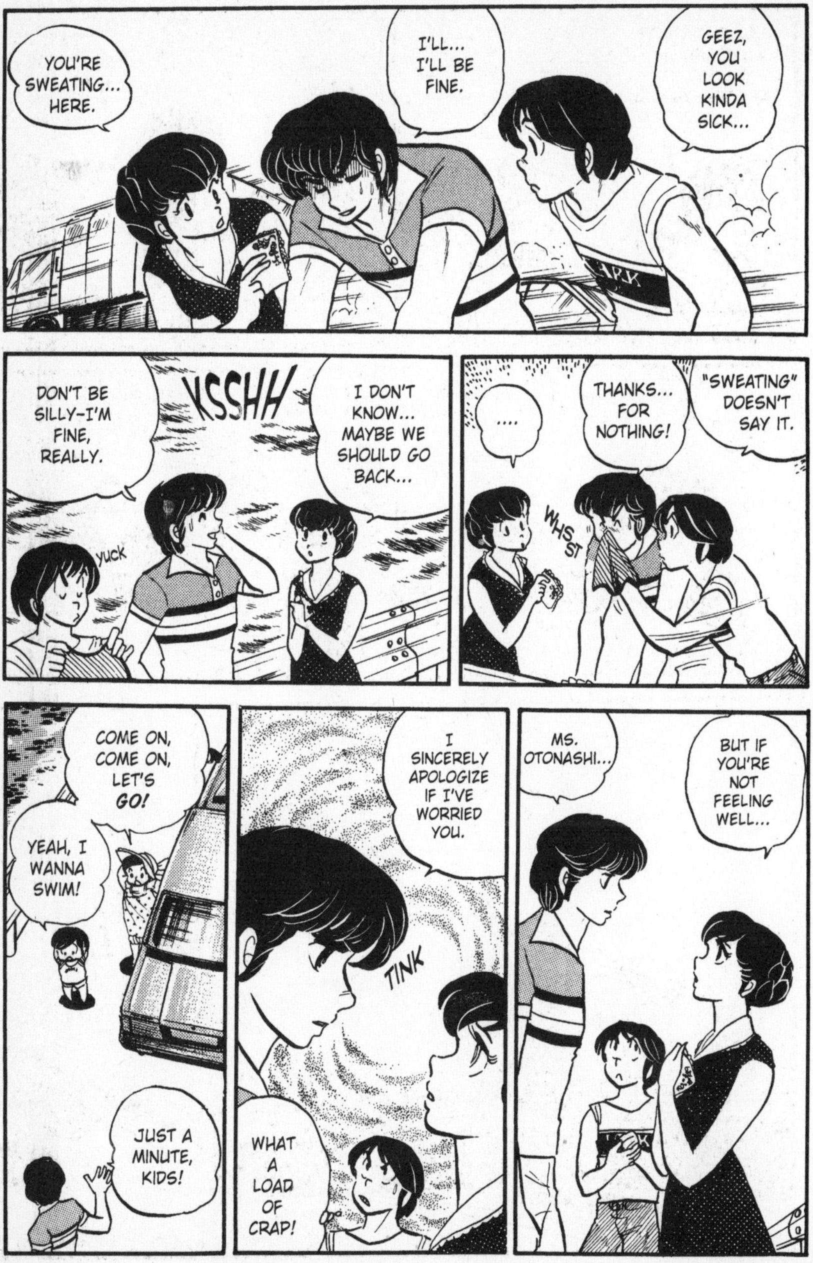
GEEZ, YOU LOOK KINDA SICK...
I'LL... I'LL BE FINE.
YOU'RE SWEATING... HERE.
"SWEATING" DOESN'T SAY IT.
THANKS... FOR NOTHING!
....
WHSST
I DON'T KNOW... MAYBE WE SHOULD GO BACK...
KSSHH
DON'T BE SILLY–I'M FINE, REALLY.
YUCK
BUT IF YOU'RE NOT FEELING WELL...
MS. OTONASHI...
I SINCERELY APOLOGIZE IF I'VE WORRIED YOU.
TINK
WHAT A LOAD OF CRAP!
COME ON, COME ON, LET'S GO!
YEAH, I WANNA SWIM!
JUST A MINUTE, KIDS!

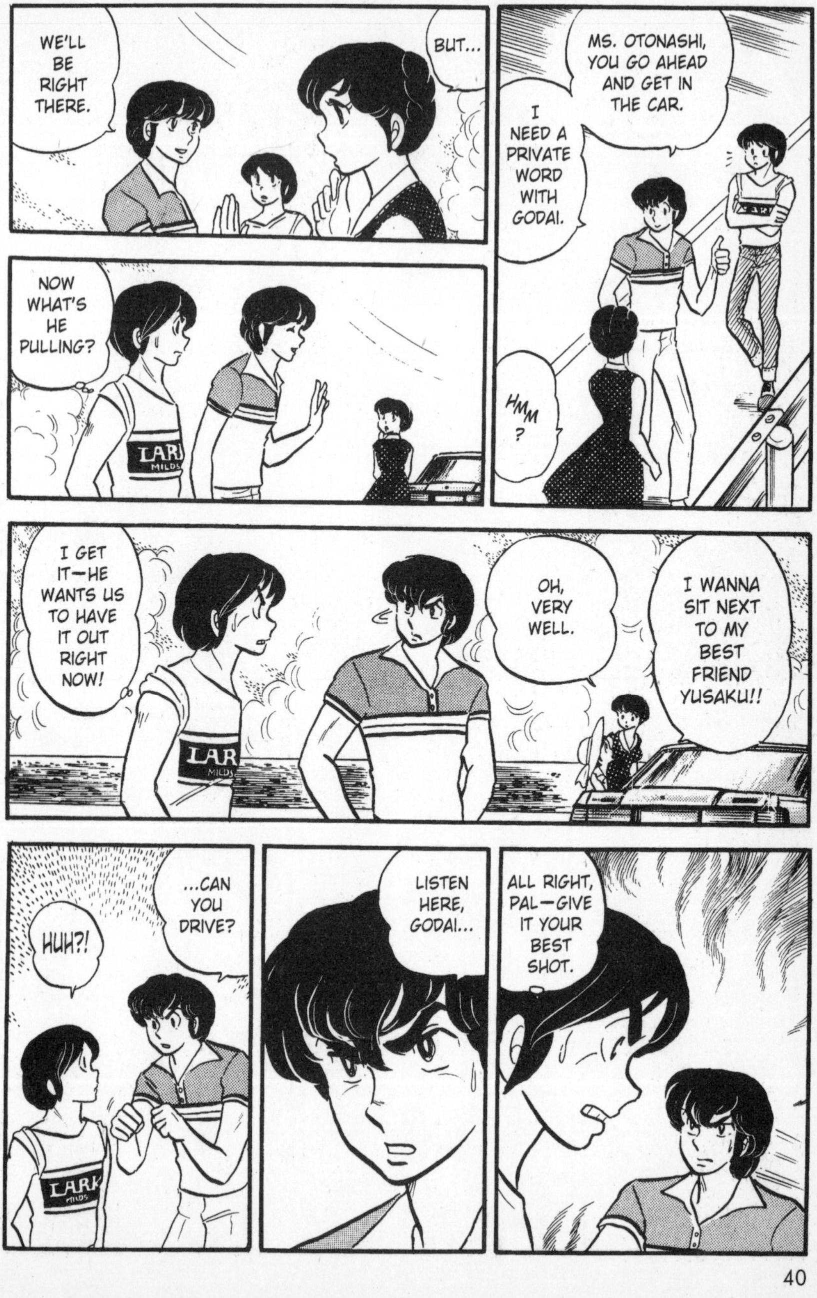
MS. OTONASHI, YOU GO AHEAD AND GET IN THE CAR.
I NEED A PRIVATE WORD WITH GODAI.
HMM?
BUT...
WE'LL BE RIGHT THERE.
NOW WHAT'S HE PULLING?
I WANNA SIT NEXT TO MY BEST FRIEND YUSAKU!!
OH, VERY WELL.
I GET IT—HE WANTS US TO HAVE IT OUT RIGHT NOW!
ALL RIGHT, PAL—GIVE IT YOUR BEST SHOT.
LISTEN HERE, GODAI...
...CAN YOU DRIVE?
HUH?!

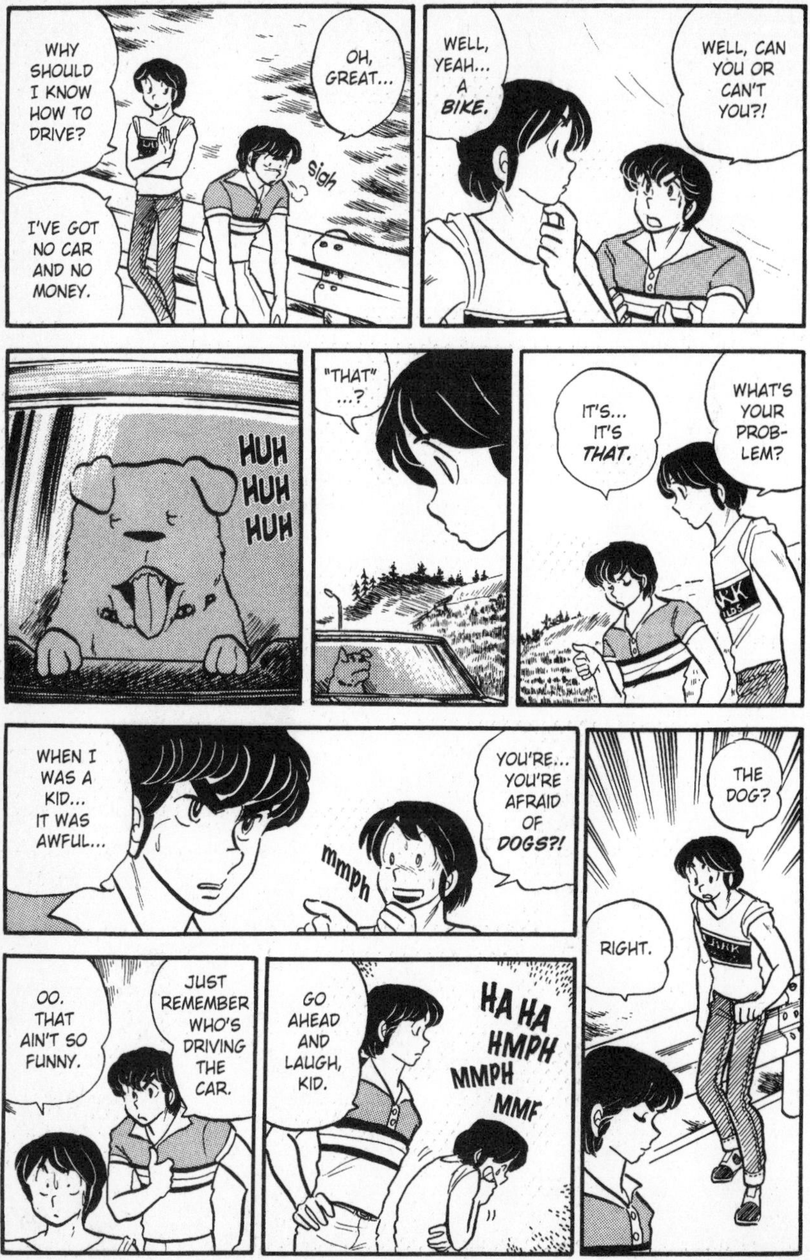
WELL, CAN YOU OR CAN'T YOU?!
WELL, YEAH... A *BIKE.*
OH, GREAT...
sigh
WHY SHOULD I KNOW HOW TO DRIVE?
I'VE GOT NO CAR AND NO MONEY.
WHAT'S YOUR PROB-LEM?
IT'S... IT'S *THAT.*
"THAT" ...?
HUH HUH HUH
THE DOG?
RIGHT.
YOU'RE... YOU'RE AFRAID OF *DOGS?!*
mmph
WHEN I WAS A KID... IT WAS AWFUL...
HA HA HMPH MMPH MMF
GO AHEAD AND LAUGH, KID.
JUST REMEMBER WHO'S DRIVING THE CAR.
OO. THAT AIN'T SO FUNNY.

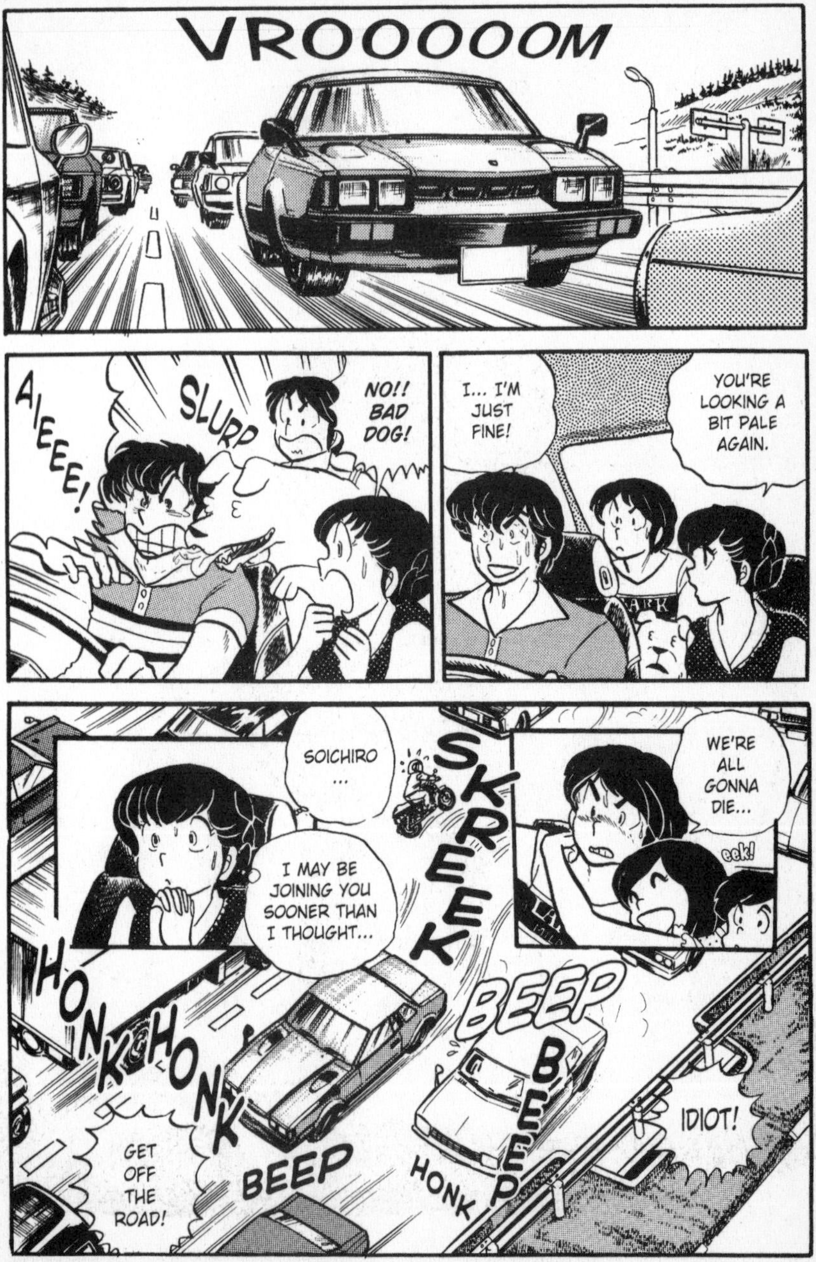
VROOOOOM
YOU'RE LOOKING A BIT PALE AGAIN.
I... I'M JUST FINE!
NO!! BAD DOG!
SLURP
AIEEEE!
WE'RE ALL GONNA DIE...
eek!
SOICHIRO ...
I MAY BE JOINING YOU SOONER THAN I THOUGHT...
SKREEK
IDIOT!
BEEP
BEEP
HONK
HONK HONK
BEEP
GET OFF THE ROAD!

PART THREE
A SALTY DOG

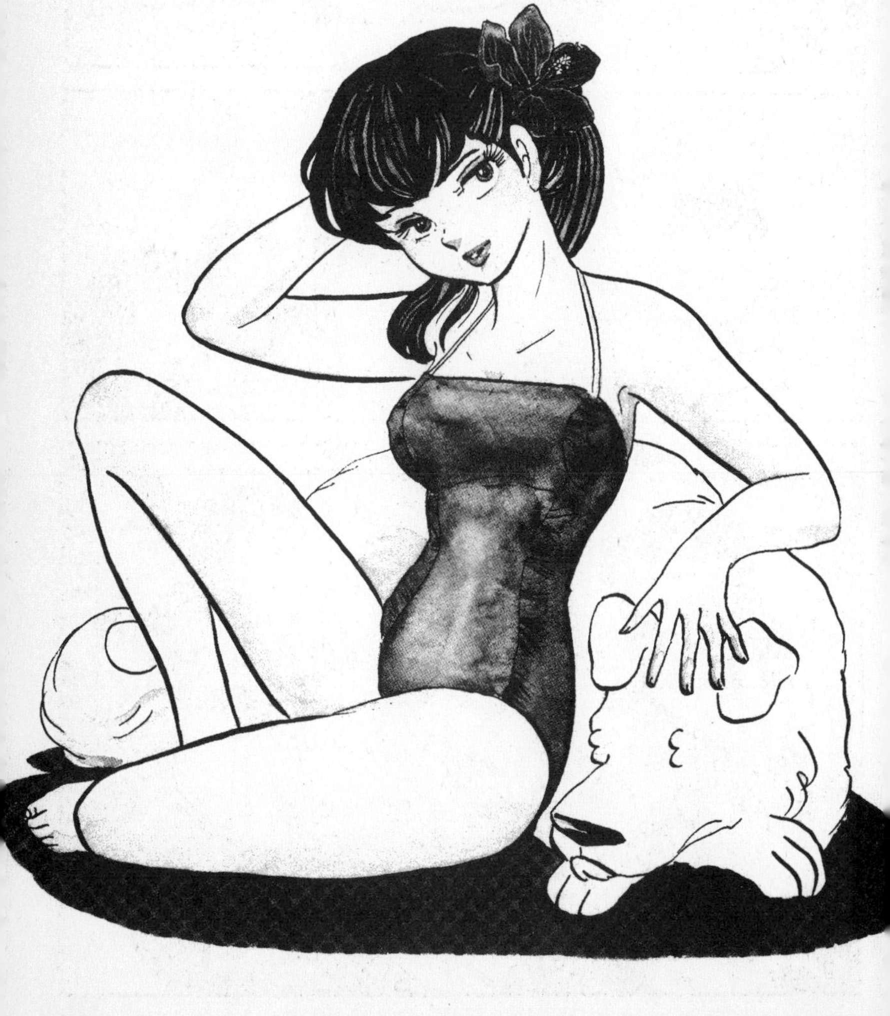

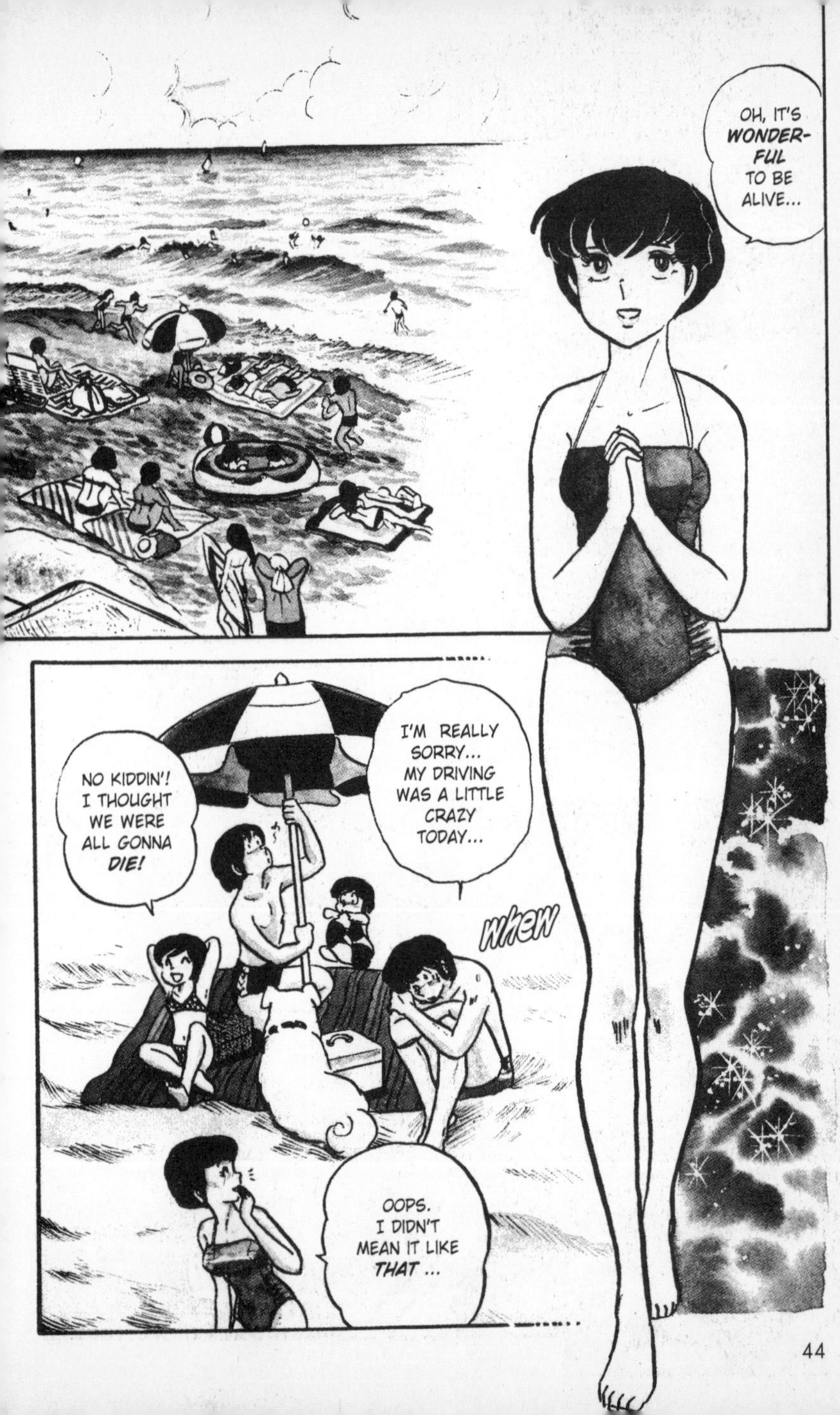
OH, IT'S *WONDERFUL* TO BE ALIVE...
I'M REALLY SORRY... MY DRIVING WAS A LITTLE CRAZY TODAY...
NO KIDDIN'! I THOUGHT WE WERE ALL GONNA *DIE!*
whew
OOPS. I DIDN'T MEAN IT LIKE *THAT* ...

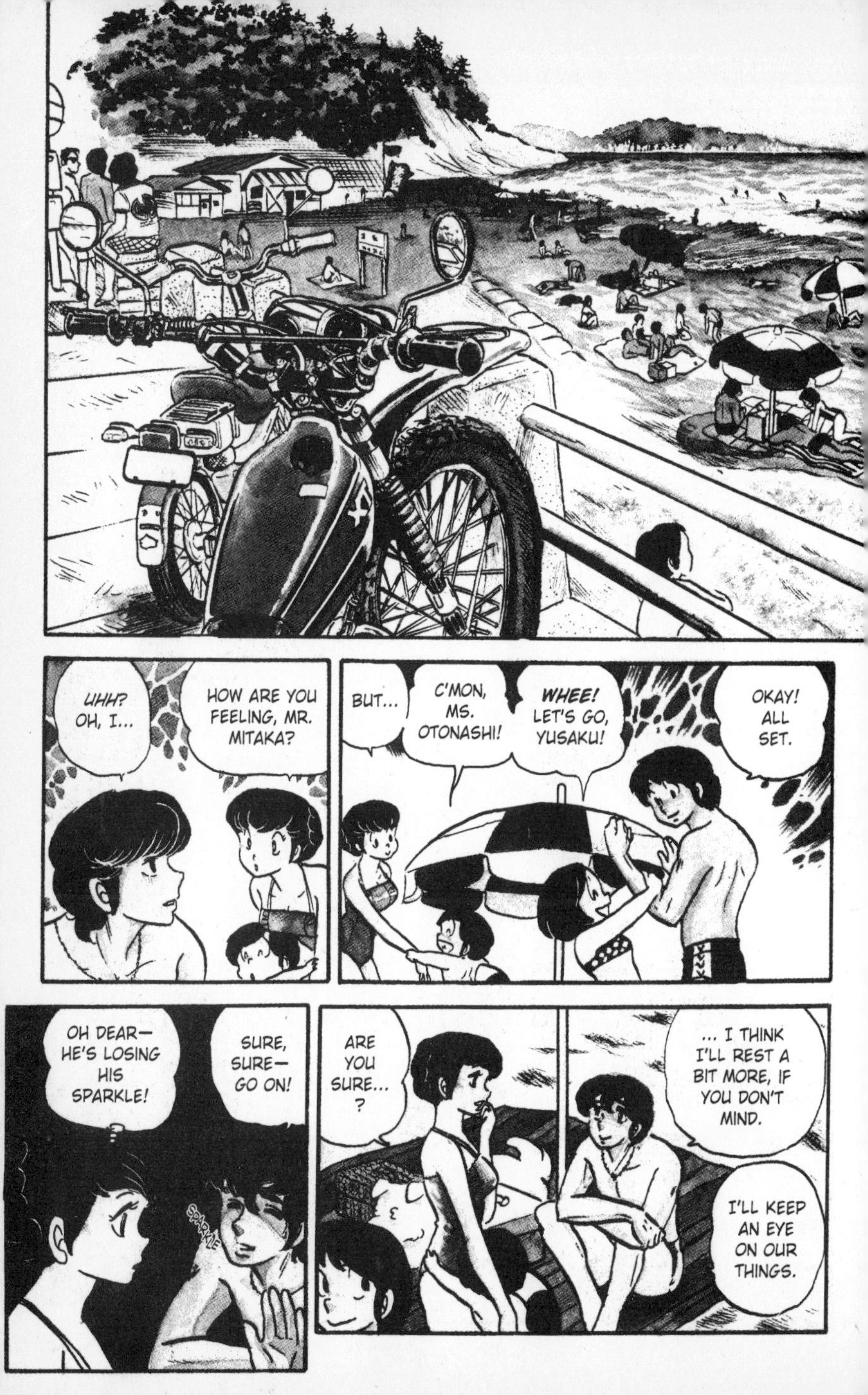
OKAY! ALL SET.
WHEE! LET'S GO, YUSAKU!
C'MON, MS. OTONASHI!
BUT...
HOW ARE YOU FEELING, MR. MITAKA?
UHH? OH, I...
... I THINK I'LL REST A BIT MORE, IF YOU DON'T MIND.
I'LL KEEP AN EYE ON OUR THINGS.
ARE YOU SURE...?
SURE, SURE— GO ON!
SPARKLE
OH DEAR— HE'S LOSING HIS SPARKLE!

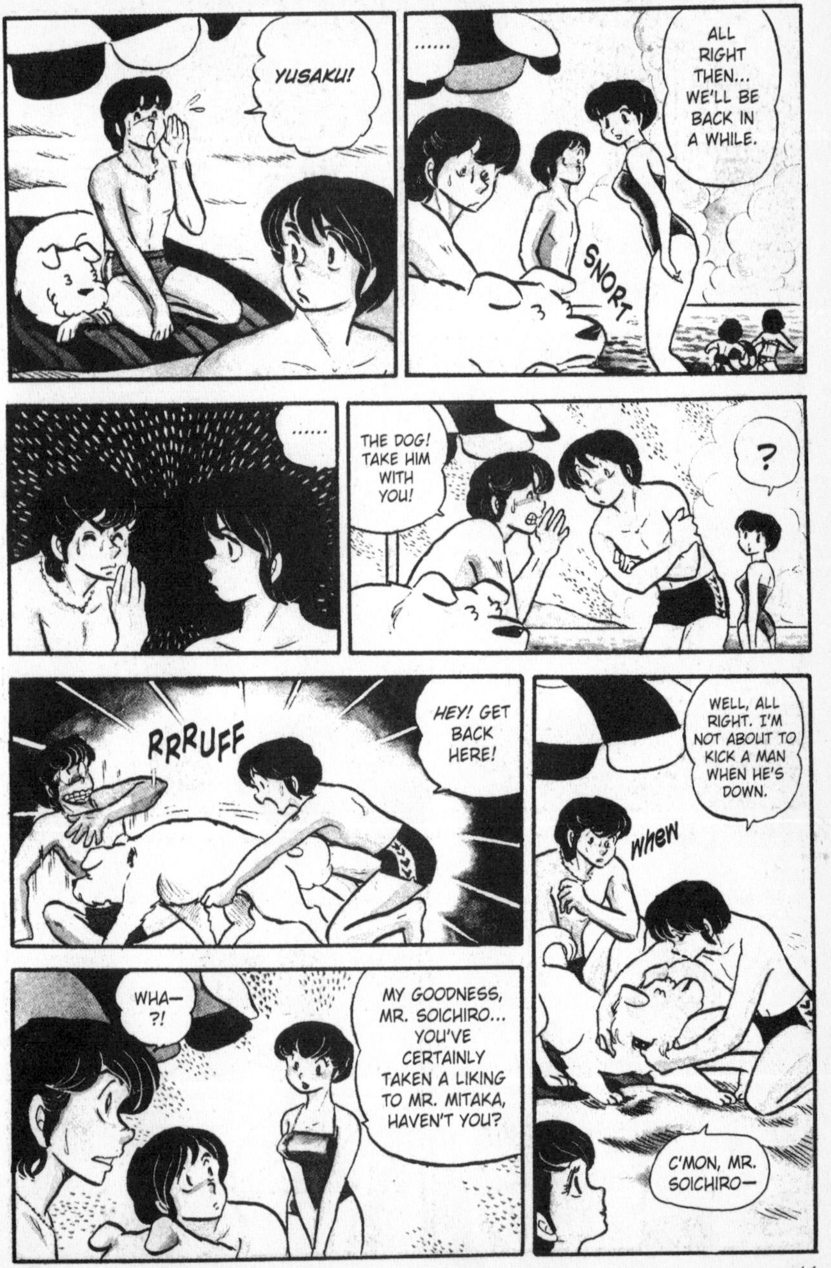
ALL RIGHT THEN... WE'LL BE BACK IN A WHILE.
......
SNORT
YUSAKU!
?
THE DOG! TAKE HIM WITH YOU!
......
WELL, ALL RIGHT. I'M NOT ABOUT TO KICK A MAN WHEN HE'S DOWN.
whew
C'MON, MR. SOICHIRO—
HEY! GET BACK HERE!
RRRUFF
MY GOODNESS, MR. SOICHIRO... YOU'VE CERTAINLY TAKEN A LIKING TO MR. MITAKA, HAVEN'T YOU?
WHA— ?!

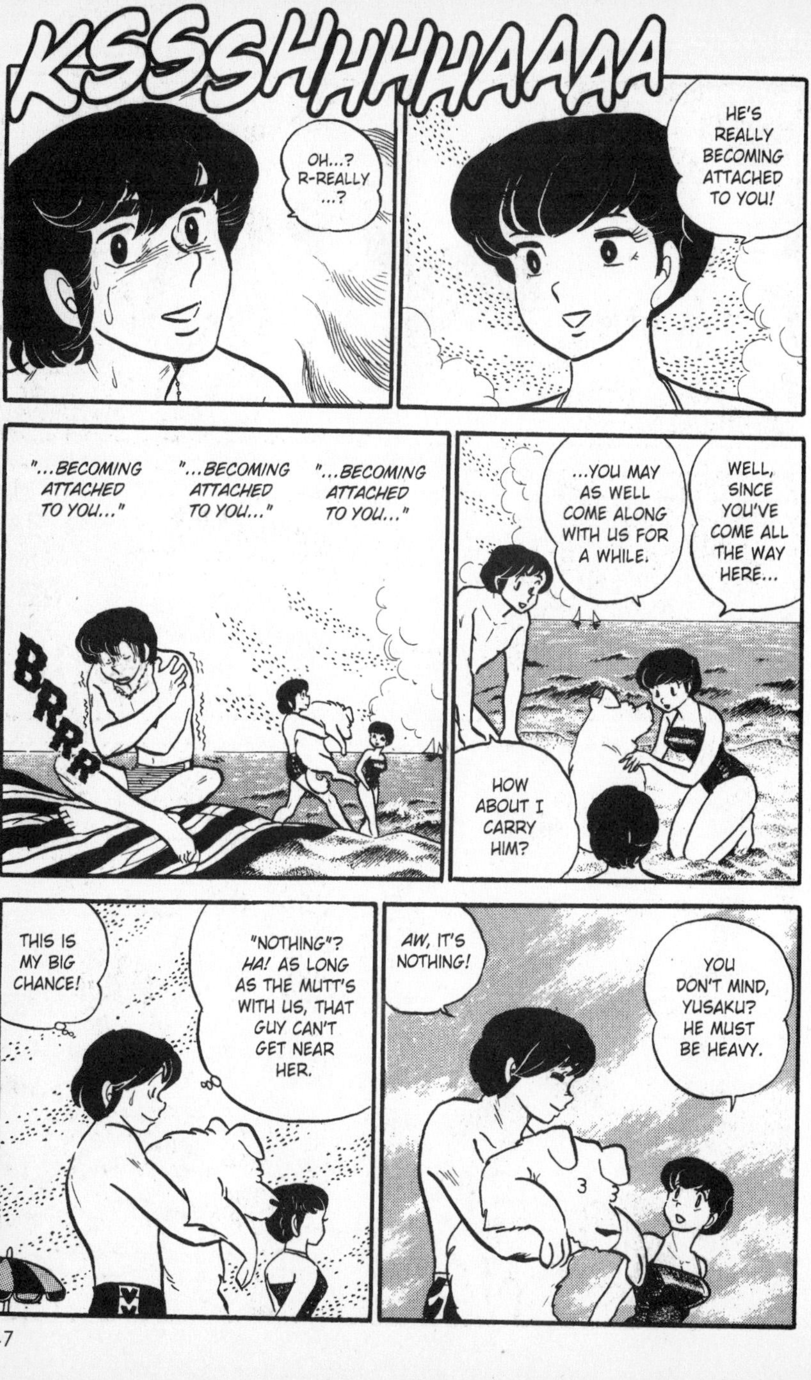
KSSSHHHAAAA
HE'S REALLY BECOMING ATTACHED TO YOU!
OH...? R-REALLY ...?
WELL, SINCE YOU'VE COME ALL THE WAY HERE...
...YOU MAY AS WELL COME ALONG WITH US FOR A WHILE.
HOW ABOUT I CARRY HIM?
"...BECOMING ATTACHED TO YOU..."
"...BECOMING ATTACHED TO YOU..."
"...BECOMING ATTACHED TO YOU..."
BRRRR
YOU DON'T MIND, YUSAKU? HE MUST BE HEAVY.
AW, IT'S NOTHING!
"NOTHING"? *HA!* AS LONG AS THE MUTT'S WITH US, THAT GUY CAN'T GET NEAR HER.
THIS IS MY BIG CHANCE!

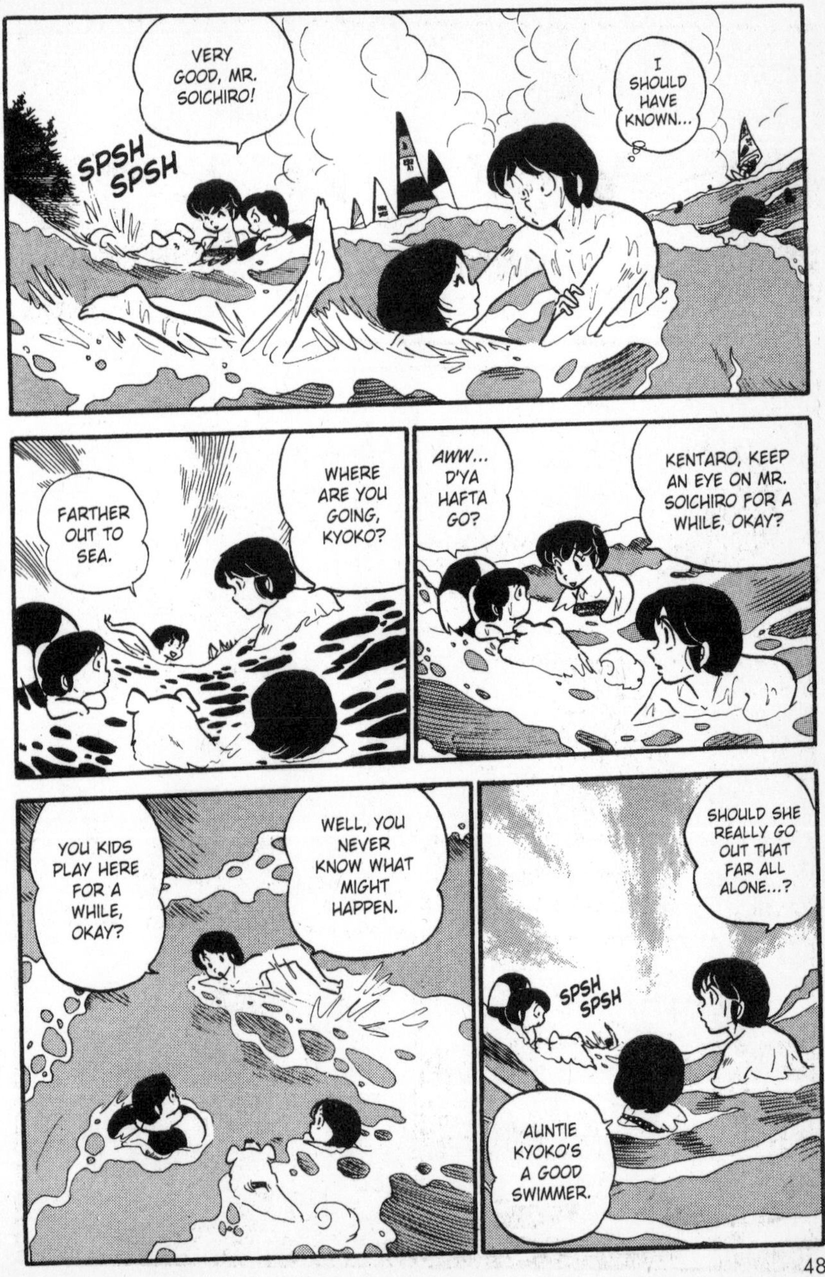
I SHOULD HAVE KNOWN...
VERY GOOD, MR. SOICHIRO!
SPSH SPSH
KENTARO, KEEP AN EYE ON MR. SOICHIRO FOR A WHILE, OKAY?
AWW... D'YA HAFTA GO?
WHERE ARE YOU GOING, KYOKO?
FARTHER OUT TO SEA.
SHOULD SHE REALLY GO OUT THAT FAR ALL ALONE...?
SPSH SPSH
AUNTIE KYOKO'S A GOOD SWIMMER.
WELL, YOU NEVER KNOW WHAT MIGHT HAPPEN.
YOU KIDS PLAY HERE FOR A WHILE, OKAY?

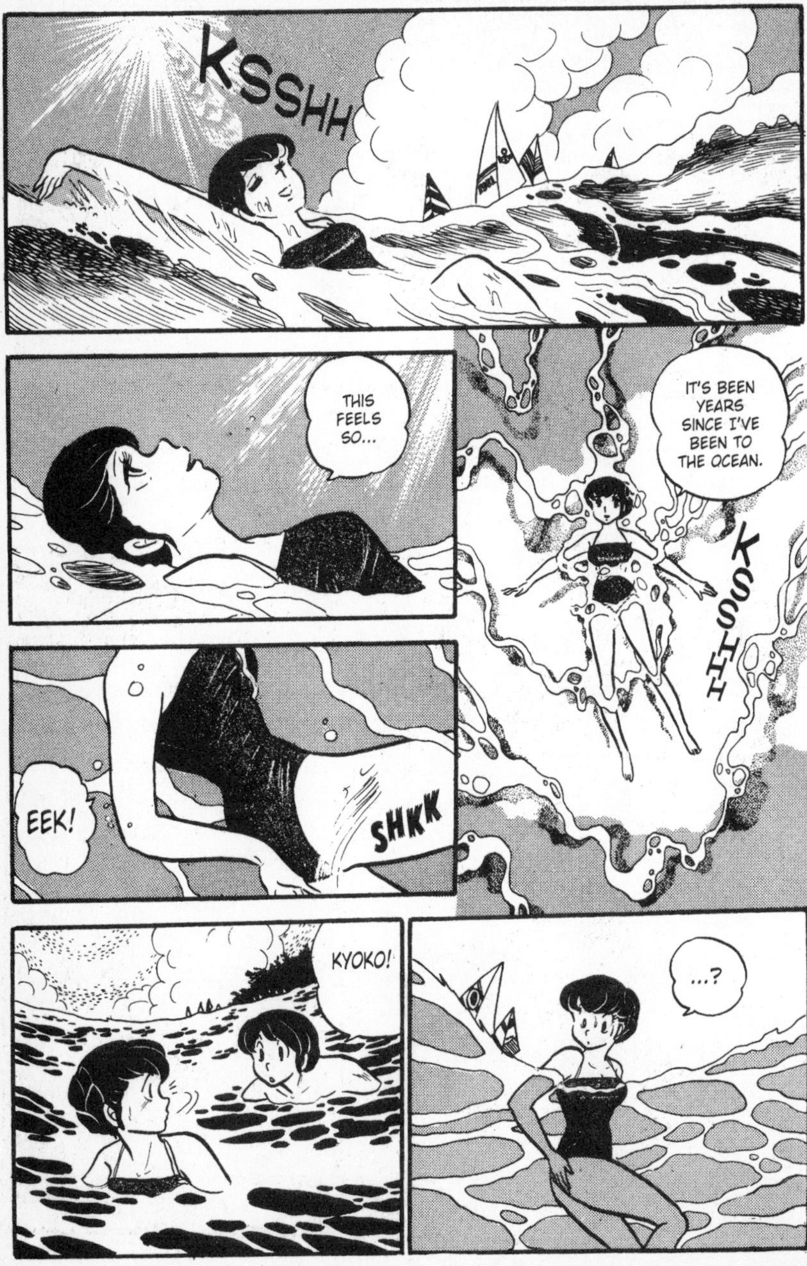
KSSHH
IT'S BEEN YEARS SINCE I'VE BEEN TO THE OCEAN.
KSSHH
THIS FEELS SO...
EEK!
SHKK
...?
KYOKO!

...?
hmph!
WHAT'S WRONG? YOU OKAY?
SPLSH
"WHAT'S WRONG," HE SAYS!
YOU SHOULDN'T BE OUT HERE BY YOURSELF! WHO KNOWS WHAT KIND OF DEVIANT MIGHT BOTHER YOU.
LOOK WHO'S TALKING!
SWAK
I DON'T BELIEVE THIS GUY!
DOES HE THINK HE CAN DO WHAT HE WANTS JUST BECAUSE I'M A WIDOW?
LOOK, YUSAKU! YOU'D BETTER LISTEN TO ME!
?

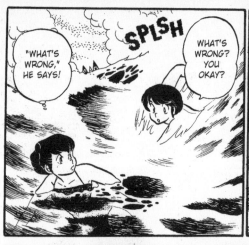

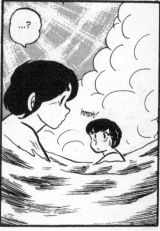

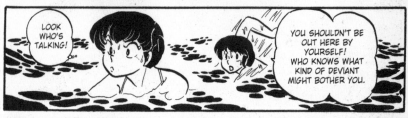

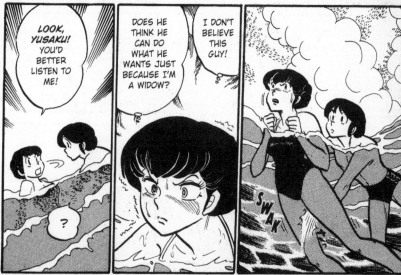

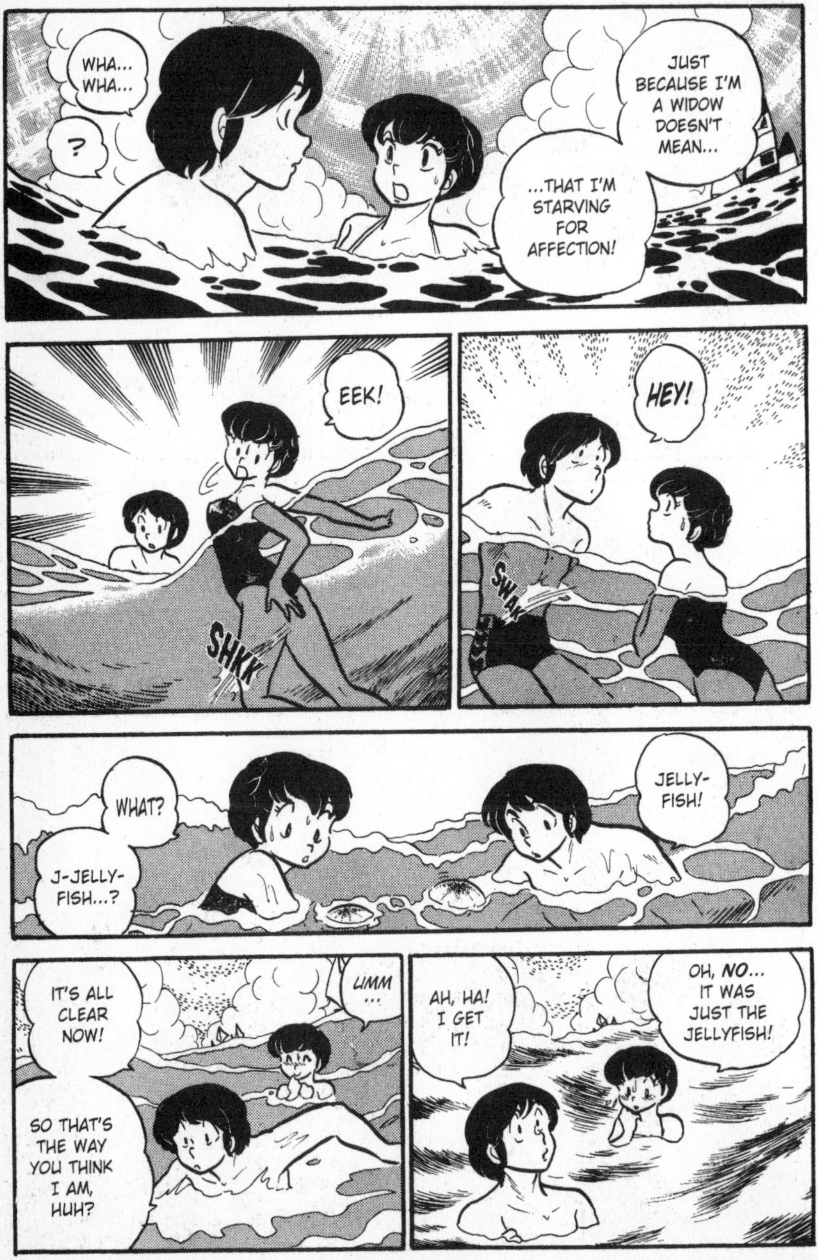
JUST BECAUSE I'M A WIDOW DOESN'T MEAN...
...THAT I'M STARVING FOR AFFECTION!
WHA... WHA...
?
HEY!
SWAK
EEK!
SHKK
JELLY-FISH!
WHAT?
J-JELLY-FISH...?
OH, NO... IT WAS JUST THE JELLYFISH!
AH, HA! I GET IT!
UMM ...
IT'S ALL CLEAR NOW!
SO THAT'S THE WAY YOU THINK I AM, HUH?

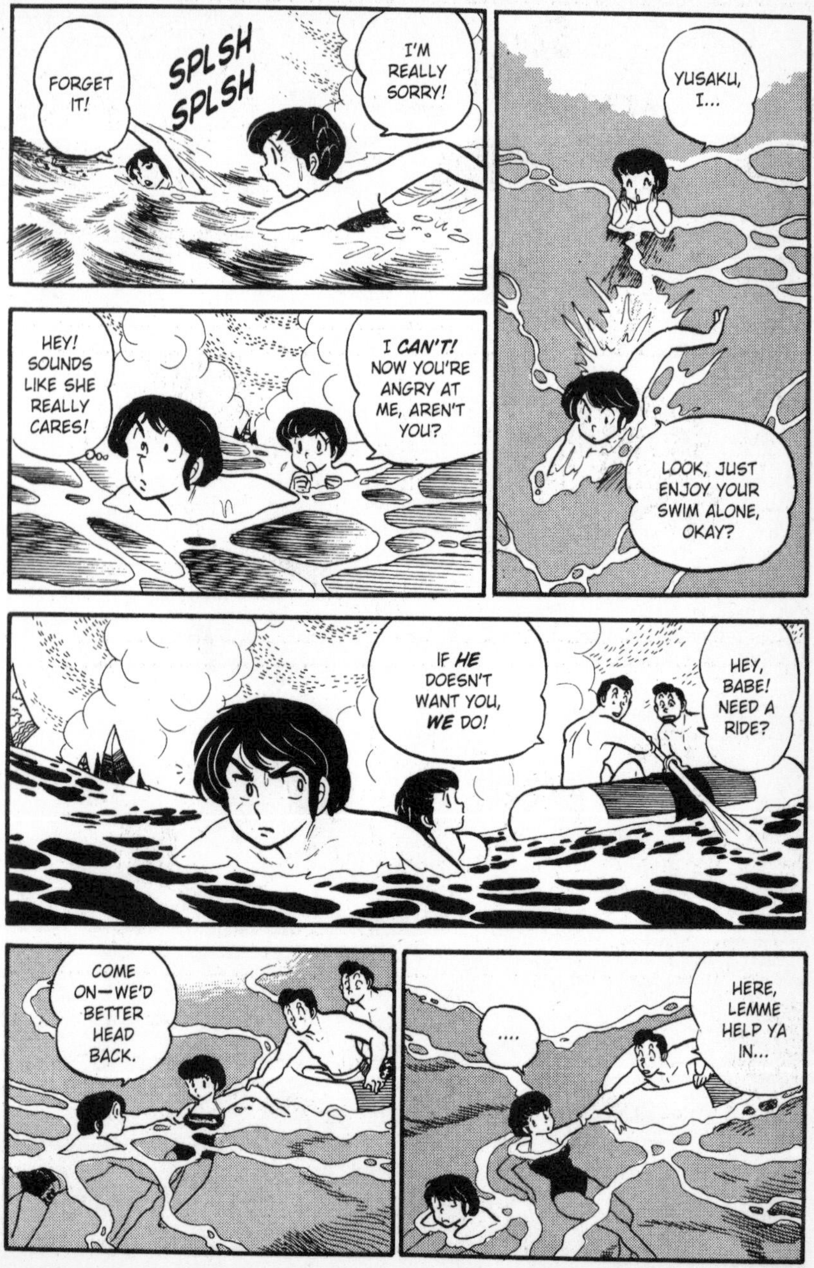
YUSAKU, I...
LOOK, JUST ENJOY YOUR SWIM ALONE, OKAY?
I'M REALLY SORRY!
SPLSH SPLSH
FORGET IT!
I CAN'T! NOW YOU'RE ANGRY AT ME, AREN'T YOU?
HEY! SOUNDS LIKE SHE REALLY CARES!
HEY, BABE! NEED A RIDE?
IF HE DOESN'T WANT YOU, WE DO!
HERE, LEMME HELP YA IN...
....
COME ON—WE'D BETTER HEAD BACK.

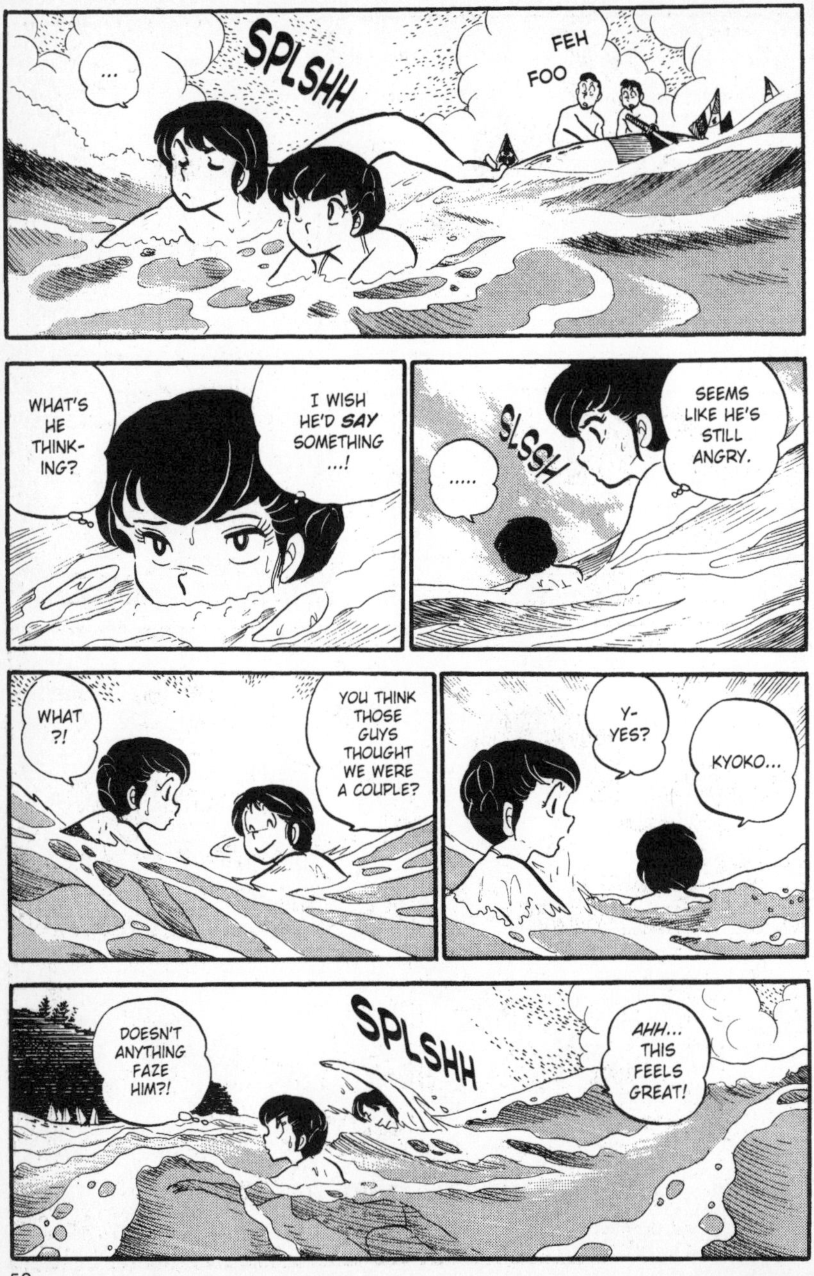
FEH
FOO
SPLSHH
...
SEEMS LIKE HE'S STILL ANGRY.
SLSSH
.....
I WISH HE'D *SAY* SOMETHING ...!
WHAT'S HE THINKING?
KYOKO...
Y- YES?
YOU THINK THOSE GUYS THOUGHT WE WERE A COUPLE?
WHAT ?!
AHH... THIS FEELS GREAT!
SPLSHH
DOESN'T ANYTHING FAZE HIM?!

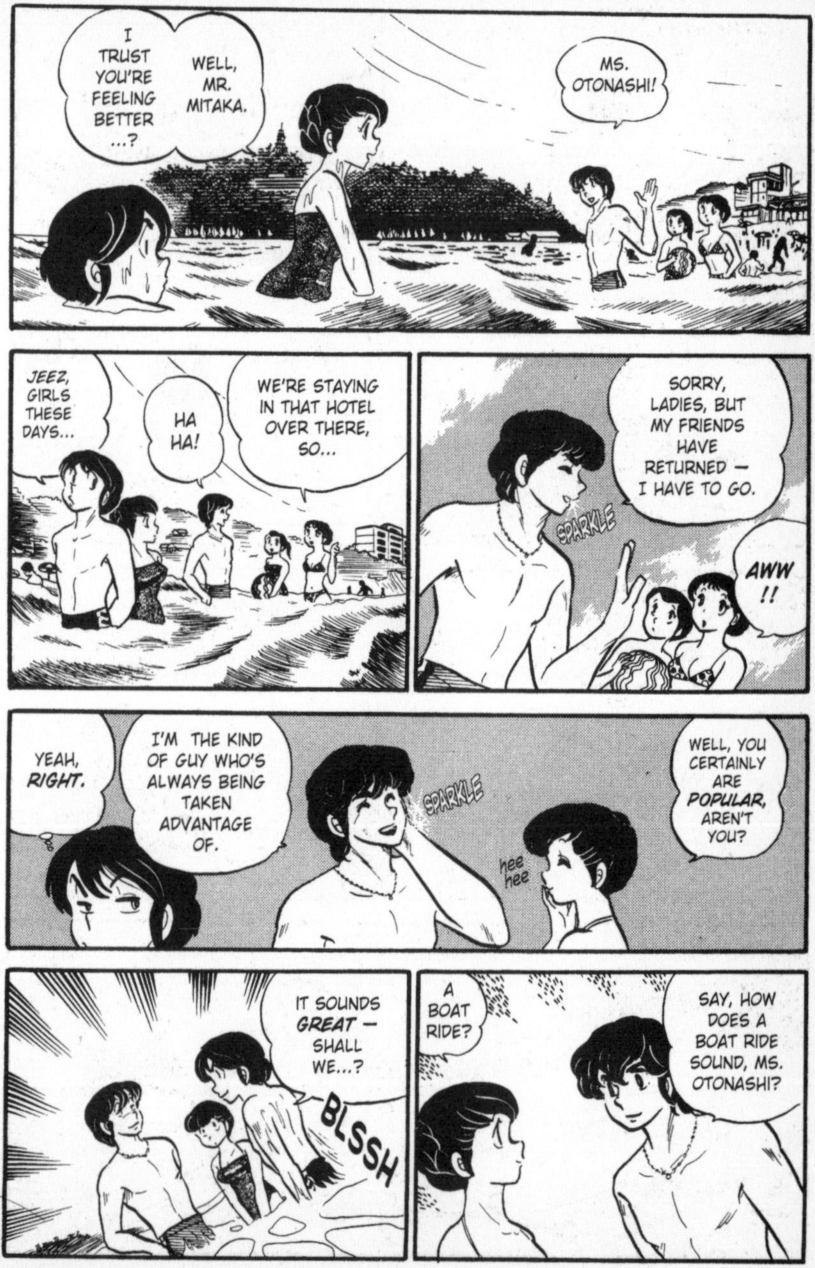
MS. OTONASHI!
WELL, MR. MITAKA.
I TRUST YOU'RE FEELING BETTER ...?
SORRY, LADIES, BUT MY FRIENDS HAVE RETURNED — I HAVE TO GO.
SPARKLE
AWW !!
WE'RE STAYING IN THAT HOTEL OVER THERE, SO...
HA HA!
JEEZ, GIRLS THESE DAYS...
WELL, YOU CERTAINLY ARE POPULAR, AREN'T YOU?
hee hee
SPARKLE
I'M THE KIND OF GUY WHO'S ALWAYS BEING TAKEN ADVANTAGE OF.
YEAH, RIGHT.
SAY, HOW DOES A BOAT RIDE SOUND, MS. OTONASHI?
A BOAT RIDE?
IT SOUNDS GREAT — SHALL WE...?
BLSSH

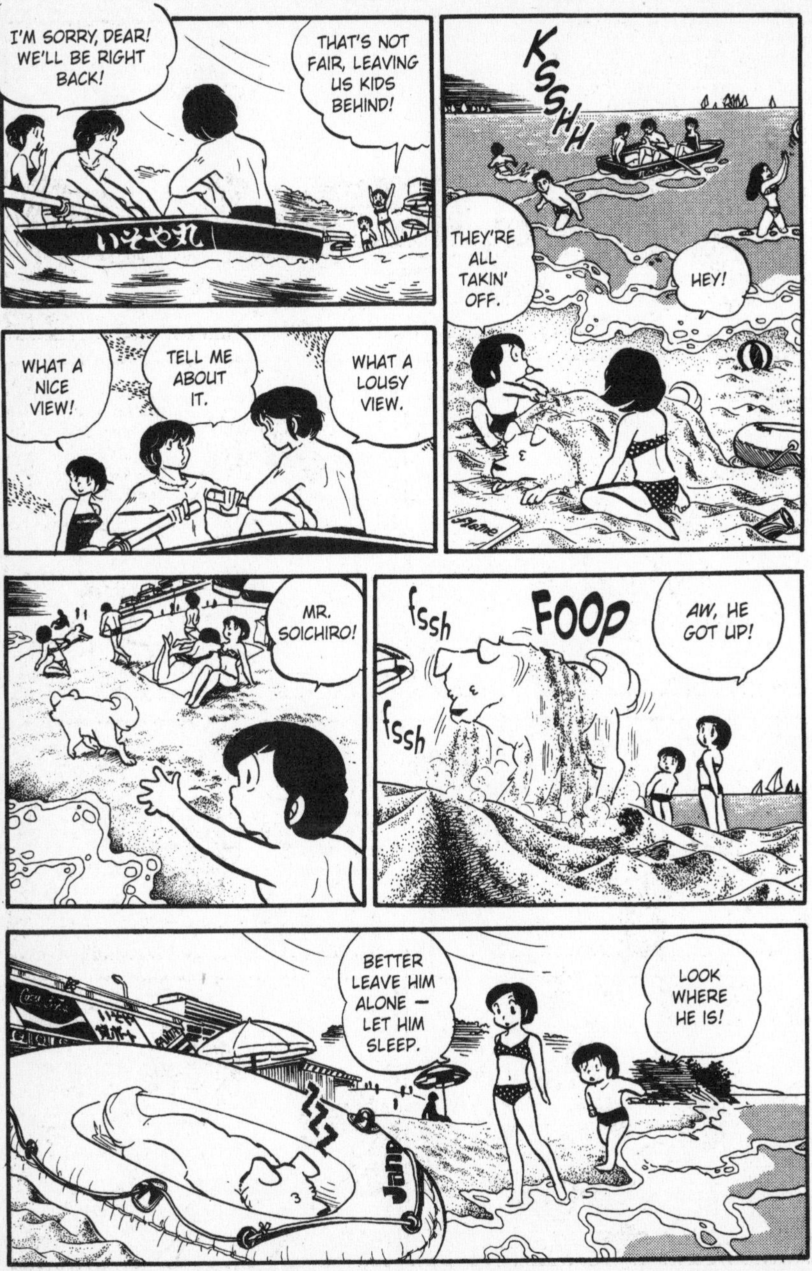
KSSHH
HEY!
THEY'RE ALL TAKIN' OFF.
THAT'S NOT FAIR, LEAVING US KIDS BEHIND!
I'M SORRY, DEAR! WE'LL BE RIGHT BACK!
いそや丸
WHAT A LOUSY VIEW.
TELL ME ABOUT IT.
WHAT A NICE VIEW!
AW, HE GOT UP!
FOOP
fssh
fssh
MR. SOICHIRO!
LOOK WHERE HE IS!
BETTER LEAVE HIM ALONE — LET HIM SLEEP.
ZZZ

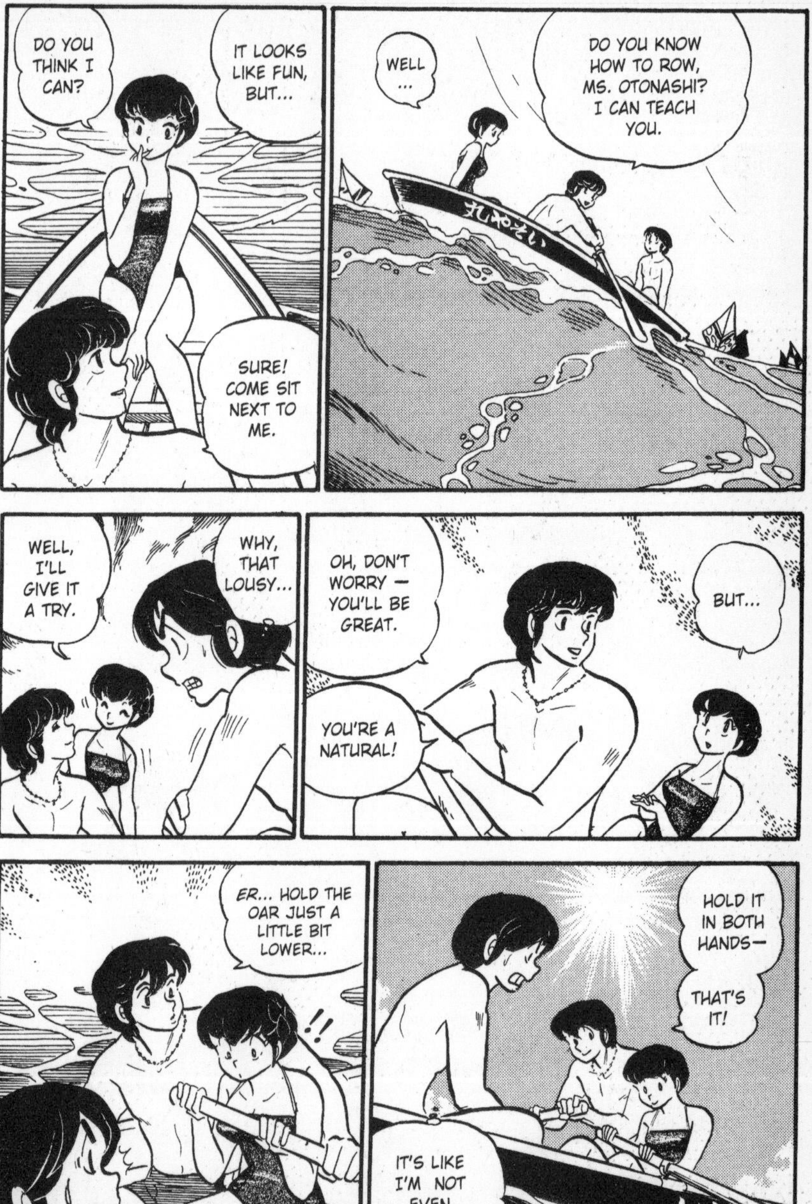
DO YOU KNOW HOW TO ROW, MS. OTONASHI? I CAN TEACH YOU.
WELL ...
IT LOOKS LIKE FUN, BUT...
DO YOU THINK I CAN?
SURE! COME SIT NEXT TO ME.
BUT...
OH, DON'T WORRY — YOU'LL BE GREAT.
YOU'RE A NATURAL!
WHY, THAT LOUSY...
WELL, I'LL GIVE IT A TRY.
HOLD IT IN BOTH HANDS—
THAT'S IT!
IT'S LIKE I'M NOT EVEN HERE!
ER... HOLD THE OAR JUST A LITTLE BIT LOWER...
!!

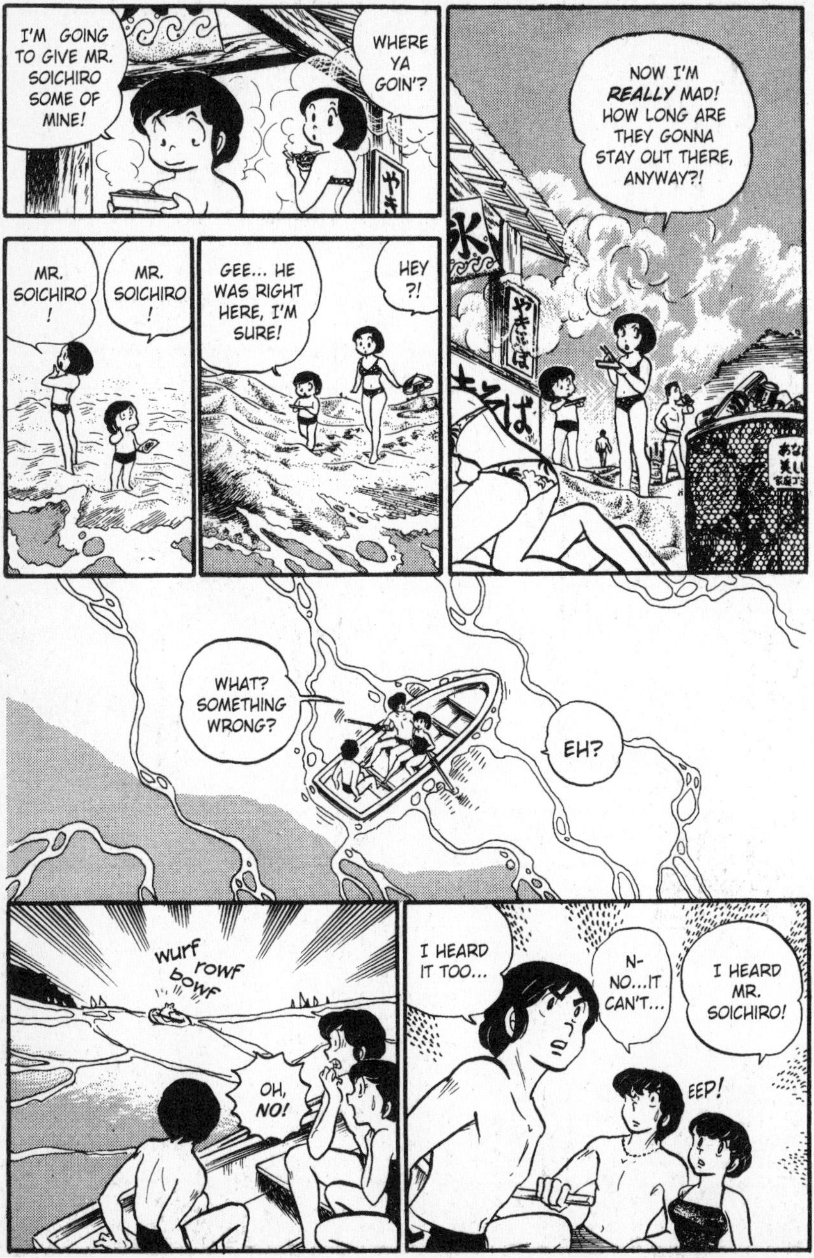
NOW I'M **REALLY** MAD! HOW LONG ARE THEY GONNA STAY OUT THERE, ANYWAY?!
氷
やきそば
WHERE YA GOIN'?
I'M GOING TO GIVE MR. SOICHIRO SOME OF MINE!
HEY ?!
GEE... HE WAS RIGHT HERE, I'M SURE!
MR. SOICHIRO!
MR. SOICHIRO!
WHAT? SOMETHING WRONG?
EH?
I HEARD MR. SOICHIRO!
N- NO...IT CAN'T...
I HEARD IT TOO...
EEP!
wurf rowf bowf
OH, **NO!**

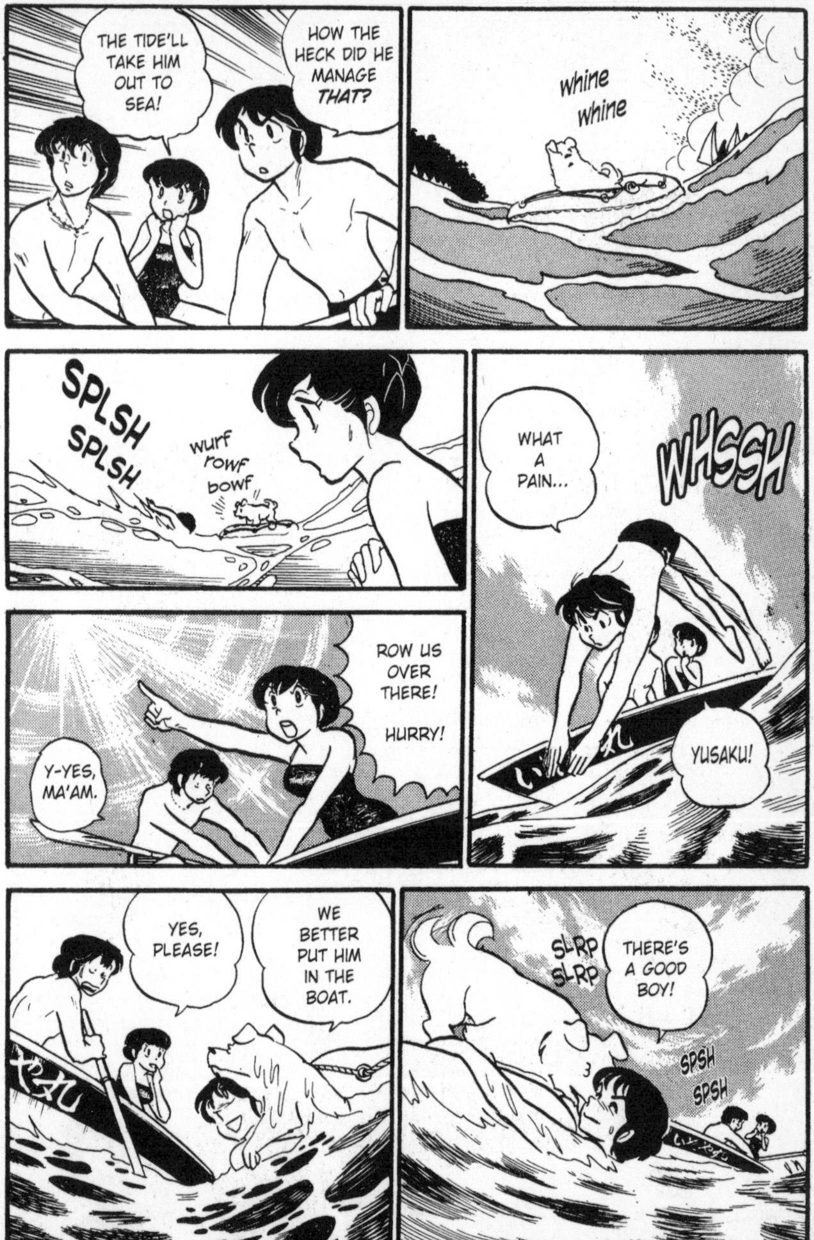
whine whine
HOW THE HECK DID HE MANAGE THAT?
THE TIDE'LL TAKE HIM OUT TO SEA!
WHSSH
WHAT A PAIN...
YUSAKU!
wurf rowf bowf
SPLSH SPLSH
ROW US OVER THERE!
HURRY!
Y-YES, MA'AM.
THERE'S A GOOD BOY!
SLRP SLRP
SPSH SPSH
WE BETTER PUT HIM IN THE BOAT.
YES, PLEASE!

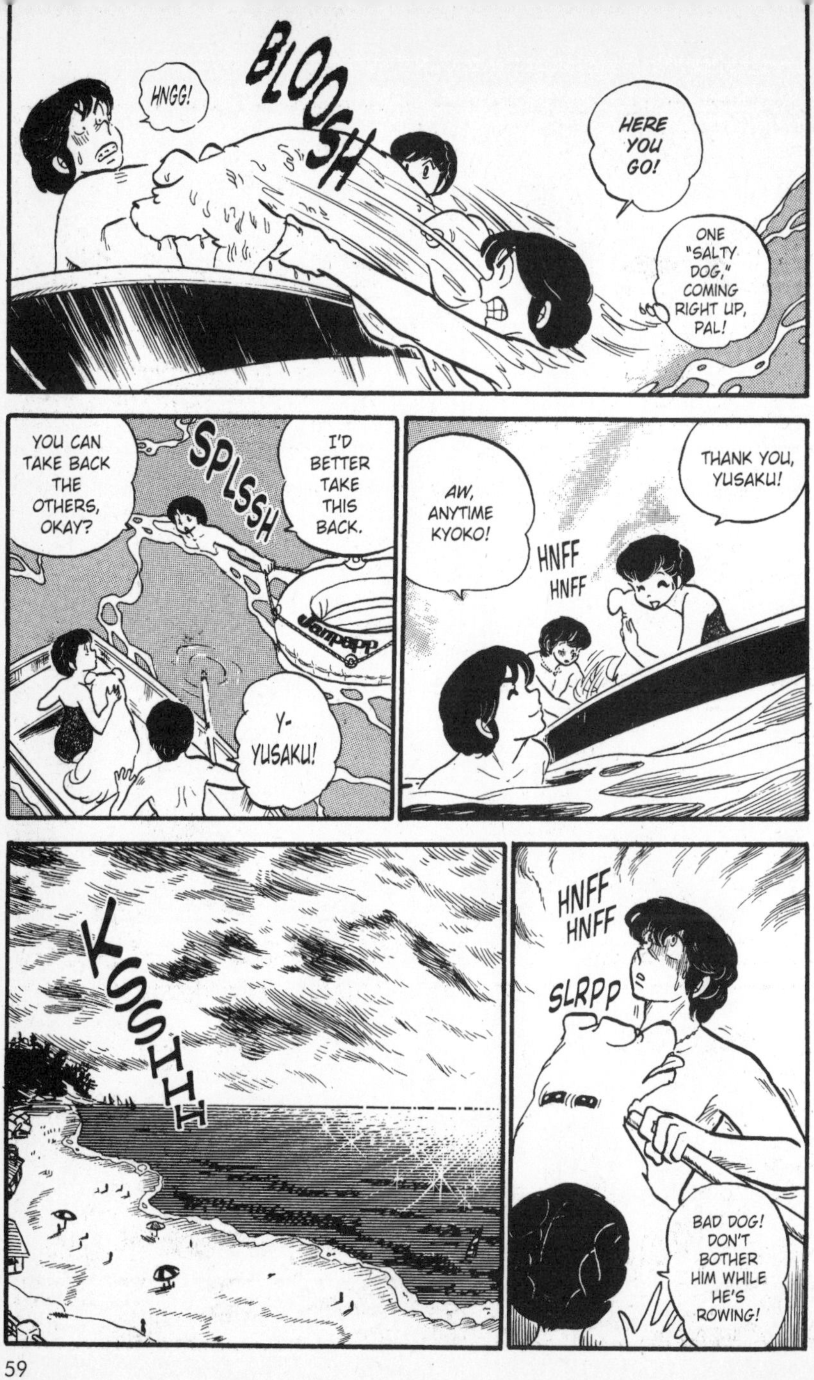
HERE YOU GO!
ONE "SALTY DOG," COMING RIGHT UP, PAL!
BLOOSH
HNGG!
THANK YOU, YUSAKU!
AW, ANYTIME KYOKO!
HNFF HNFF
I'D BETTER TAKE THIS BACK.
SPLSSH
YOU CAN TAKE BACK THE OTHERS, OKAY?
Y-YUSAKU!
HNFF HNFF
SLRPP
BAD DOG! DON'T BOTHER HIM WHILE HE'S ROWING!
KSSHHH

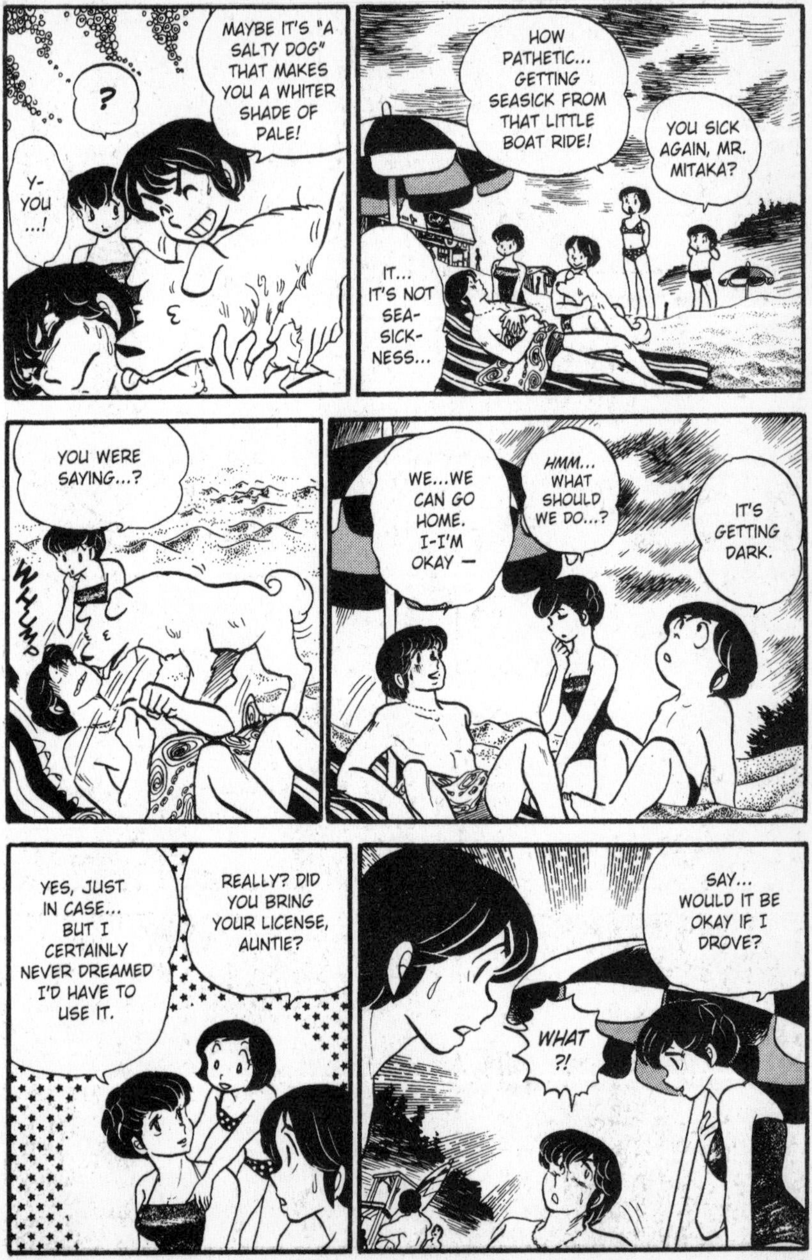
YOU SICK AGAIN, MR. MITAKA?
HOW PATHETIC... GETTING SEASICK FROM THAT LITTLE BOAT RIDE!
IT... IT'S NOT SEA-SICK-NESS...
MAYBE IT'S "A SALTY DOG" THAT MAKES YOU A WHITER SHADE OF PALE!
?
Y-YOU ...!
IT'S GETTING DARK.
HMM... WHAT SHOULD WE DO...?
WE...WE CAN GO HOME. I-I'M OKAY —
YOU WERE SAYING...?
WHUMP
SAY... WOULD IT BE OKAY IF I DROVE?
WHAT ?!
REALLY? DID YOU BRING YOUR LICENSE, AUNTIE?
YES, JUST IN CASE... BUT I CERTAINLY NEVER DREAMED I'D HAVE TO USE IT.

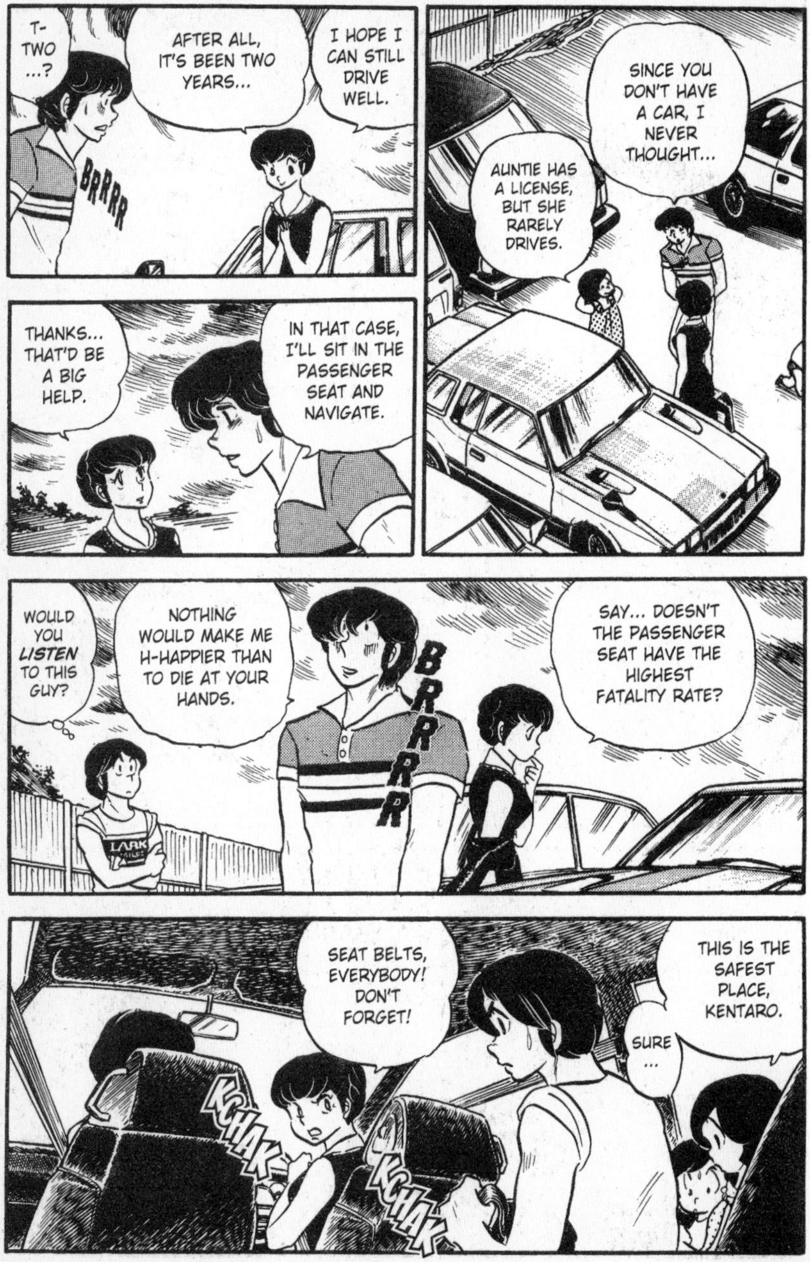
SINCE YOU DON'T HAVE A CAR, I NEVER THOUGHT...
AUNTIE HAS A LICENSE, BUT SHE RARELY DRIVES.
I HOPE I CAN STILL DRIVE WELL.
AFTER ALL, IT'S BEEN TWO YEARS...
T-TWO ...?
BRRRR
IN THAT CASE, I'LL SIT IN THE PASSENGER SEAT AND NAVIGATE.
THANKS... THAT'D BE A BIG HELP.
SAY... DOESN'T THE PASSENGER SEAT HAVE THE HIGHEST FATALITY RATE?
BRRRRR
NOTHING WOULD MAKE ME H-HAPPIER THAN TO DIE AT YOUR HANDS.
WOULD YOU *LISTEN* TO THIS GUY?
THIS IS THE SAFEST PLACE, KENTARO.
SURE ...
SEAT BELTS, EVERYBODY! DON'T FORGET!
KCHAK
KCHAK

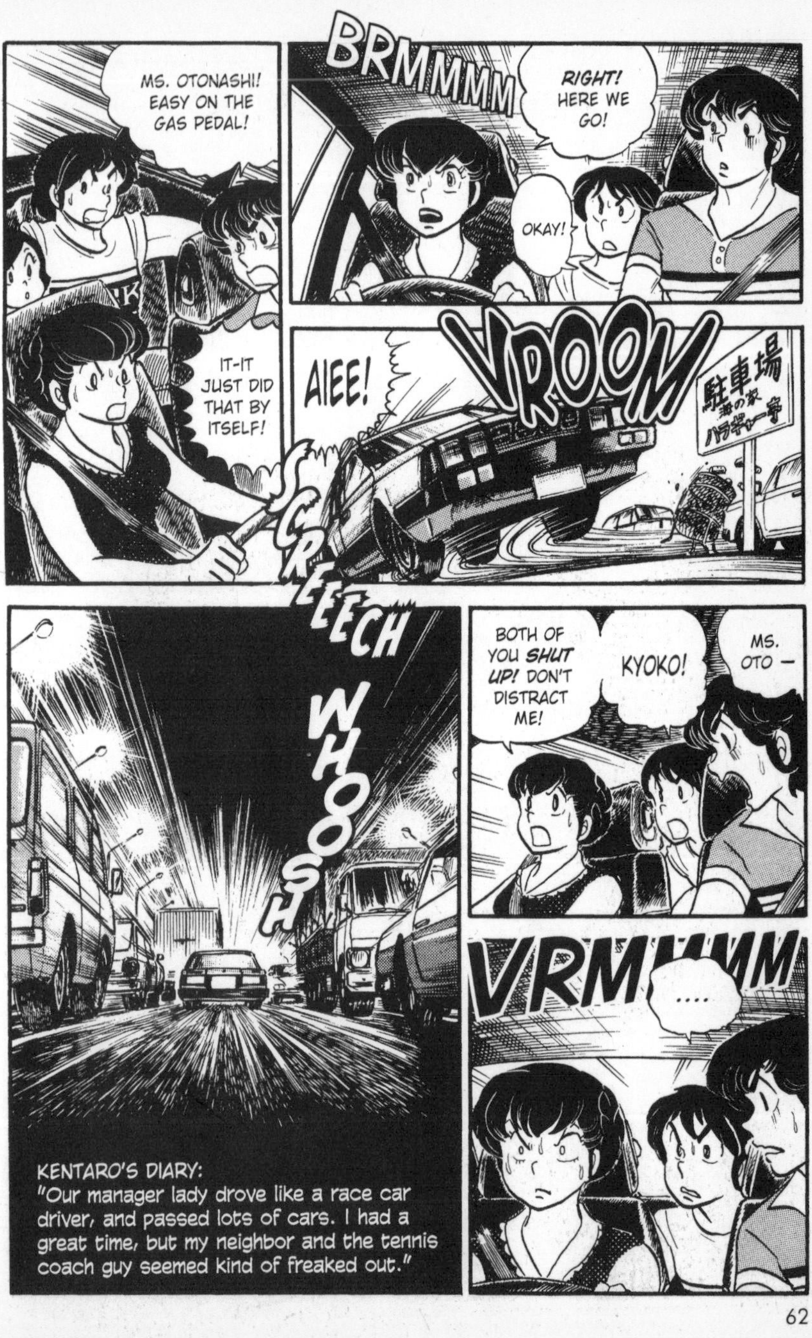

BRMMMMM
MS. OTONASHI! EASY ON THE GAS PEDAL!
RIGHT! HERE WE GO!
OKAY!
IT-IT JUST DID THAT BY ITSELF!
AIEE!
VROOM
駐車場
CREEEECH
WHOOSH
MS. OTO —
KYOKO!
BOTH OF YOU SHUT UP! DON'T DISTRACT ME!
VRMMMM
....
KENTARO'S DIARY:
"Our manager lady drove like a race car driver, and passed lots of cars. I had a great time, but my neighbor and the tennis coach guy seemed kind of freaked out."

PART FOUR

MEMORIAL COOKING

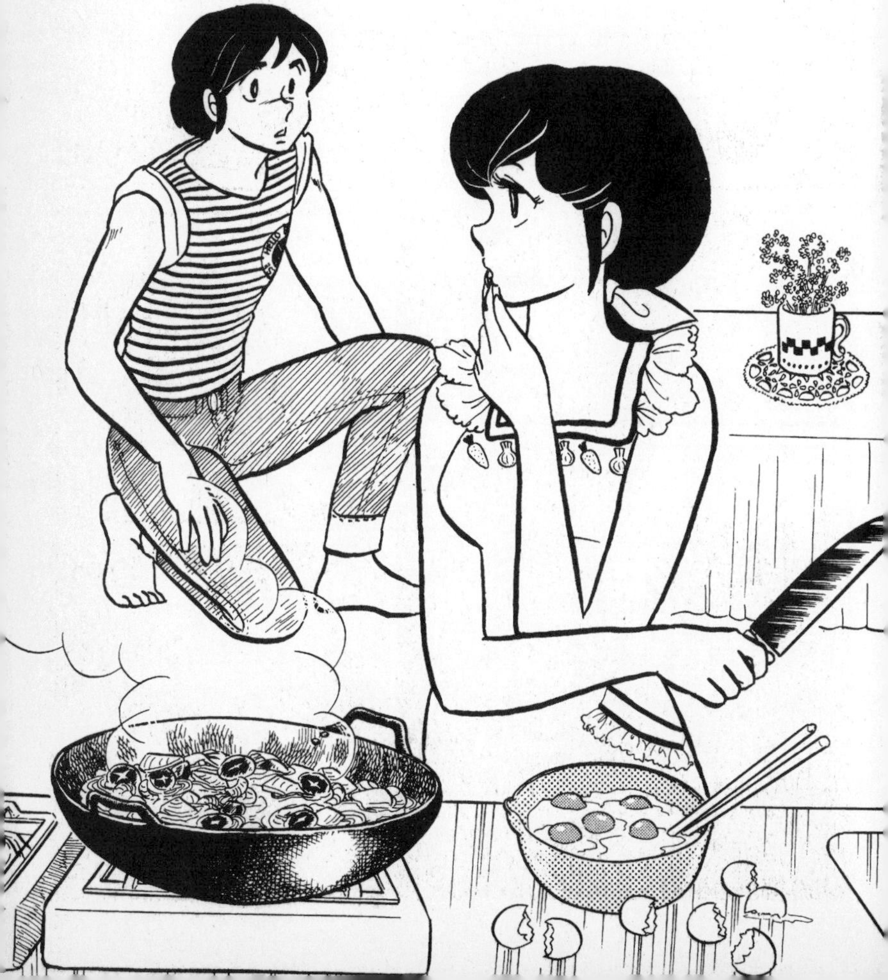

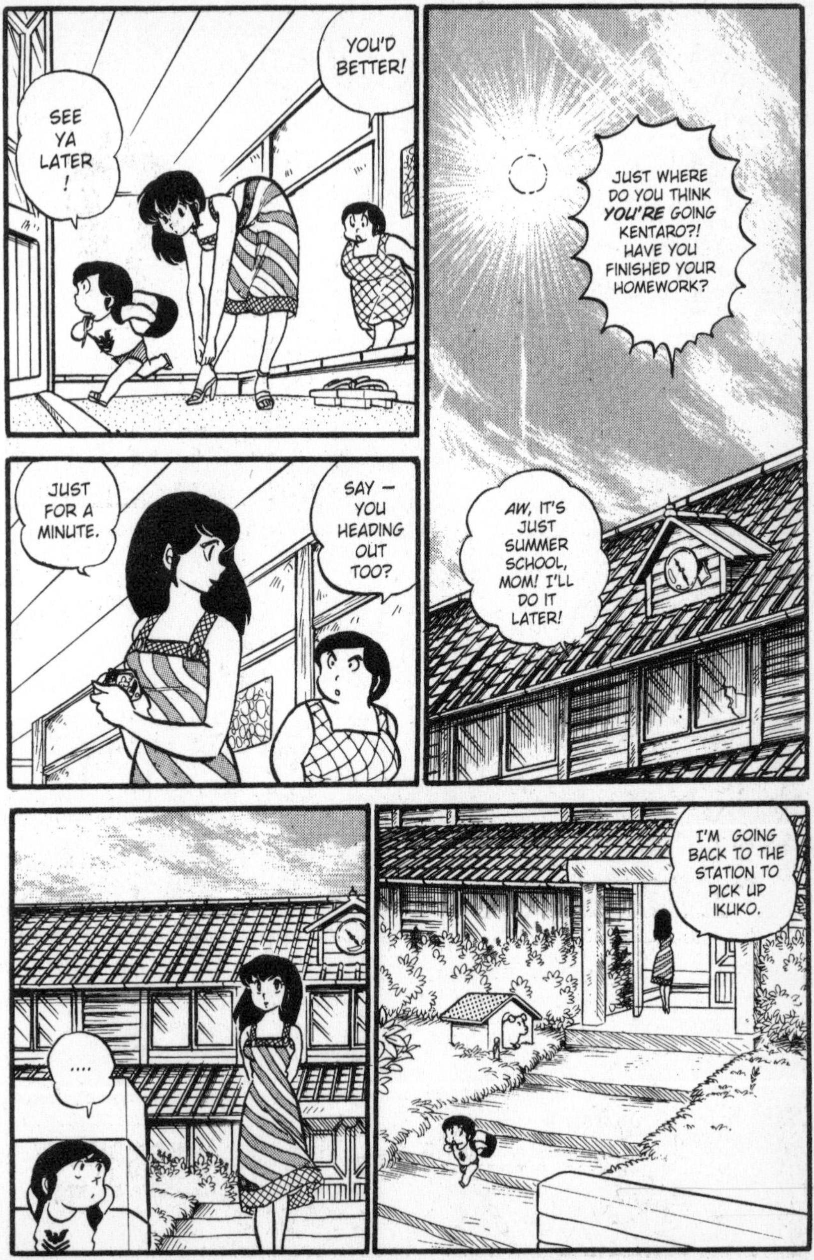
JUST WHERE DO YOU THINK YOU'RE GOING KENTARO?! HAVE YOU FINISHED YOUR HOMEWORK?
AW, IT'S JUST SUMMER SCHOOL, MOM! I'LL DO IT LATER!
YOU'D BETTER!
SEE YA LATER!
SAY — YOU HEADING OUT TOO?
JUST FOR A MINUTE.
I'M GOING BACK TO THE STATION TO PICK UP IKUKO.
....

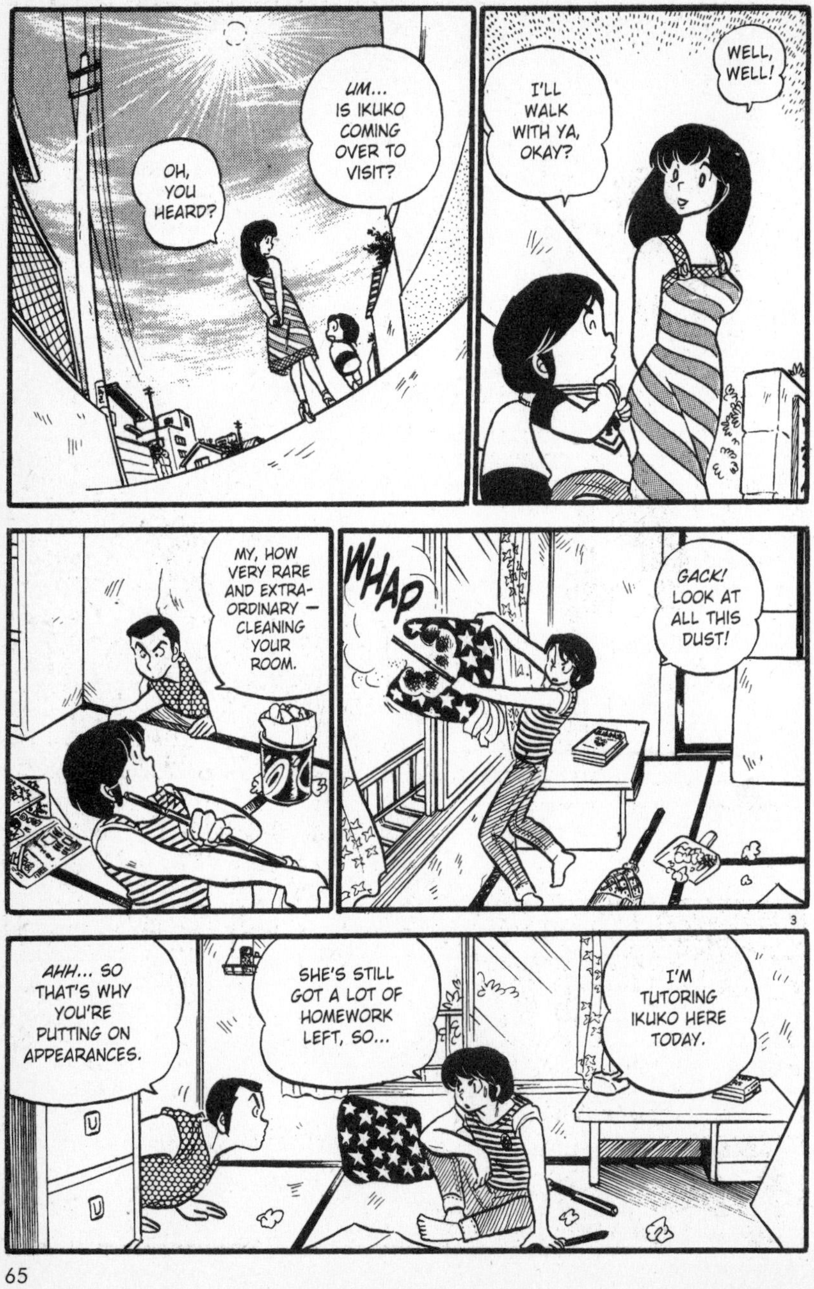
WELL, WELL!
I'LL WALK WITH YA, OKAY?
UM... IS IKUKO COMING OVER TO VISIT?
OH, YOU HEARD?
WHAP
GACK! LOOK AT ALL THIS DUST!
MY, HOW VERY RARE AND EXTRA-ORDINARY — CLEANING YOUR ROOM.
I'M TUTORING IKUKO HERE TODAY.
SHE'S STILL GOT A LOT OF HOMEWORK LEFT, SO...
AHH... SO THAT'S WHY YOU'RE PUTTING ON APPEARANCES.

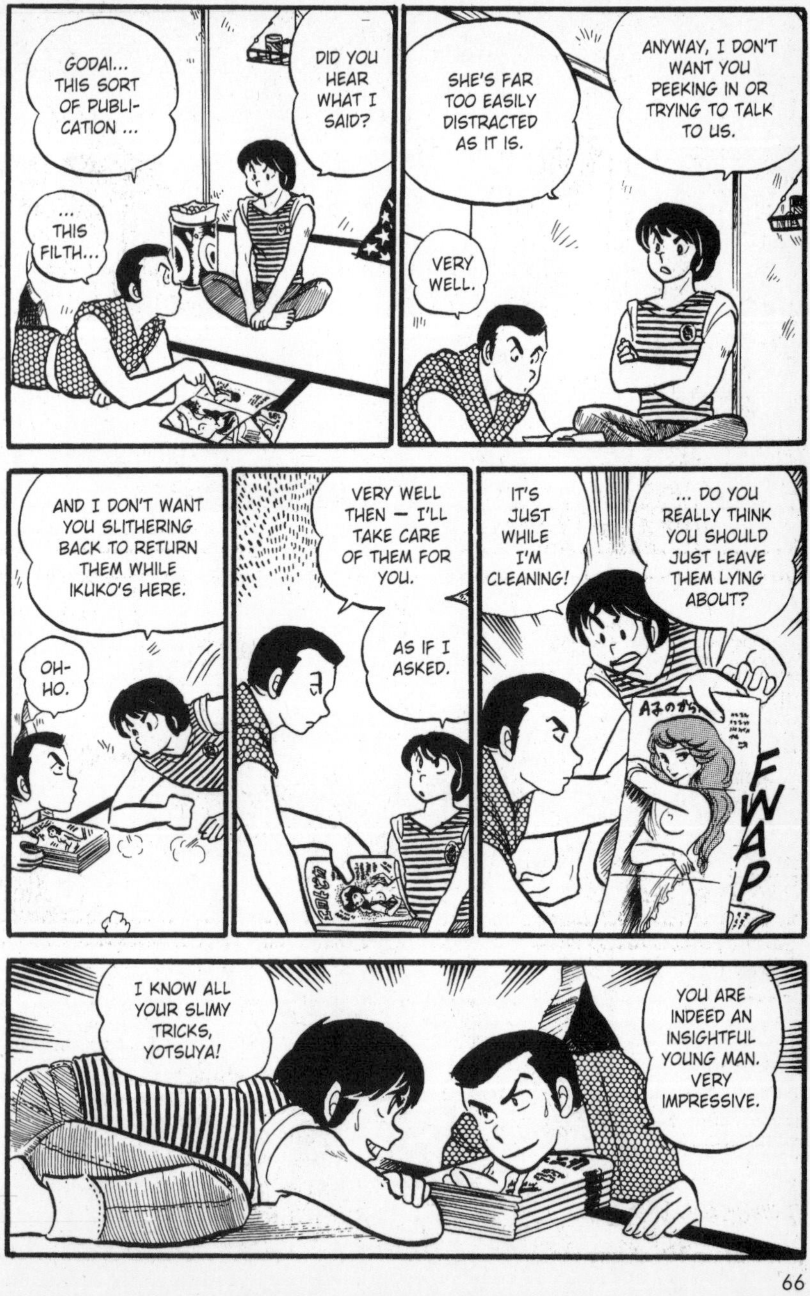
ANYWAY, I DON'T WANT YOU PEEKING IN OR TRYING TO TALK TO US.
SHE'S FAR TOO EASILY DISTRACTED AS IT IS.
VERY WELL.
DID YOU HEAR WHAT I SAID?
GODAI... THIS SORT OF PUBLICATION ...
... THIS FILTH...
... DO YOU REALLY THINK YOU SHOULD JUST LEAVE THEM LYING ABOUT?
IT'S JUST WHILE I'M CLEANING!
FWAP
VERY WELL THEN — I'LL TAKE CARE OF THEM FOR YOU.
AS IF I ASKED.
AND I DON'T WANT YOU SLITHERING BACK TO RETURN THEM WHILE IKUKO'S HERE.
OH-HO.
YOU ARE INDEED AN INSIGHTFUL YOUNG MAN. VERY IMPRESSIVE.
I KNOW ALL YOUR SLIMY TRICKS, YOTSUYA!

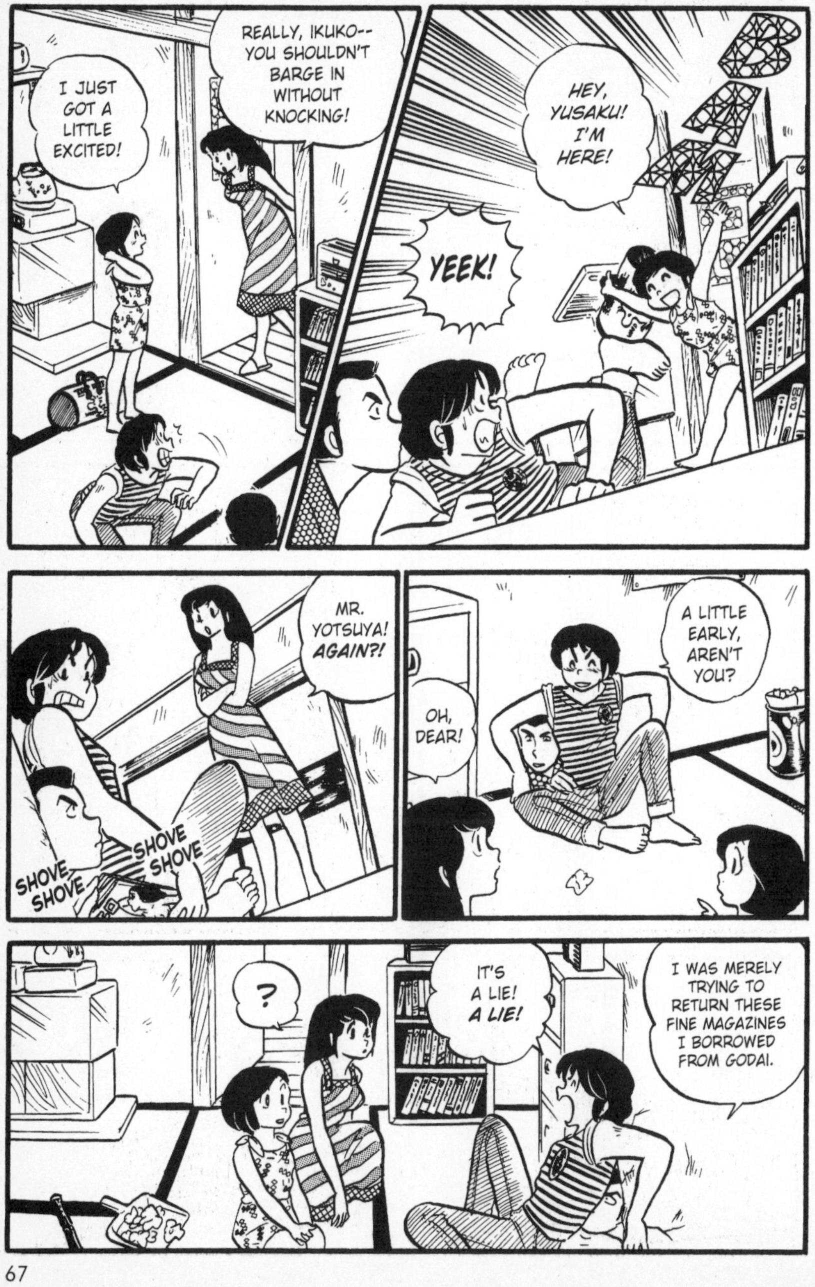

BAM
HEY, YUSAKU! I'M HERE!
YEEK!
REALLY, IKUKO-- YOU SHOULDN'T BARGE IN WITHOUT KNOCKING!
I JUST GOT A LITTLE EXCITED!
A LITTLE EARLY, AREN'T YOU?
OH, DEAR!
MR. YOTSUYA! AGAIN?!
SHOVE SHOVE
SHOVE SHOVE
I WAS MERELY TRYING TO RETURN THESE FINE MAGAZINES I BORROWED FROM GODAI.
IT'S A LIE! A LIE!
?

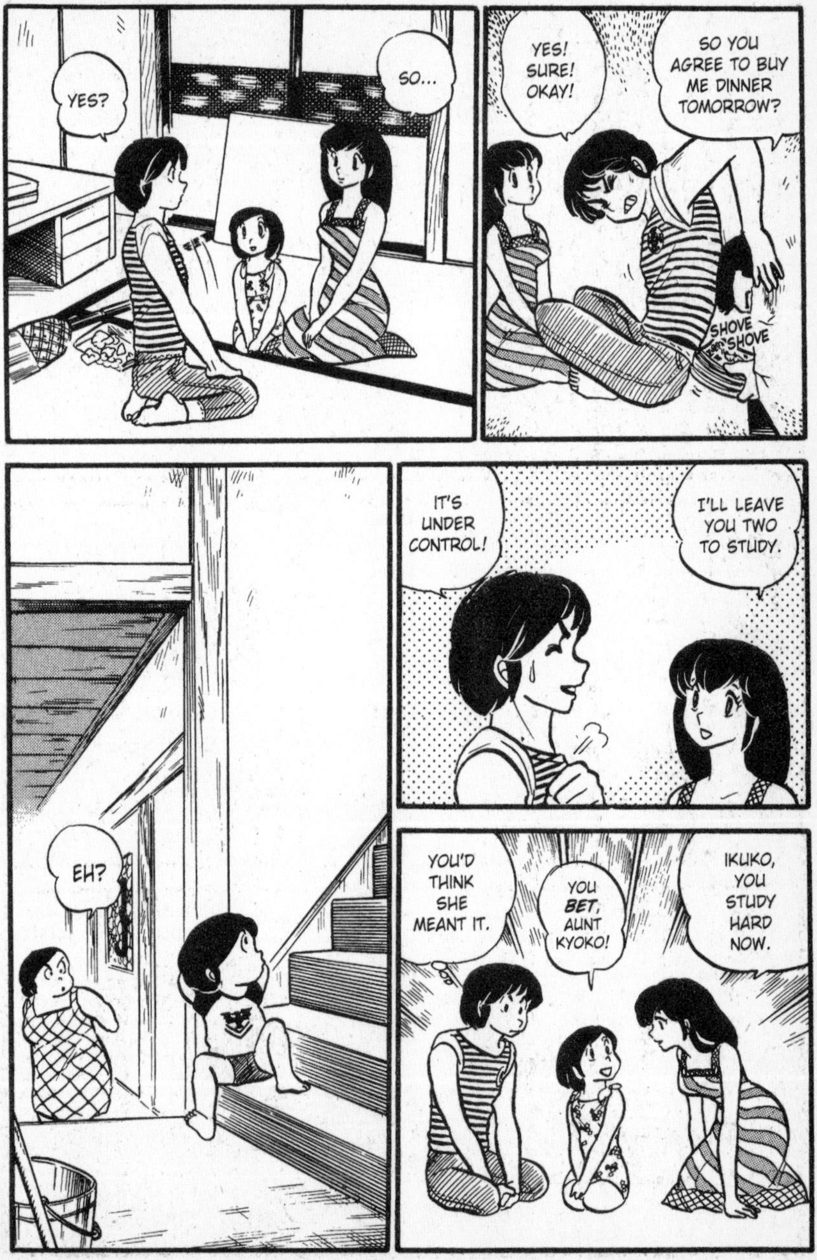
SO YOU AGREE TO BUY ME DINNER TOMORROW?
YES! SURE! OKAY!
SHOVE SHOVE
SO...
YES?
I'LL LEAVE YOU TWO TO STUDY.
IT'S UNDER CONTROL!
IKUKO, YOU STUDY HARD NOW.
YOU BET, AUNT KYOKO!
YOU'D THINK SHE MEANT IT.
EH?

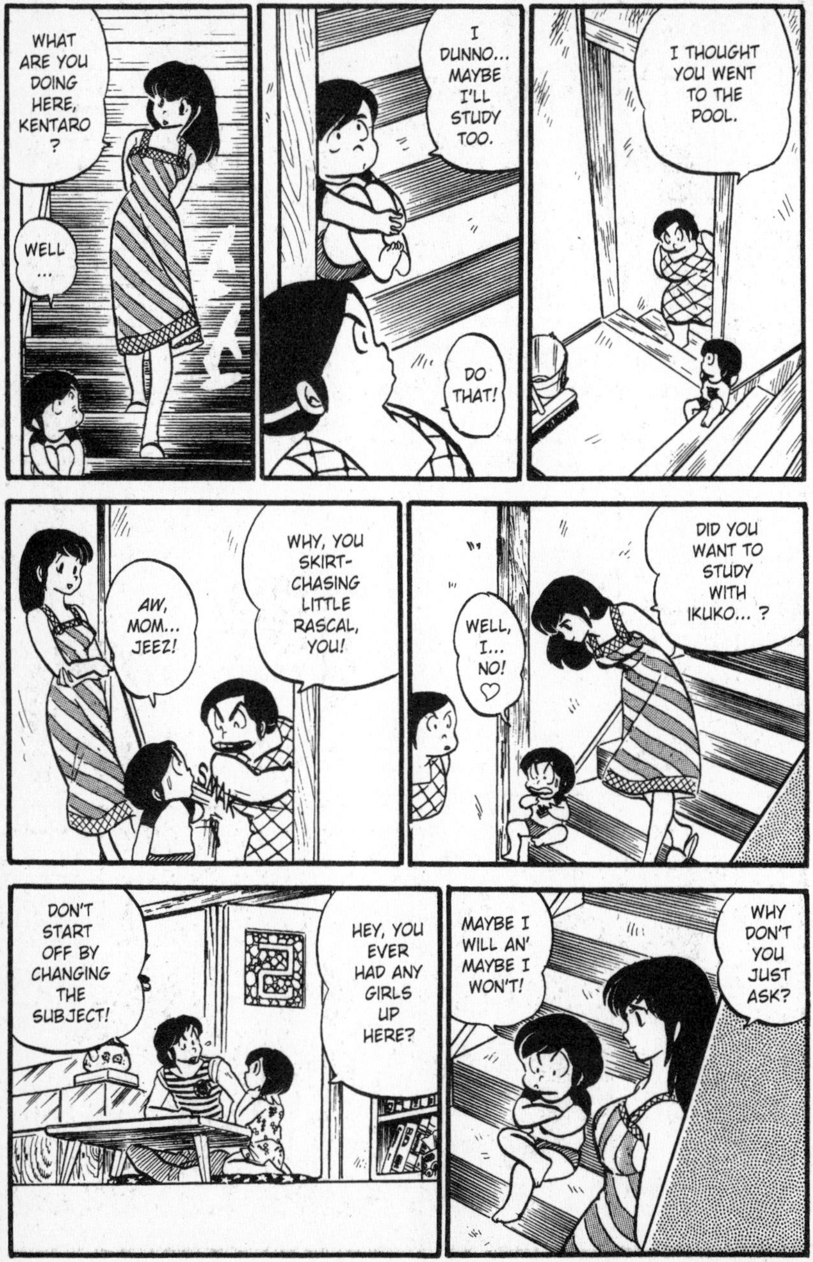
I THOUGHT YOU WENT TO THE POOL.
I DUNNO... MAYBE I'LL STUDY TOO.
DO THAT!
WHAT ARE YOU DOING HERE, KENTARO?
WELL...
DID YOU WANT TO STUDY WITH IKUKO... ?
WELL, I... NO! ♡
WHY, YOU SKIRT-CHASING LITTLE RASCAL, YOU!
AW, MOM... JEEZ!
SMAK
WHY DON'T YOU JUST ASK?
MAYBE I WILL AN' MAYBE I WON'T!
HEY, YOU EVER HAD ANY GIRLS UP HERE?
DON'T START OFF BY CHANGING THE SUBJECT!

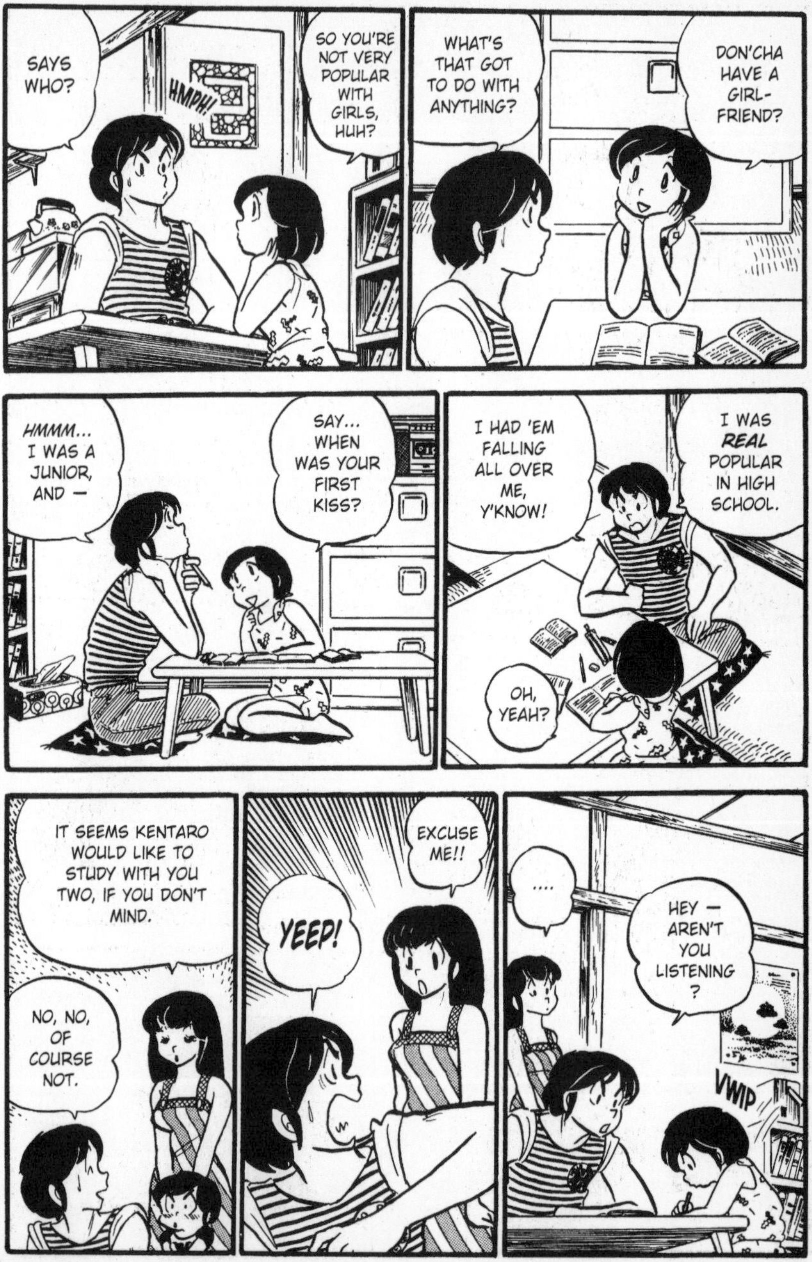
DON'CHA HAVE A GIRL-FRIEND?
WHAT'S THAT GOT TO DO WITH ANYTHING?
SO YOU'RE NOT VERY POPULAR WITH GIRLS, HUH?
HMPH!
SAYS WHO?
I WAS REAL POPULAR IN HIGH SCHOOL.
I HAD 'EM FALLING ALL OVER ME, Y'KNOW!
OH, YEAH?
SAY... WHEN WAS YOUR FIRST KISS?
HMMM... I WAS A JUNIOR, AND —
HEY — AREN'T YOU LISTENING ?
....
VWIP
EXCUSE ME!!
YEEP!
IT SEEMS KENTARO WOULD LIKE TO STUDY WITH YOU TWO, IF YOU DON'T MIND.
NO, NO, OF COURSE NOT.

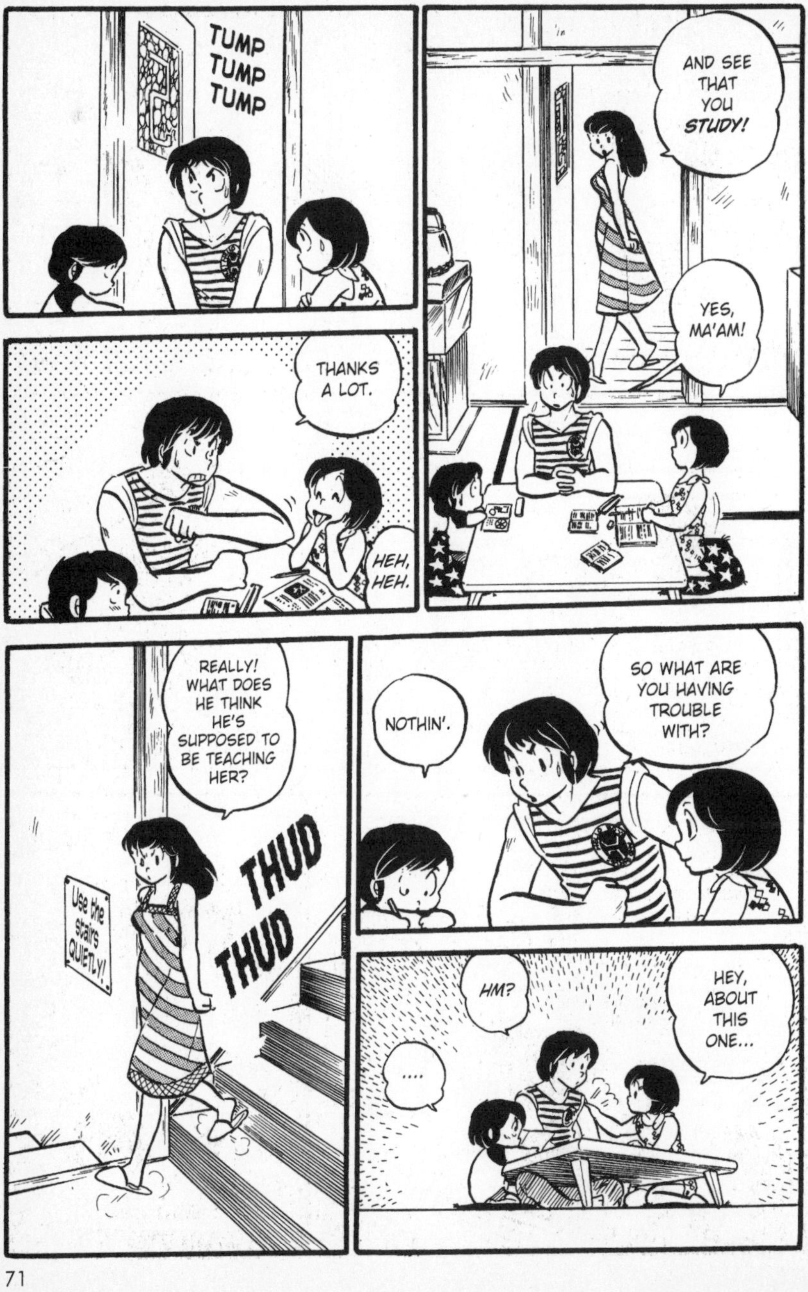
AND SEE THAT YOU *STUDY!*
YES, MA'AM!
TUMP TUMP TUMP
THANKS A LOT.
HEH, HEH.
SO WHAT ARE YOU HAVING TROUBLE WITH?
NOTHIN'.
HEY, ABOUT THIS ONE...
HM?
....
REALLY! WHAT DOES HE THINK HE'S SUPPOSED TO BE TEACHING HER?
THUD THUD
Use the stairs QUIETLY!

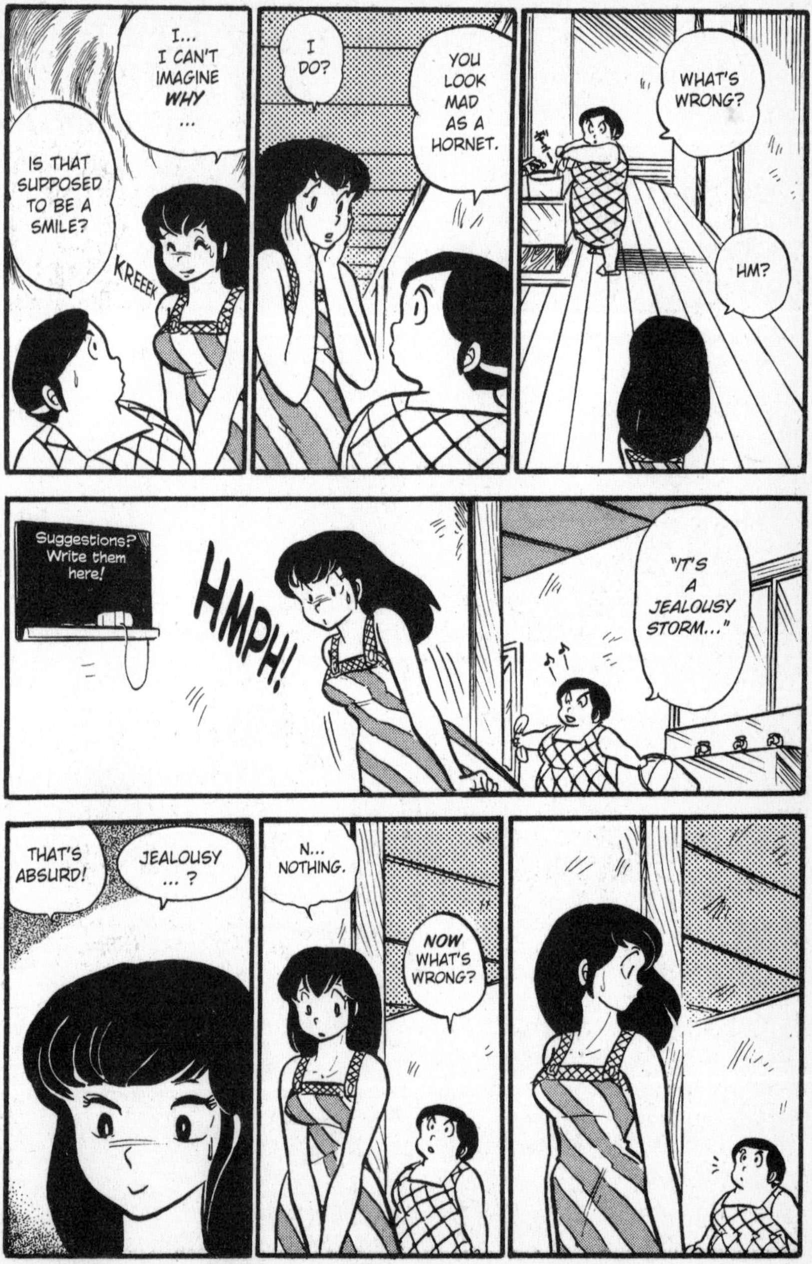
WHAT'S WRONG?
HM?
YOU LOOK MAD AS A HORNET.
I DO?
I... I CAN'T IMAGINE *WHY* ...
IS THAT SUPPOSED TO BE A SMILE?
KREEEK
"IT'S A JEALOUSY STORM..."
HMPH!
Suggestions? Write them here!
NOW WHAT'S WRONG?
N... NOTHING.
JEALOUSY ... ?
THAT'S ABSURD!

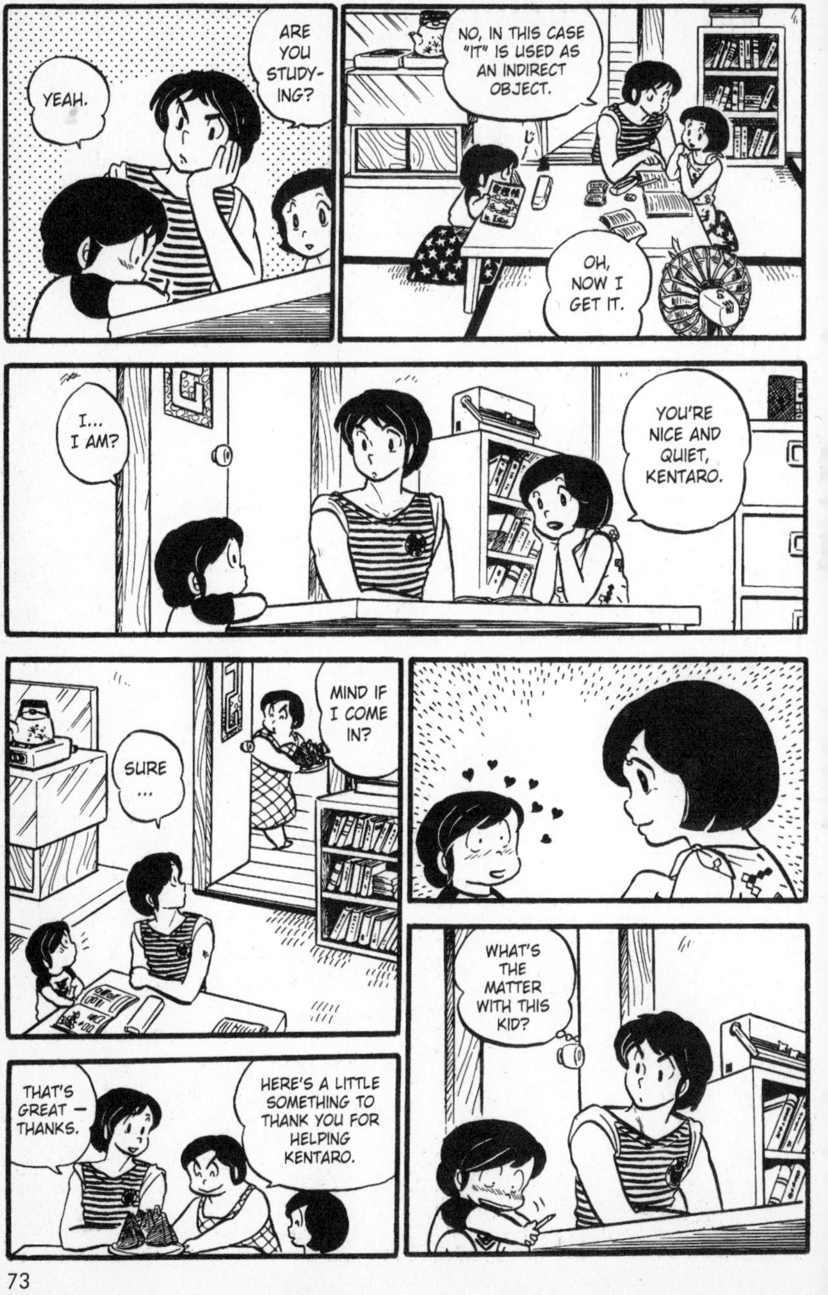
NO, IN THIS CASE "IT" IS USED AS AN INDIRECT OBJECT.
OH, NOW I GET IT.
ARE YOU STUDY-ING?
YEAH.
YOU'RE NICE AND QUIET, KENTARO.
I... I AM?
WHAT'S THE MATTER WITH THIS KID?
MIND IF I COME IN?
SURE ...
HERE'S A LITTLE SOMETHING TO THANK YOU FOR HELPING KENTARO.
THAT'S GREAT — THANKS.

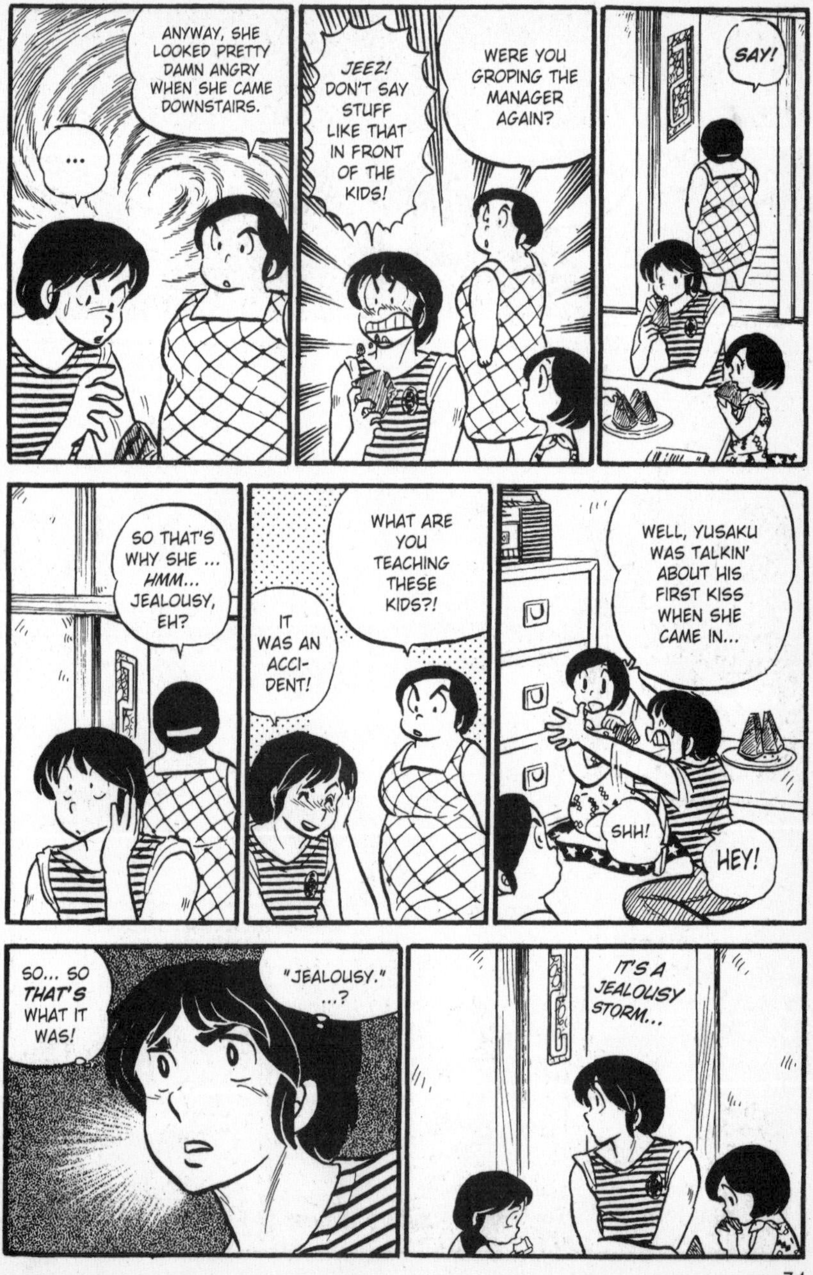
SAY!
WERE YOU GROPING THE MANAGER AGAIN?
JEEZ! DON'T SAY STUFF LIKE THAT IN FRONT OF THE KIDS!
ANYWAY, SHE LOOKED PRETTY DAMN ANGRY WHEN SHE CAME DOWNSTAIRS.
...
WELL, YUSAKU WAS TALKIN' ABOUT HIS FIRST KISS WHEN SHE CAME IN...
SHH!
HEY!
WHAT ARE YOU TEACHING THESE KIDS?!
IT WAS AN ACCIDENT!
SO THAT'S WHY SHE ... HMM... JEALOUSY, EH?
IT'S A JEALOUSY STORM...
"JEALOUSY." ...?
SO... SO THAT'S WHAT IT WAS!

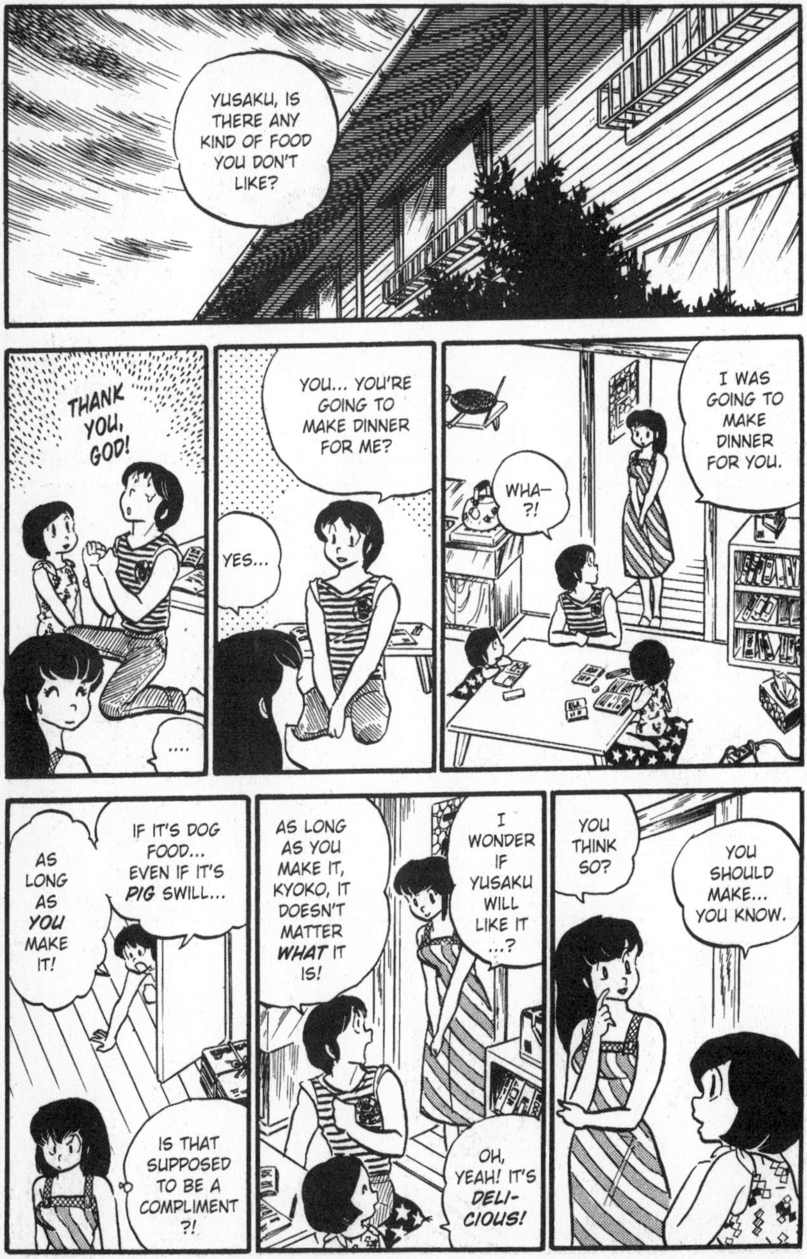
YUSAKU, IS THERE ANY KIND OF FOOD YOU DON'T LIKE?
I WAS GOING TO MAKE DINNER FOR YOU.
WHA—?!
YOU... YOU'RE GOING TO MAKE DINNER FOR ME?
YES...
THANK YOU, GOD!
....
YOU SHOULD MAKE... YOU KNOW.
YOU THINK SO?
I WONDER IF YUSAKU WILL LIKE IT ...?
AS LONG AS YOU MAKE IT, KYOKO, IT DOESN'T MATTER *WHAT* IT IS!
OH, YEAH! IT'S *DELICIOUS!*
IF IT'S DOG FOOD... EVEN IF IT'S *PIG* SWILL...
AS LONG AS *YOU* MAKE IT!
IS THAT SUPPOSED TO BE A COMPLIMENT?!

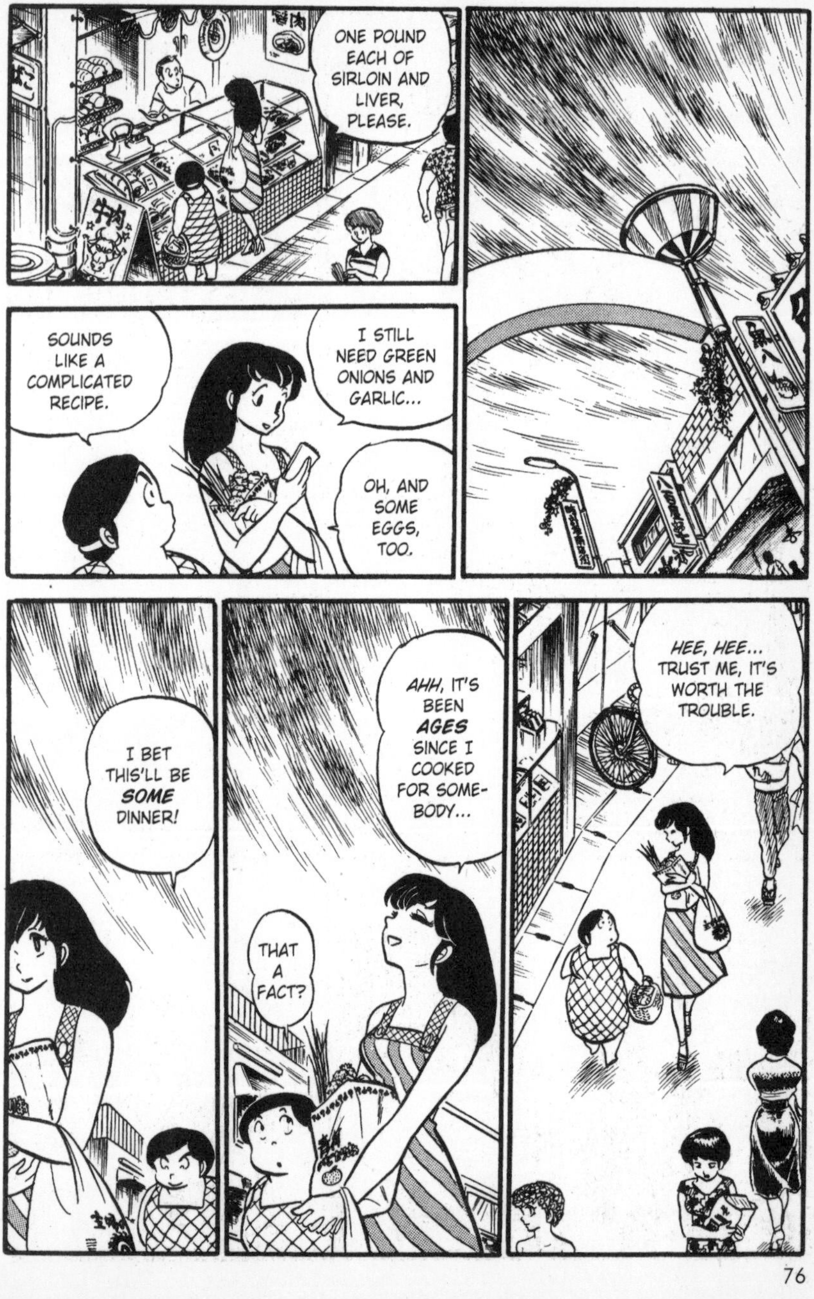
ONE POUND EACH OF SIRLOIN AND LIVER, PLEASE.
I STILL NEED GREEN ONIONS AND GARLIC...
OH, AND SOME EGGS, TOO.
SOUNDS LIKE A COMPLICATED RECIPE.
HEE, HEE... TRUST ME, IT'S WORTH THE TROUBLE.
AHH, IT'S BEEN ***AGES*** SINCE I COOKED FOR SOME-BODY...
THAT A FACT?
I BET THIS'LL BE ***SOME*** DINNER!

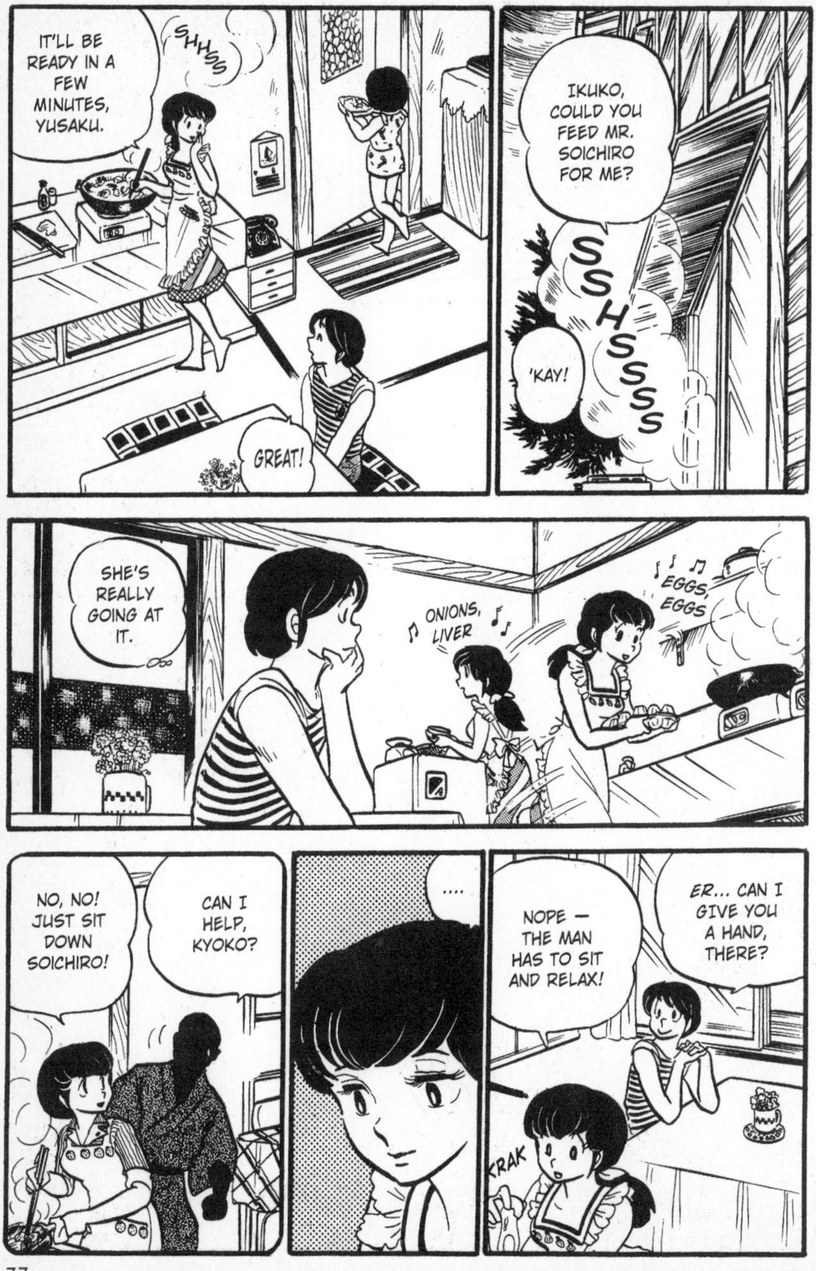
IKUKO, COULD YOU FEED MR. SOICHIRO FOR ME?
SSHSSSS
'KAY!
IT'LL BE READY IN A FEW MINUTES, YUSAKU.
SHHSS
GREAT!
EGGS, EGGS
ONIONS, LIVER
SHE'S REALLY GOING AT IT.
ER... CAN I GIVE YOU A HAND, THERE?
NOPE — THE MAN HAS TO SIT AND RELAX!
KRAK
....
CAN I HELP, KYOKO?
NO, NO! JUST SIT DOWN SOICHIRO!

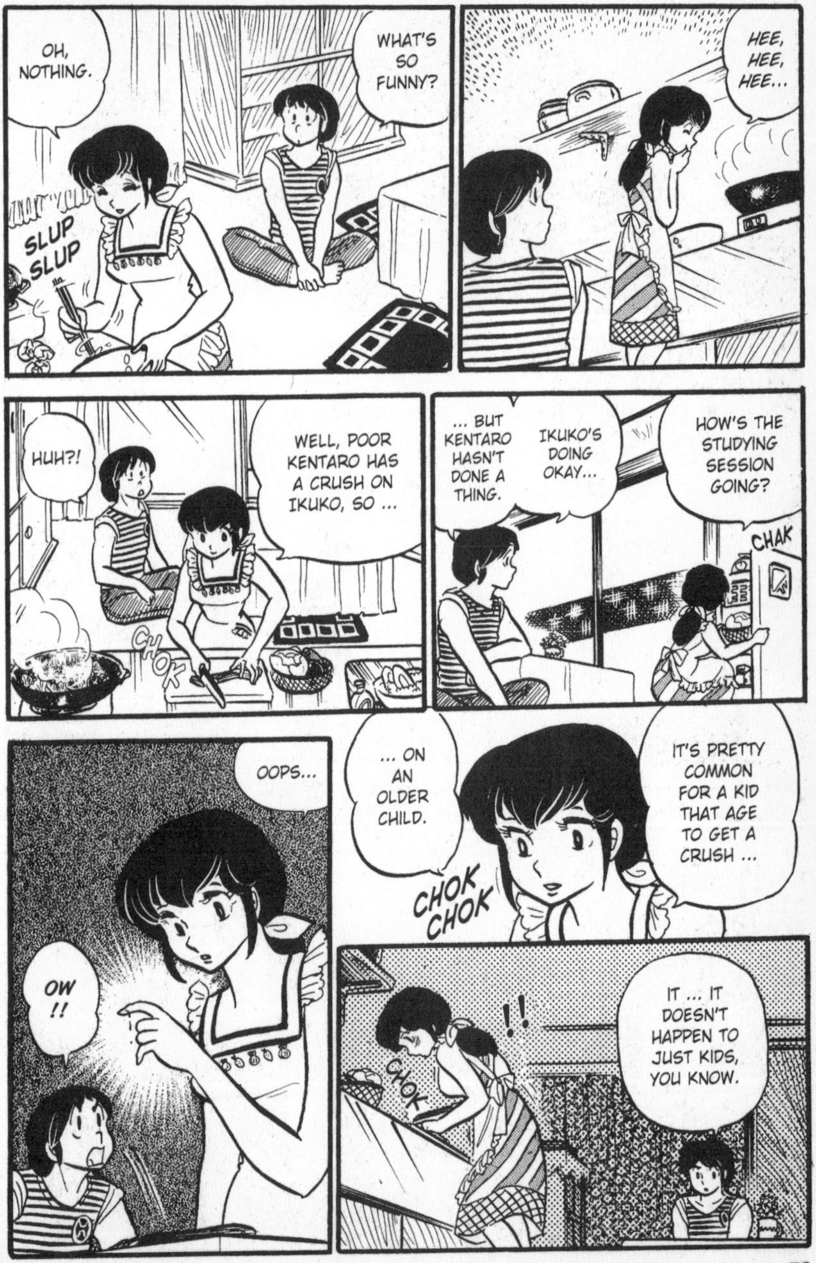
HEE, HEE, HEE...
WHAT'S SO FUNNY?
OH, NOTHING.
SLUP SLUP
HOW'S THE STUDYING SESSION GOING?
IKUKO'S DOING OKAY...
... BUT KENTARO HASN'T DONE A THING.
CHAK
WELL, POOR KENTARO HAS A CRUSH ON IKUKO, SO ...
HUH?!
CHOK
IT'S PRETTY COMMON FOR A KID THAT AGE TO GET A CRUSH ...
... ON AN OLDER CHILD.
CHOK CHOK
IT ... IT DOESN'T HAPPEN TO JUST KIDS, YOU KNOW.
!!
CHOK
OOPS...
OW !!

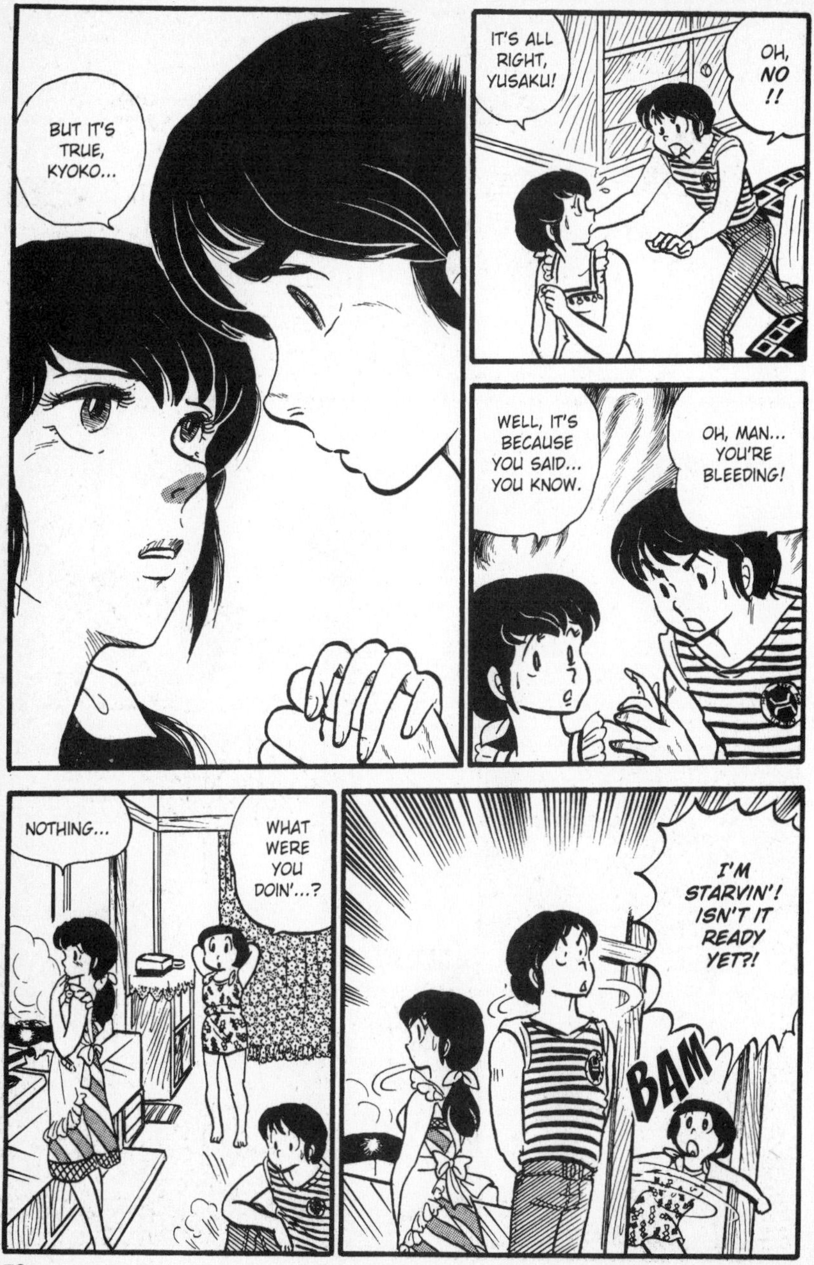
OH, NO !!
IT'S ALL RIGHT, YUSAKU!
OH, MAN... YOU'RE BLEEDING!
WELL, IT'S BECAUSE YOU SAID... YOU KNOW.
BUT IT'S TRUE, KYOKO...
I'M STARVIN'! ISN'T IT READY YET?!
BAM
WHAT WERE YOU DOIN'...?
NOTHING...

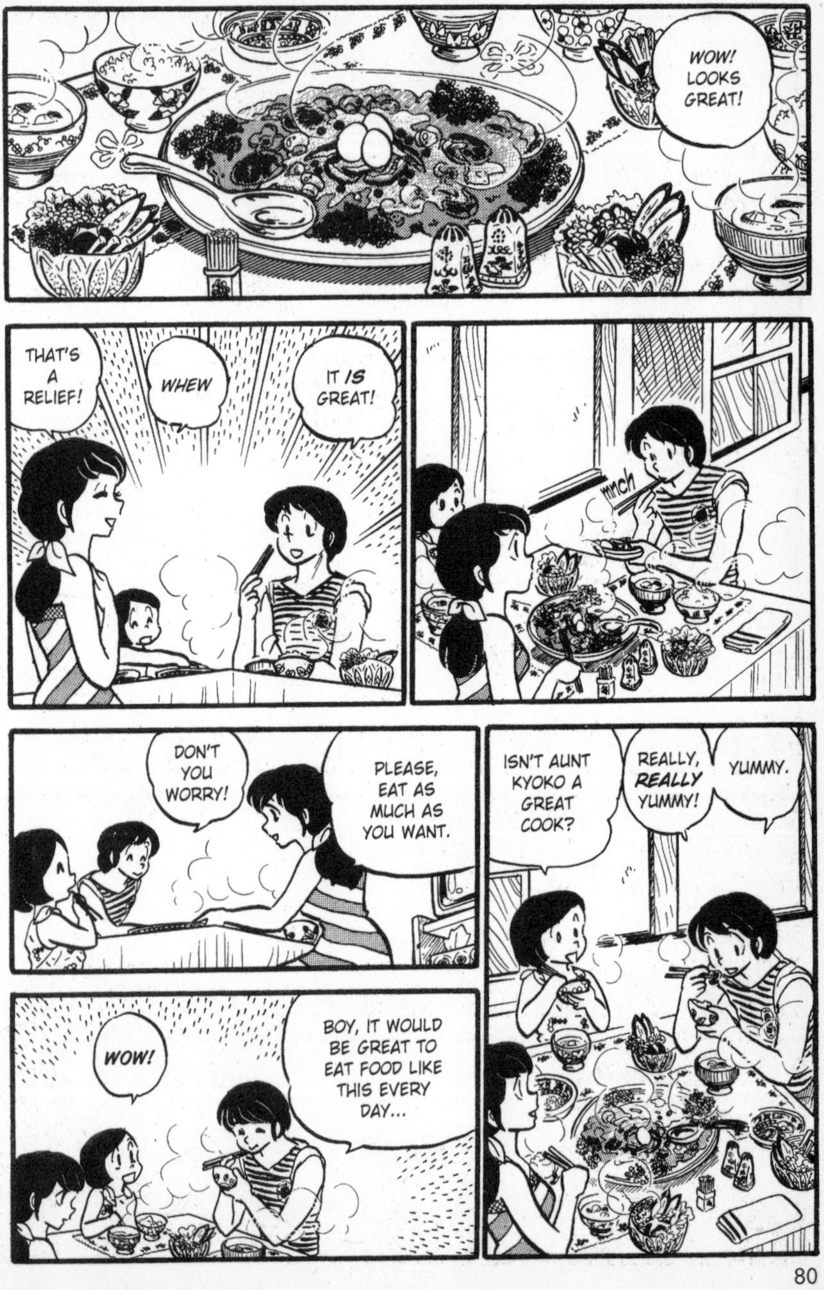
WOW! LOOKS GREAT!
mnch
IT *IS* GREAT!
WHEW
THAT'S A RELIEF!
YUMMY.
REALLY, ***REALLY*** YUMMY!
ISN'T AUNT KYOKO A GREAT COOK?
PLEASE, EAT AS MUCH AS YOU WANT.
DON'T YOU WORRY!
BOY, IT WOULD BE GREAT TO EAT FOOD LIKE THIS EVERY DAY...
WOW!

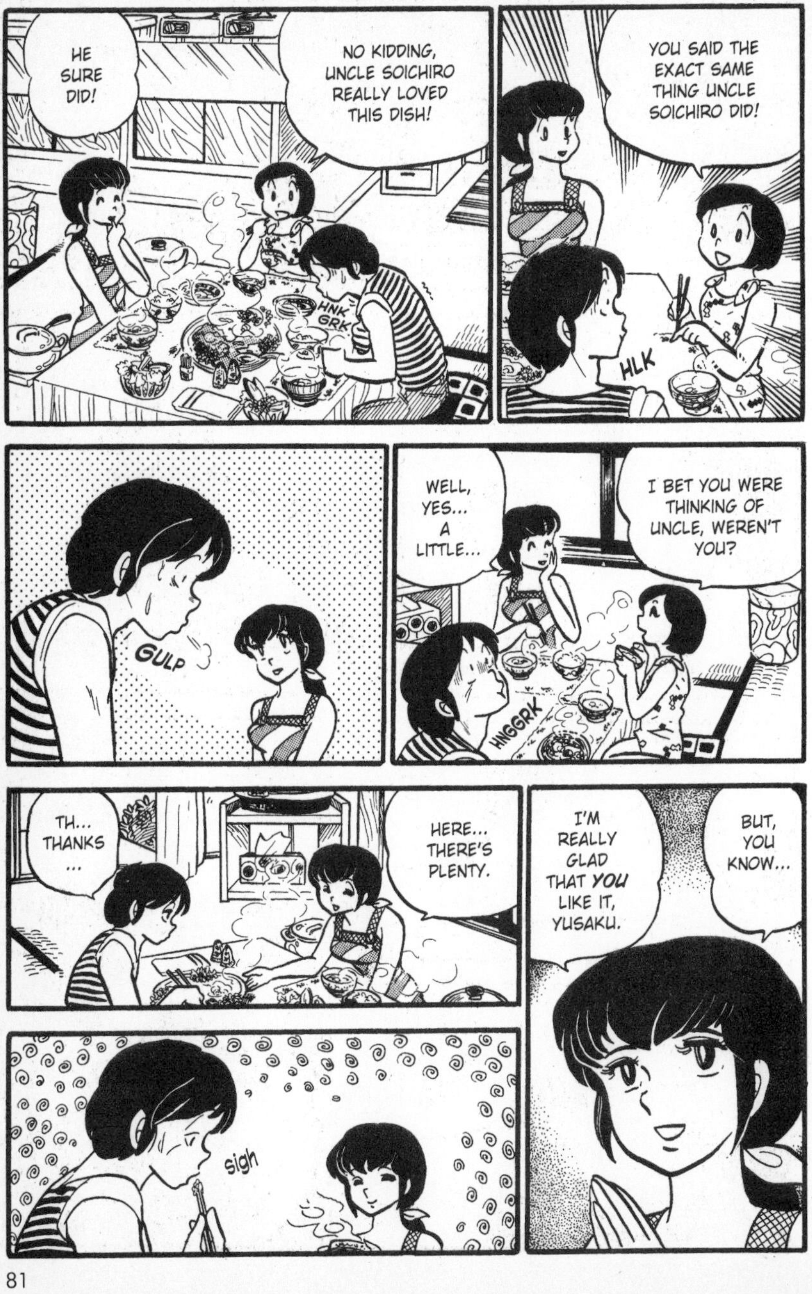
YOU SAID THE EXACT SAME THING UNCLE SOICHIRO DID!
HLK
NO KIDDING, UNCLE SOICHIRO REALLY LOVED THIS DISH!
HE SURE DID!
HNK GRK
I BET YOU WERE THINKING OF UNCLE, WEREN'T YOU?
WELL, YES... A LITTLE...
HNGGRK
GULP
BUT, YOU KNOW...
I'M REALLY GLAD THAT *YOU* LIKE IT, YUSAKU.
HERE... THERE'S PLENTY.
TH... THANKS ...
sigh

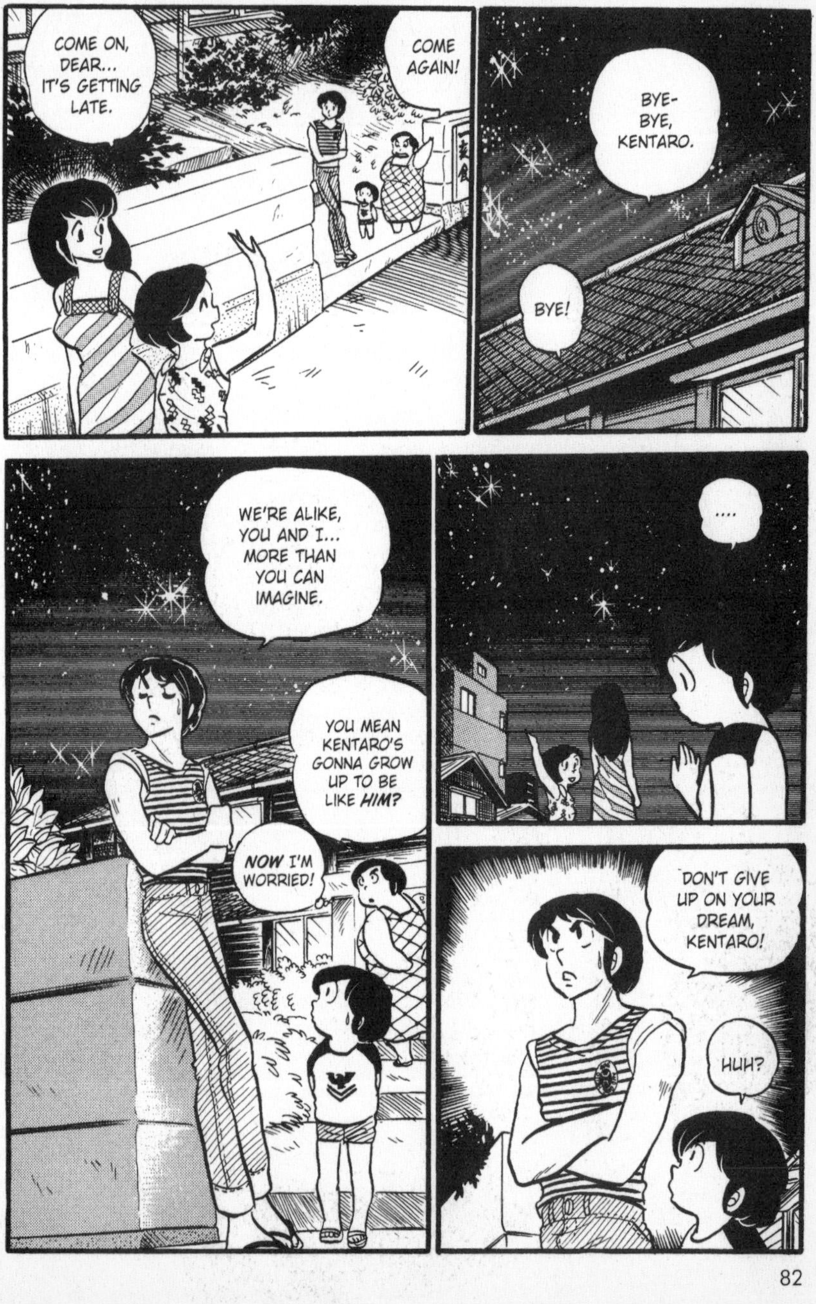
BYE-BYE, KENTARO.
BYE!
COME AGAIN!
COME ON, DEAR... IT'S GETTING LATE.
....
DON'T GIVE UP ON YOUR DREAM, KENTARO!
HUH?
WE'RE ALIKE, YOU AND I... MORE THAN YOU CAN IMAGINE.
YOU MEAN KENTARO'S GONNA GROW UP TO BE LIKE *HIM*?
NOW I'M WORRIED!

PART FIVE

ONE ENTANGLED EVENING

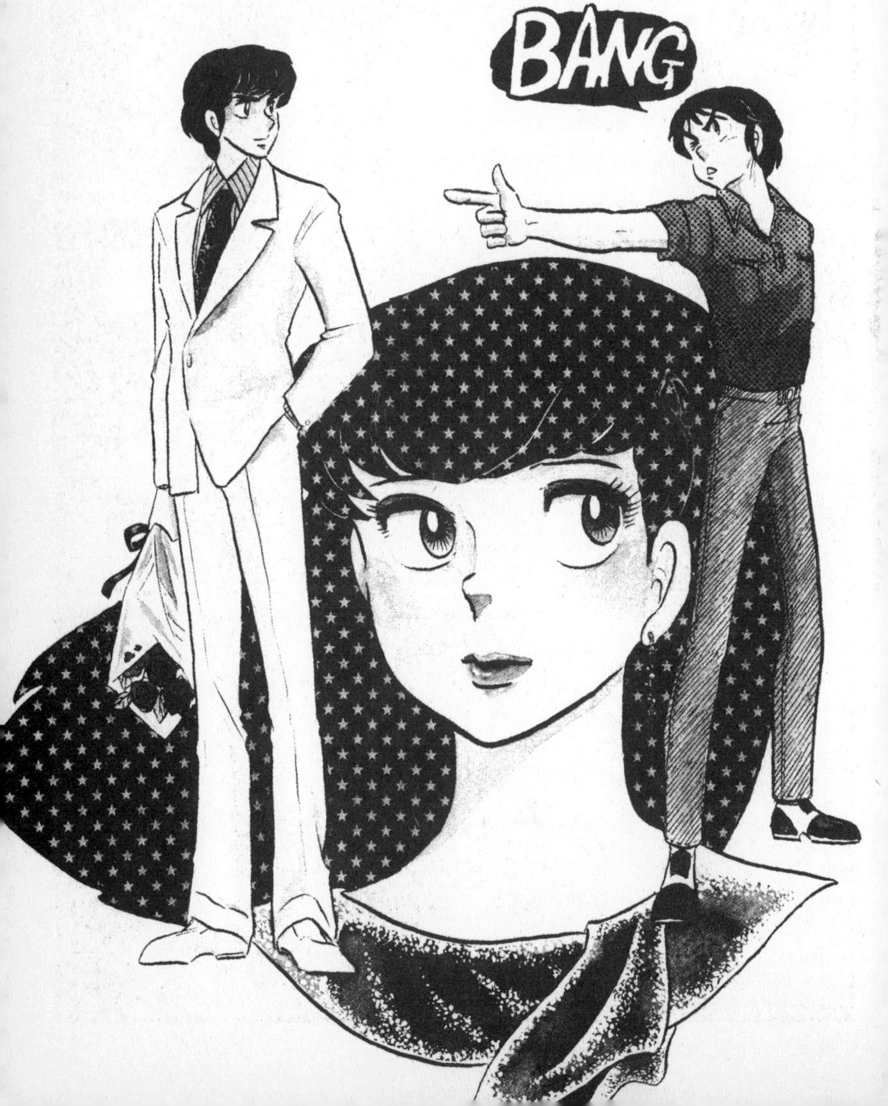
BANG

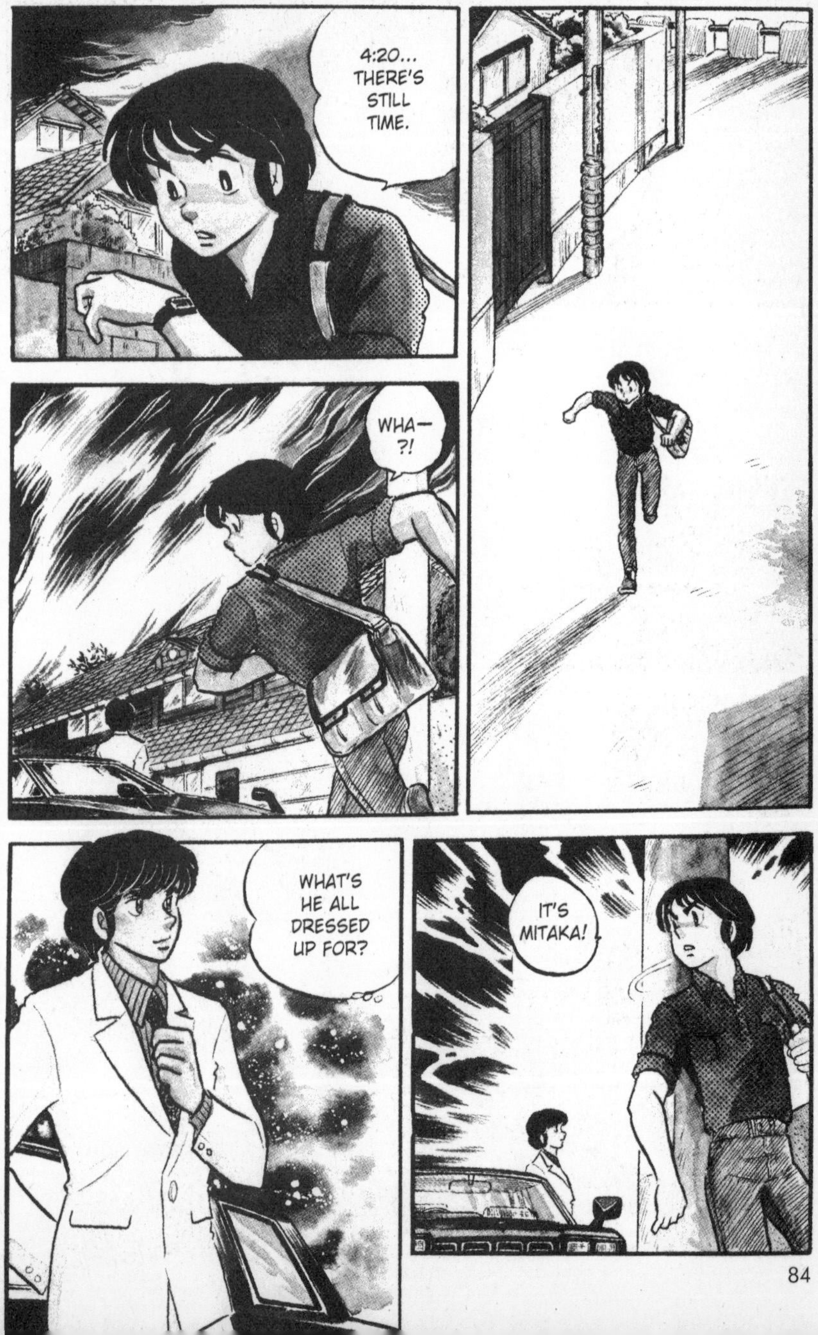
4:20... THERE'S STILL TIME.
WHA— ?!
IT'S MITAKA!
WHAT'S HE ALL DRESSED UP FOR?

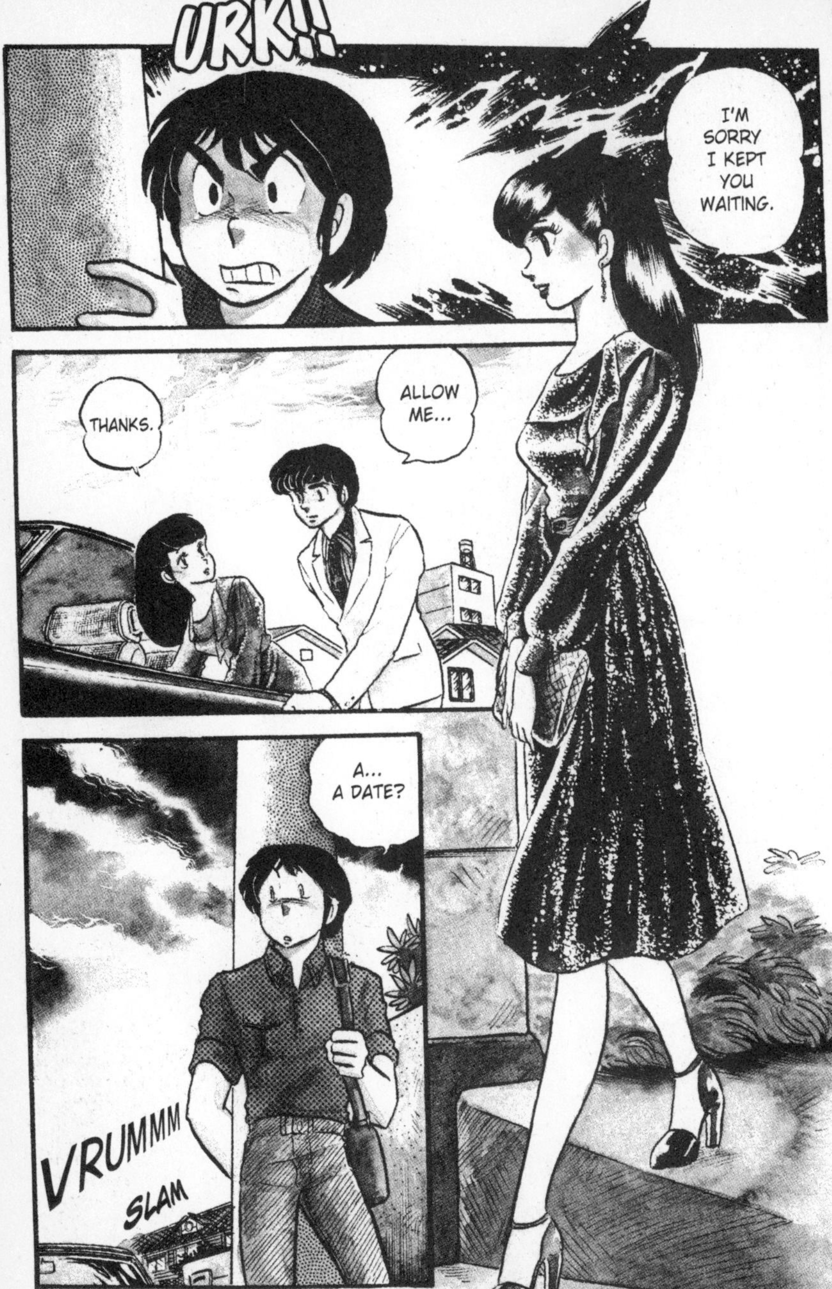
I'M SORRY I KEPT YOU WAITING.
URK!!
ALLOW ME...
THANKS.
A... A DATE?
VRUMMM
SLAM

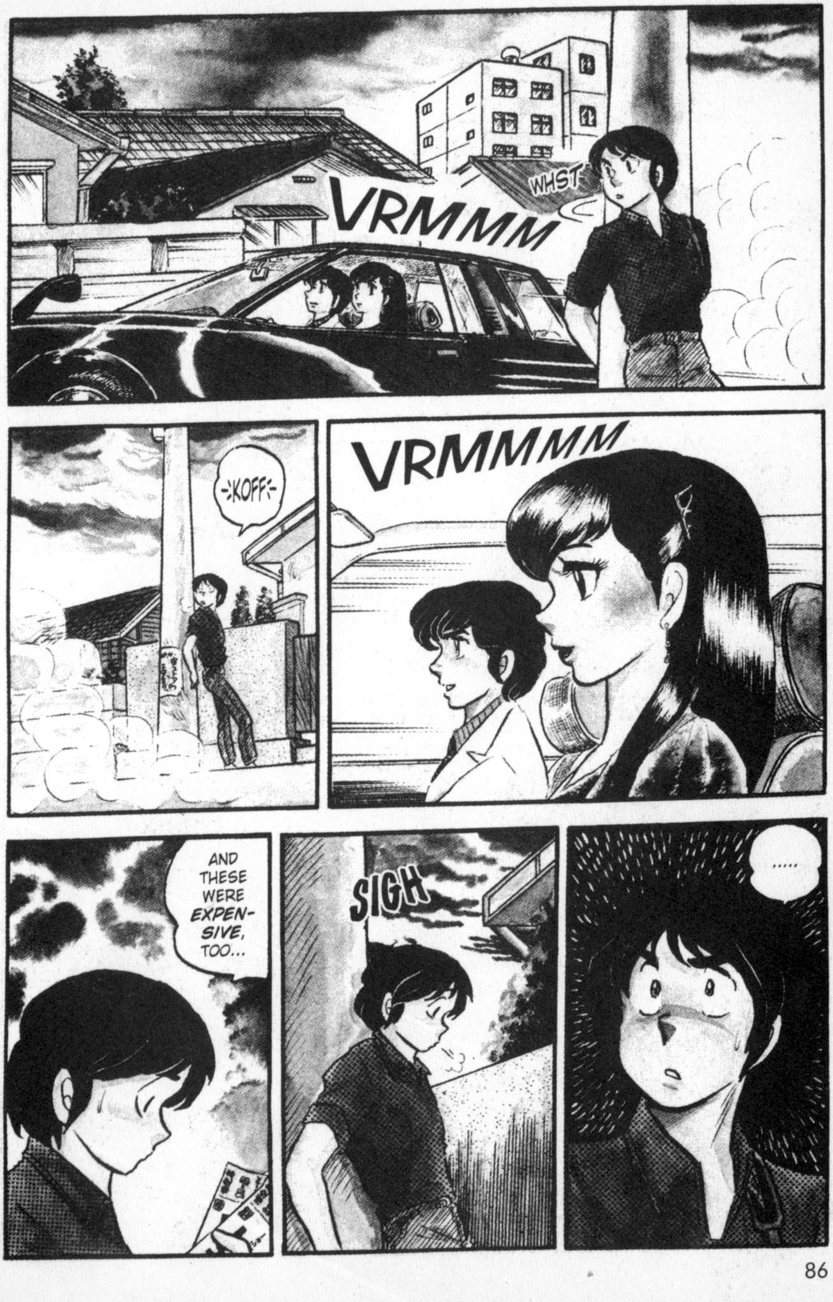
WHST
VRMMMM
VRMMMMM
-KOFF-
.....
SIGH
AND THESE WERE EXPENSIVE, TOO...

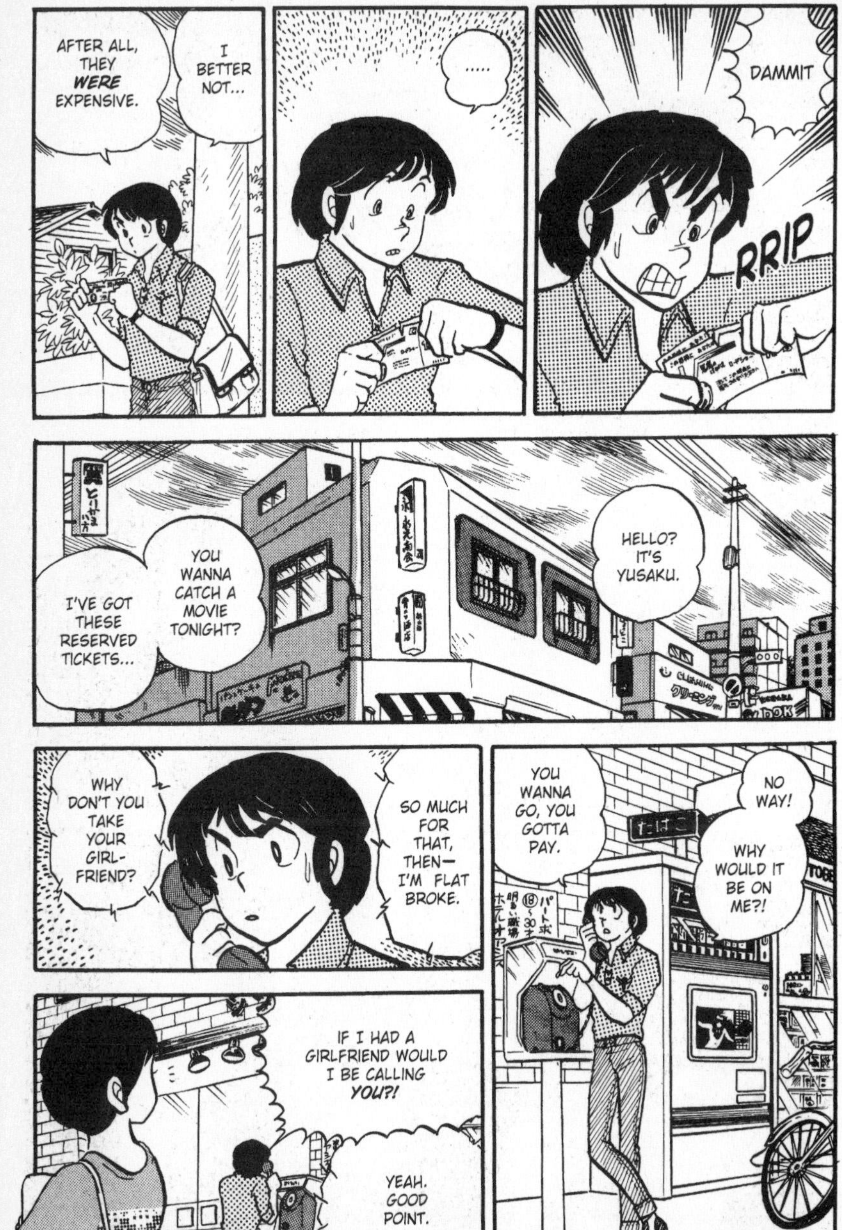
DAMMIT
RRIP
.....
I BETTER NOT...
AFTER ALL, THEY ***WERE*** EXPENSIVE.
HELLO? IT'S YUSAKU.
YOU WANNA CATCH A MOVIE TONIGHT?
I'VE GOT THESE RESERVED TICKETS...
NO WAY!
WHY WOULD IT BE ON ME?!
YOU WANNA GO, YOU GOTTA PAY.
たばこ
SO MUCH FOR THAT, THEN— I'M FLAT BROKE.
WHY DON'T YOU TAKE YOUR GIRL-FRIEND?
IF I HAD A GIRLFRIEND WOULD I BE CALLING ***YOU?!***
YEAH. GOOD POINT.

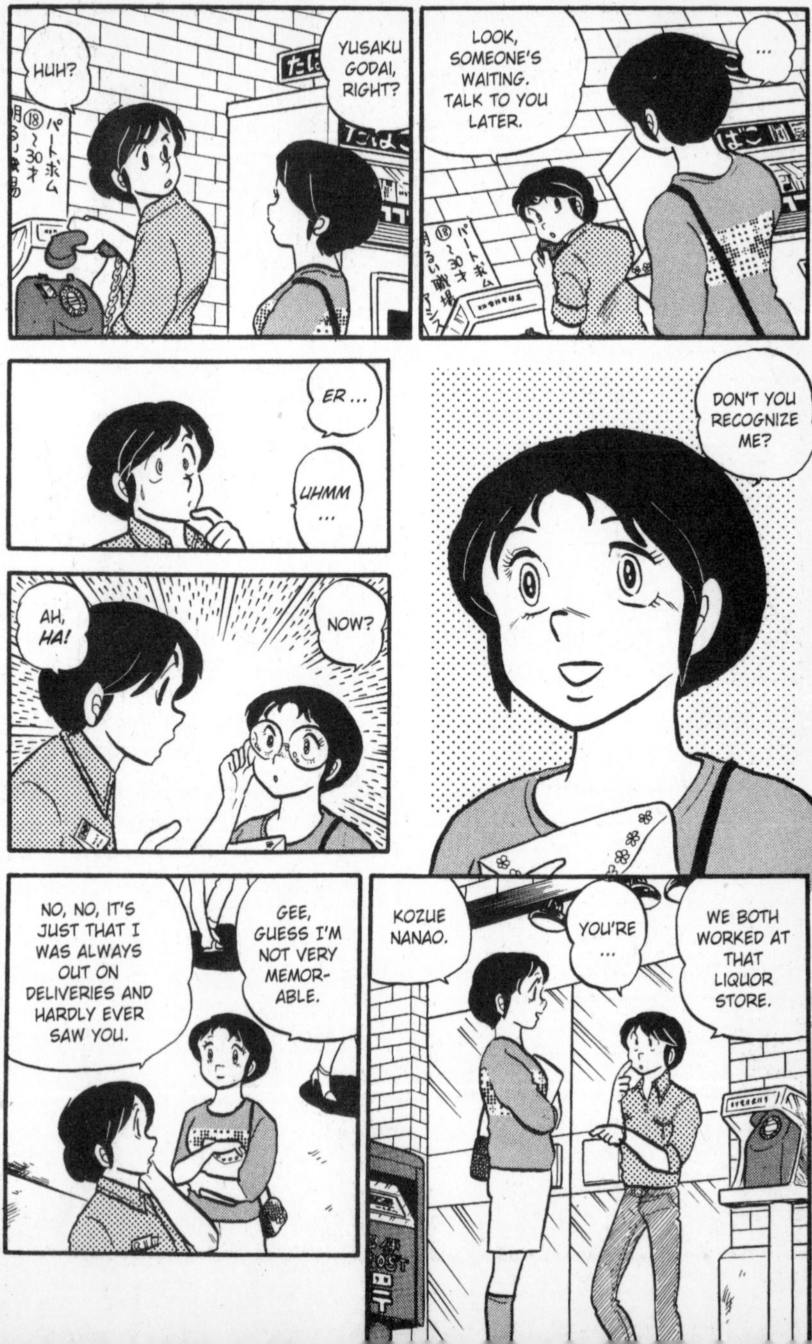
LOOK, SOMEONE'S WAITING. TALK TO YOU LATER.
...
YUSAKU GODAI, RIGHT?
HUH?
DON'T YOU RECOGNIZE ME?
ER ...
UHMM ...
NOW?
AH, *HA!*
WE BOTH WORKED AT THAT LIQUOR STORE.
YOU'RE ...
KOZUE NANAO.
GEE, GUESS I'M NOT VERY MEMORABLE.
NO, NO, IT'S JUST THAT I WAS ALWAYS OUT ON DELIVERIES AND HARDLY EVER SAW YOU.

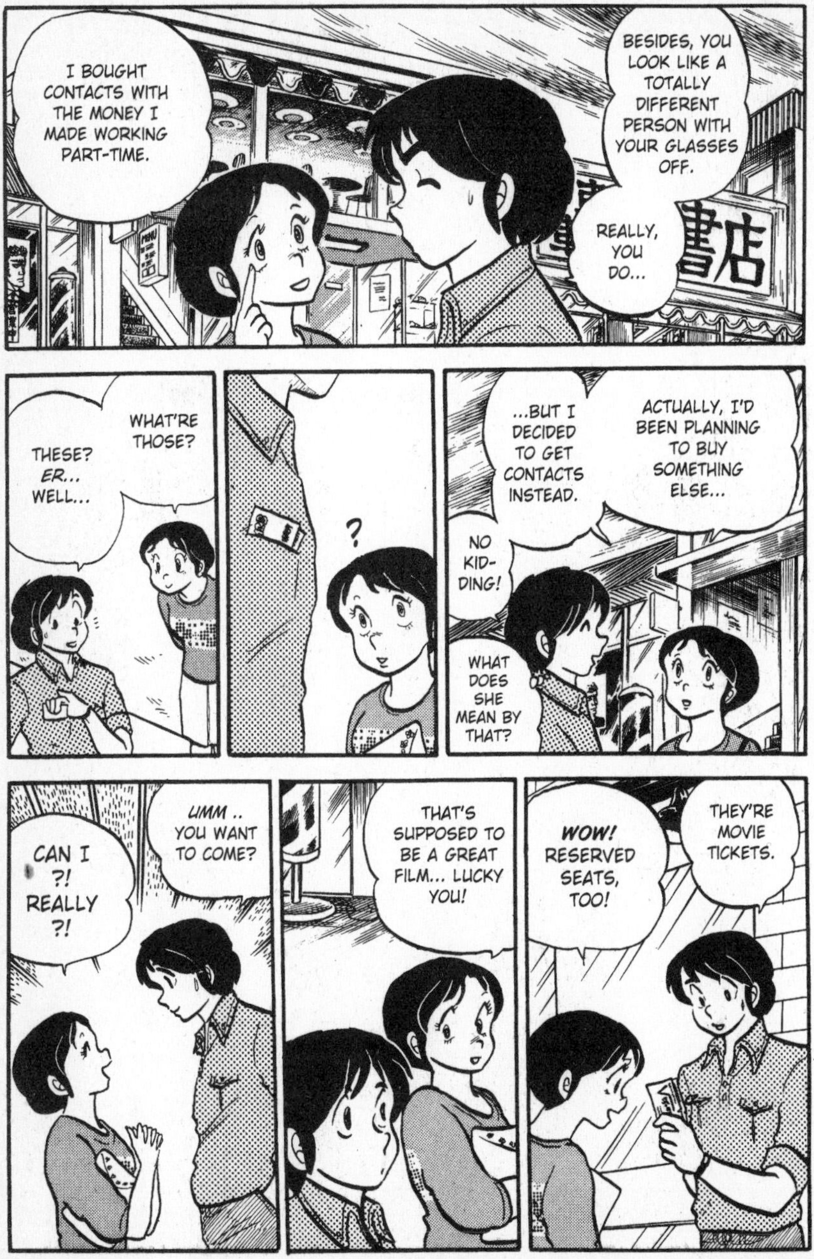
BESIDES, YOU LOOK LIKE A TOTALLY DIFFERENT PERSON WITH YOUR GLASSES OFF.
REALLY, YOU DO...
I BOUGHT CONTACTS WITH THE MONEY I MADE WORKING PART-TIME.
ACTUALLY, I'D BEEN PLANNING TO BUY SOMETHING ELSE...
...BUT I DECIDED TO GET CONTACTS INSTEAD.
NO KID-DING!
WHAT DOES SHE MEAN BY THAT?
?
WHAT'RE THOSE?
THESE? *ER...* WELL...
THEY'RE MOVIE TICKETS.
WOW! RESERVED SEATS, TOO!
THAT'S SUPPOSED TO BE A GREAT FILM... LUCKY YOU!
UMM .. YOU WANT TO COME?
CAN I ?! REALLY ?!

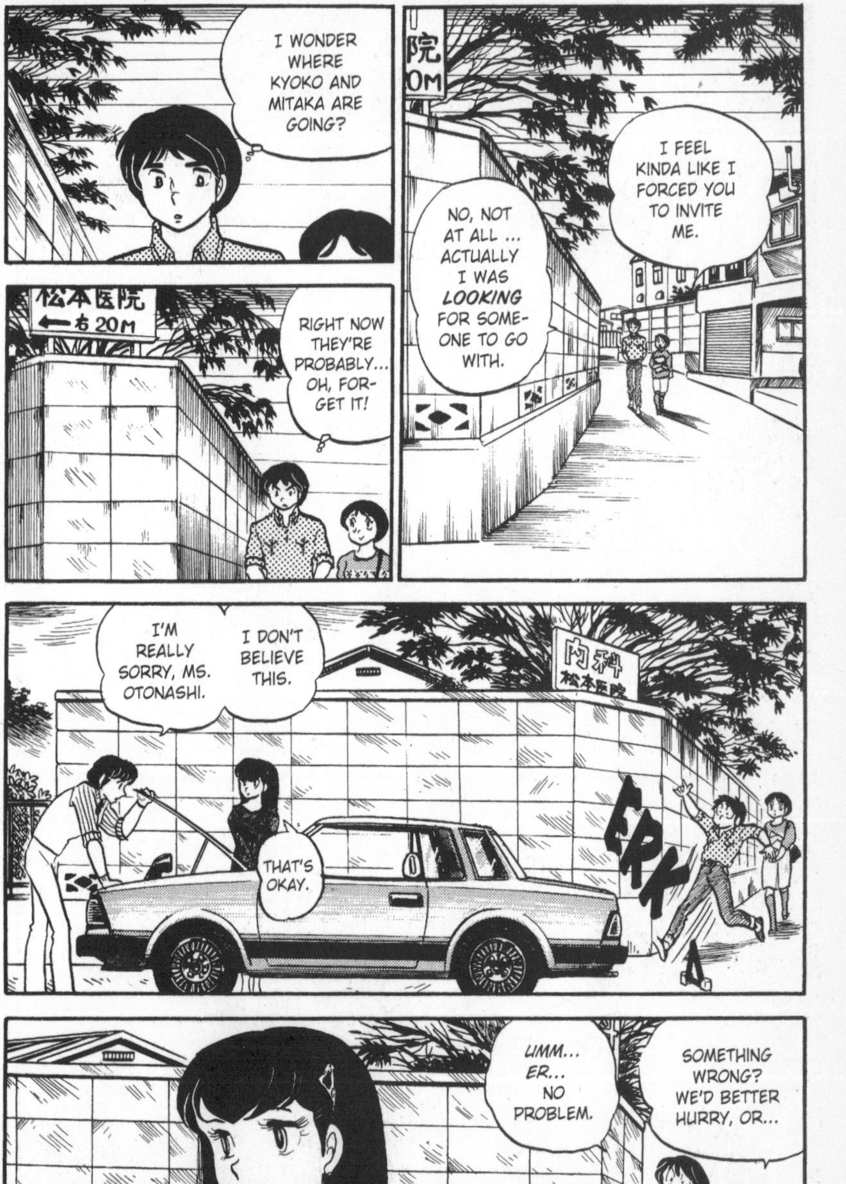
I FEEL KINDA LIKE I FORCED YOU TO INVITE ME.
NO, NOT AT ALL ... ACTUALLY I WAS ***LOOKING*** FOR SOMEONE TO GO WITH.
I WONDER WHERE KYOKO AND MITAKA ARE GOING?
松本医院
←右20M
RIGHT NOW THEY'RE PROBABLY... OH, FORGET IT!
内科
松本医院
ERK
I DON'T BELIEVE THIS.
I'M REALLY SORRY, MS. OTONASHI.
THAT'S OKAY.
SOMETHING WRONG? WE'D BETTER HURRY, OR...
UMM... ER... NO PROBLEM.

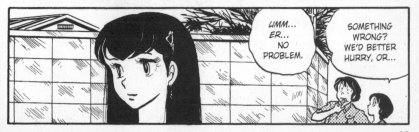

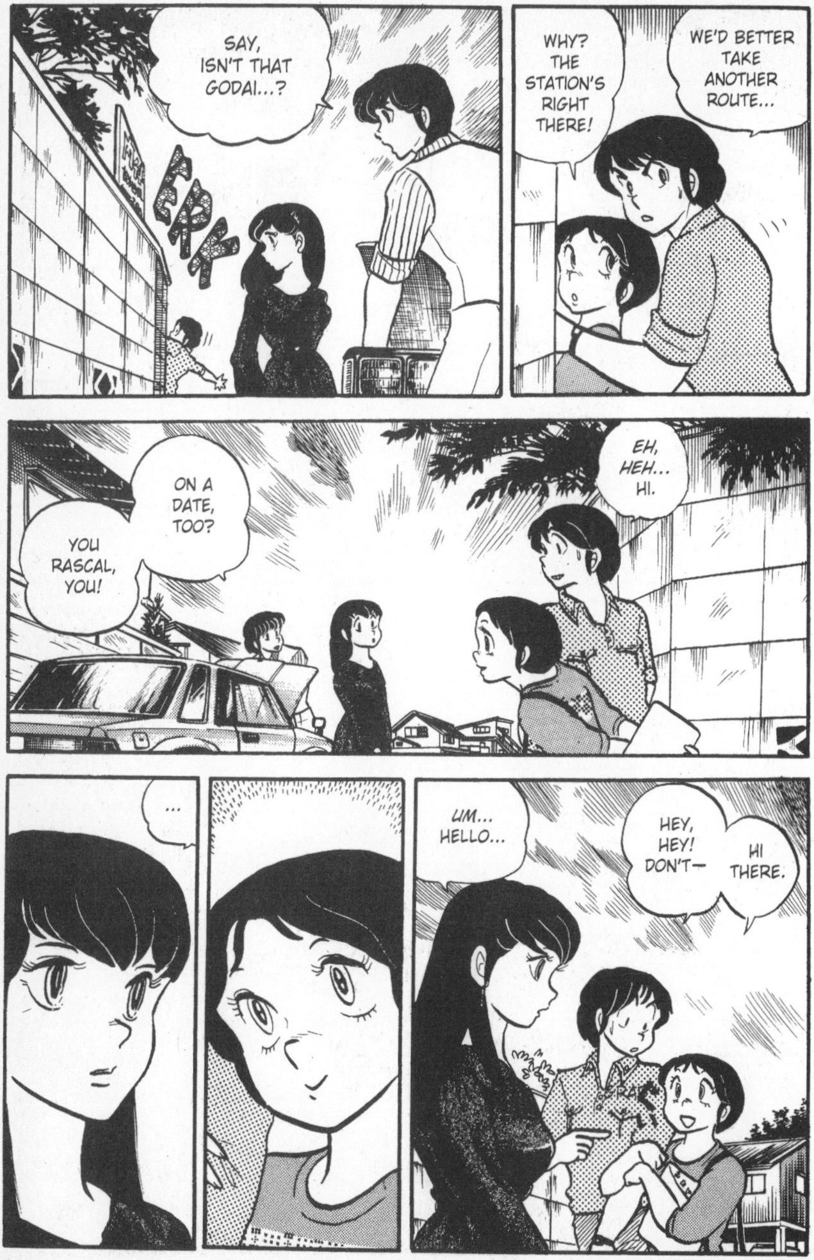
WE'D BETTER TAKE ANOTHER ROUTE...
WHY? THE STATION'S RIGHT THERE!
SAY, ISN'T THAT GODAI...?
ERK
EH, HEH... HI.
ON A DATE, TOO?
YOU RASCAL, YOU!
HI THERE.
HEY, HEY! DON'T—
UM... HELLO...
...

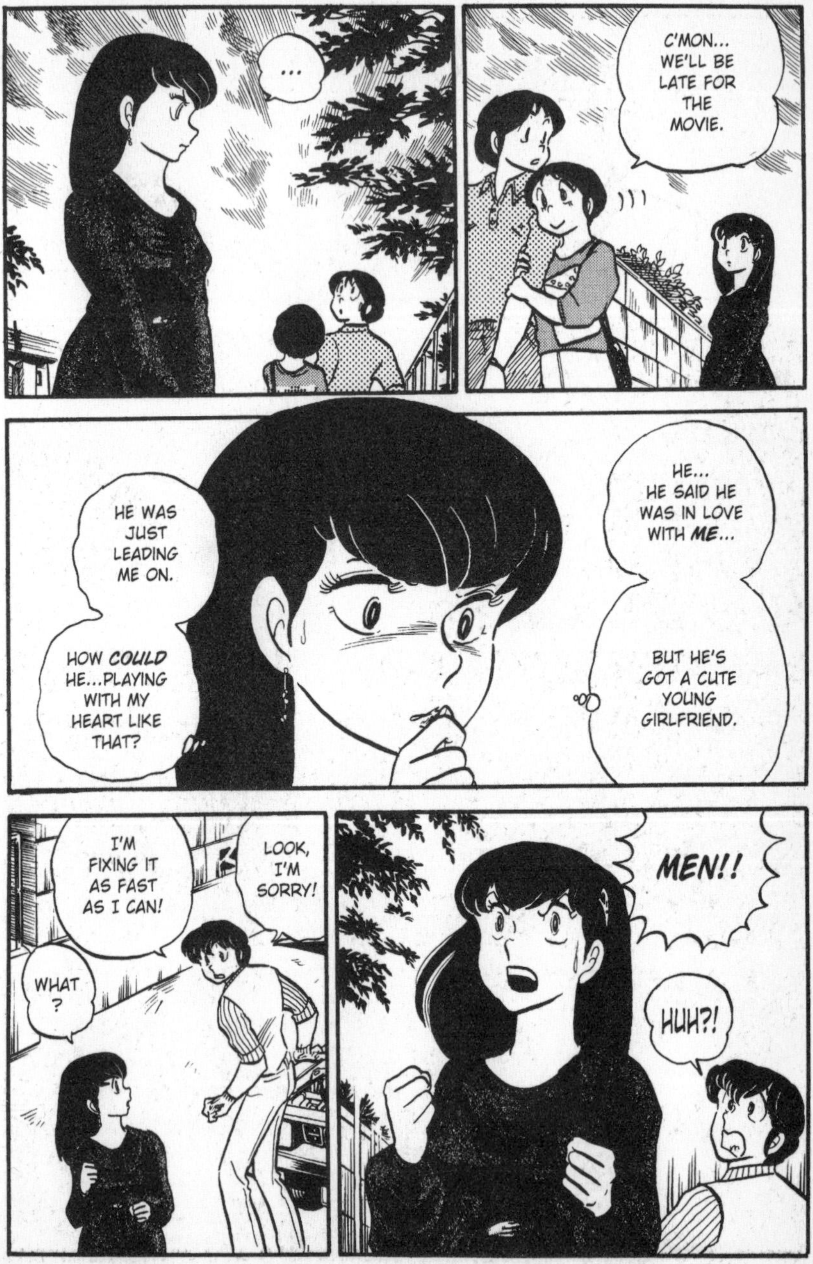
C'MON... WE'LL BE LATE FOR THE MOVIE.
...
HE... HE SAID HE WAS IN LOVE WITH *ME*...
BUT HE'S GOT A CUTE YOUNG GIRLFRIEND.
HE WAS JUST LEADING ME ON.
HOW *COULD* HE...PLAYING WITH MY HEART LIKE THAT?
MEN!!
HUH?!
LOOK, I'M SORRY!
I'M FIXING IT AS FAST AS I CAN!
WHAT?

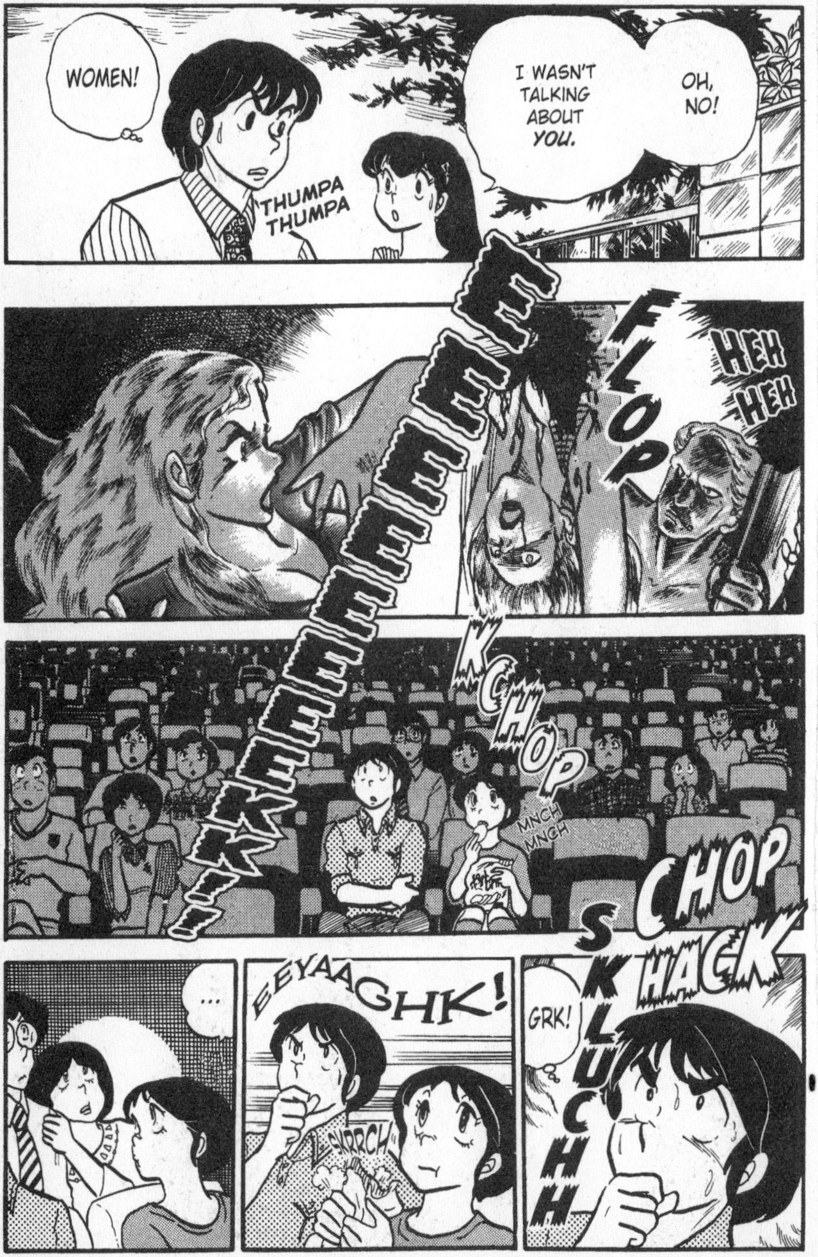
OH, NO!
I WASN'T TALKING ABOUT YOU.
THUMPA THUMPA
WOMEN!
HEH HEH
FLOP
EEEEEEEEEEEK!!!
KCHOP
MNCH MNCH
CHOP
HACK
SKLUCHHH
GRK!
EEYAAGHK!
SKRRCH
...

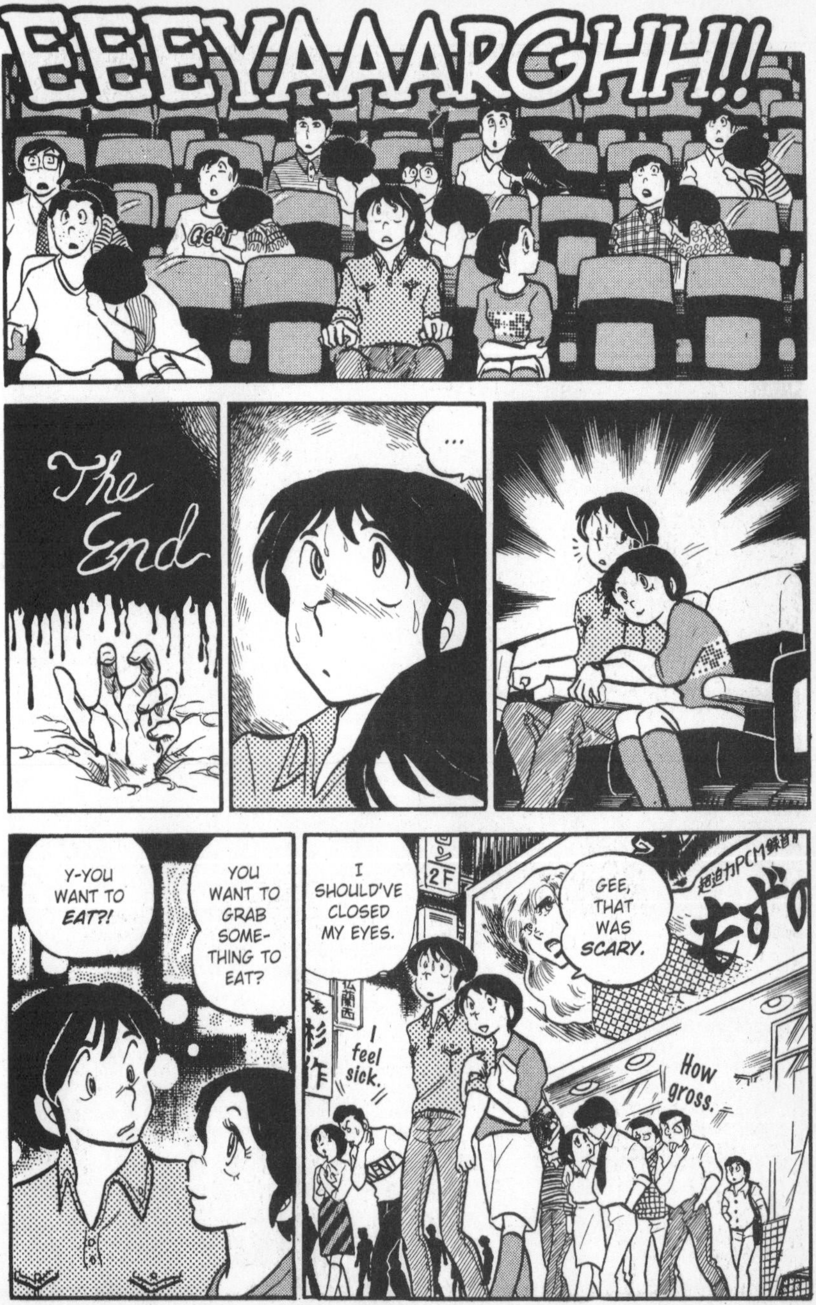
EEEYAAARGHH!!
...
The End
GEE, THAT WAS SCARY.
I SHOULD'VE CLOSED MY EYES.
2F
How gross.
I feel sick.
YOU WANT TO GRAB SOMETHING TO EAT?
Y-YOU WANT TO EAT?!

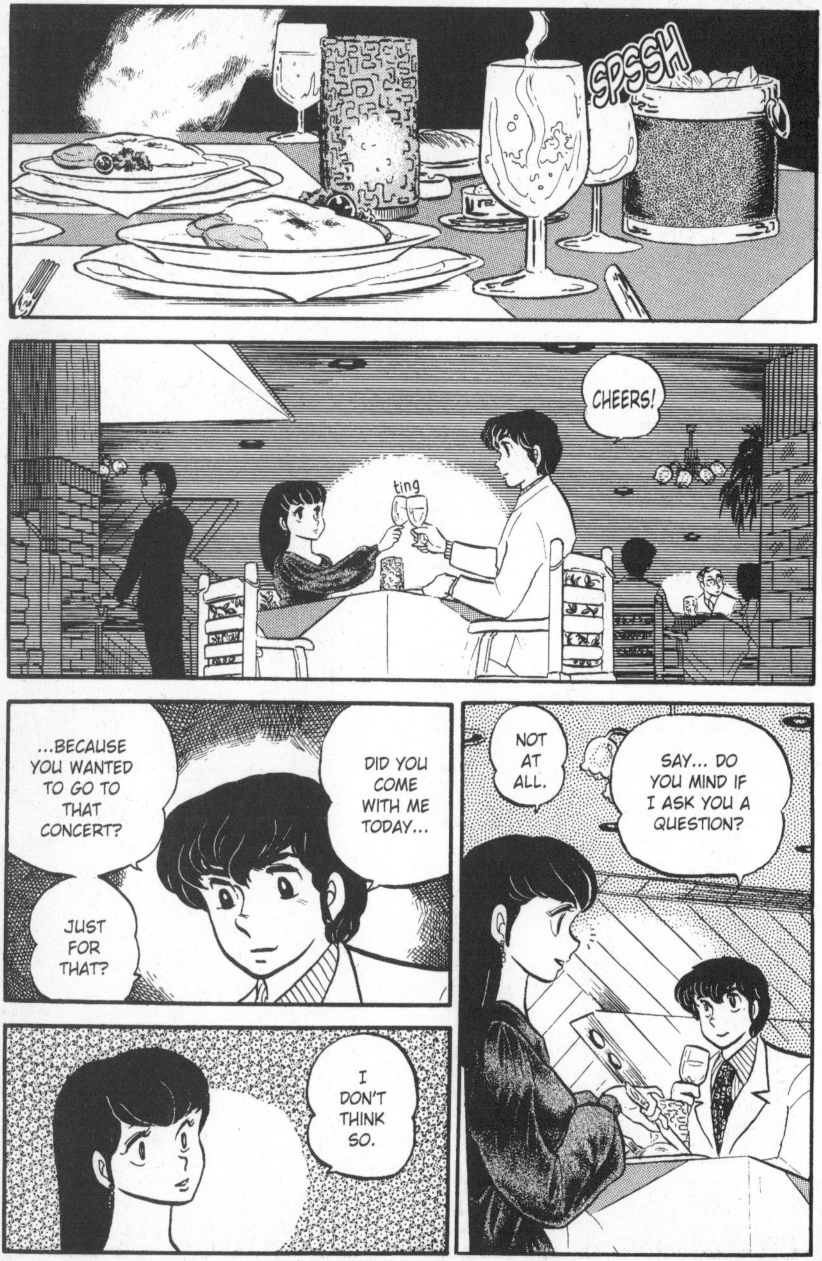
SPSSH
ting
CHEERS!
SAY... DO YOU MIND IF I ASK YOU A QUESTION?
NOT AT ALL.
DID YOU COME WITH ME TODAY...
...BECAUSE YOU WANTED TO GO TO THAT CONCERT?
JUST FOR THAT?
I DON'T THINK SO.

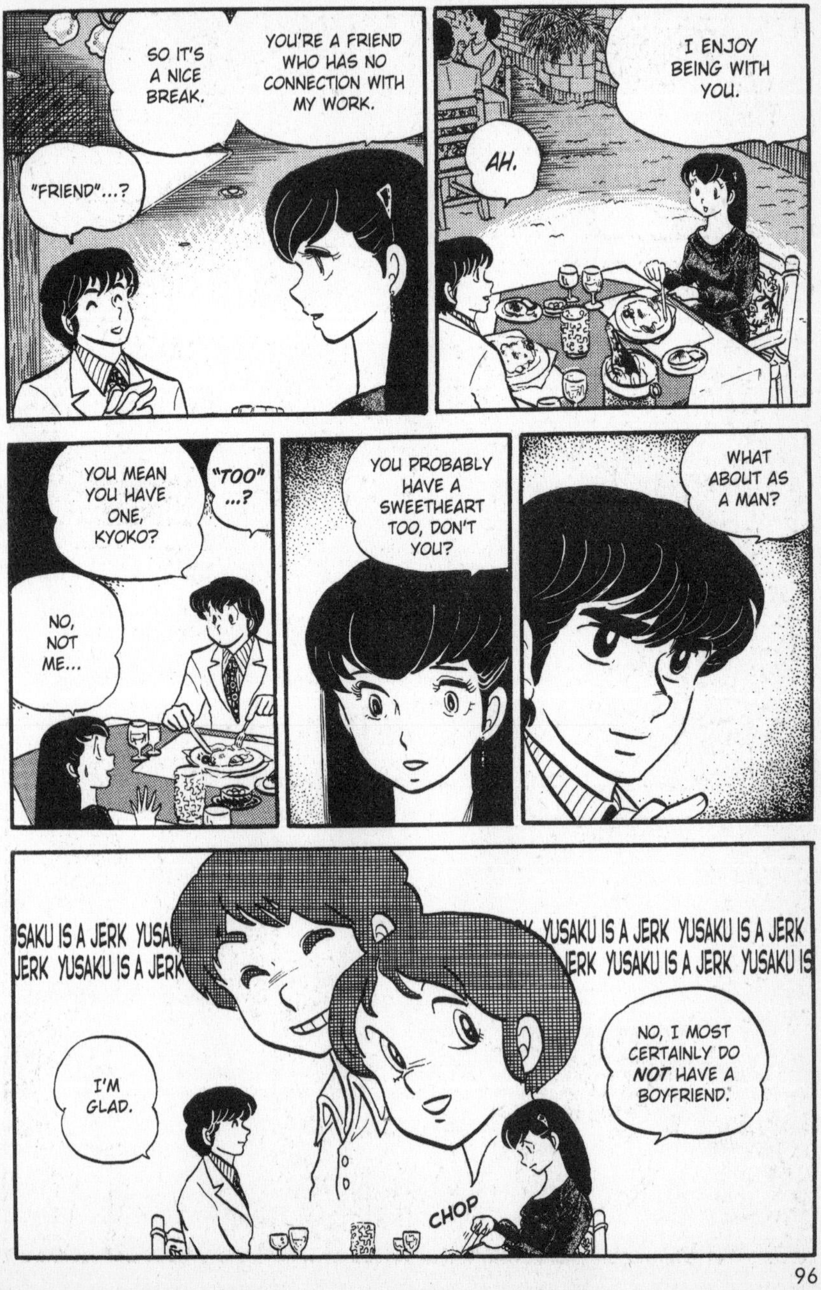
I ENJOY BEING WITH YOU.
AH.
YOU'RE A FRIEND WHO HAS NO CONNECTION WITH MY WORK.
SO IT'S A NICE BREAK.
"FRIEND"...?
WHAT ABOUT AS A MAN?
YOU PROBABLY HAVE A SWEETHEART TOO, DON'T YOU?
"TOO" ...?
YOU MEAN YOU HAVE ONE, KYOKO?
NO, NOT ME...
YUSAKU IS A JERK YUSAKU IS A JERK
JERK YUSAKU IS A JERK YUSAKU IS
NO, I MOST CERTAINLY DO **NOT** HAVE A BOYFRIEND.
SAKU IS A JERK
JERK YUSAKU IS A JERK
I'M GLAD.
CHOP

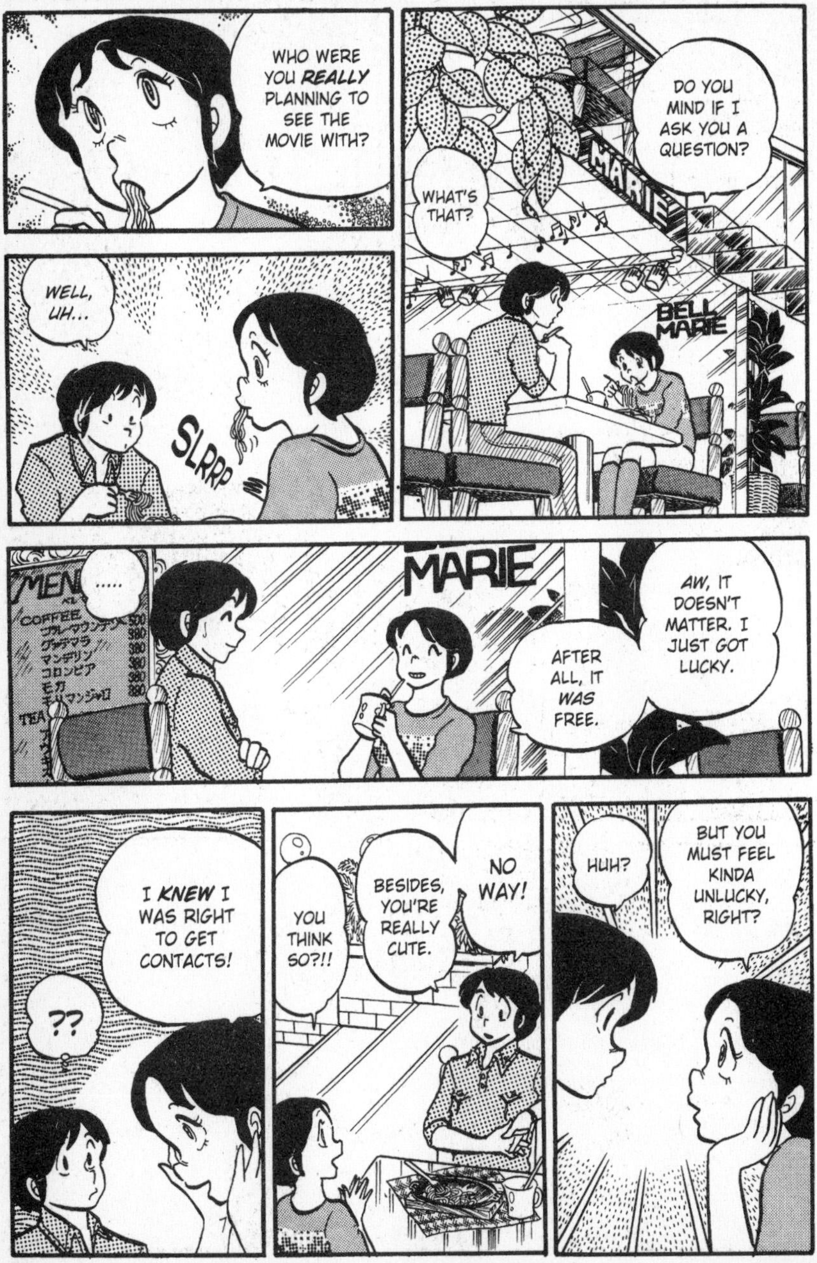
DO YOU MIND IF I ASK YOU A QUESTION?
WHAT'S THAT?
MARIE
BELL MARIE
WHO WERE YOU *REALLY* PLANNING TO SEE THE MOVIE WITH?
WELL, UH...
SLRRP
AW, IT DOESN'T MATTER. I JUST GOT LUCKY.
AFTER ALL, IT *WAS* FREE.
MARIE
.....
COFFEE
TEA
BUT YOU MUST FEEL KINDA UNLUCKY, RIGHT?
HUH?
NO WAY!
BESIDES, YOU'RE REALLY CUTE.
YOU THINK SO?!!
I *KNEW* I WAS RIGHT TO GET CONTACTS!
??

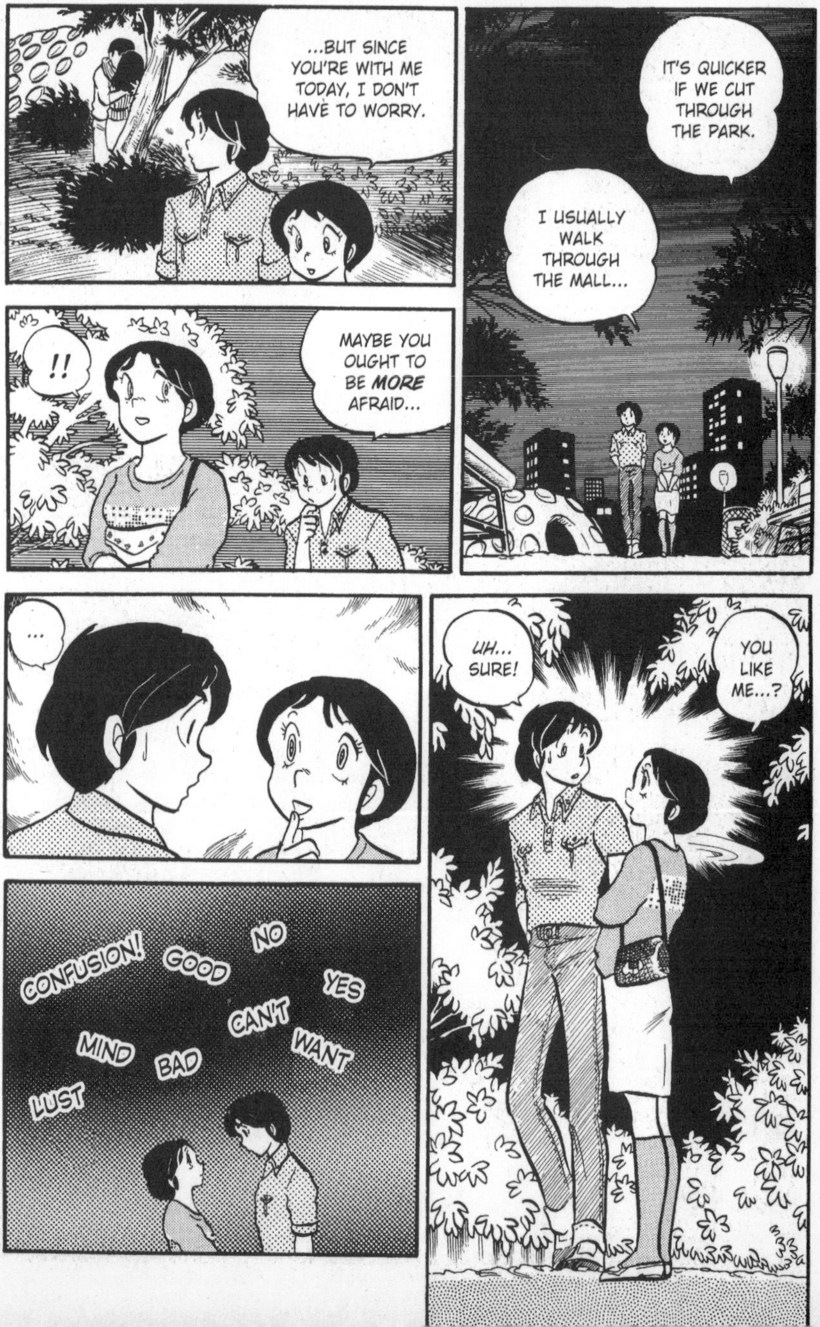
IT'S QUICKER IF WE CUT THROUGH THE PARK.
I USUALLY WALK THROUGH THE MALL...
...BUT SINCE YOU'RE WITH ME TODAY, I DON'T HAVE TO WORRY.
MAYBE YOU OUGHT TO BE *MORE* AFRAID...
!!
YOU LIKE ME...?
UH... SURE!
...
NO
YES
GOOD
CONFUSION!
CAN'T
WANT
MIND
BAD
LUST

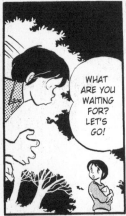

N-NO!
I CAN'T JUST LOSE CONTROL IN THE HEAT OF THE MOMENT...
BUT HELL!
WHAT'S ONE LITTLE KISS?!
WHAT ARE YOU WAITING FOR? LET'S GO!
I WONDER ...
IS SHE INTERESTED IN ME?
CAN WE SEE EACH OTHER AGAIN?
KOZUE, HUH?
BOWF

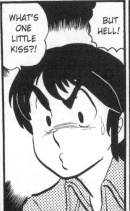

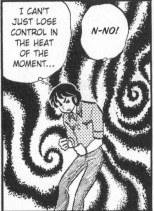

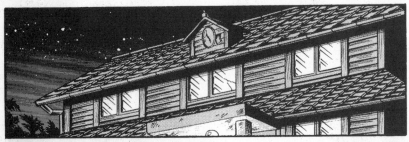

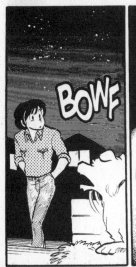

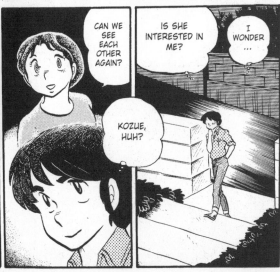

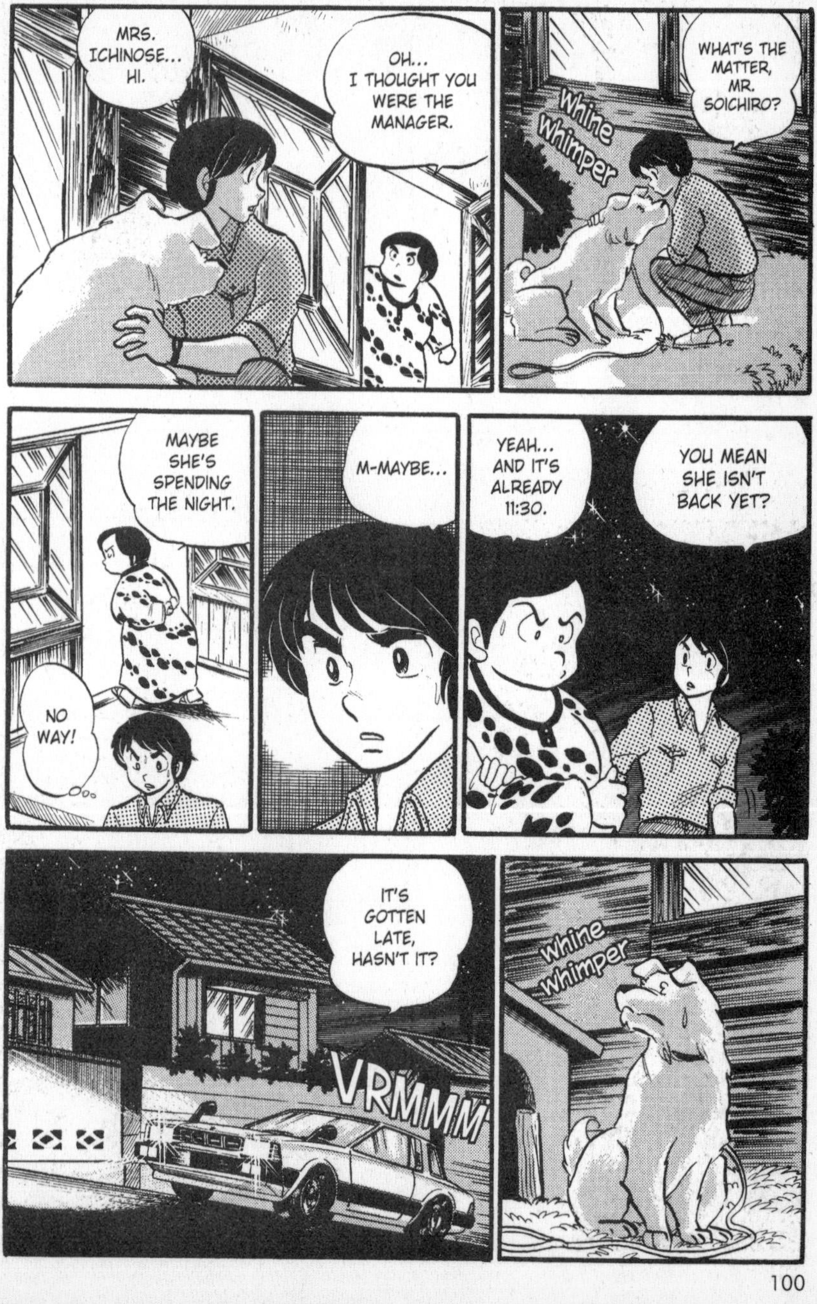
WHAT'S THE MATTER, MR. SOICHIRO?
Whine Whimper
OH... I THOUGHT YOU WERE THE MANAGER.
MRS. ICHINOSE... HI.
YOU MEAN SHE ISN'T BACK YET?
YEAH... AND IT'S ALREADY 11:30.
M-MAYBE...
MAYBE SHE'S SPENDING THE NIGHT.
NO WAY!
Whine Whimper
IT'S GOTTEN LATE, HASN'T IT?
VRMMM

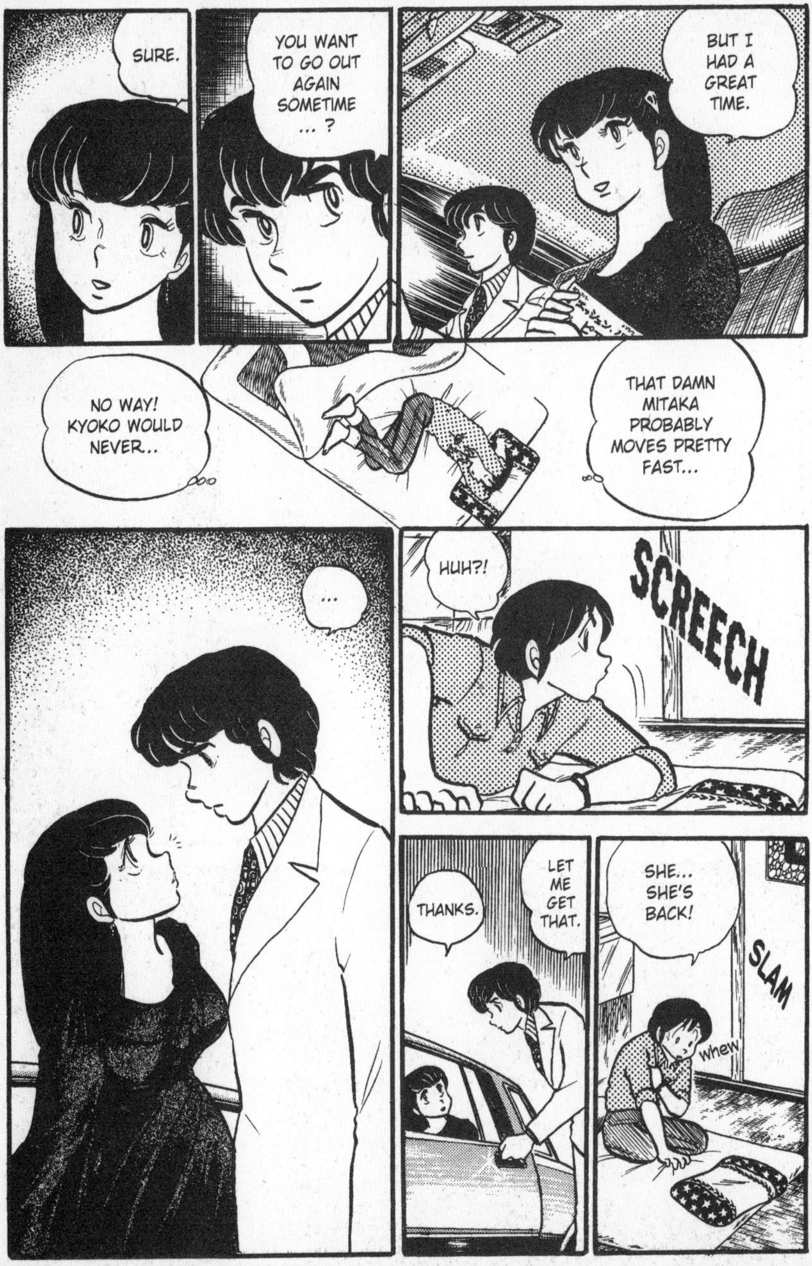
BUT I HAD A GREAT TIME.
YOU WANT TO GO OUT AGAIN SOMETIME ... ?
SURE.
THAT DAMN MITAKA PROBABLY MOVES PRETTY FAST...
NO WAY! KYOKO WOULD NEVER..
SCREECH
HUH?!
SHE... SHE'S BACK!
SLAM
whew
LET ME GET THAT.
THANKS.
...

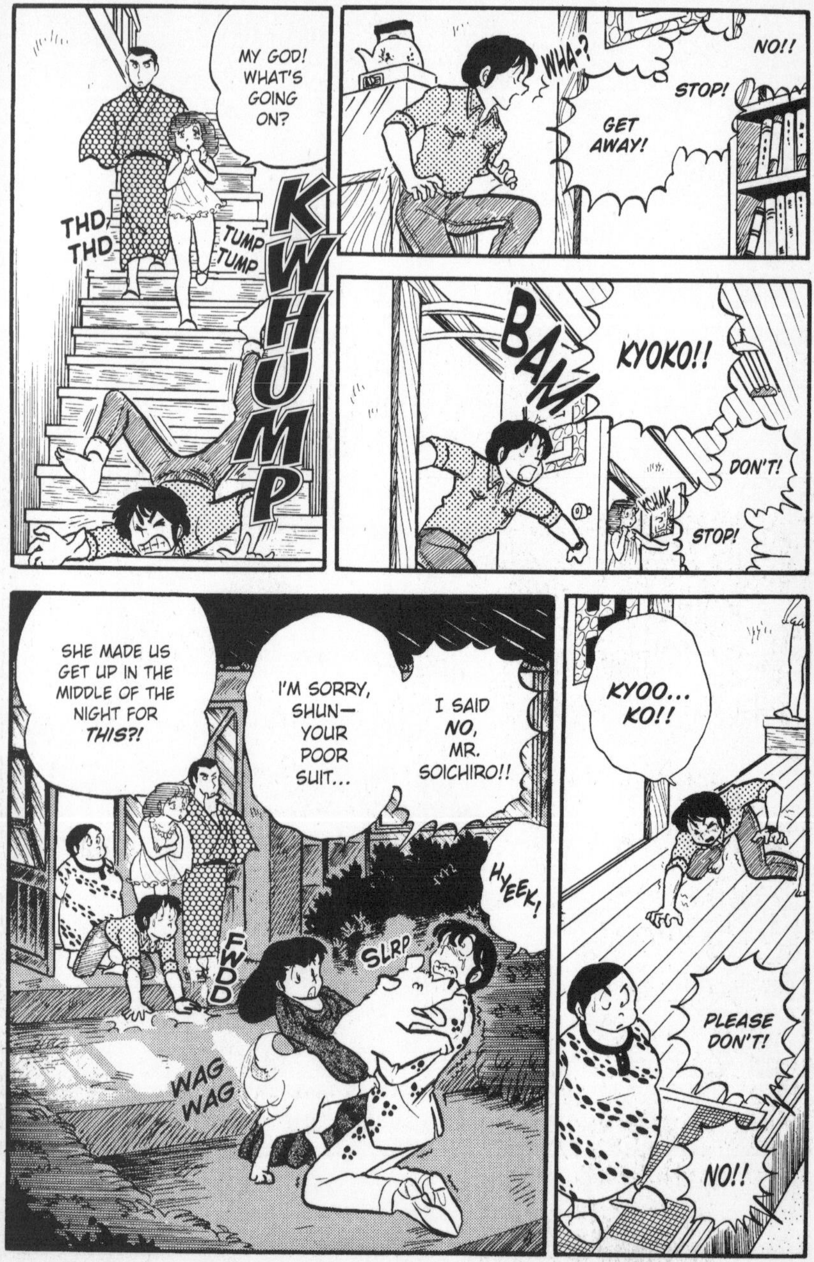

NO!!
STOP!
GET AWAY!
WHA-?
KYOKO!!
BAM
DON'T!
KCHAK
STOP!
MY GOD! WHAT'S GOING ON?
KWHUMP
TUMP TUMP
THD THD
KYOO... KO!!
PLEASE DON'T!
NO!!
I SAID NO, MR. SOICHIRO!!
HYEEK!
I'M SORRY, SHUN— YOUR POOR SUIT...
SHE MADE US GET UP IN THE MIDDLE OF THE NIGHT FOR THIS?!
SLRP
FWDD
WAG WAG

PART SIX

1-900-TROUBLE

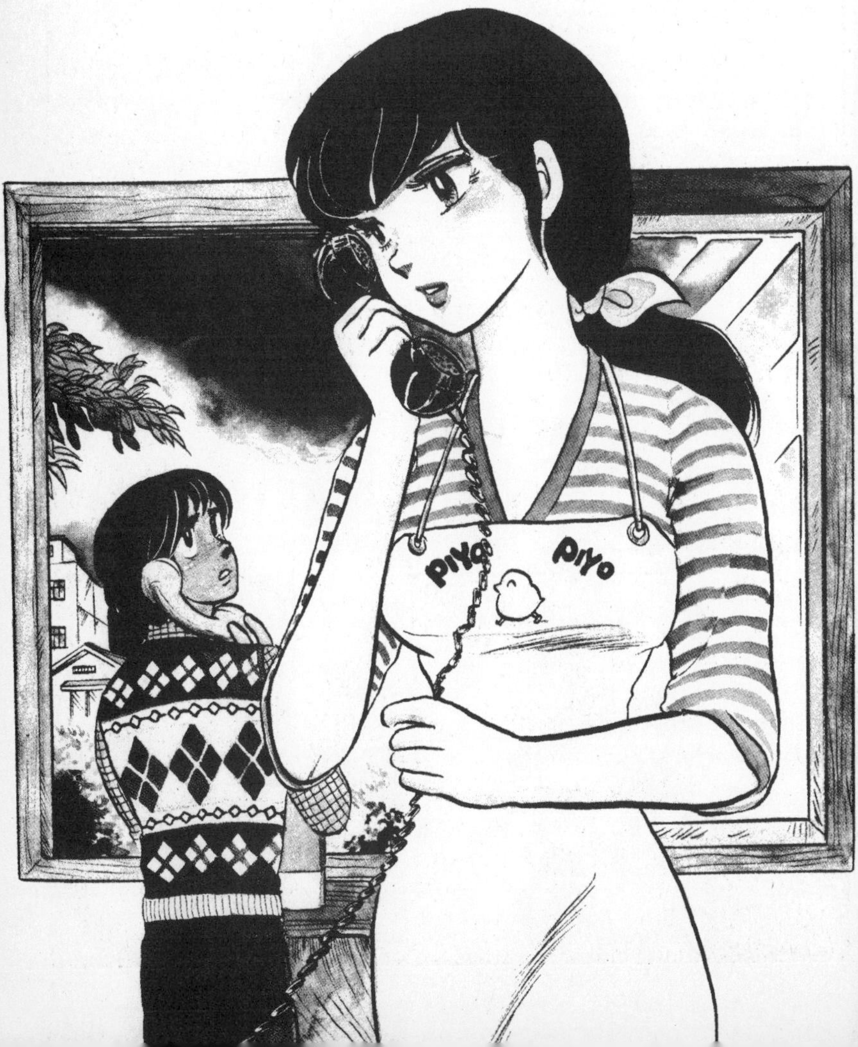
piyo
piyo

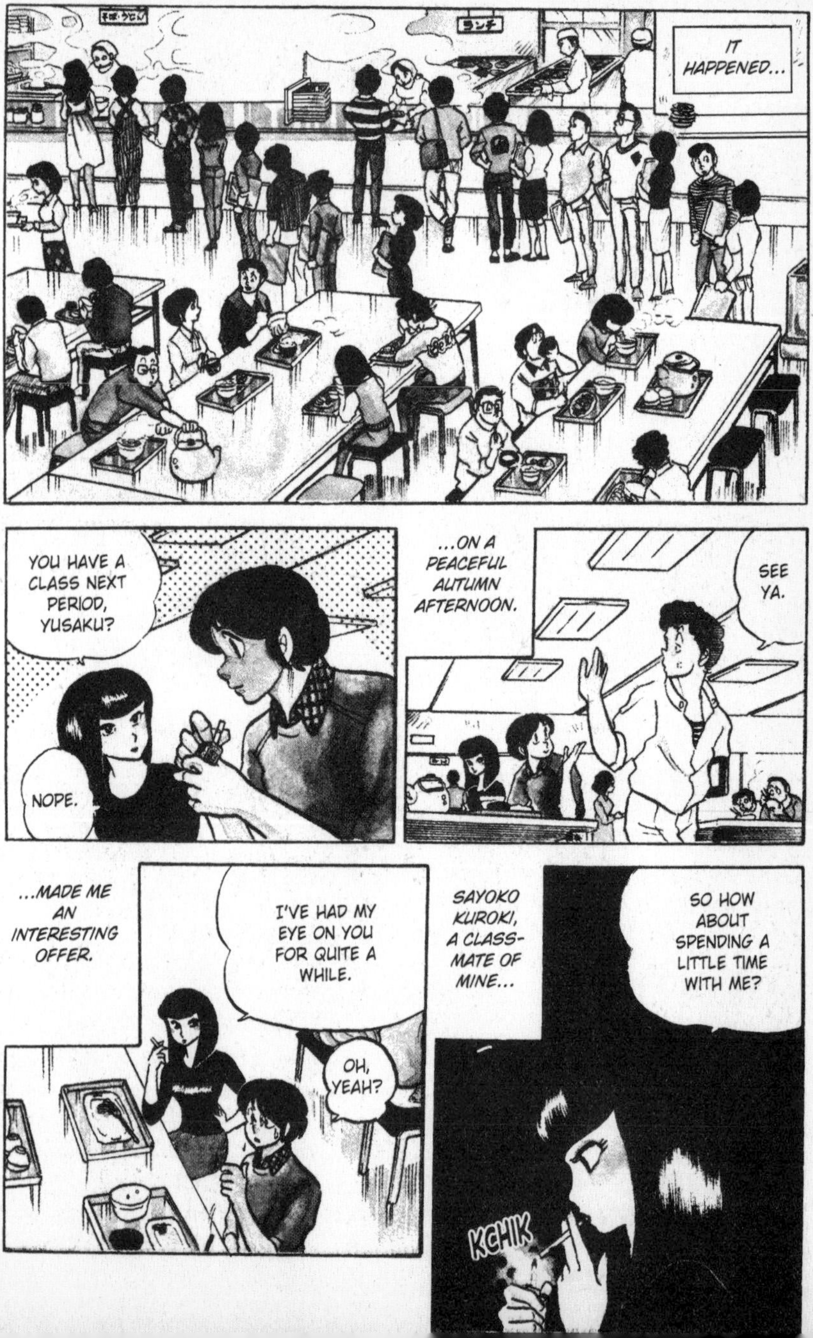
IT HAPPENED...
ランチ
そば・うどん
...ON A PEACEFUL AUTUMN AFTERNOON.
SEE YA.
YOU HAVE A CLASS NEXT PERIOD, YUSAKU?
NOPE.
SAYOKO KUROKI, A CLASS-MATE OF MINE...
SO HOW ABOUT SPENDING A LITTLE TIME WITH ME?
KCHIK
...MADE ME AN INTERESTING OFFER.
I'VE HAD MY EYE ON YOU FOR QUITE A WHILE.
OH, YEAH?

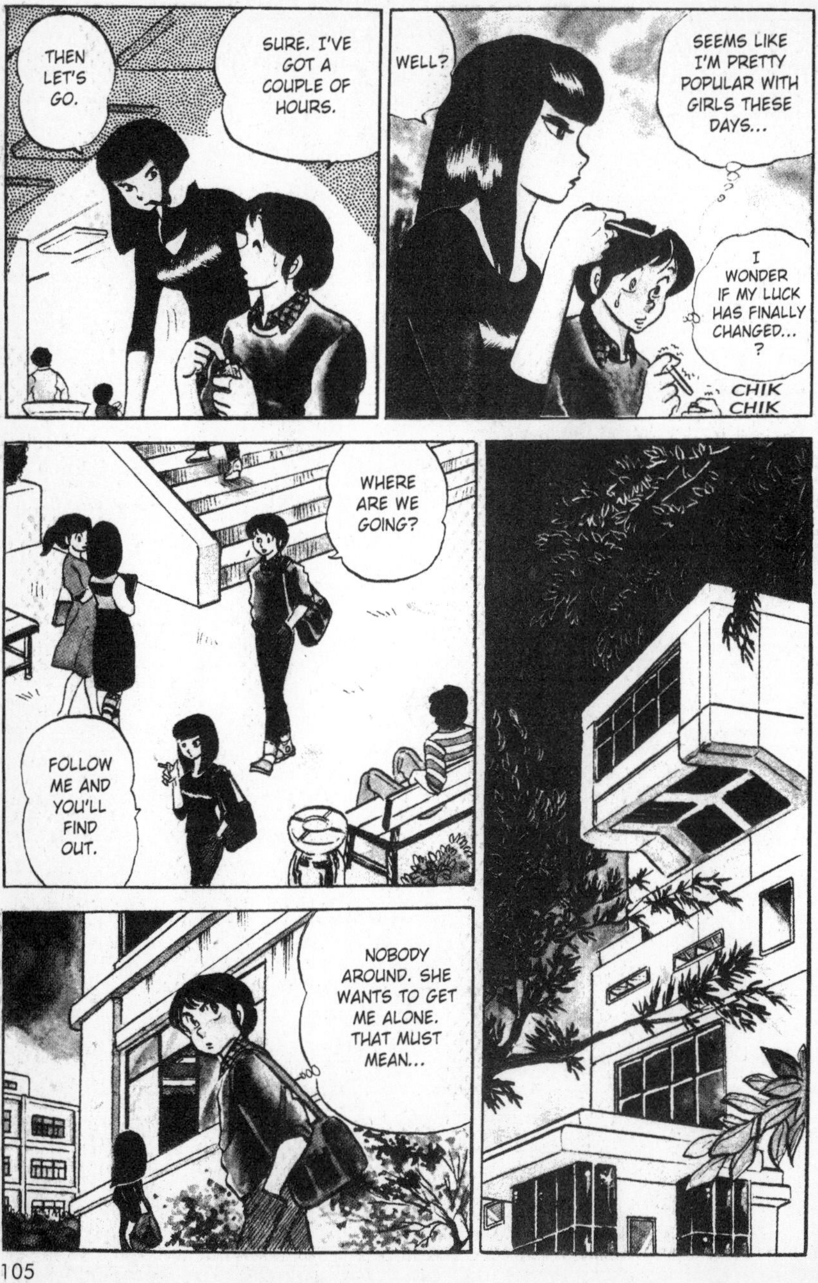
SEEMS LIKE I'M PRETTY POPULAR WITH GIRLS THESE DAYS...
WELL?
I WONDER IF MY LUCK HAS FINALLY CHANGED...?
CHIK CHIK
SURE. I'VE GOT A COUPLE OF HOURS.
THEN LET'S GO.
WHERE ARE WE GOING?
FOLLOW ME AND YOU'LL FIND OUT.
NOBODY AROUND. SHE WANTS TO GET ME ALONE. THAT MUST MEAN...

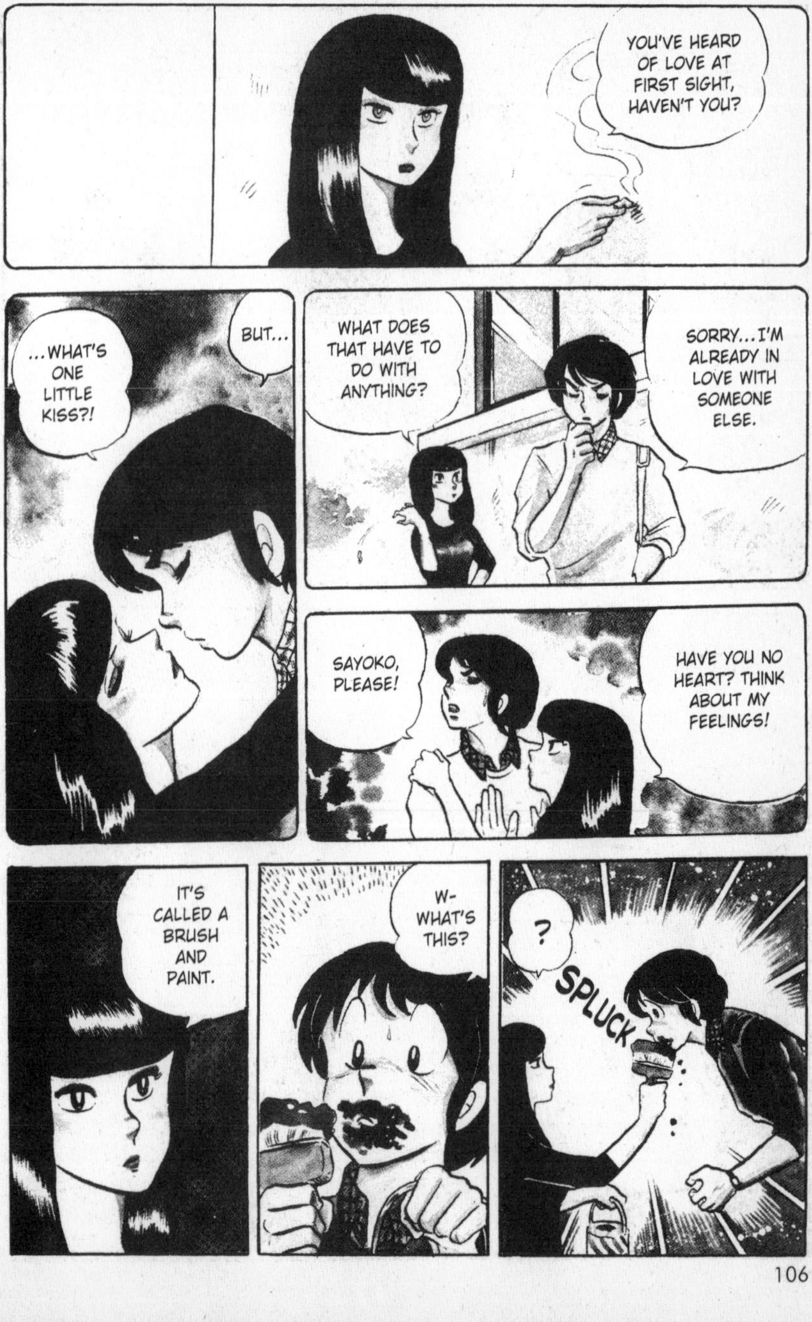
YOU'VE HEARD OF LOVE AT FIRST SIGHT, HAVEN'T YOU?
SORRY...I'M ALREADY IN LOVE WITH SOMEONE ELSE.
WHAT DOES THAT HAVE TO DO WITH ANYTHING?
HAVE YOU NO HEART? THINK ABOUT MY FEELINGS!
SAYOKO, PLEASE!
BUT...
...WHAT'S ONE LITTLE KISS?!
?
SPLUCK
W-WHAT'S THIS?
IT'S CALLED A BRUSH AND PAINT.

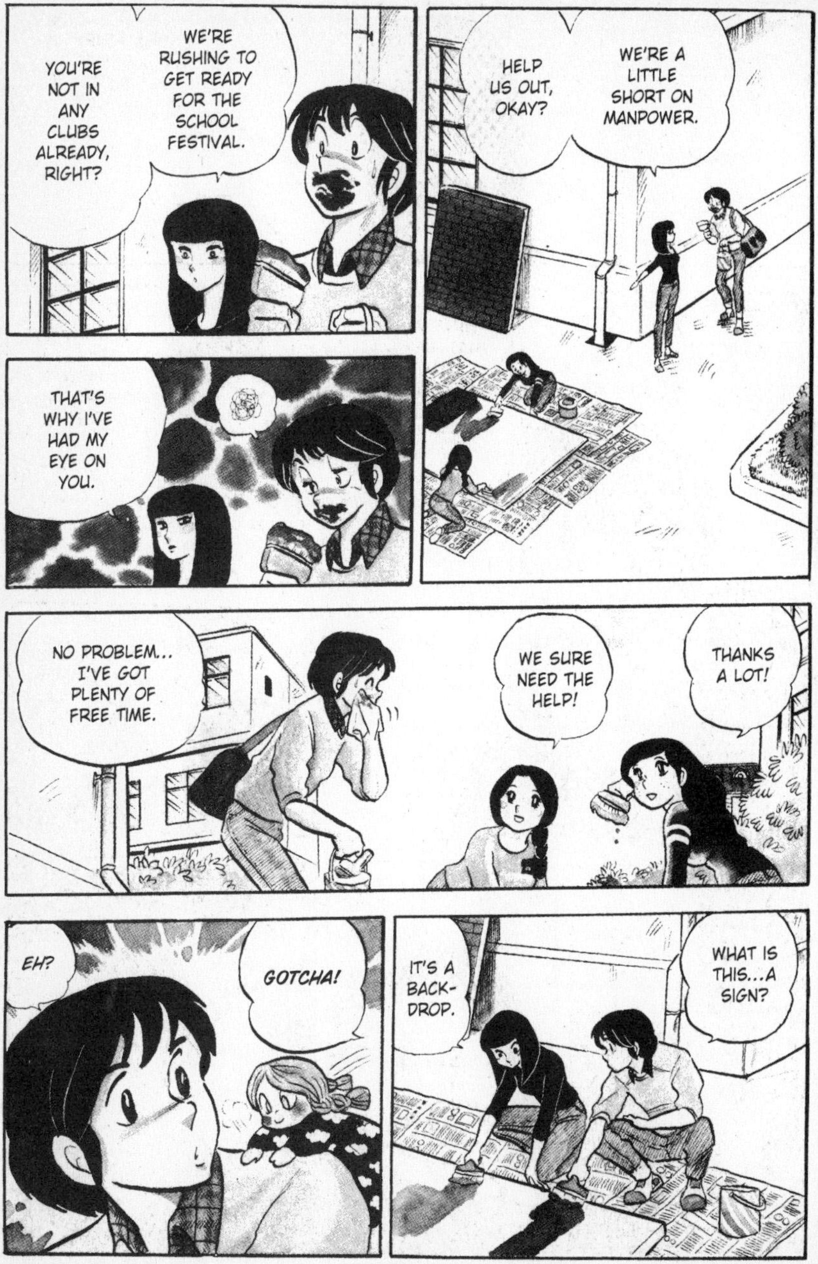
WE'RE A LITTLE SHORT ON MANPOWER.
HELP US OUT, OKAY?
WE'RE RUSHING TO GET READY FOR THE SCHOOL FESTIVAL.
YOU'RE NOT IN ANY CLUBS ALREADY, RIGHT?
THAT'S WHY I'VE HAD MY EYE ON YOU.
THANKS A LOT!
WE SURE NEED THE HELP!
NO PROBLEM... I'VE GOT PLENTY OF FREE TIME.
WHAT IS THIS...A SIGN?
IT'S A BACK-DROP.
GOTCHA!
EH?

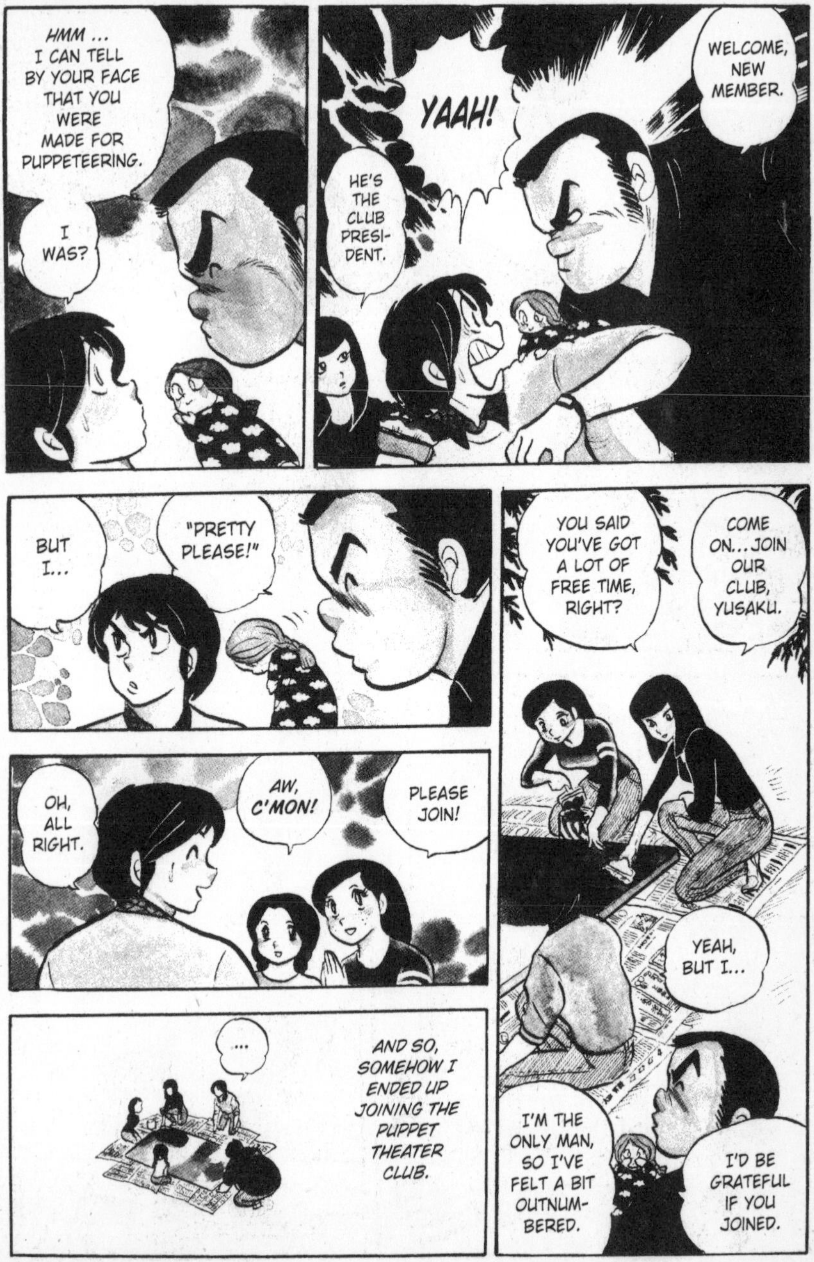
HMM ... I CAN TELL BY YOUR FACE THAT YOU WERE MADE FOR PUPPETEERING.
I WAS?
YAAH!
HE'S THE CLUB PRESI-DENT.
WELCOME, NEW MEMBER.
COME ON... JOIN OUR CLUB, YUSAKU.
YOU SAID YOU'VE GOT A LOT OF FREE TIME, RIGHT?
YEAH, BUT I...
I'M THE ONLY MAN, SO I'VE FELT A BIT OUTNUM-BERED.
I'D BE GRATEFUL IF YOU JOINED.
BUT I...
"PRETTY PLEASE!"
OH, ALL RIGHT.
AW, C'MON!
PLEASE JOIN!
...
AND SO, SOMEHOW I ENDED UP JOINING THE PUPPET THEATER CLUB.

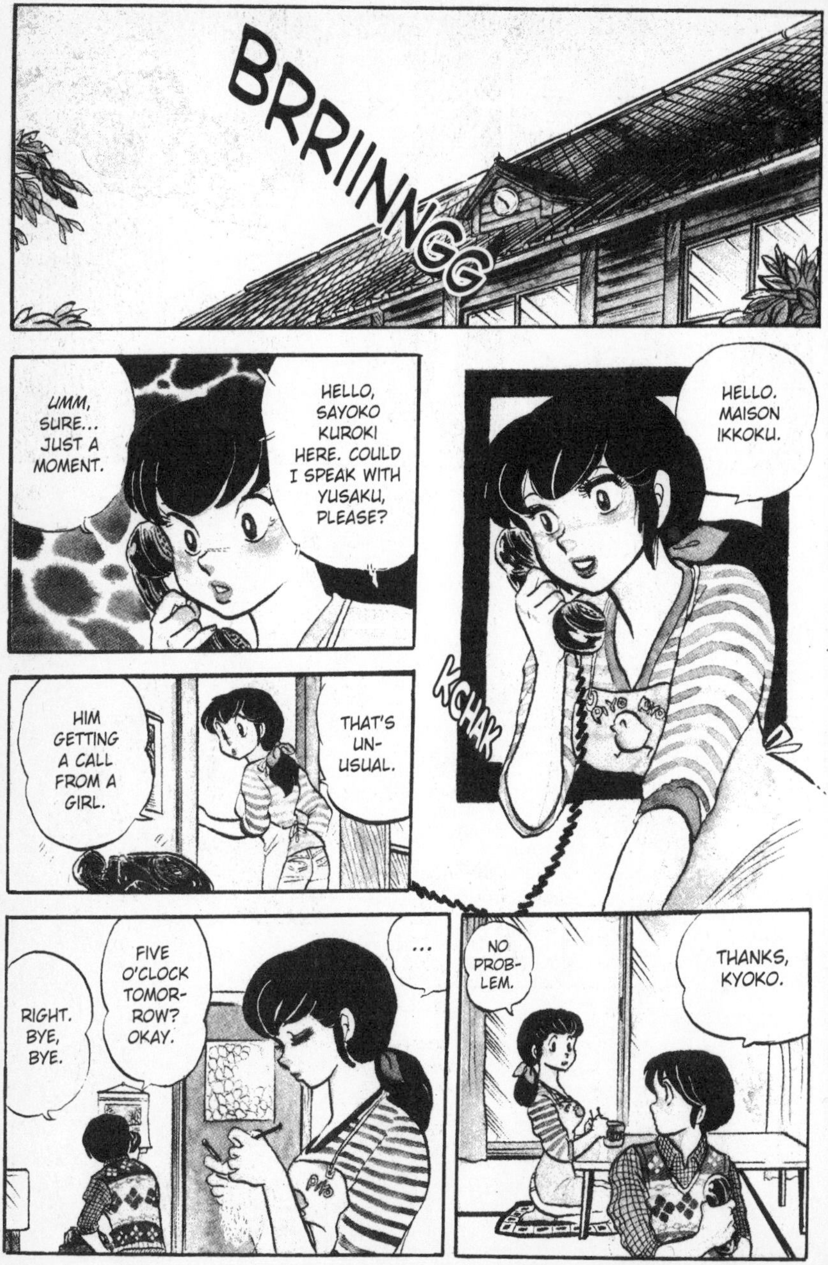
BRRIINNGG
HELLO. MAISON IKKOKU.
KCHAK
HELLO, SAYOKO KUROKI HERE. COULD I SPEAK WITH YUSAKU, PLEASE?
UMM, SURE... JUST A MOMENT.
THAT'S UN-USUAL.
HIM GETTING A CALL FROM A GIRL.
THANKS, KYOKO.
NO PROB-LEM.
...
FIVE O'CLOCK TOMOR-ROW? OKAY.
RIGHT. BYE, BYE.

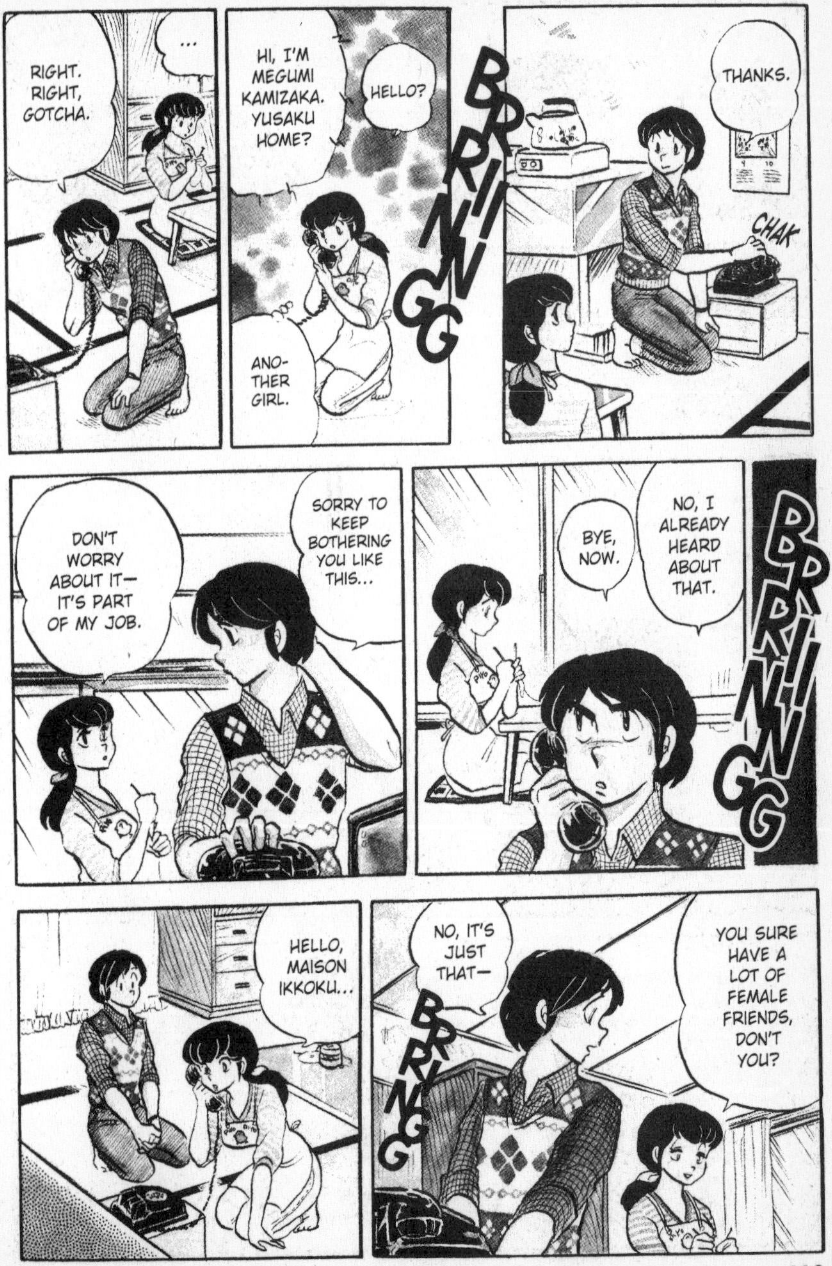
THANKS.
CHAK
BRRIIINNGG
HELLO?
HI, I'M MEGUMI KAMIZAKA. YUSAKU HOME?
ANO-THER GIRL.
...
RIGHT. RIGHT, GOTCHA.
BRRRIIINNGG
NO, I ALREADY HEARD ABOUT THAT.
BYE, NOW.
SORRY TO KEEP BOTHERING YOU LIKE THIS...
DON'T WORRY ABOUT IT—IT'S PART OF MY JOB.
YOU SURE HAVE A LOT OF FEMALE FRIENDS, DON'T YOU?
NO, IT'S JUST THAT—
BRRING
HELLO, MAISON IKKOKU...

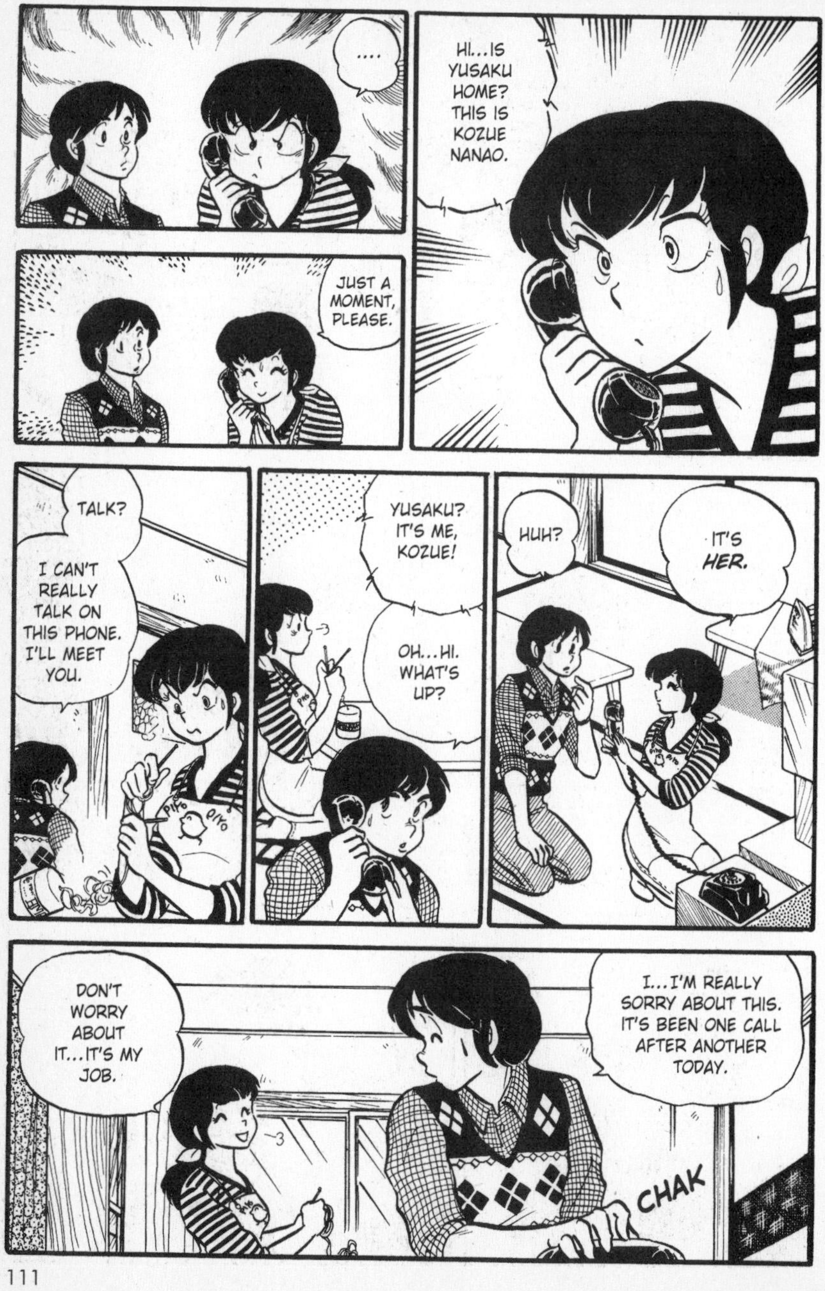
HI...IS YUSAKU HOME? THIS IS KOZUE NANAO.
....
JUST A MOMENT, PLEASE.
IT'S *HER.*
HUH?
YUSAKU? IT'S ME, KOZUE!
OH...HI. WHAT'S UP?
TALK?
I CAN'T REALLY TALK ON THIS PHONE. I'LL MEET YOU.
I...I'M REALLY SORRY ABOUT THIS. IT'S BEEN ONE CALL AFTER ANOTHER TODAY.
CHAK
DON'T WORRY ABOUT IT...IT'S MY JOB.

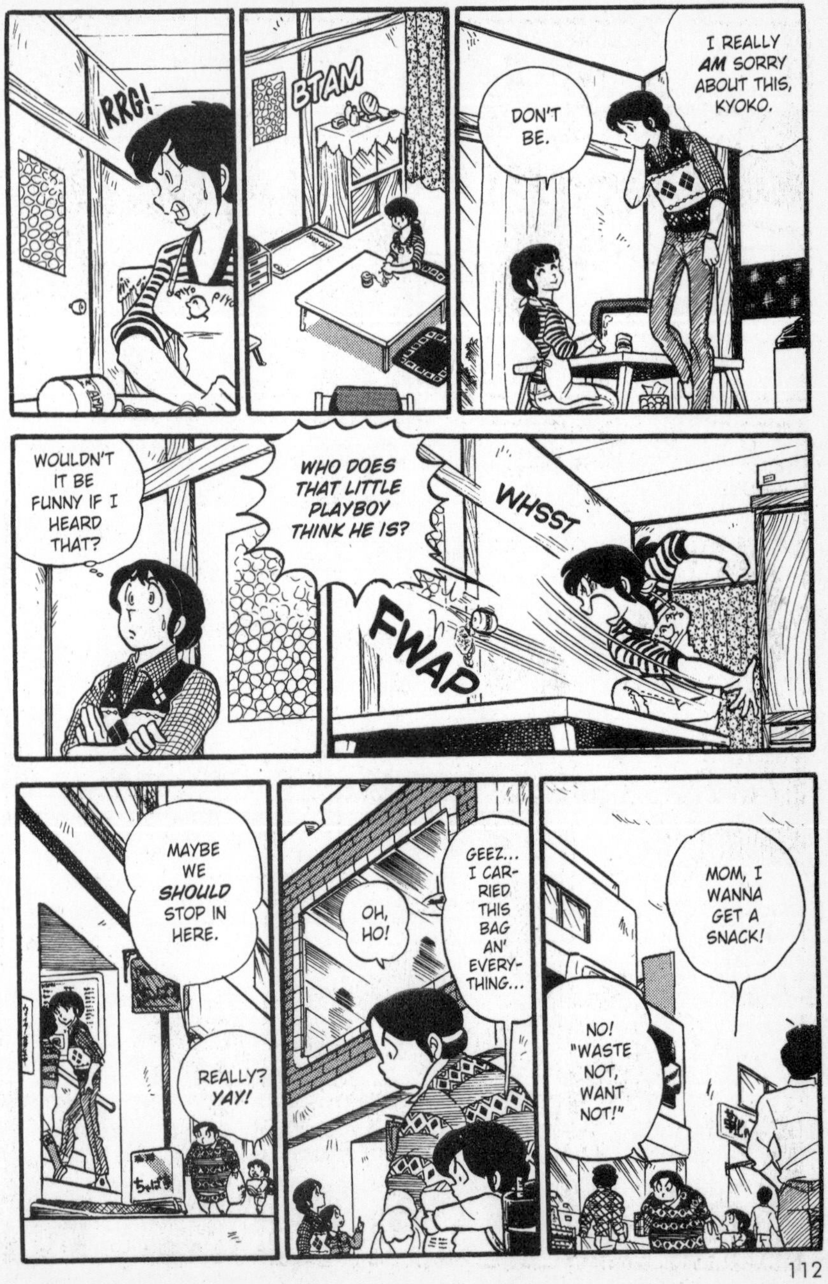
I REALLY AM SORRY ABOUT THIS, KYOKO.
DON'T BE.
BTAM
RRG!
WHO DOES THAT LITTLE PLAYBOY THINK HE IS?
WHSST
FWAP
WOULDN'T IT BE FUNNY IF I HEARD THAT?
MOM, I WANNA GET A SNACK!
NO! "WASTE NOT, WANT NOT!"
GEEZ... I CARRIED THIS BAG AN' EVERYTHING...
OH, HO!
MAYBE WE SHOULD STOP IN HERE.
REALLY? YAY!

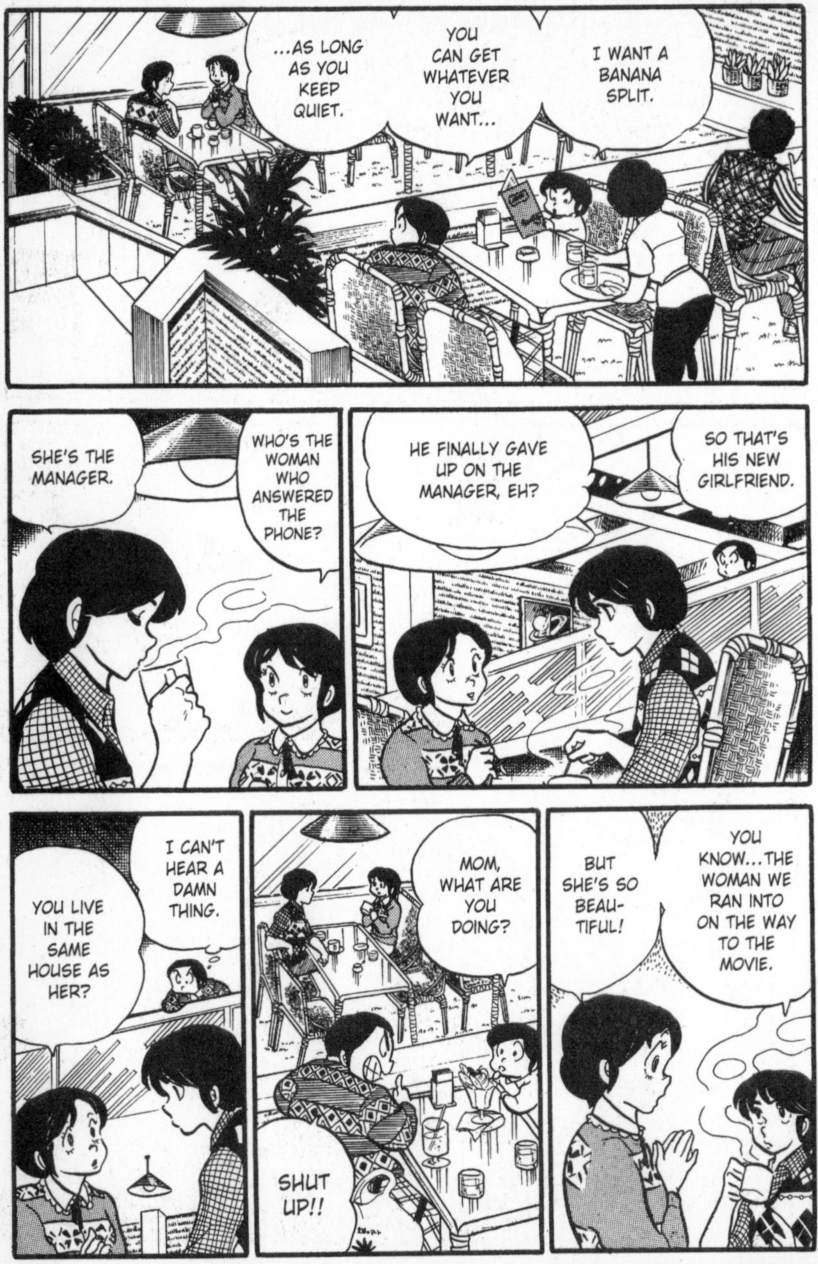
I WANT A BANANA SPLIT.
YOU CAN GET WHATEVER YOU WANT...
...AS LONG AS YOU KEEP QUIET.
SO THAT'S HIS NEW GIRLFRIEND.
HE FINALLY GAVE UP ON THE MANAGER, EH?
WHO'S THE WOMAN WHO ANSWERED THE PHONE?
SHE'S THE MANAGER.
YOU KNOW...THE WOMAN WE RAN INTO ON THE WAY TO THE MOVIE.
BUT SHE'S SO BEAU-TIFUL!
MOM, WHAT ARE YOU DOING?
SHUT UP!!
I CAN'T HEAR A DAMN THING.
YOU LIVE IN THE SAME HOUSE AS HER?

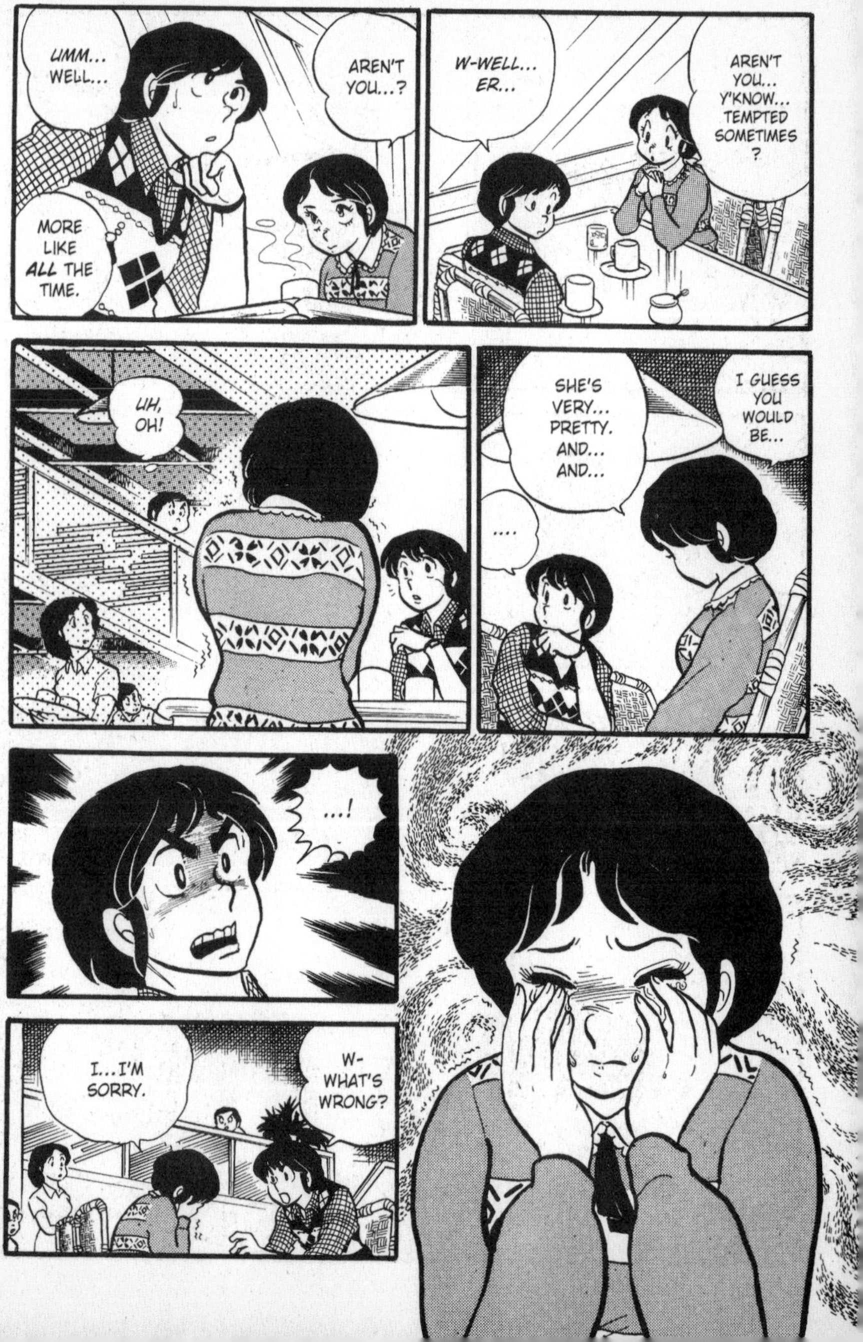
AREN'T YOU... Y'KNOW... TEMPTED SOMETIMES?
W-WELL... ER...
AREN'T YOU...?
UMM... WELL...
MORE LIKE ALL THE TIME.
I GUESS YOU WOULD BE...
SHE'S VERY... PRETTY. AND... AND...
....
UH, OH!
...!
W- WHAT'S WRONG?
I... I'M SORRY.

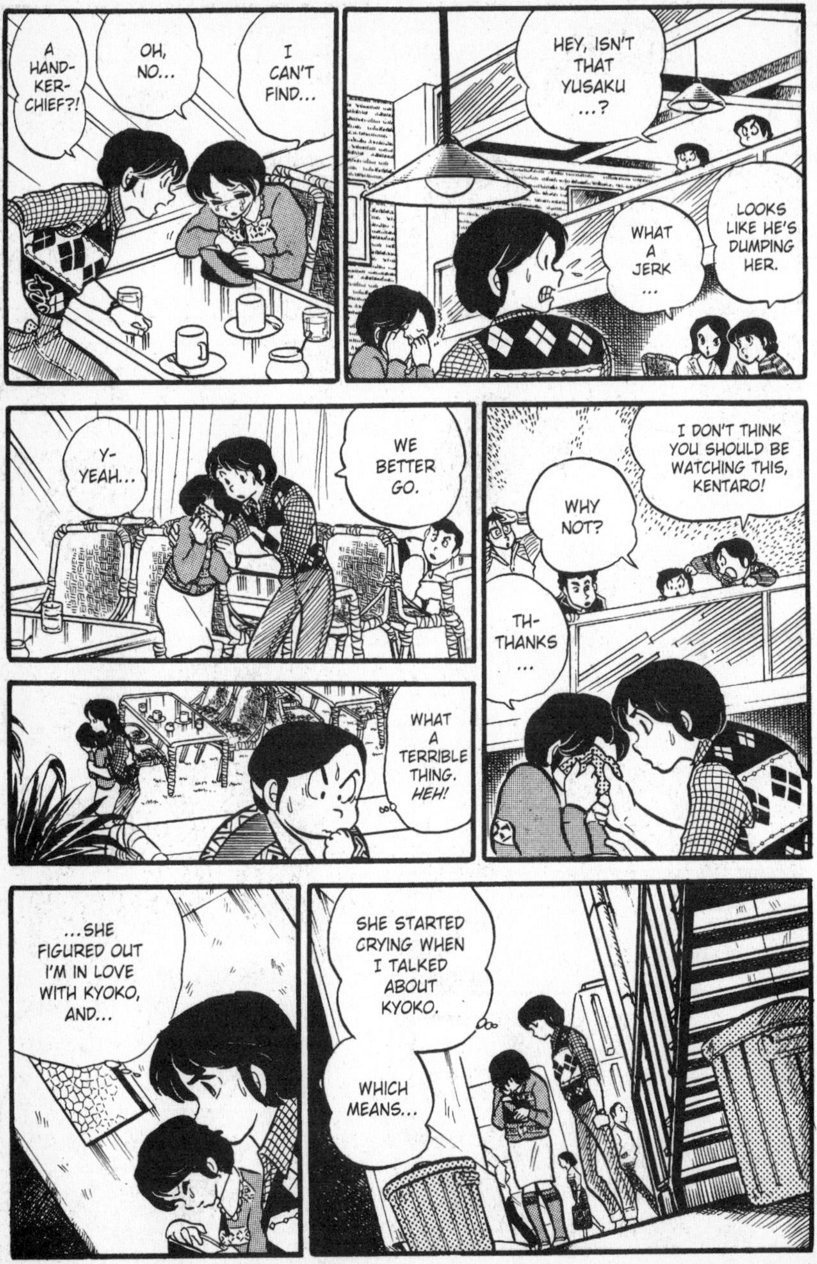
HEY, ISN'T THAT YUSAKU ...?
LOOKS LIKE HE'S DUMPING HER.
WHAT A JERK ...
I CAN'T FIND...
OH, NO...
A HAND-KER-CHIEF?!
I DON'T THINK YOU SHOULD BE WATCHING THIS, KENTARO!
WHY NOT?
TH-THANKS ...
WE BETTER GO.
Y-YEAH...
WHAT A TERRIBLE THING. *HEH!*
SHE STARTED CRYING WHEN I TALKED ABOUT KYOKO.
WHICH MEANS...
...SHE FIGURED OUT I'M IN LOVE WITH KYOKO, AND...

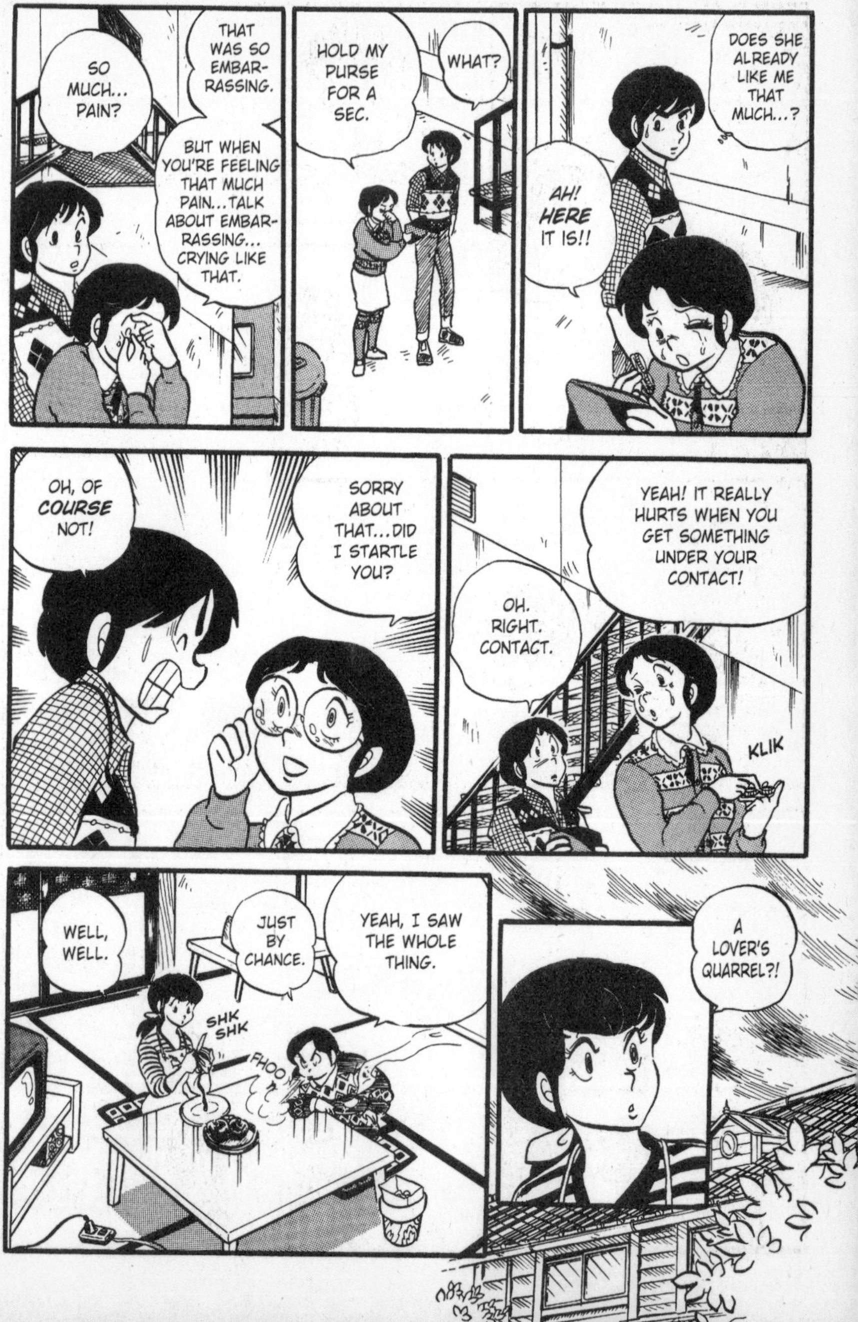
DOES SHE ALREADY LIKE ME THAT MUCH...?
AH! HERE IT IS!!
WHAT?
HOLD MY PURSE FOR A SEC.
THAT WAS SO EMBARRASSING.
BUT WHEN YOU'RE FEELING THAT MUCH PAIN...TALK ABOUT EMBARRASSING... CRYING LIKE THAT.
SO MUCH... PAIN?
YEAH! IT REALLY HURTS WHEN YOU GET SOMETHING UNDER YOUR CONTACT!
OH. RIGHT. CONTACT.
KLIK
SORRY ABOUT THAT...DID I STARTLE YOU?
OH, OF COURSE NOT!
A LOVER'S QUARREL?!
YEAH, I SAW THE WHOLE THING.
JUST BY CHANCE.
WELL, WELL.
SHK SHK
FHOO

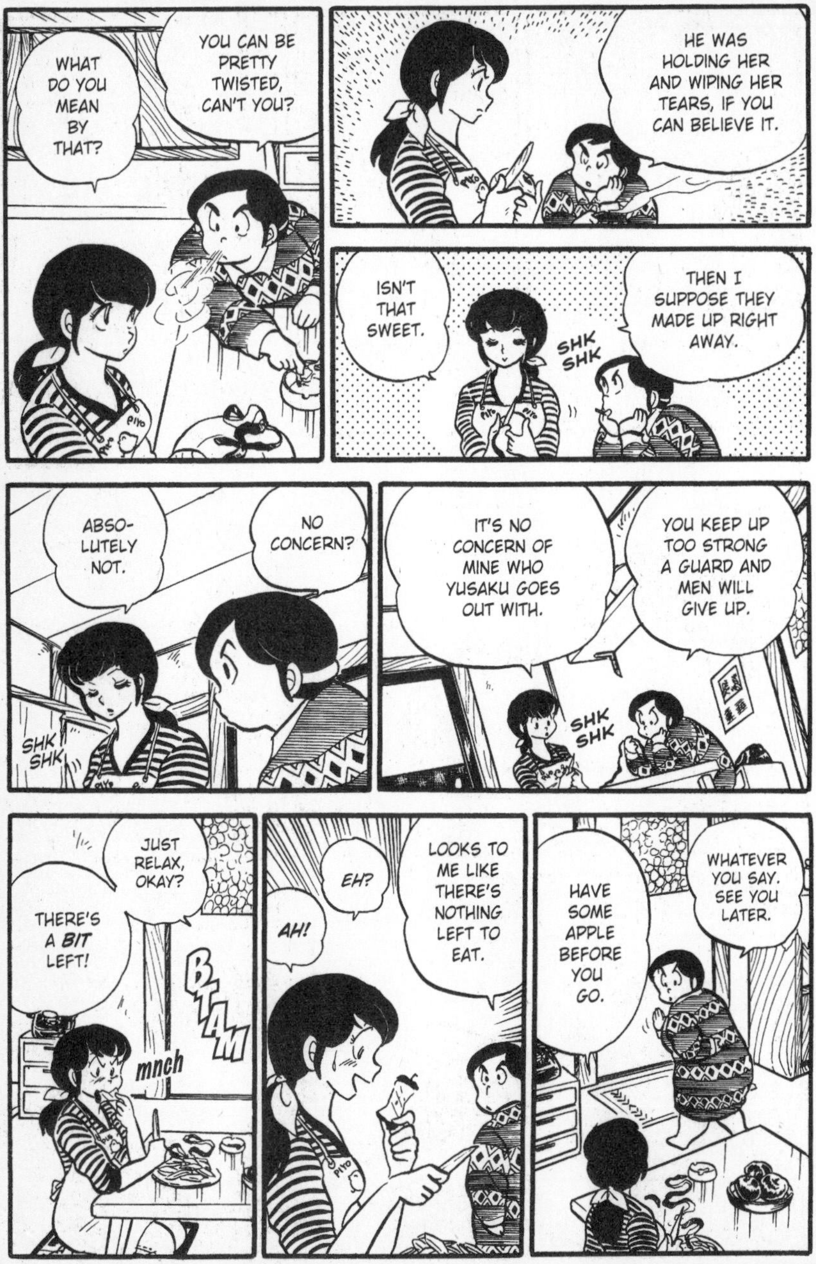
HE WAS HOLDING HER AND WIPING HER TEARS, IF YOU CAN BELIEVE IT.
THEN I SUPPOSE THEY MADE UP RIGHT AWAY.
ISN'T THAT SWEET.
SHK SHK
YOU CAN BE PRETTY TWISTED, CAN'T YOU?
WHAT DO YOU MEAN BY THAT?
YOU KEEP UP TOO STRONG A GUARD AND MEN WILL GIVE UP.
IT'S NO CONCERN OF MINE WHO YUSAKU GOES OUT WITH.
SHK SHK
NO CONCERN?
ABSO-LUTELY NOT.
SHK SHK
WHATEVER YOU SAY. SEE YOU LATER.
HAVE SOME APPLE BEFORE YOU GO.
LOOKS TO ME LIKE THERE'S NOTHING LEFT TO EAT.
EH?
AH!
JUST RELAX, OKAY?
BTAM
THERE'S A *BIT* LEFT!
mnch

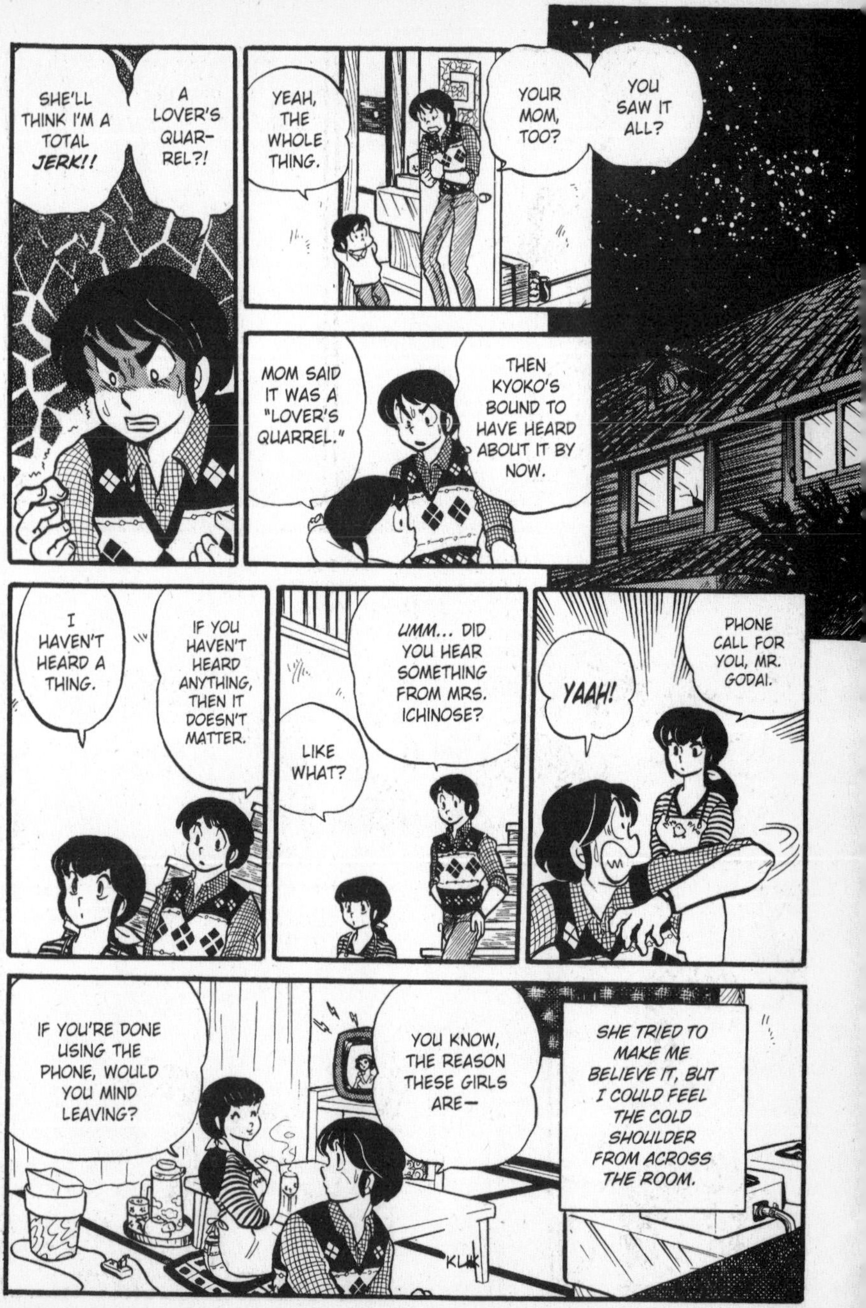
YOU SAW IT ALL?
YOUR MOM, TOO?
YEAH, THE WHOLE THING.
THEN KYOKO'S BOUND TO HAVE HEARD ABOUT IT BY NOW.
MOM SAID IT WAS A "LOVER'S QUARREL."
A LOVER'S QUARREL?!
SHE'LL THINK I'M A TOTAL *JERK!!*
PHONE CALL FOR YOU, MR. GODAI.
YAAH!
UMM... DID YOU HEAR SOMETHING FROM MRS. ICHINOSE?
LIKE WHAT?
IF YOU HAVEN'T HEARD ANYTHING, THEN IT DOESN'T MATTER.
I HAVEN'T HEARD A THING.
SHE TRIED TO MAKE ME BELIEVE IT, BUT I COULD FEEL THE COLD SHOULDER FROM ACROSS THE ROOM.
YOU KNOW, THE REASON THESE GIRLS ARE—
IF YOU'RE DONE USING THE PHONE, WOULD YOU MIND LEAVING?
KLIK

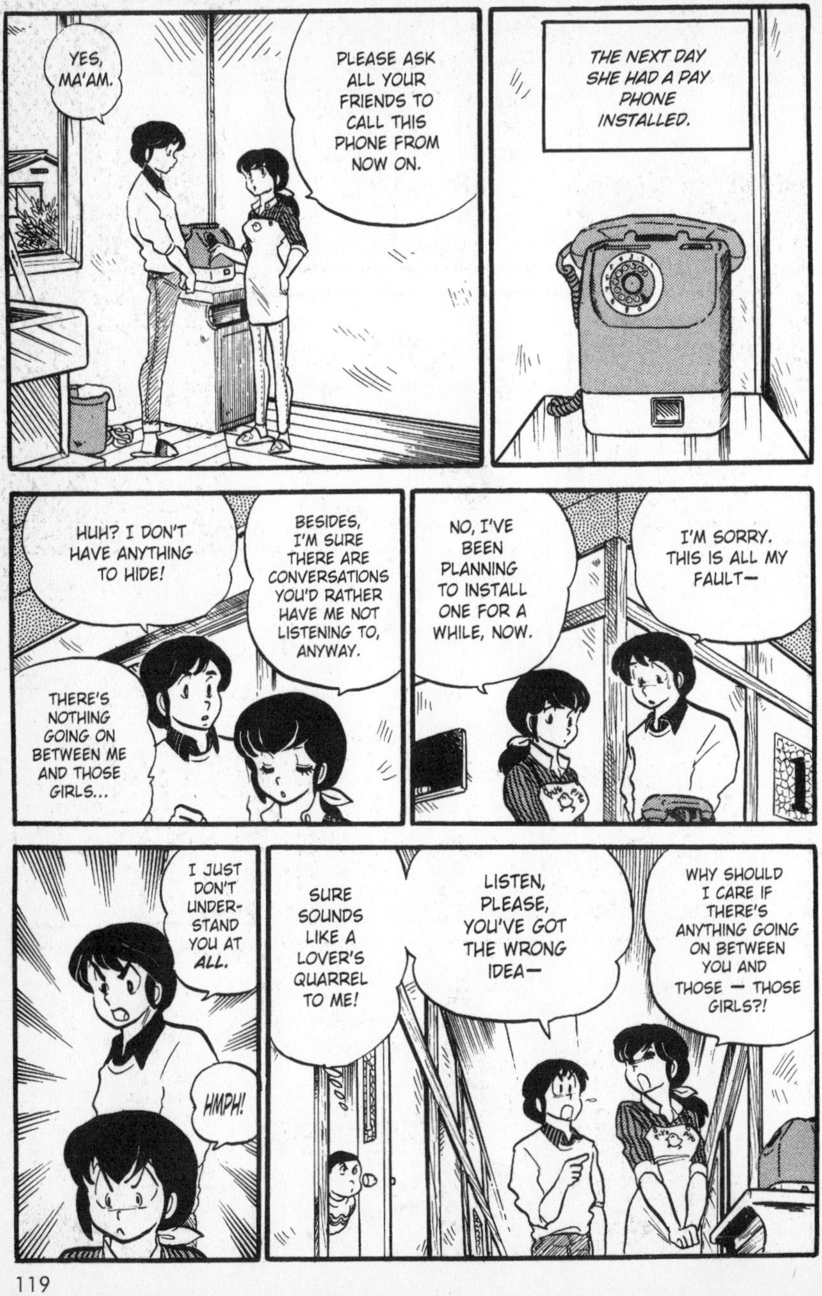
THE NEXT DAY SHE HAD A PAY PHONE INSTALLED.
PLEASE ASK ALL YOUR FRIENDS TO CALL THIS PHONE FROM NOW ON.
YES, MA'AM.
I'M SORRY. THIS IS ALL MY FAULT—
NO, I'VE BEEN PLANNING TO INSTALL ONE FOR A WHILE, NOW.
BESIDES, I'M SURE THERE ARE CONVERSATIONS YOU'D RATHER HAVE ME NOT LISTENING TO, ANYWAY.
HUH? I DON'T HAVE ANYTHING TO HIDE!
THERE'S NOTHING GOING ON BETWEEN ME AND THOSE GIRLS...
WHY SHOULD I CARE IF THERE'S ANYTHING GOING ON BETWEEN YOU AND THOSE — THOSE GIRLS?!
LISTEN, PLEASE, YOU'VE GOT THE WRONG IDEA—
SURE SOUNDS LIKE A LOVER'S QUARREL TO ME!
I JUST DON'T UNDER-STAND YOU AT ALL.
HMPH!

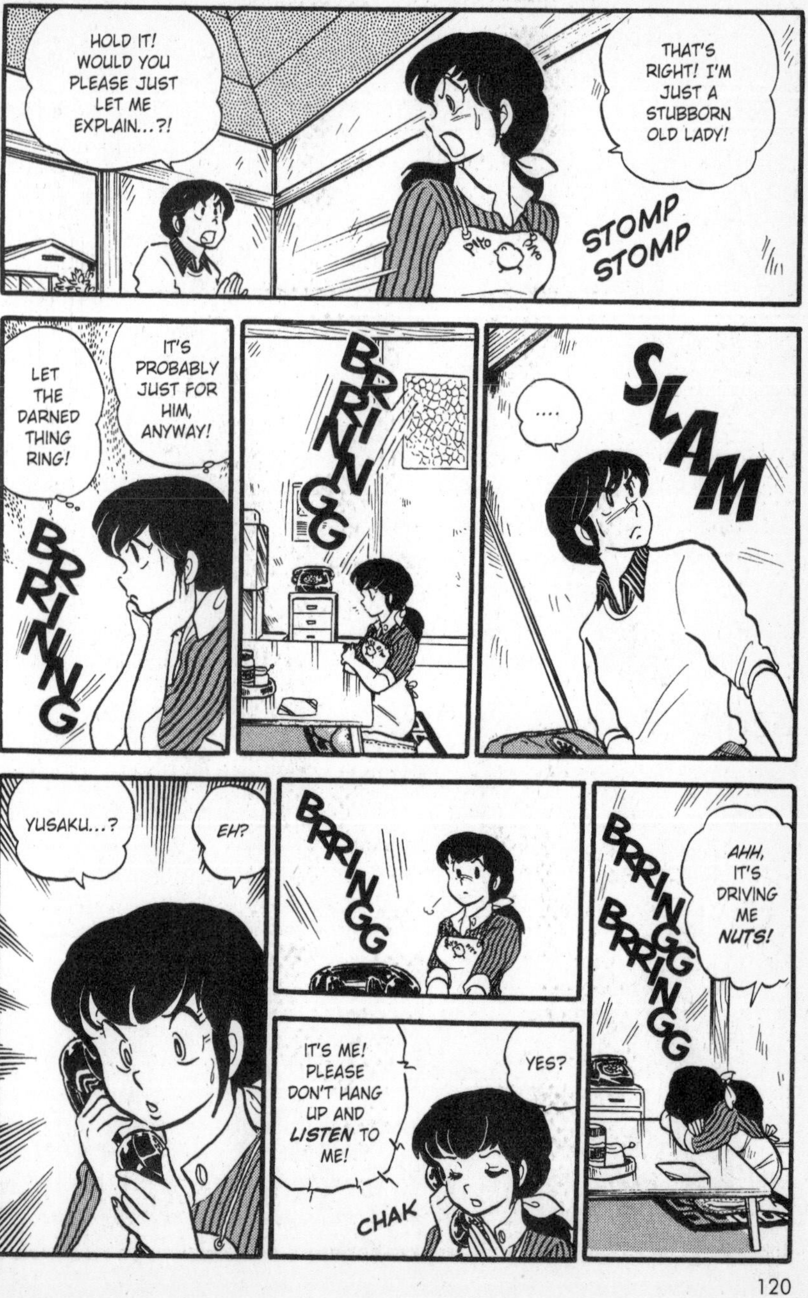
THAT'S RIGHT! I'M JUST A STUBBORN OLD LADY!
HOLD IT! WOULD YOU PLEASE JUST LET ME EXPLAIN...?!
STOMP STOMP
SLAM
....
BRRINNGG
IT'S PROBABLY JUST FOR HIM, ANYWAY!
LET THE DARNED THING RING!
BRRINNNG
BRRRINGG BRRRINGG
AHH, IT'S DRIVING ME NUTS!
BRRRINGG
YES?
IT'S ME! PLEASE DON'T HANG UP AND LISTEN TO ME!
CHAK
EH?
YUSAKU...?

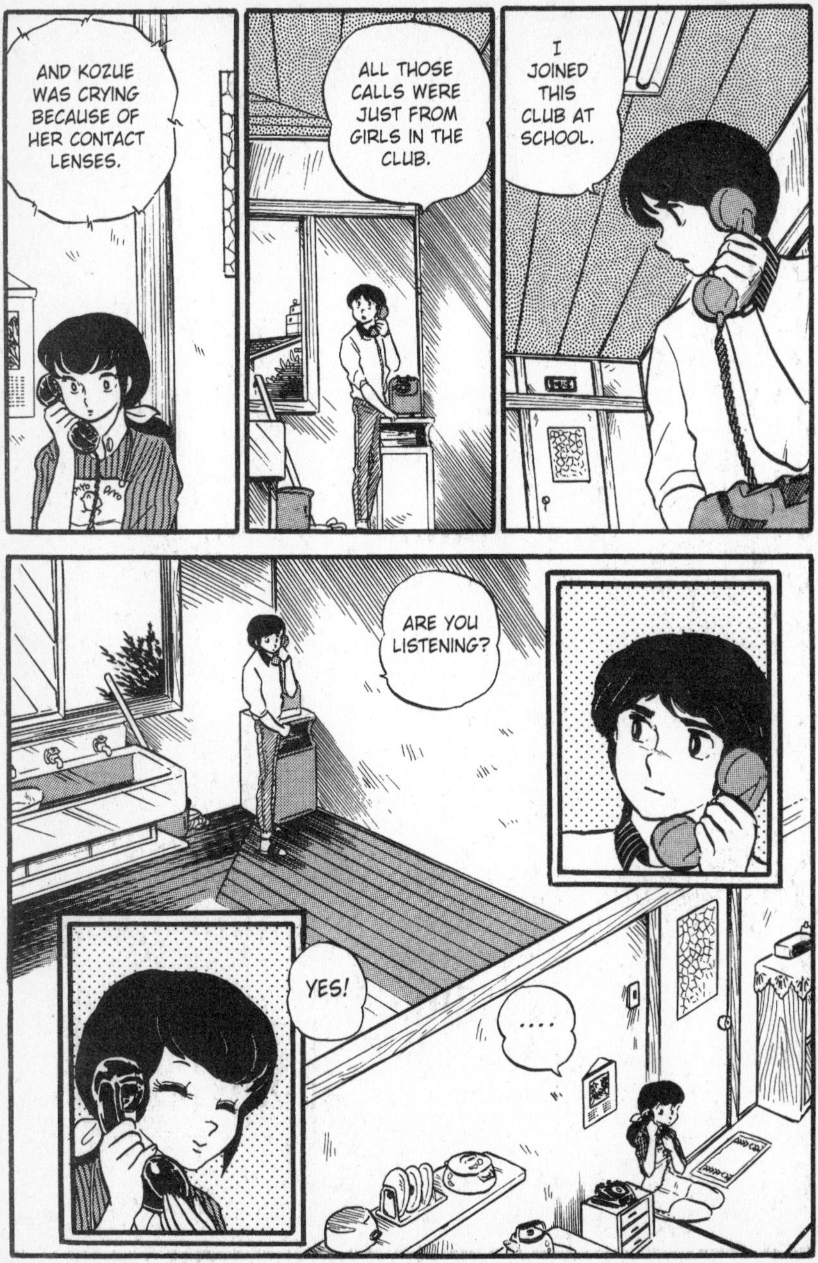
I JOINED THIS CLUB AT SCHOOL.
ALL THOSE CALLS WERE JUST FROM GIRLS IN THE CLUB.
AND KOZUE WAS CRYING BECAUSE OF HER CONTACT LENSES.
ARE YOU LISTENING?
YES!
....

PART SEVEN

WITH A LITTLE NONCHALANCE

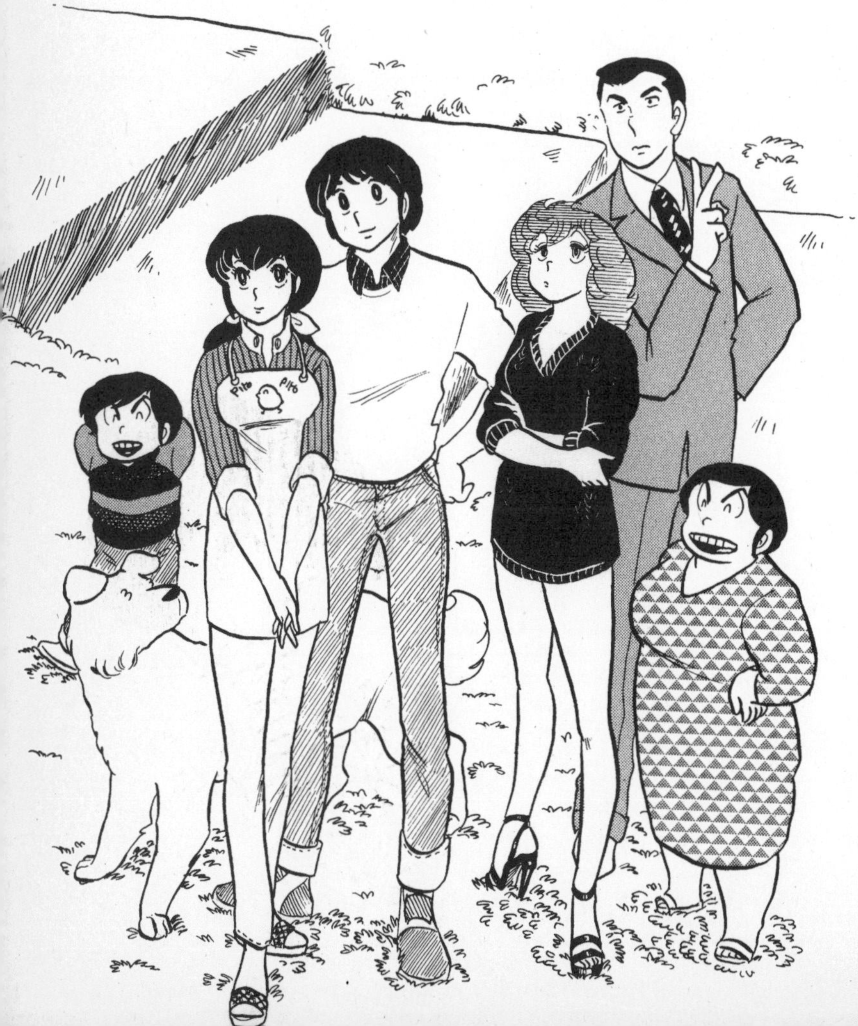

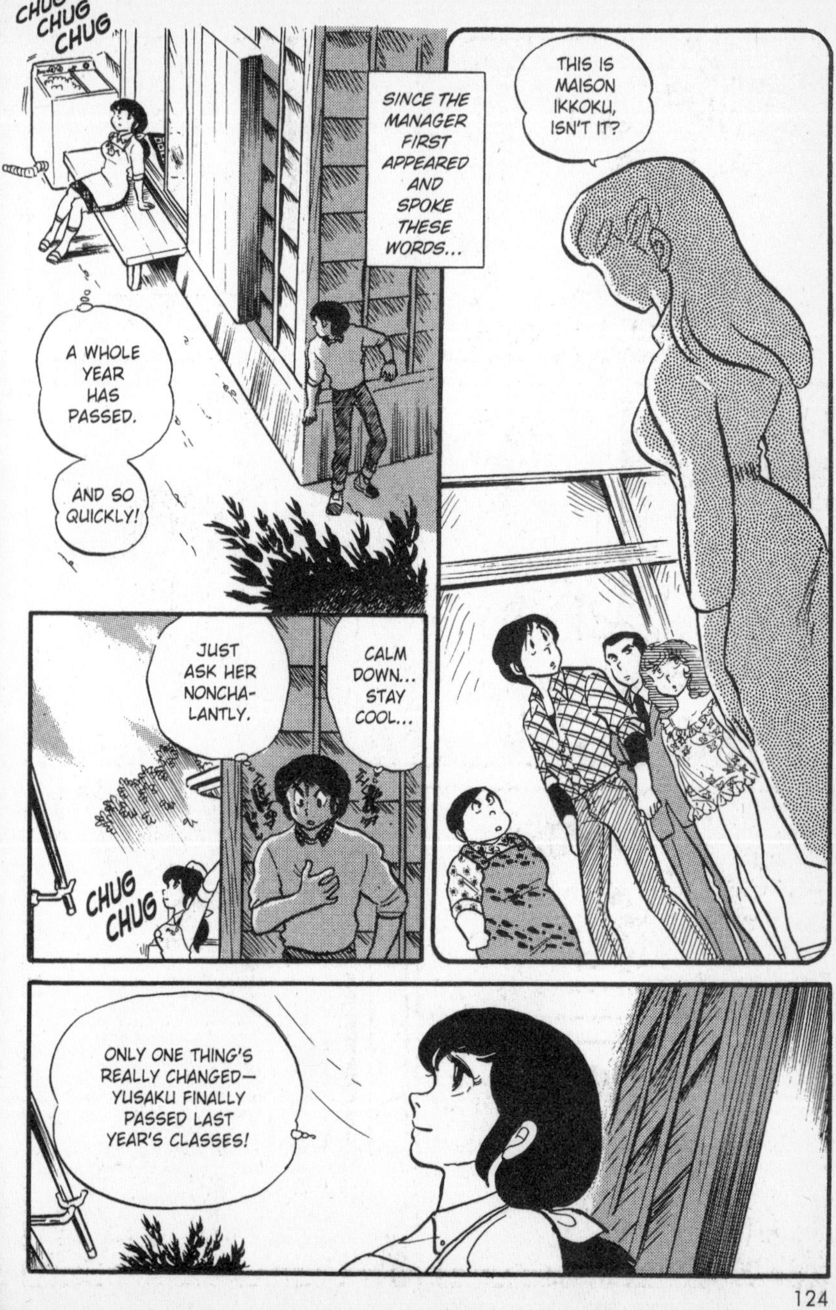
THIS IS MAISON IKKOKU, ISN'T IT?
SINCE THE MANAGER FIRST APPEARED AND SPOKE THESE WORDS...
CHUG CHUG CHUG
A WHOLE YEAR HAS PASSED.
AND SO QUICKLY!
CALM DOWN... STAY COOL...
JUST ASK HER NONCHALANTLY.
CHUG CHUG
ONLY ONE THING'S REALLY CHANGED—YUSAKU FINALLY PASSED LAST YEAR'S CLASSES!

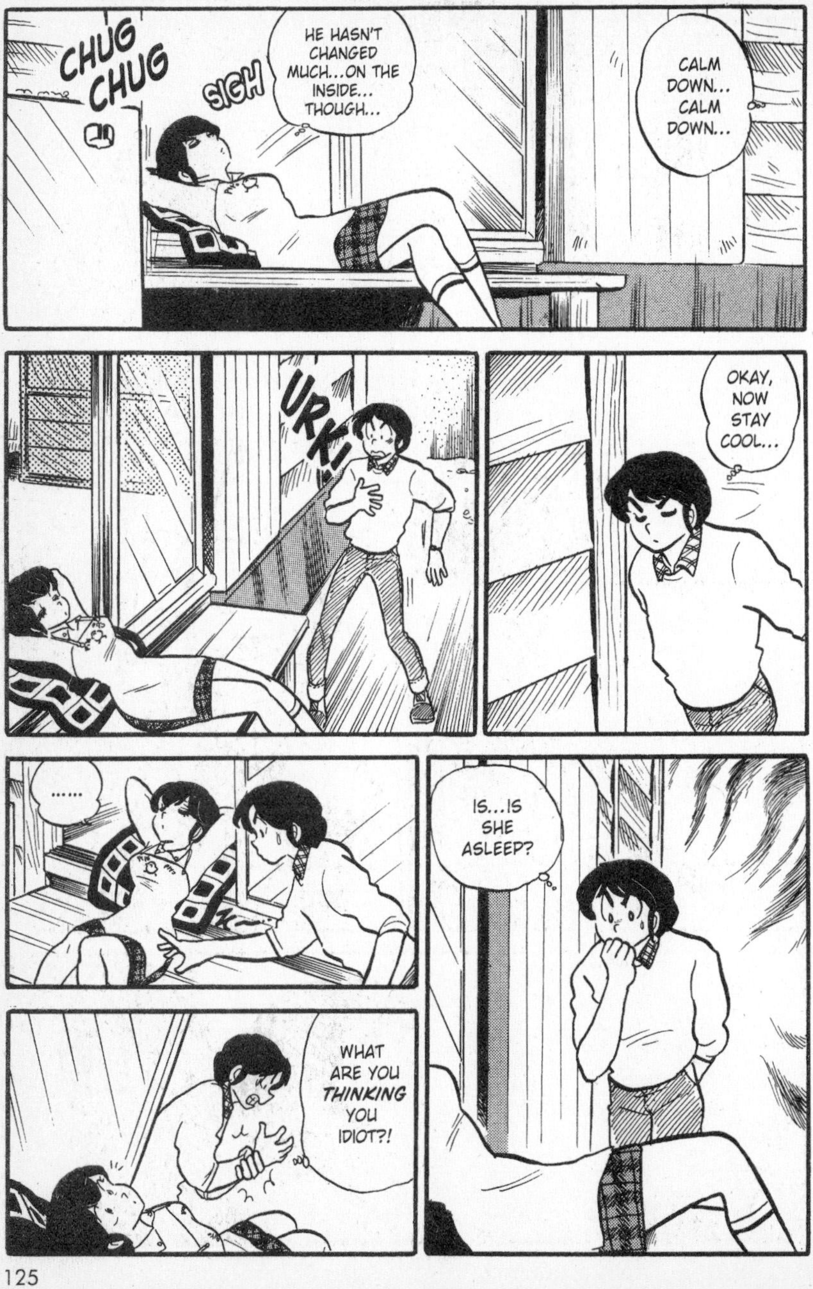
CALM DOWN... CALM DOWN...
HE HASN'T CHANGED MUCH...ON THE INSIDE... THOUGH...
SIGH
CHUG CHUG
OKAY, NOW STAY COOL...
URK!
IS...IS SHE ASLEEP?
......
WHAT ARE YOU *THINKING* YOU IDIOT?!

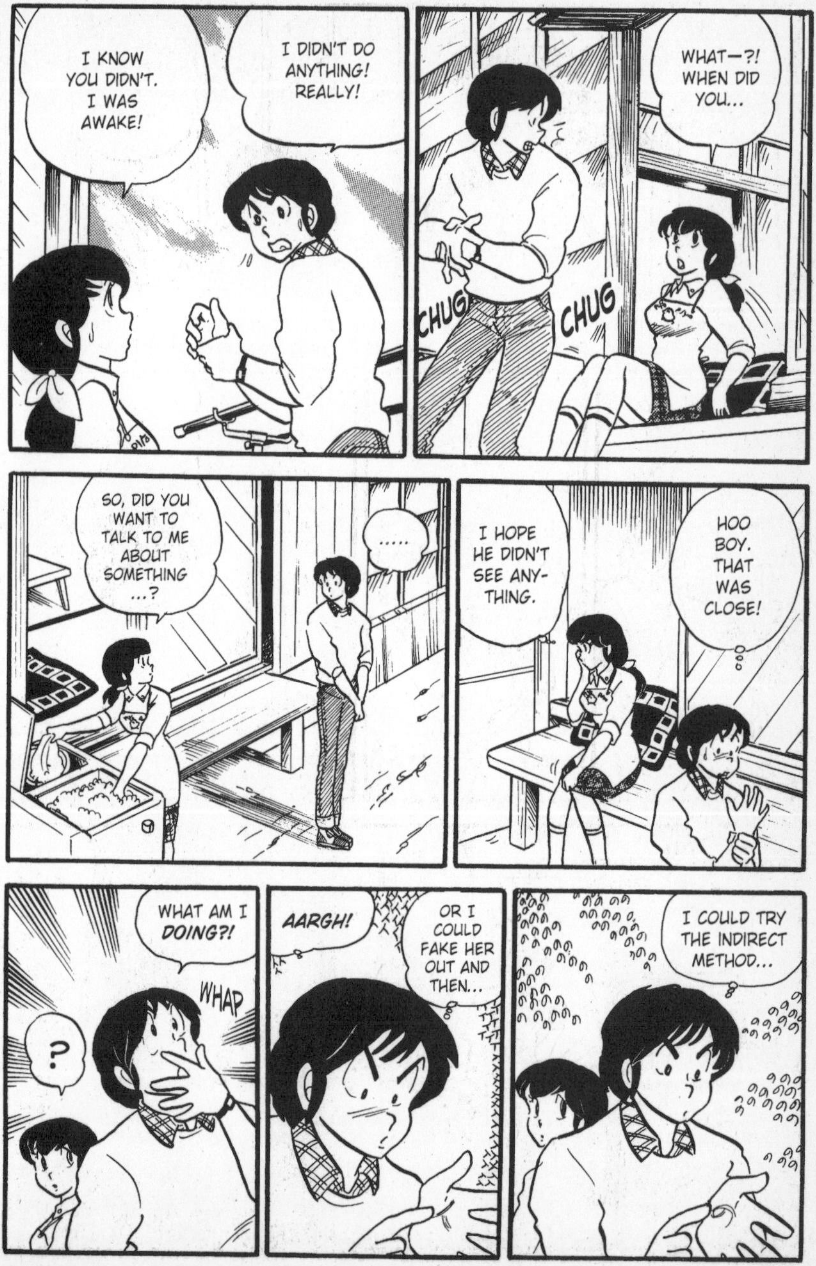
WHAT—?! WHEN DID YOU...
CHUG
CHUG
I DIDN'T DO ANYTHING! REALLY!
I KNOW YOU DIDN'T. I WAS AWAKE!
HOO BOY. THAT WAS CLOSE!
I HOPE HE DIDN'T SEE ANY-THING.
......
SO, DID YOU WANT TO TALK TO ME ABOUT SOMETHING ...?
I COULD TRY THE INDIRECT METHOD...
OR I COULD FAKE HER OUT AND THEN...
AARGH!
WHAT AM I *DOING?!*
WHAP
?

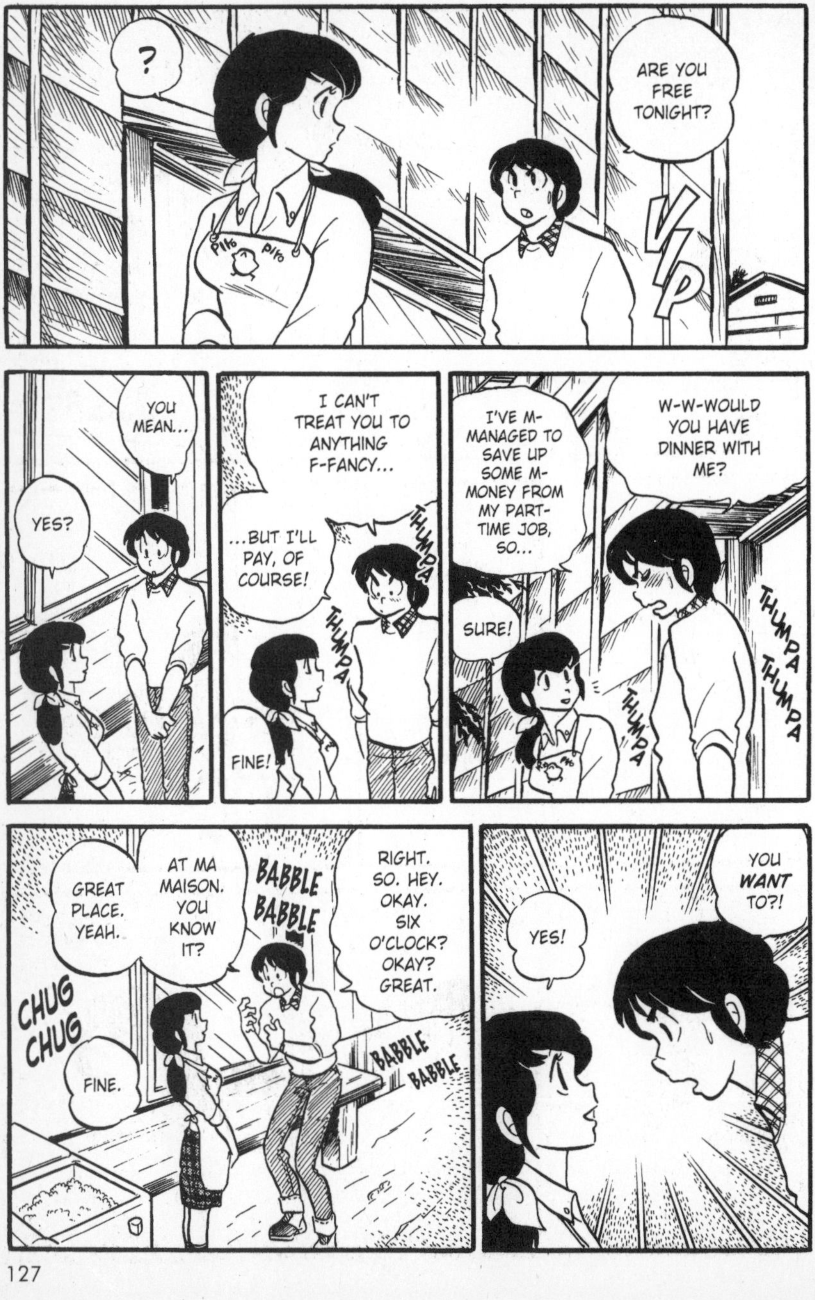
ARE YOU FREE TONIGHT?
?
VIP
W-W-WOULD YOU HAVE DINNER WITH ME?
I'VE M-MANAGED TO SAVE UP SOME M-MONEY FROM MY PART-TIME JOB, SO...
THUMPA THUMPA
SURE!
THUMPA
I CAN'T TREAT YOU TO ANYTHING F-FANCY...
THUMPA
...BUT I'LL PAY, OF COURSE!
THUMPA
FINE!
YOU MEAN...
YES?
YOU WANT TO?!
YES!
RIGHT. SO. HEY. OKAY. SIX O'CLOCK? OKAY? GREAT.
BABBLE BABBLE
AT MA MAISON. YOU KNOW IT?
GREAT PLACE. YEAH.
BABBLE BABBLE
CHUG CHUG
FINE.

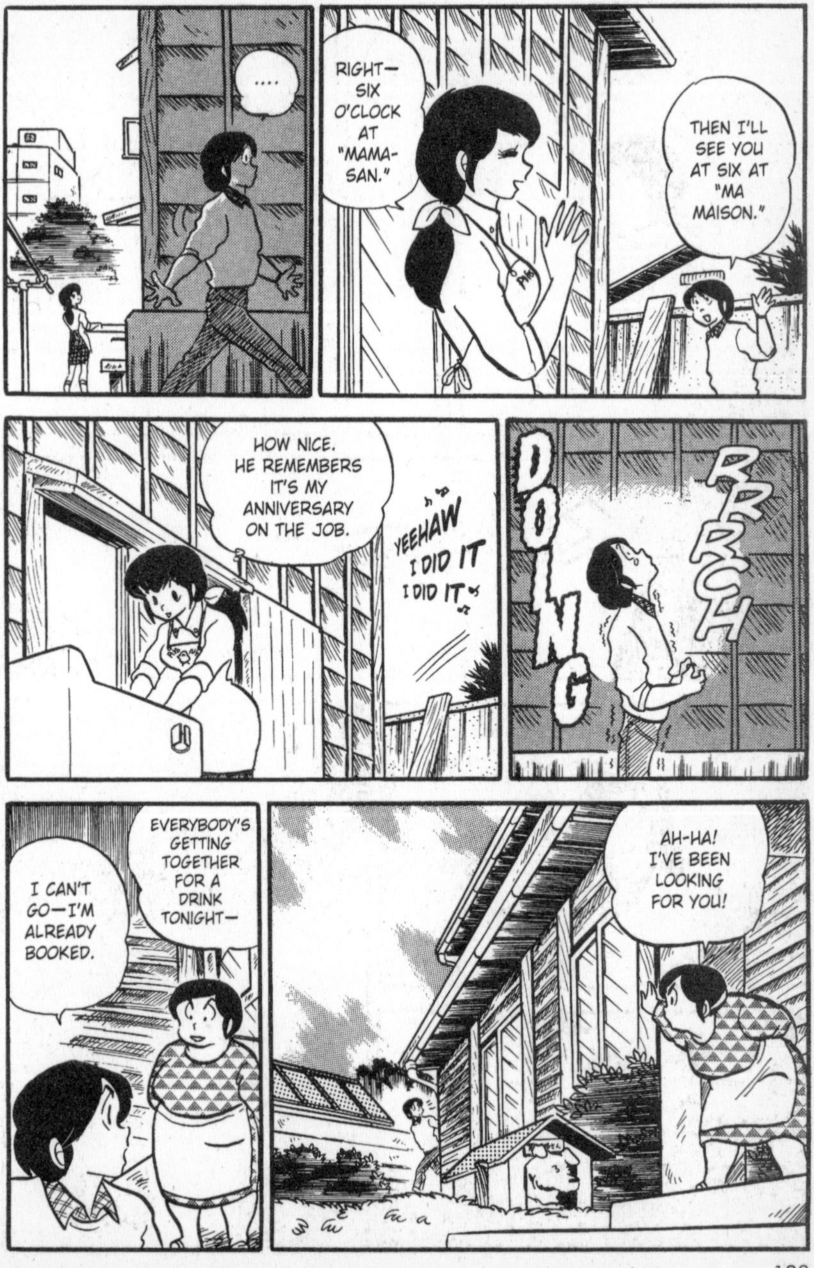
THEN I'LL SEE YOU AT SIX AT "MA MAISON."
RIGHT— SIX O'CLOCK AT "MAMA-SAN."
....
RRRCH
DOING
HOW NICE. HE REMEMBERS IT'S MY ANNIVERSARY ON THE JOB.
YEEHAW I DID IT I DID IT
AH-HA! I'VE BEEN LOOKING FOR YOU!
EVERYBODY'S GETTING TOGETHER FOR A DRINK TONIGHT—
I CAN'T GO—I'M ALREADY BOOKED.

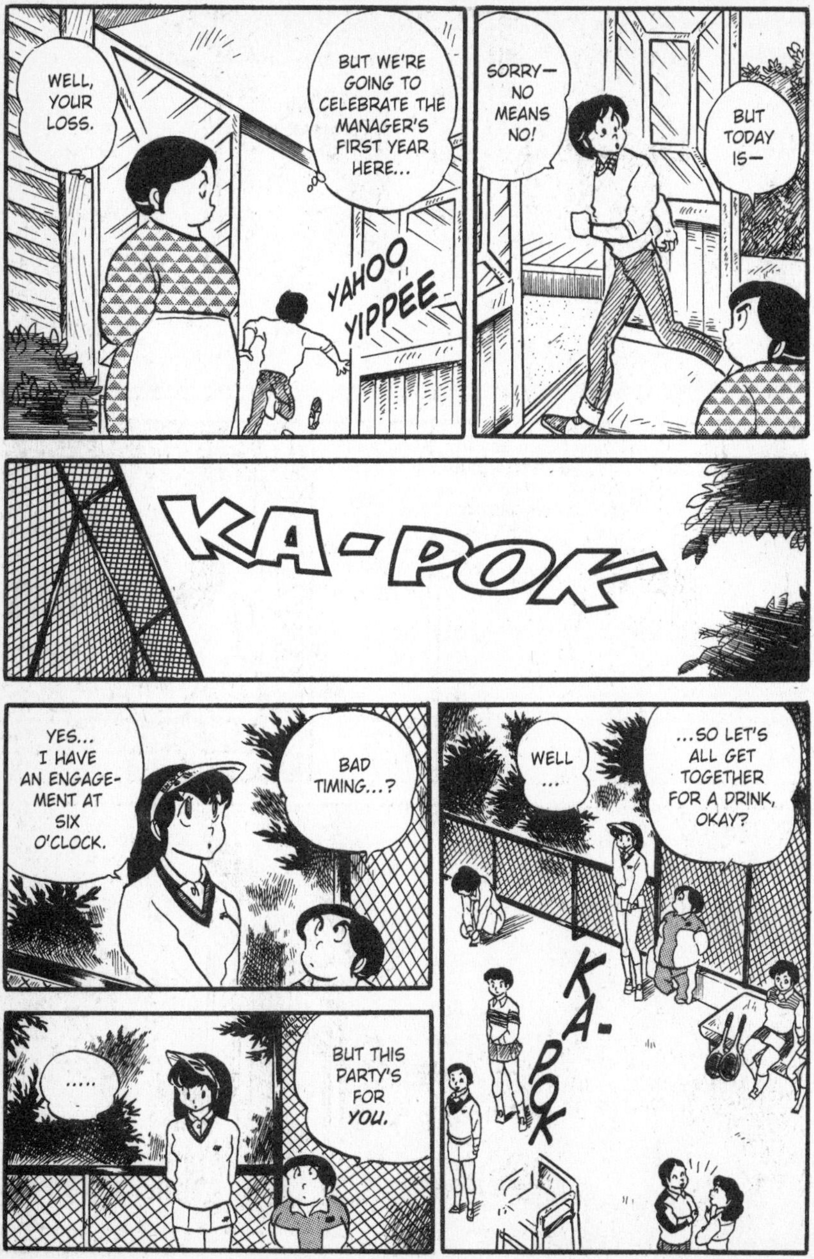
BUT TODAY IS—
SORRY— NO MEANS NO!
BUT WE'RE GOING TO CELEBRATE THE MANAGER'S FIRST YEAR HERE...
YAHOO YIPPEE
WELL, YOUR LOSS.
KA-POK
...SO LET'S ALL GET TOGETHER FOR A DRINK, OKAY?
WELL ...
KA-POK
BAD TIMING...?
YES... I HAVE AN ENGAGEMENT AT SIX O'CLOCK.
BUT THIS PARTY'S FOR *YOU.*
.....

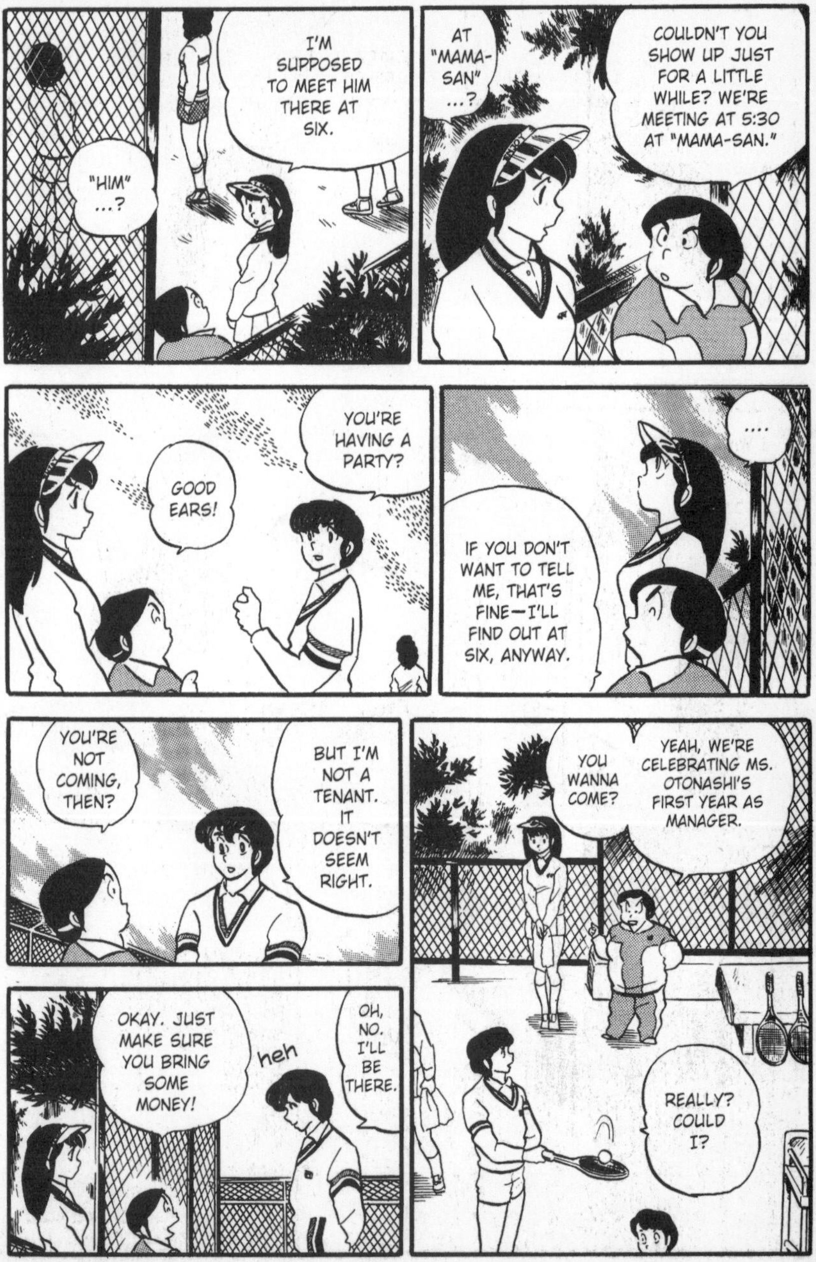
COULDN'T YOU SHOW UP JUST FOR A LITTLE WHILE? WE'RE MEETING AT 5:30 AT "MAMA-SAN."
AT "MAMA-SAN" ...?
I'M SUPPOSED TO MEET HIM THERE AT SIX.
"HIM" ...?
....
IF YOU DON'T WANT TO TELL ME, THAT'S FINE—I'LL FIND OUT AT SIX, ANYWAY.
YOU'RE HAVING A PARTY?
GOOD EARS!
YEAH, WE'RE CELEBRATING MS. OTONASHI'S FIRST YEAR AS MANAGER.
YOU WANNA COME?
REALLY? COULD I?
BUT I'M NOT A TENANT. IT DOESN'T SEEM RIGHT.
YOU'RE NOT COMING, THEN?
OH, NO. I'LL BE THERE.
heh
OKAY. JUST MAKE SURE YOU BRING SOME MONEY!

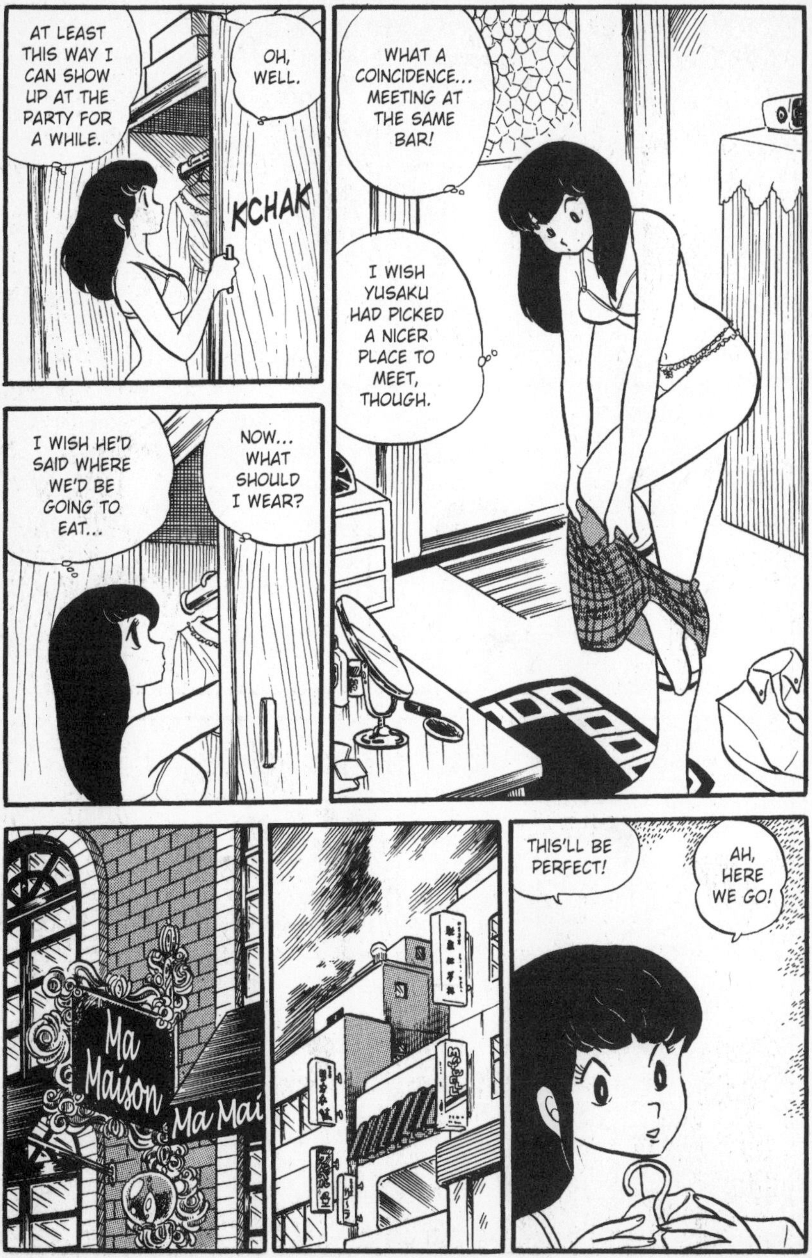
WHAT A COINCIDENCE... MEETING AT THE SAME BAR!
I WISH YUSAKU HAD PICKED A NICER PLACE TO MEET, THOUGH.
OH, WELL.
AT LEAST THIS WAY I CAN SHOW UP AT THE PARTY FOR A WHILE.
KCHAK
NOW... WHAT SHOULD I WEAR?
I WISH HE'D SAID WHERE WE'D BE GOING TO EAT...
AH, HERE WE GO!
THIS'LL BE PERFECT!
Ma Maison
Ma Mai

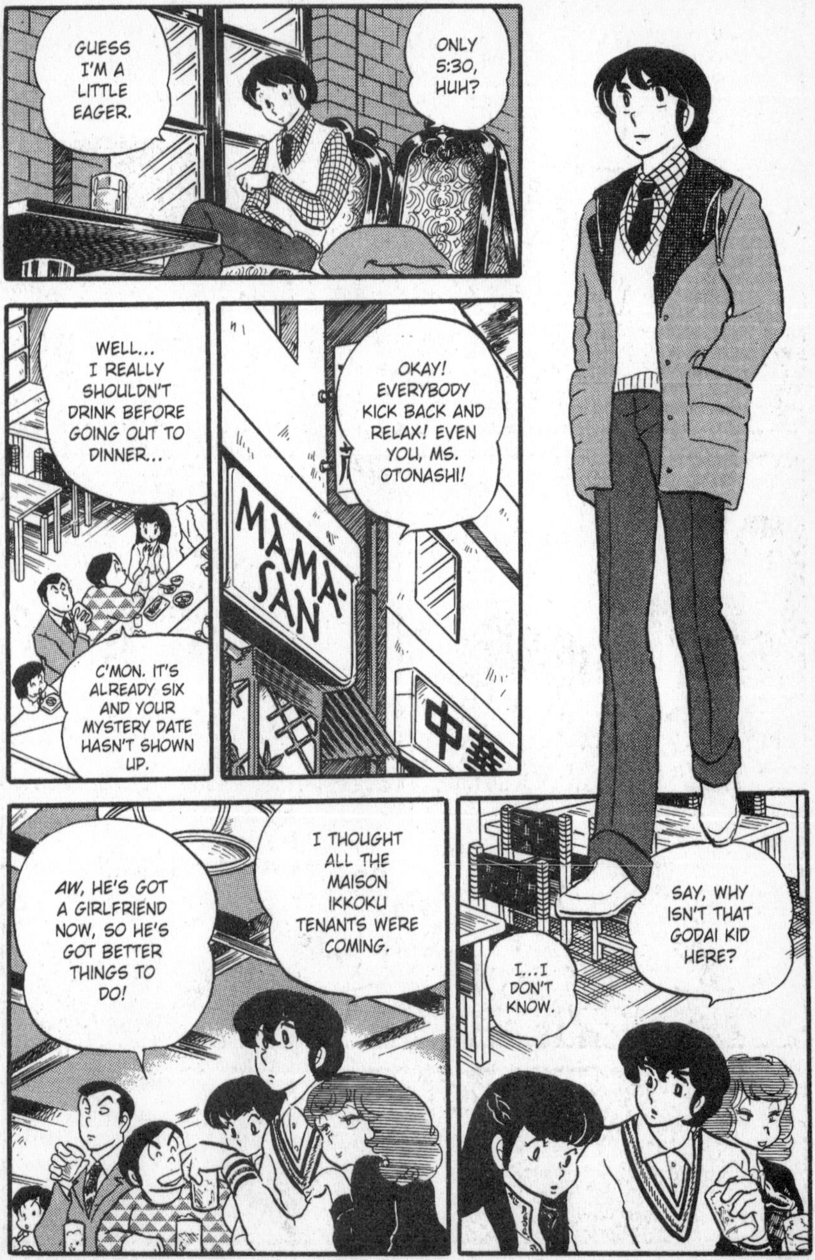
ONLY 5:30, HUH?
GUESS I'M A LITTLE EAGER.
OKAY! EVERYBODY KICK BACK AND RELAX! EVEN YOU, MS. OTONASHI!
MAMA-SAN
中華
WELL... I REALLY SHOULDN'T DRINK BEFORE GOING OUT TO DINNER...
C'MON. IT'S ALREADY SIX AND YOUR MYSTERY DATE HASN'T SHOWN UP.
SAY, WHY ISN'T THAT GODAI KID HERE?
I...I DON'T KNOW.
I THOUGHT ALL THE MAISON IKKOKU TENANTS WERE COMING.
AW, HE'S GOT A GIRLFRIEND NOW, SO HE'S GOT BETTER THINGS TO DO!

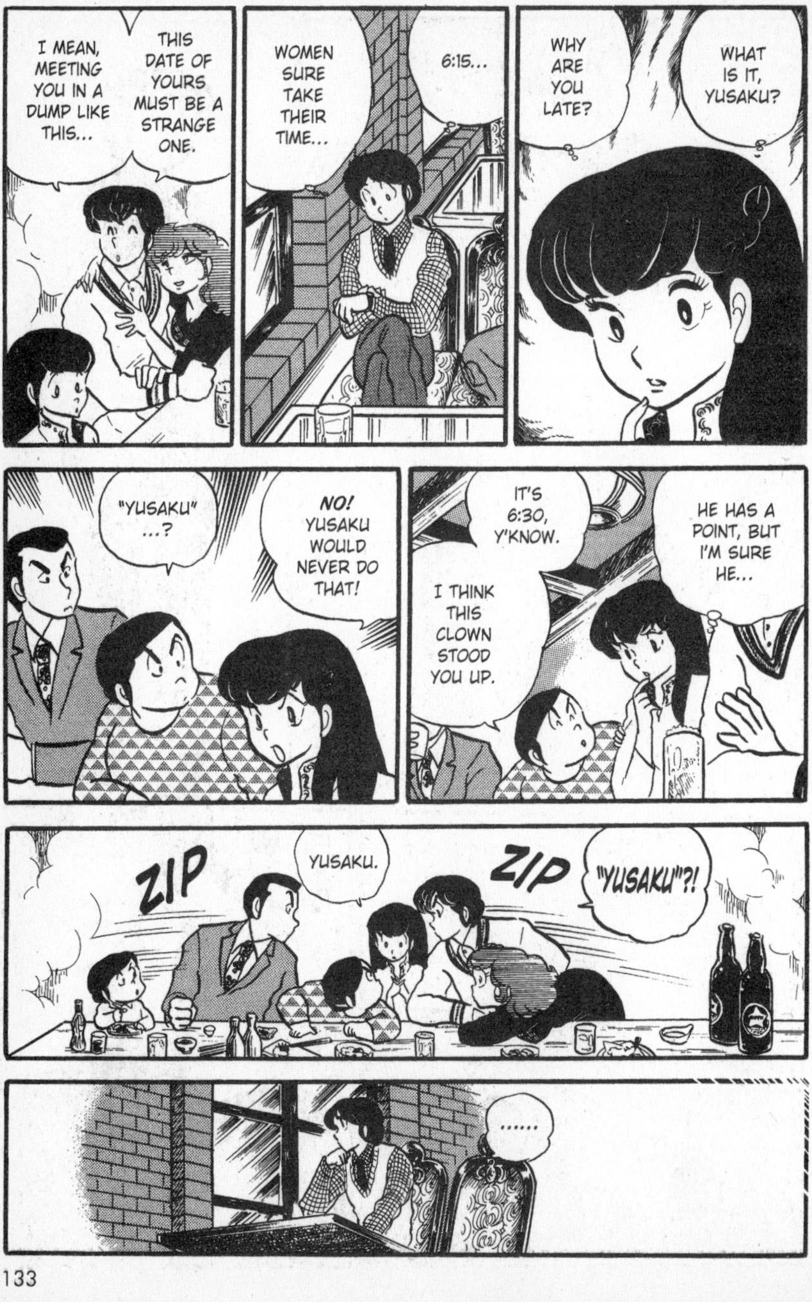
WHAT IS IT, YUSAKU?
WHY ARE YOU LATE?
6:15...
WOMEN SURE TAKE THEIR TIME...
THIS DATE OF YOURS MUST BE A STRANGE ONE.
I MEAN, MEETING YOU IN A DUMP LIKE THIS...
HE HAS A POINT, BUT I'M SURE HE...
IT'S 6:30, Y'KNOW.
I THINK THIS CLOWN STOOD YOU UP.
NO! YUSAKU WOULD NEVER DO THAT!
"YUSAKU" ...?
"YUSAKU"?!
ZIP
YUSAKU.
ZIP
......

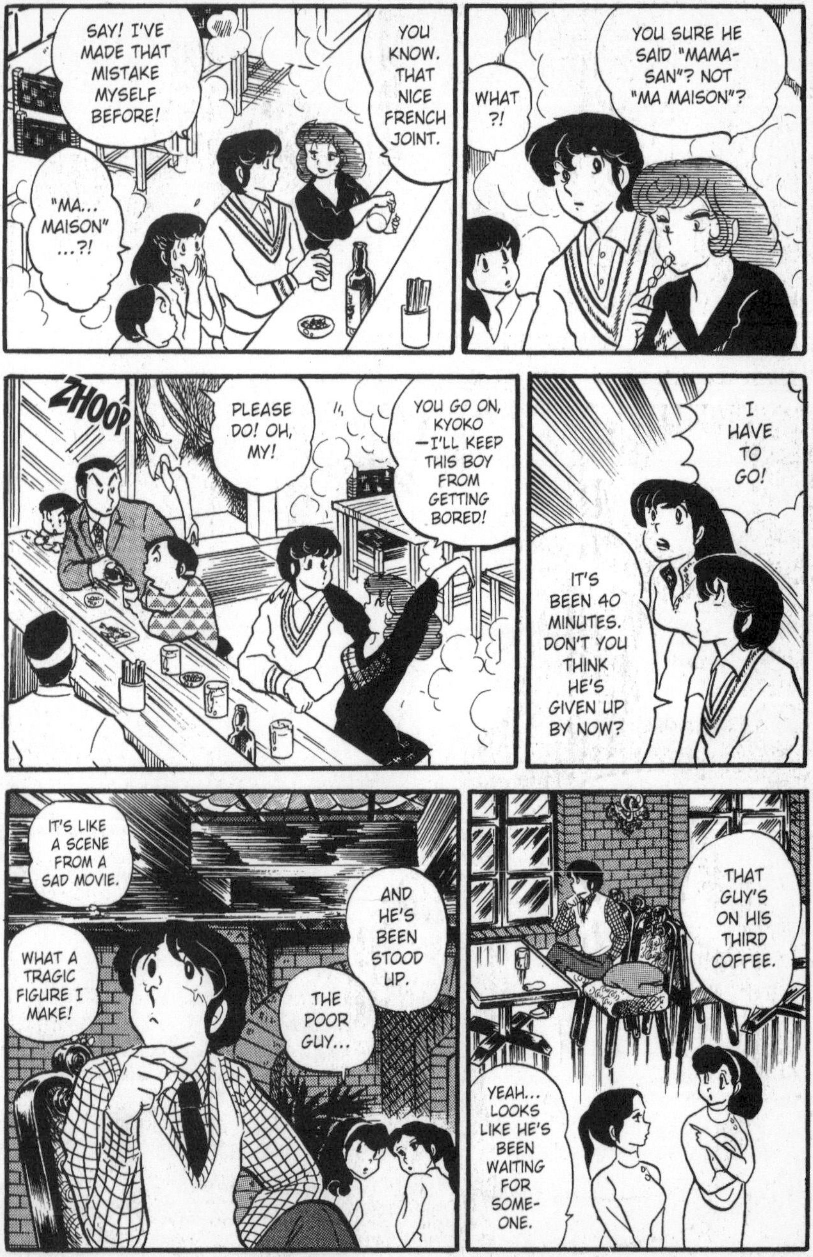
YOU KNOW. THAT NICE FRENCH JOINT.
"MA... MAISON" ...?!
SAY! I'VE MADE THAT MISTAKE MYSELF BEFORE!
YOU SURE HE SAID "MAMA-SAN"? NOT "MA MAISON"?
WHAT ?!
ZHOOP
YOU GO ON, KYOKO —I'LL KEEP THIS BOY FROM GETTING BORED!
PLEASE DO! OH, MY!
I HAVE TO GO!
IT'S BEEN 40 MINUTES. DON'T YOU THINK HE'S GIVEN UP BY NOW?
IT'S LIKE A SCENE FROM A SAD MOVIE.
WHAT A TRAGIC FIGURE I MAKE!
AND HE'S BEEN STOOD UP.
THE POOR GUY...
THAT GUY'S ON HIS THIRD COFFEE.
YEAH... LOOKS LIKE HE'S BEEN WAITING FOR SOME-ONE.

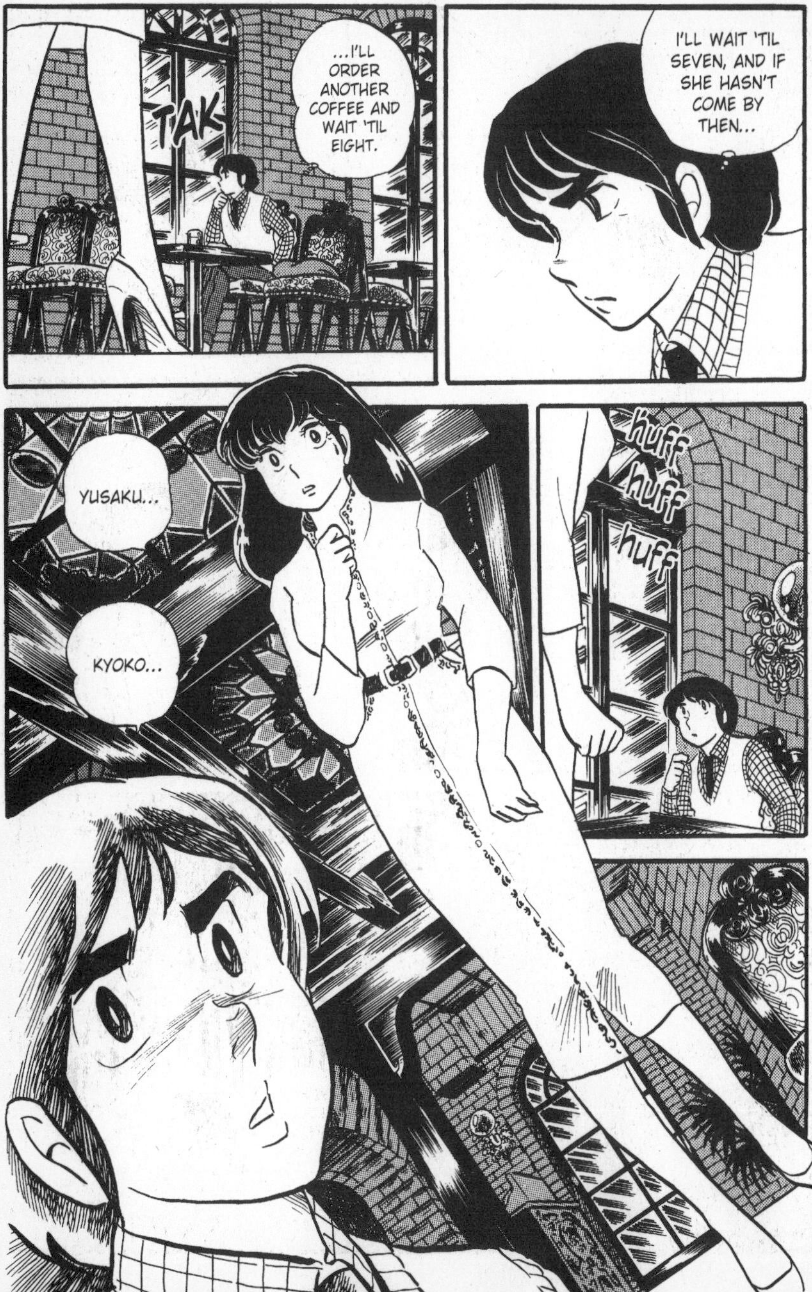
I'LL WAIT 'TIL SEVEN, AND IF SHE HASN'T COME BY THEN...
...I'LL ORDER ANOTHER COFFEE AND WAIT 'TIL EIGHT.
TAK
huff
huff
huff
YUSAKU...
KYOKO...

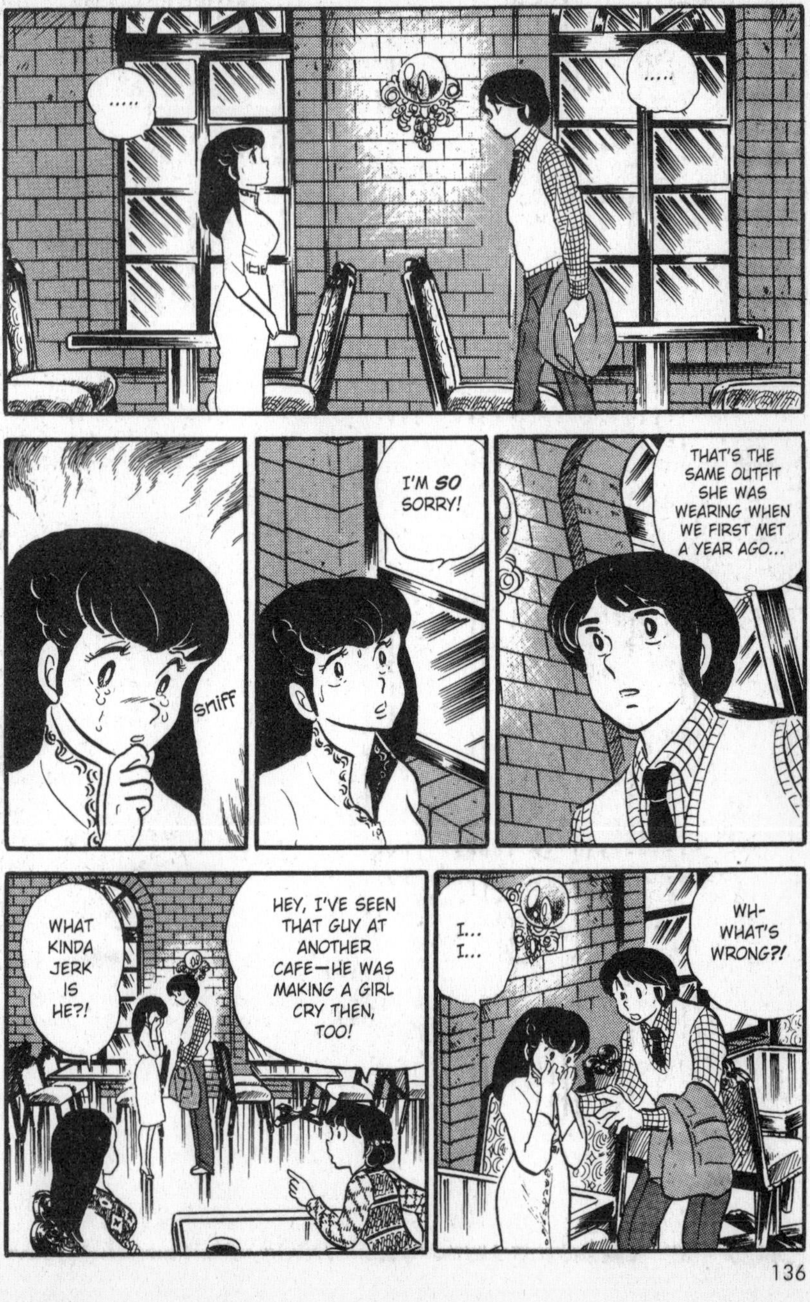
......
......
THAT'S THE SAME OUTFIT SHE WAS WEARING WHEN WE FIRST MET A YEAR AGO...
I'M SO SORRY!
sniff
WH- WHAT'S WRONG?!
I... I...
HEY, I'VE SEEN THAT GUY AT ANOTHER CAFE—HE WAS MAKING A GIRL CRY THEN, TOO!
WHAT KINDA JERK IS HE?!

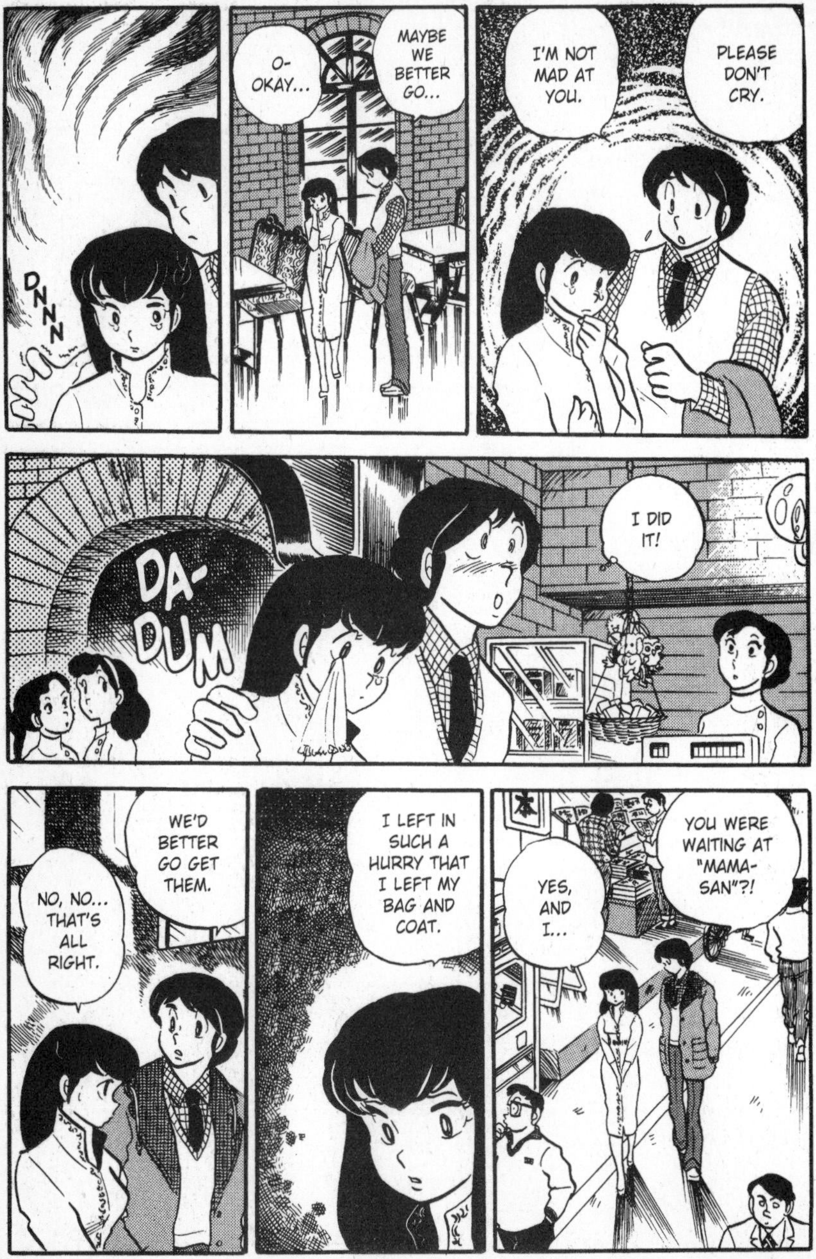
PLEASE DON'T CRY.
I'M NOT MAD AT YOU.
MAYBE WE BETTER GO...
O-OKAY...
DNNN
I DID IT!
DA-DUM
YOU WERE WAITING AT "MAMA-SAN"?!
YES, AND I...
I LEFT IN SUCH A HURRY THAT I LEFT MY BAG AND COAT.
WE'D BETTER GO GET THEM.
NO, NO... THAT'S ALL RIGHT.

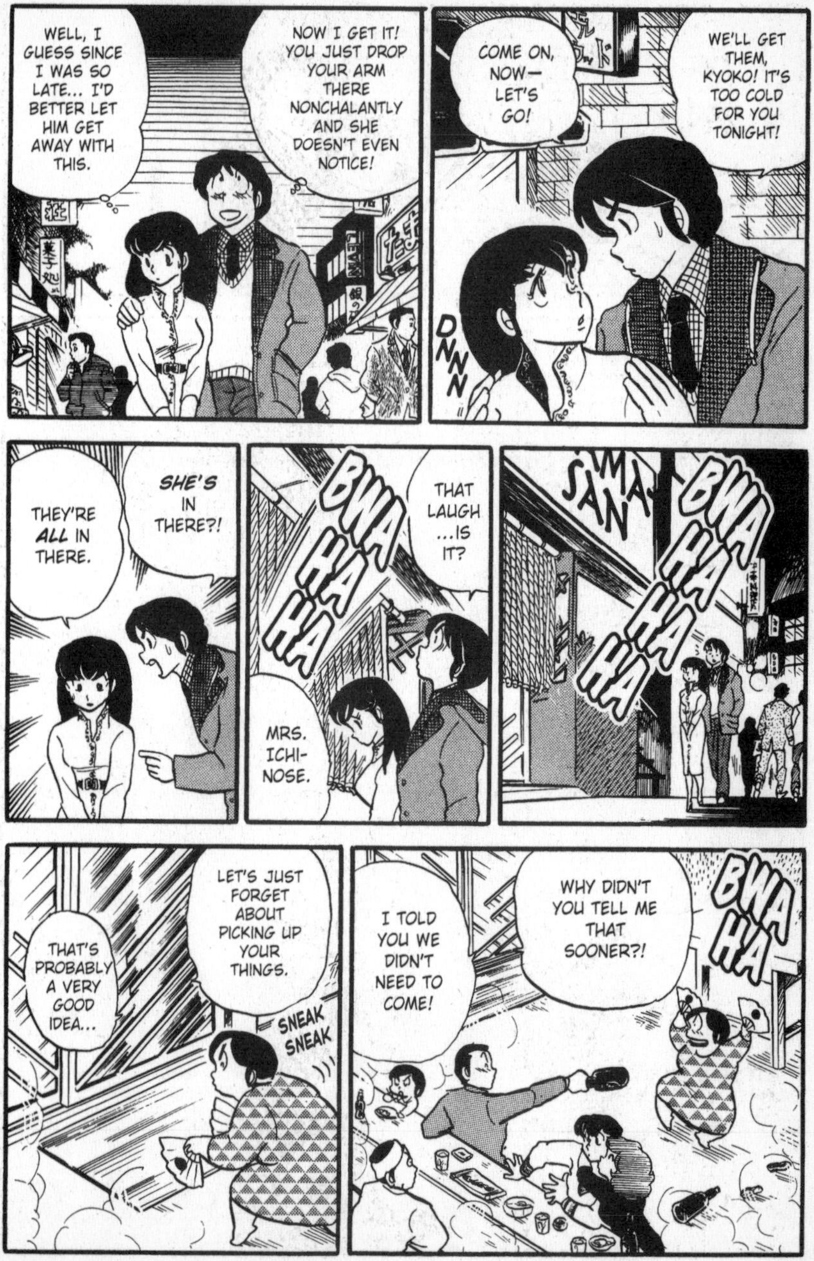
WE'LL GET THEM, KYOKO! IT'S TOO COLD FOR YOU TONIGHT!
COME ON, NOW— LET'S GO!
DNNN
NOW I GET IT! YOU JUST DROP YOUR ARM THERE NONCHALANTLY AND SHE DOESN'T EVEN NOTICE!
WELL, I GUESS SINCE I WAS SO LATE... I'D BETTER LET HIM GET AWAY WITH THIS.
BWA HA HA HA HA
THAT LAUGH ...IS IT?
BWA HA HA HA
MRS. ICHINOSE.
SHE'S IN THERE?!
THEY'RE ALL IN THERE.
BWA HA
WHY DIDN'T YOU TELL ME THAT SOONER?!
I TOLD YOU WE DIDN'T NEED TO COME!
LET'S JUST FORGET ABOUT PICKING UP YOUR THINGS.
THAT'S PROBABLY A VERY GOOD IDEA...
SNEAK SNEAK

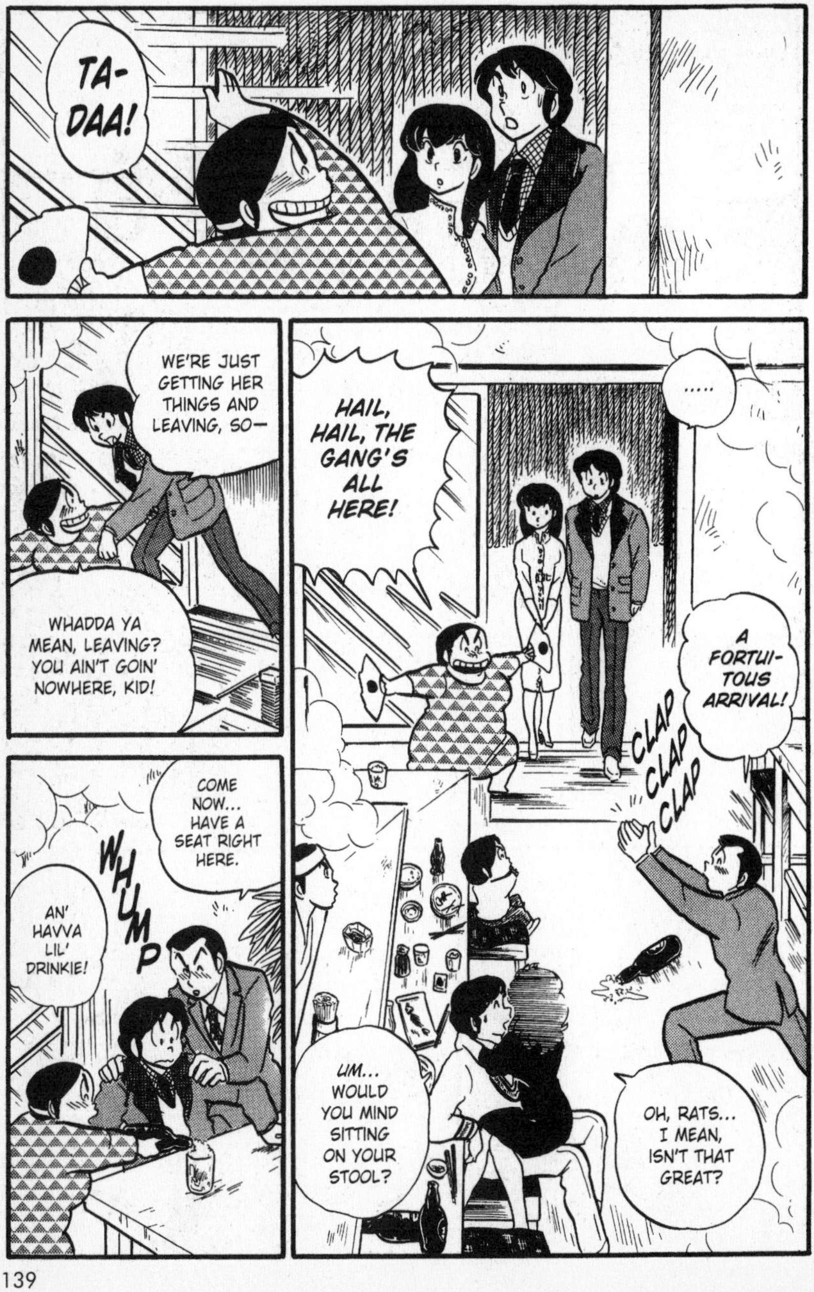
TA-DAA!
.....
HAIL, HAIL, THE GANG'S ALL HERE!
A FORTUITOUS ARRIVAL!
CLAP CLAP CLAP
OH, RATS... I MEAN, ISN'T THAT GREAT?
UM... WOULD YOU MIND SITTING ON YOUR STOOL?
WE'RE JUST GETTING HER THINGS AND LEAVING, SO—
WHADDA YA MEAN, LEAVING? YOU AIN'T GOIN' NOWHERE, KID!
COME NOW... HAVE A SEAT RIGHT HERE.
WHUMP
AN' HAVVA LIL' DRINKIE!

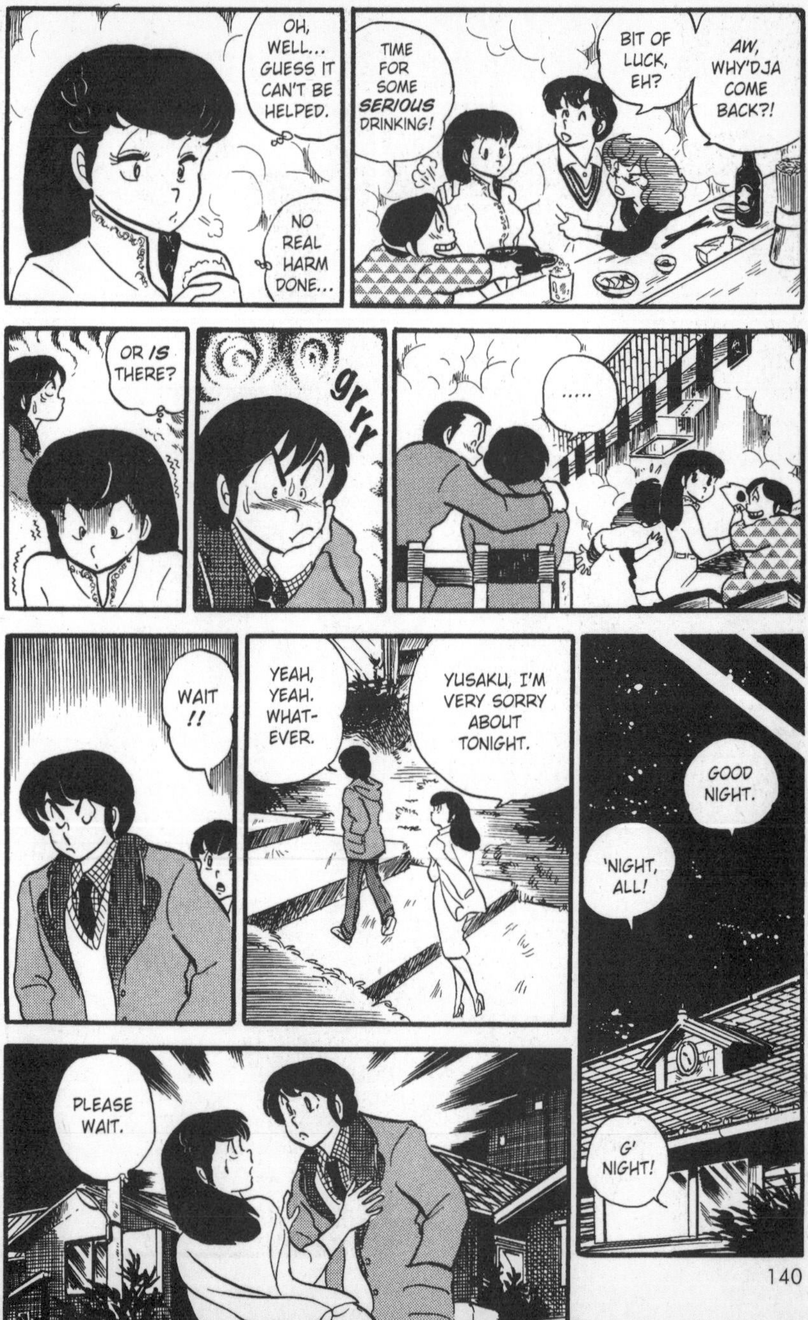
AW, WHY'DJA COME BACK?!
BIT OF LUCK, EH?
TIME FOR SOME SERIOUS DRINKING!
OH, WELL... GUESS IT CAN'T BE HELPED.
NO REAL HARM DONE...
......
grrr
OR IS THERE?
GOOD NIGHT.
'NIGHT, ALL!
G' NIGHT!
YUSAKU, I'M VERY SORRY ABOUT TONIGHT.
YEAH, YEAH. WHATEVER.
WAIT !!
PLEASE WAIT.

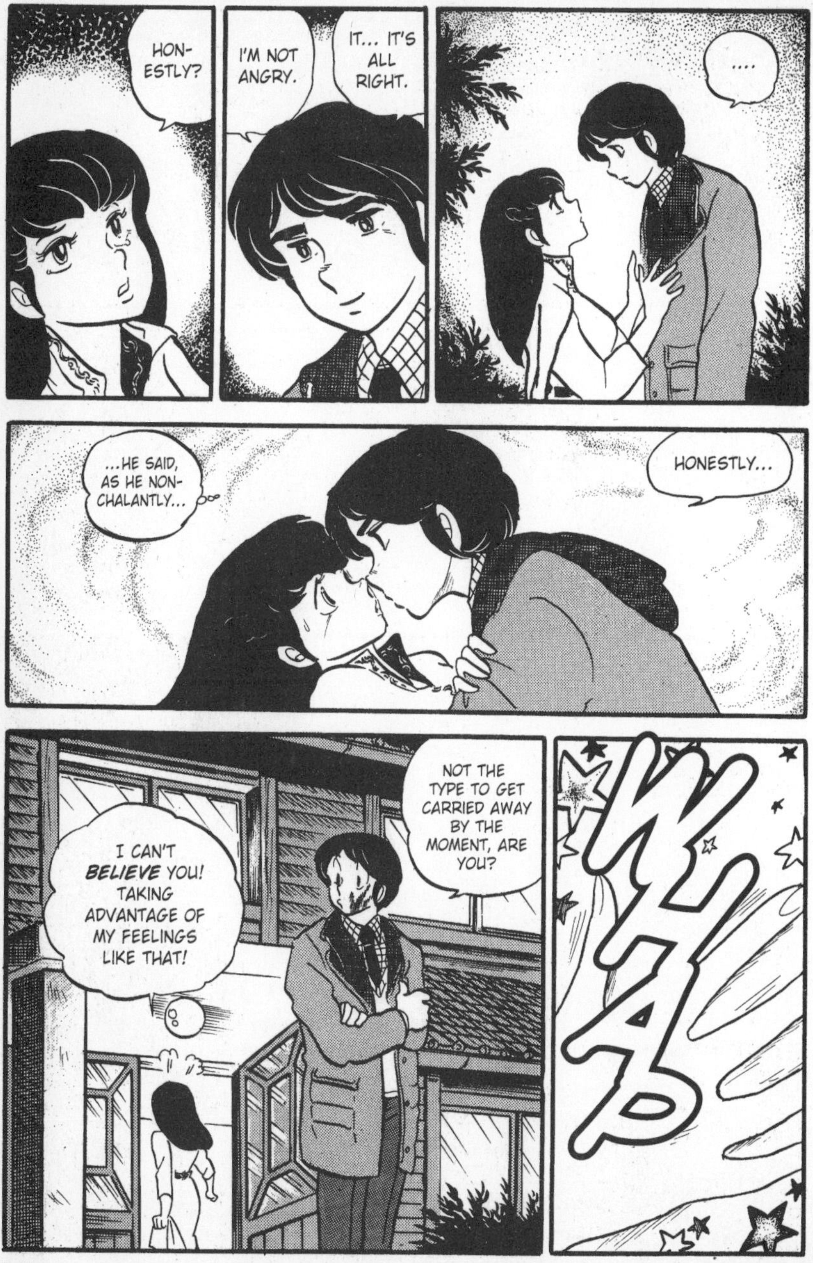
....
IT... IT'S ALL RIGHT.
I'M NOT ANGRY.
HON-ESTLY?
HONESTLY...
...HE SAID, AS HE NON-CHALANTLY...
WHAP
NOT THE TYPE TO GET CARRIED AWAY BY THE MOMENT, ARE YOU?
I CAN'T **BELIEVE** YOU! TAKING ADVANTAGE OF MY FEELINGS LIKE THAT!

PART EIGHT

CAMPUS DOLL

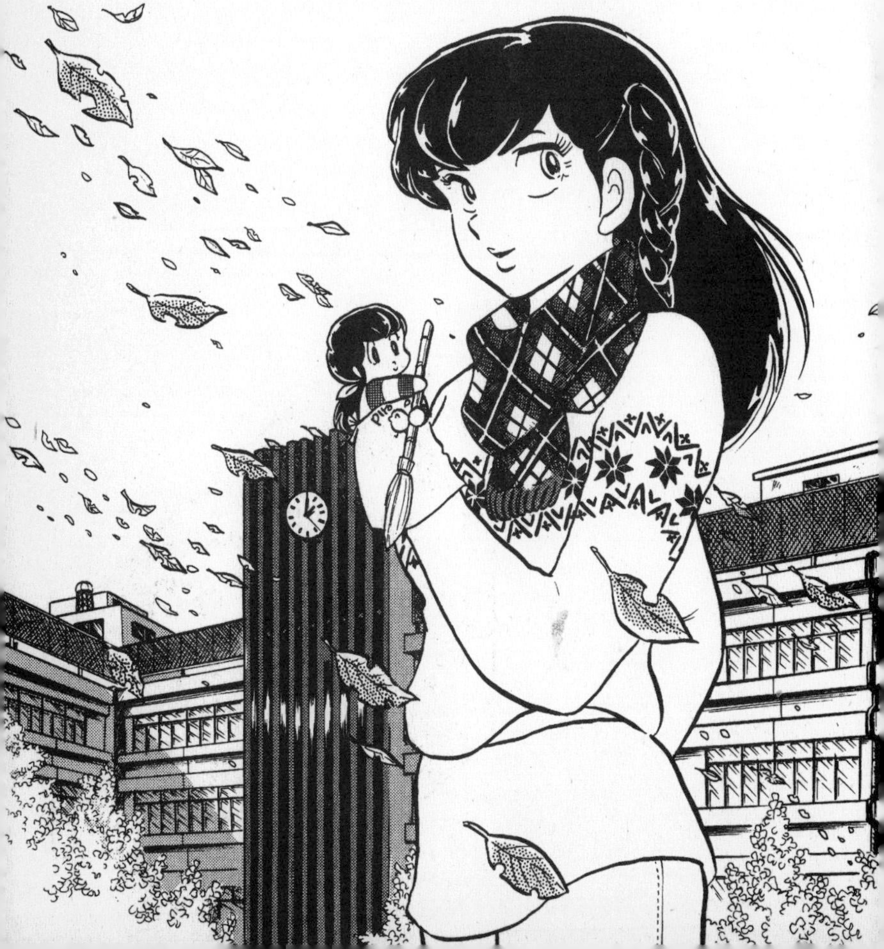

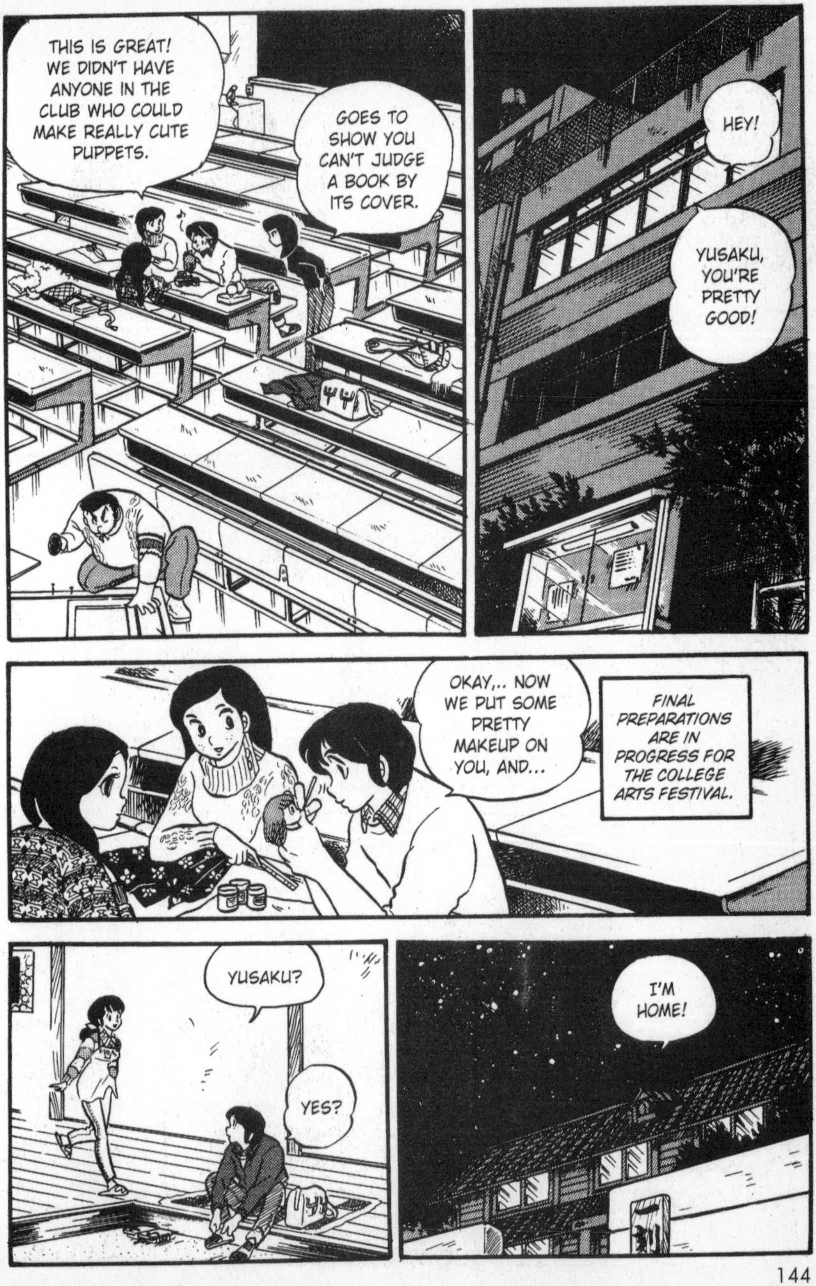
HEY!
YUSAKU, YOU'RE PRETTY GOOD!
THIS IS GREAT! WE DIDN'T HAVE ANYONE IN THE CLUB WHO COULD MAKE REALLY CUTE PUPPETS.
GOES TO SHOW YOU CAN'T JUDGE A BOOK BY ITS COVER.
FINAL PREPARATIONS ARE IN PROGRESS FOR THE COLLEGE ARTS FESTIVAL.
OKAY,.. NOW WE PUT SOME PRETTY MAKEUP ON YOU, AND...
I'M HOME!
YUSAKU?
YES?

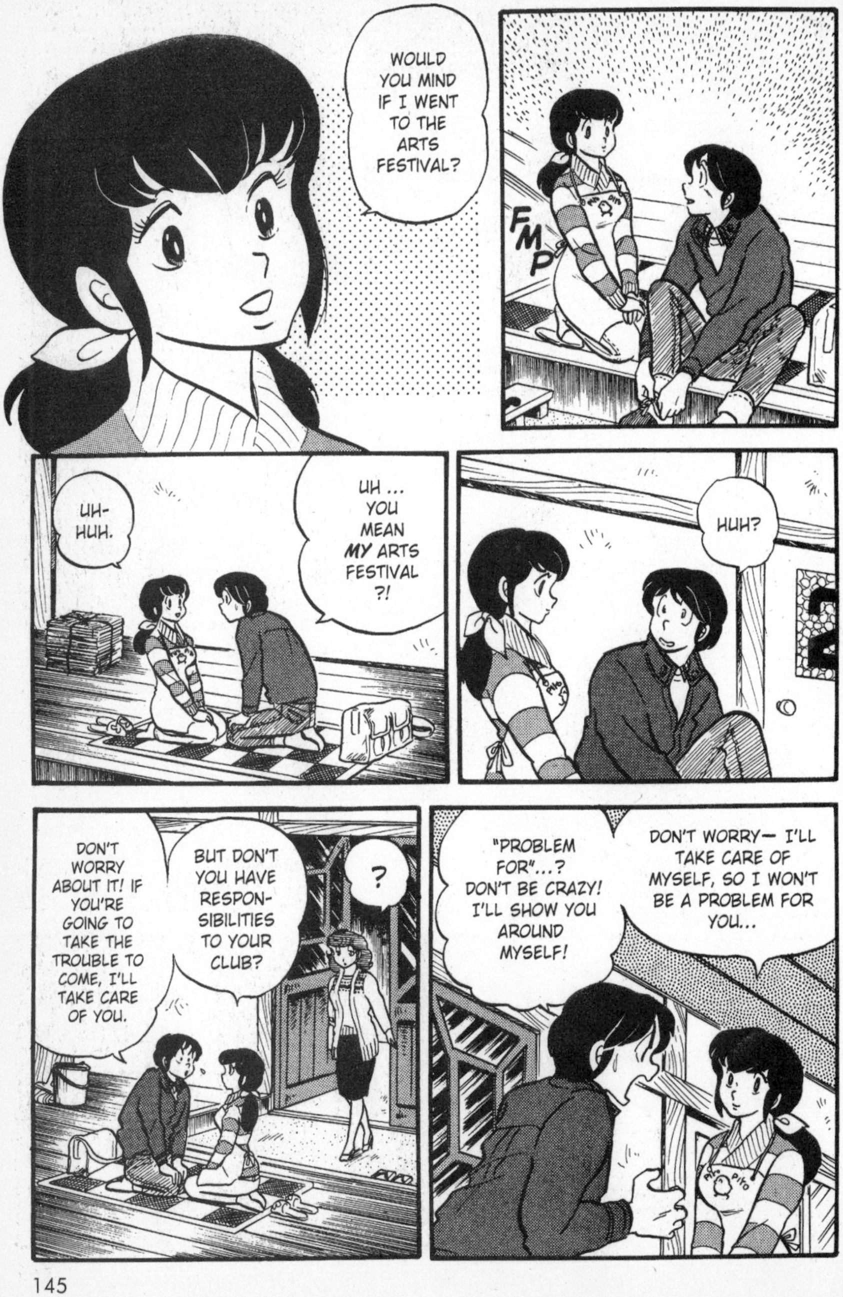
FMP
WOULD YOU MIND IF I WENT TO THE ARTS FESTIVAL?
HUH?
UH ... YOU MEAN **MY** ARTS FESTIVAL ?!
UH-HUH.
DON'T WORRY— I'LL TAKE CARE OF MYSELF, SO I WON'T BE A PROBLEM FOR YOU...
"PROBLEM FOR"...? DON'T BE CRAZY! I'LL SHOW YOU AROUND MYSELF!
?
BUT DON'T YOU HAVE RESPON-SIBILITIES TO YOUR CLUB?
DON'T WORRY ABOUT IT! IF YOU'RE GOING TO TAKE THE TROUBLE TO COME, I'LL TAKE CARE OF YOU.

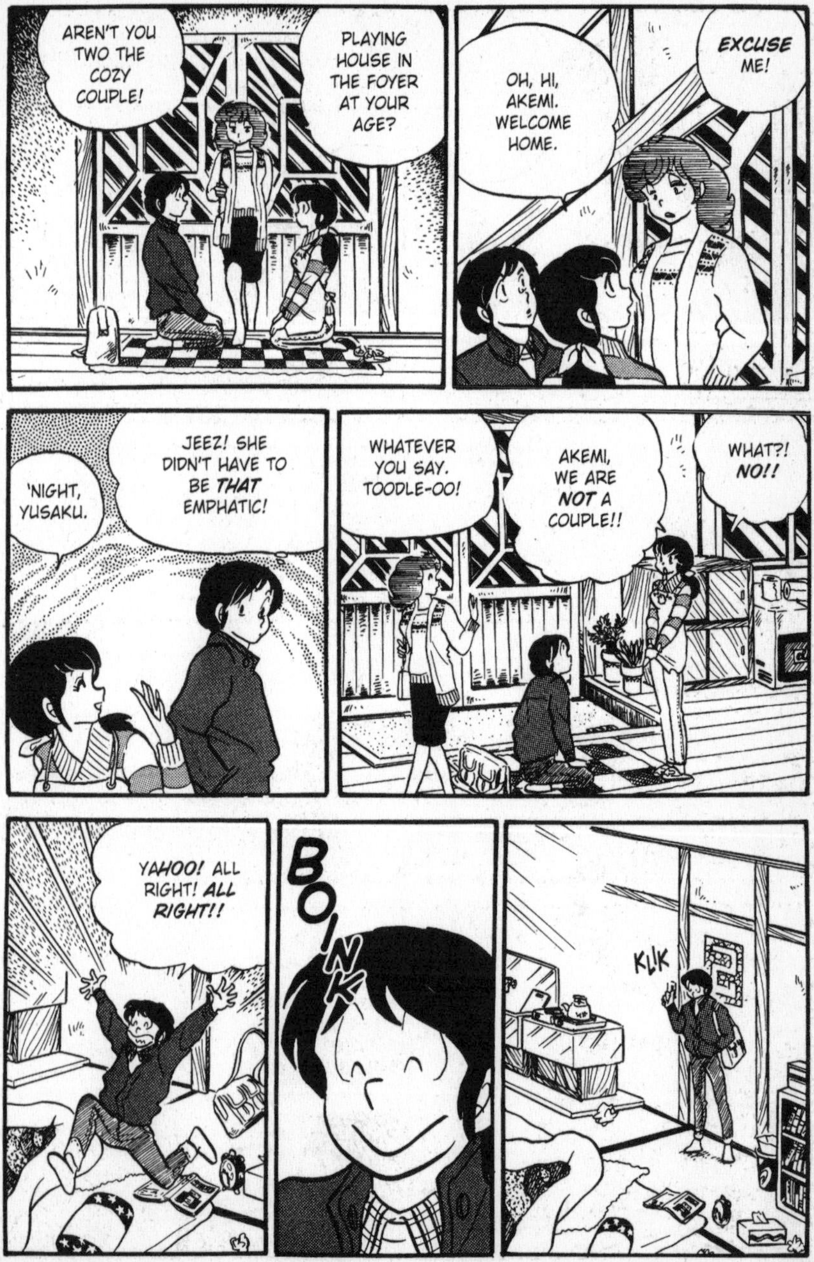

EXCUSE ME!
OH, HI, AKEMI. WELCOME HOME.
PLAYING HOUSE IN THE FOYER AT YOUR AGE?
AREN'T YOU TWO THE COZY COUPLE!
WHAT?! NO!!
AKEMI, WE ARE NOT A COUPLE!!
WHATEVER YOU SAY. TOODLE-OO!
JEEZ! SHE DIDN'T HAVE TO BE THAT EMPHATIC!
'NIGHT, YUSAKU.
KLIK
BOINK
YAHOO! ALL RIGHT! ALL RIGHT!!

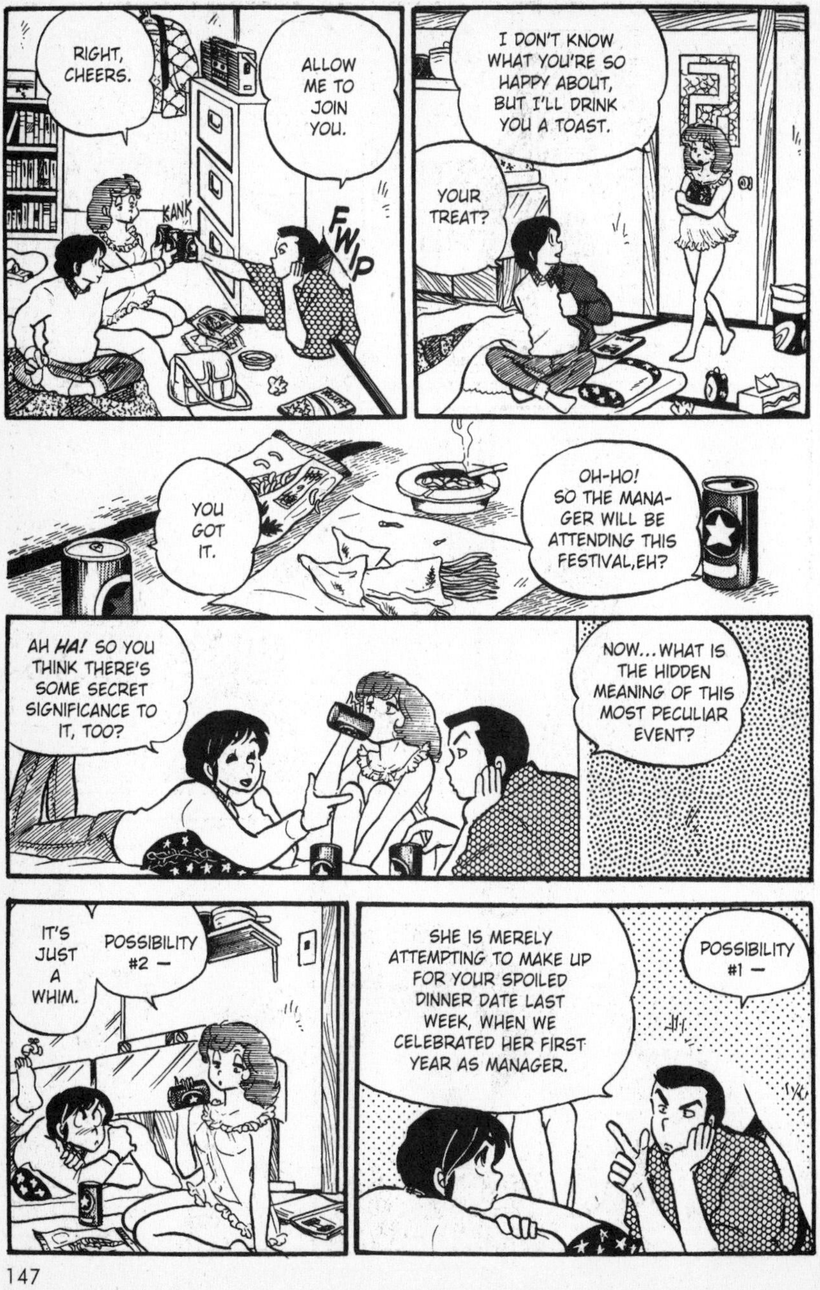
I DON'T KNOW WHAT YOU'RE SO HAPPY ABOUT, BUT I'LL DRINK YOU A TOAST.
YOUR TREAT?
ALLOW ME TO JOIN YOU.
RIGHT, CHEERS.
FWIP
KANK
OH-HO! SO THE MANA-GER WILL BE ATTENDING THIS FESTIVAL,EH?
YOU GOT IT.
NOW...WHAT IS THE HIDDEN MEANING OF THIS MOST PECULIAR EVENT?
AH HA! SO YOU THINK THERE'S SOME SECRET SIGNIFICANCE TO IT, TOO?
POSSIBILITY #1 —
SHE IS MERELY ATTEMPTING TO MAKE UP FOR YOUR SPOILED DINNER DATE LAST WEEK, WHEN WE CELEBRATED HER FIRST YEAR AS MANAGER.
POSSIBILITY #2 —
IT'S JUST A WHIM.

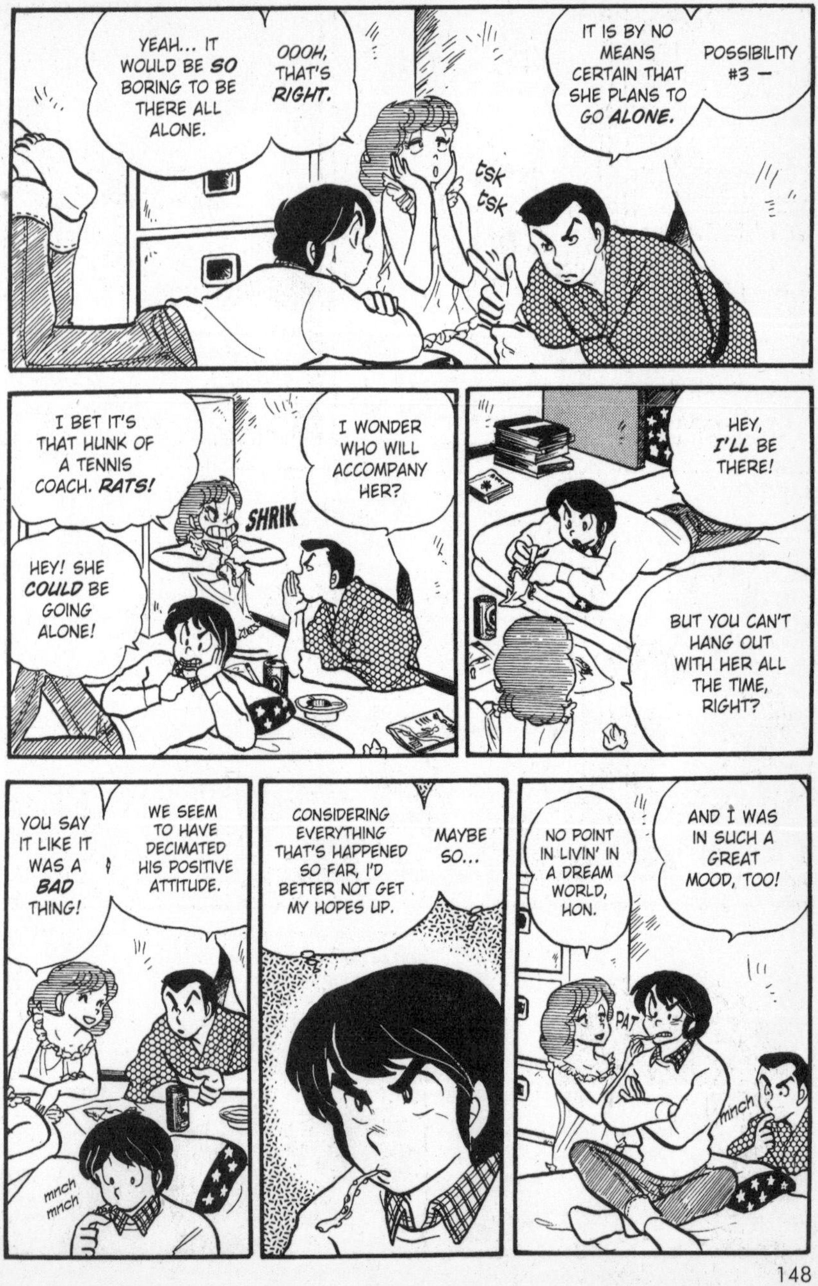
POSSIBILITY #3 —
IT IS BY NO MEANS CERTAIN THAT SHE PLANS TO GO ALONE.
tsk tsk
OOOH, THAT'S RIGHT.
YEAH... IT WOULD BE SO BORING TO BE THERE ALL ALONE.
HEY, I'LL BE THERE!
BUT YOU CAN'T HANG OUT WITH HER ALL THE TIME, RIGHT?
I WONDER WHO WILL ACCOMPANY HER?
I BET IT'S THAT HUNK OF A TENNIS COACH. RATS!
SHRIK
HEY! SHE COULD BE GOING ALONE!
AND I WAS IN SUCH A GREAT MOOD, TOO!
NO POINT IN LIVIN' IN A DREAM WORLD, HON.
PAT
mnch
MAYBE SO...
CONSIDERING EVERYTHING THAT'S HAPPENED SO FAR, I'D BETTER NOT GET MY HOPES UP.
WE SEEM TO HAVE DECIMATED HIS POSITIVE ATTITUDE.
YOU SAY IT LIKE IT WAS A BAD THING!
mnch mnch

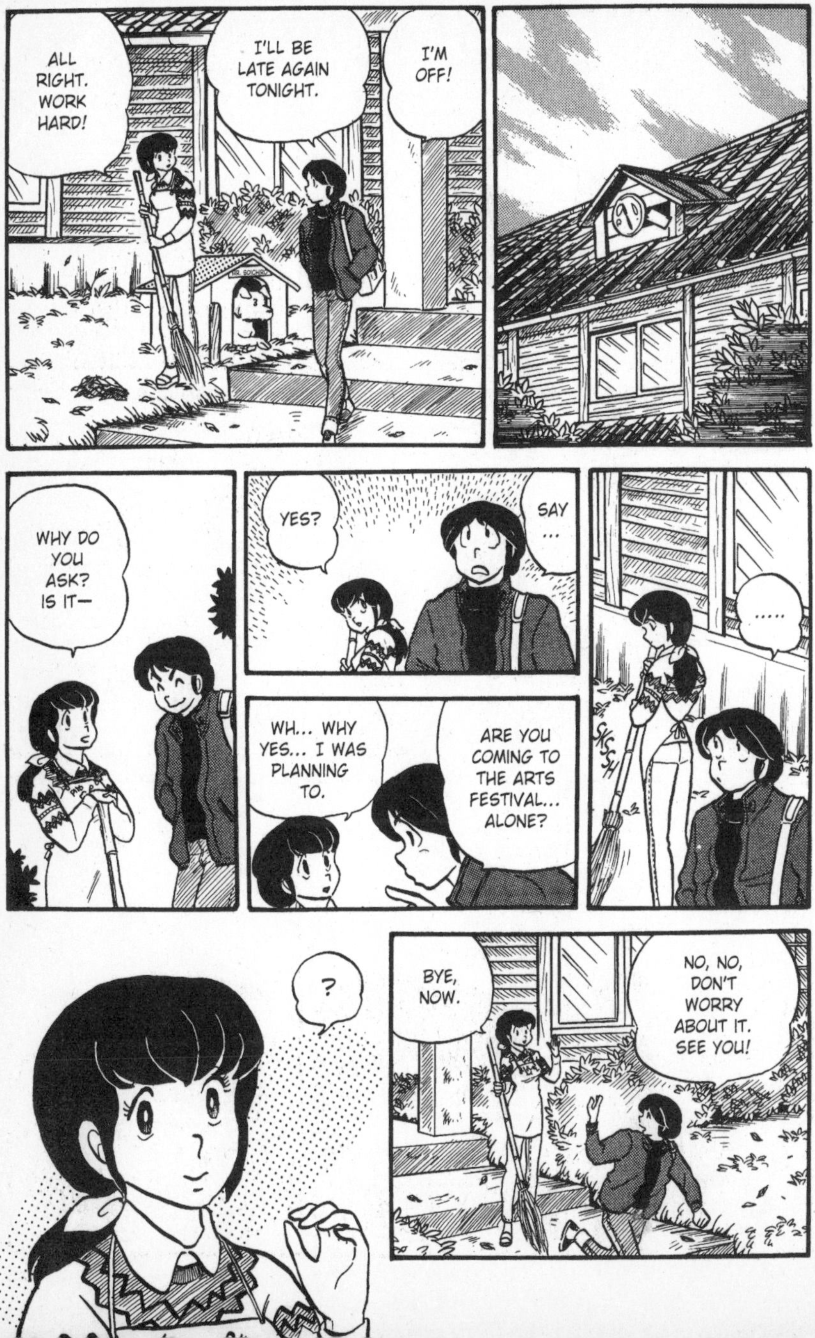
I'M OFF!
I'LL BE LATE AGAIN TONIGHT.
ALL RIGHT. WORK HARD!
.....
SKSSH
SAY ...
YES?
ARE YOU COMING TO THE ARTS FESTIVAL... ALONE?
WH... WHY YES... I WAS PLANNING TO.
WHY DO YOU ASK? IS IT—
NO, NO, DON'T WORRY ABOUT IT. SEE YOU!
BYE, NOW.
?

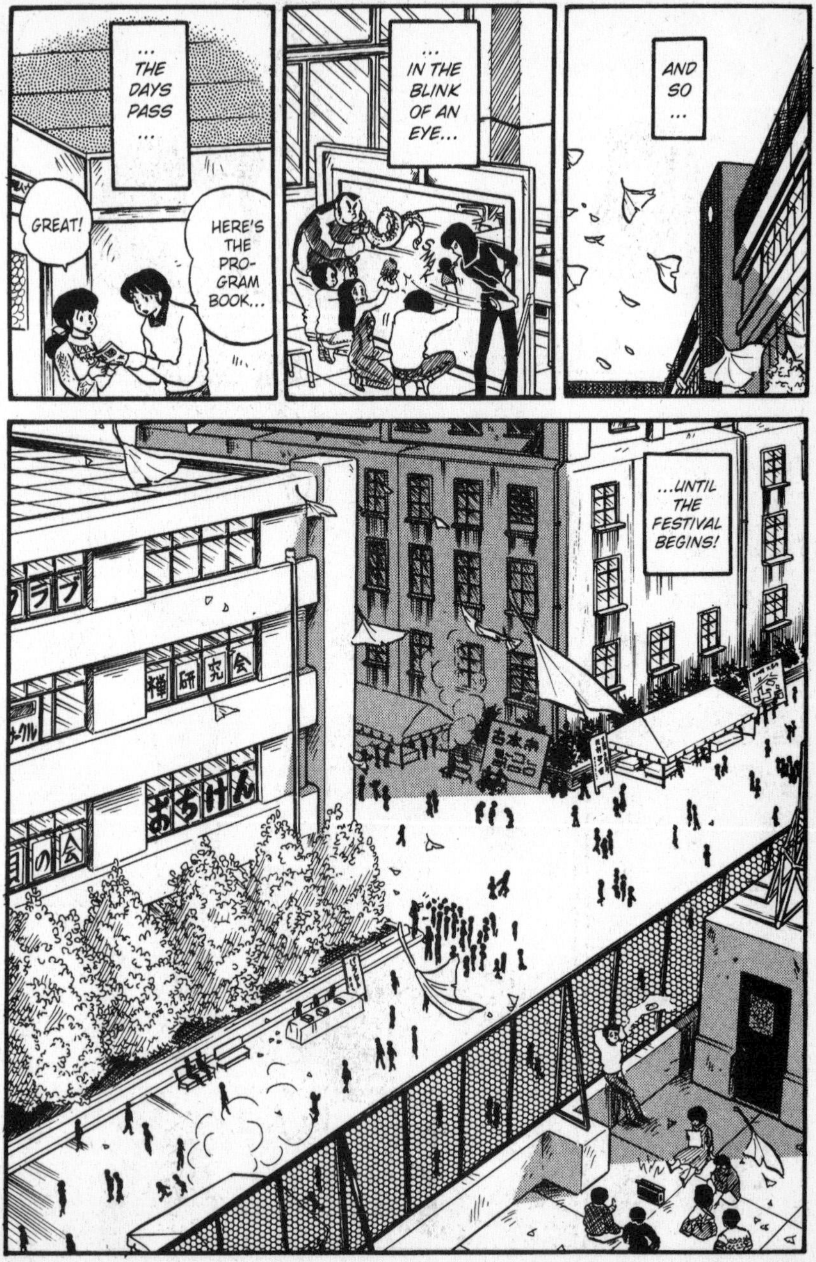
AND SO ...
... IN THE BLINK OF AN EYE...
... THE DAYS PASS ...
HERE'S THE PRO-GRAM BOOK...
GREAT!
...UNTIL THE FESTIVAL BEGINS!
禅研究会
おちけん

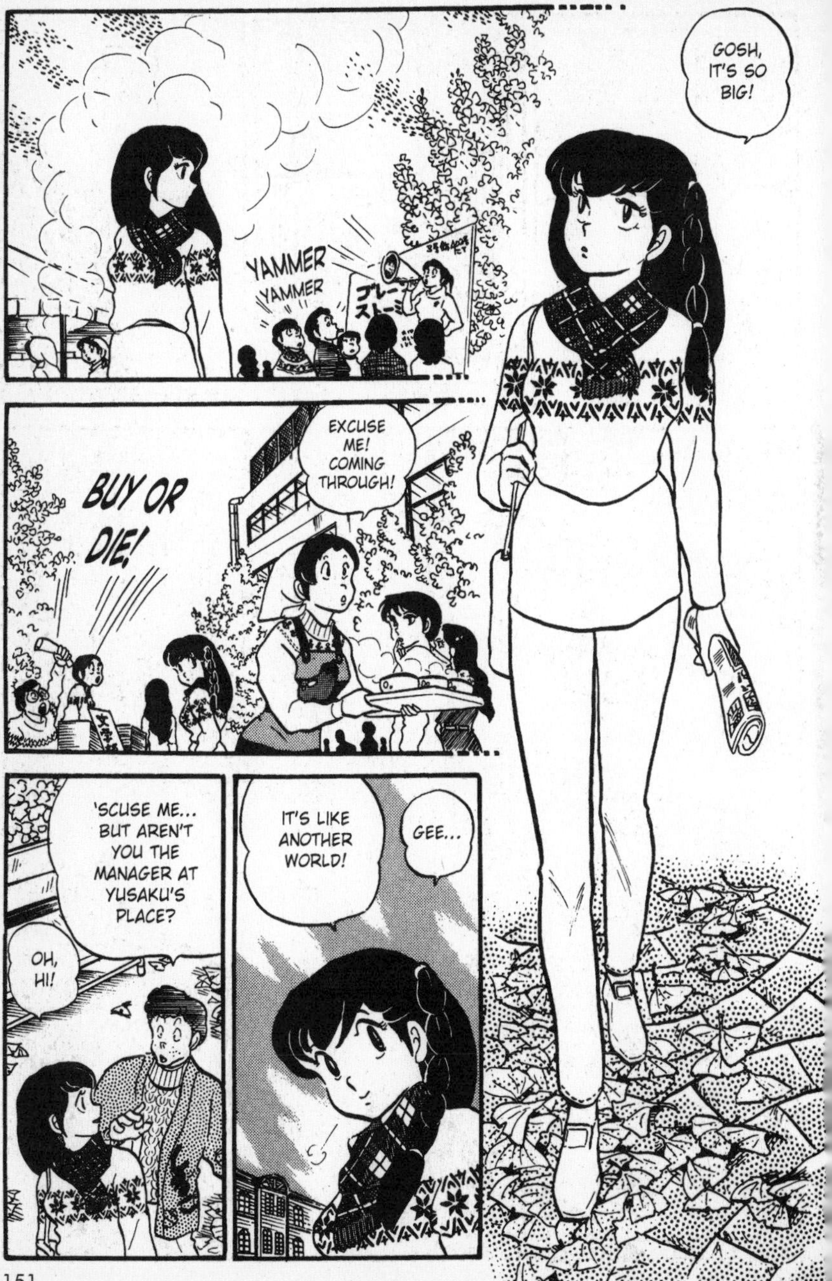
GOSH, IT'S SO BIG!
YAMMER
YAMMER
EXCUSE ME! COMING THROUGH!
BUY OR DIE!
GEE...
IT'S LIKE ANOTHER WORLD!
'SCUSE ME... BUT AREN'T YOU THE MANAGER AT YUSAKU'S PLACE?
OH, HI!

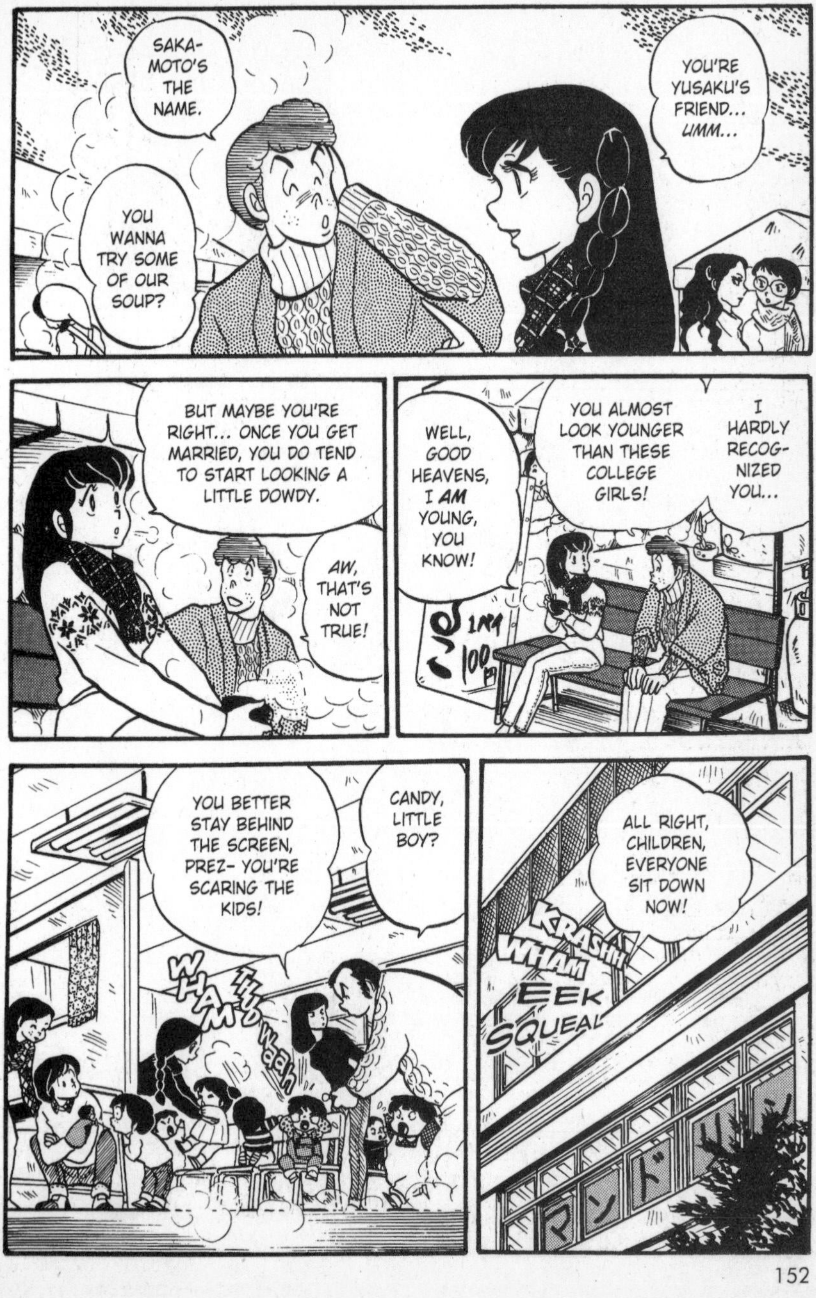
YOU'RE YUSAKU'S FRIEND... UMM...
SAKA-MOTO'S THE NAME.
YOU WANNA TRY SOME OF OUR SOUP?
I HARDLY RECOG-NIZED YOU...
YOU ALMOST LOOK YOUNGER THAN THESE COLLEGE GIRLS!
WELL, GOOD HEAVENS, I *AM* YOUNG, YOU KNOW!
BUT MAYBE YOU'RE RIGHT... ONCE YOU GET MARRIED, YOU DO TEND TO START LOOKING A LITTLE DOWDY.
AW, THAT'S NOT TRUE!
ALL RIGHT, CHILDREN, EVERYONE SIT DOWN NOW!
KRASHH
WHAM
EEK
SQUEAL
CANDY, LITTLE BOY?
YOU BETTER STAY BEHIND THE SCREEN, PREZ- YOU'RE SCARING THE KIDS!
WHAM
THUD
WAAH

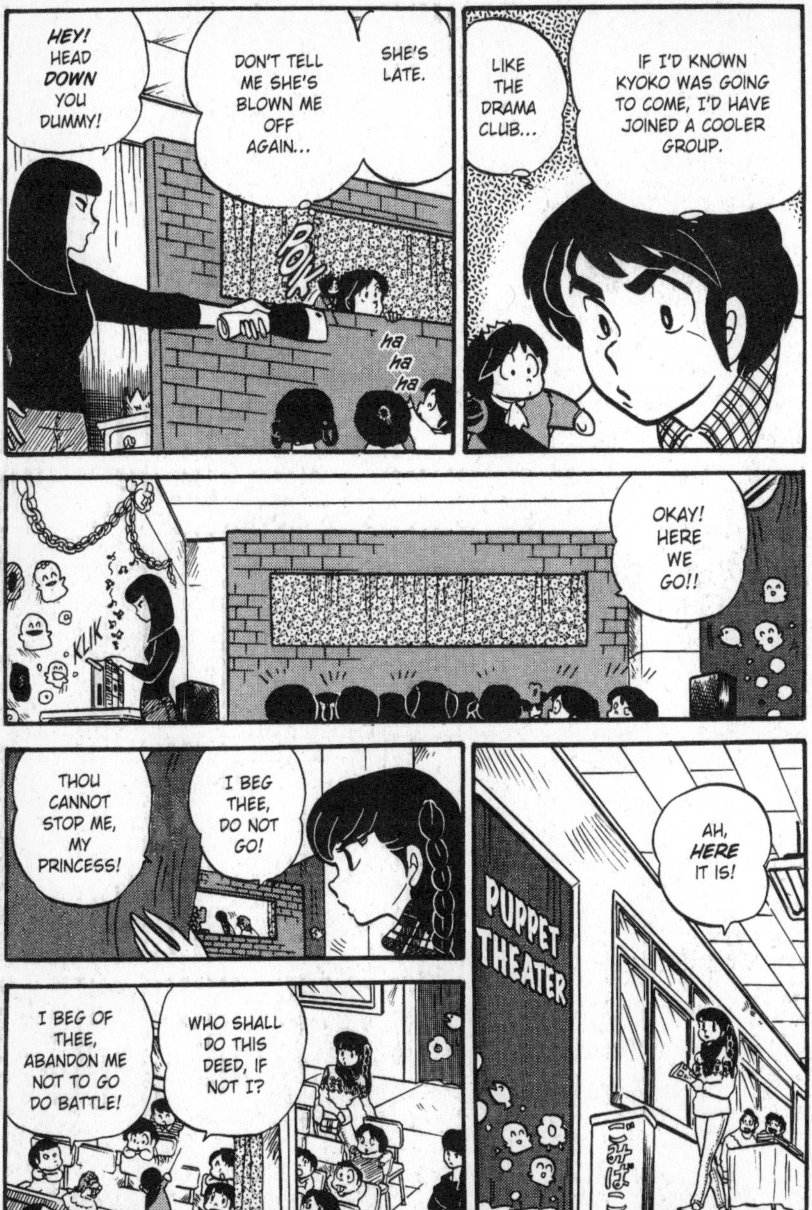
IF I'D KNOWN KYOKO WAS GOING TO COME, I'D HAVE JOINED A COOLER GROUP.
LIKE THE DRAMA CLUB...
SHE'S LATE.
DON'T TELL ME SHE'S BLOWN ME OFF AGAIN...
HEY! HEAD DOWN YOU DUMMY!
POK
ha ha ha
OKAY! HERE WE GO!!
KLIK
AH, HERE IT IS!
PUPPET THEATER
I BEG THEE, DO NOT GO!
THOU CANNOT STOP ME, MY PRINCESS!
WHO SHALL DO THIS DEED, IF NOT I?
I BEG OF THEE, ABANDON ME NOT TO GO DO BATTLE!

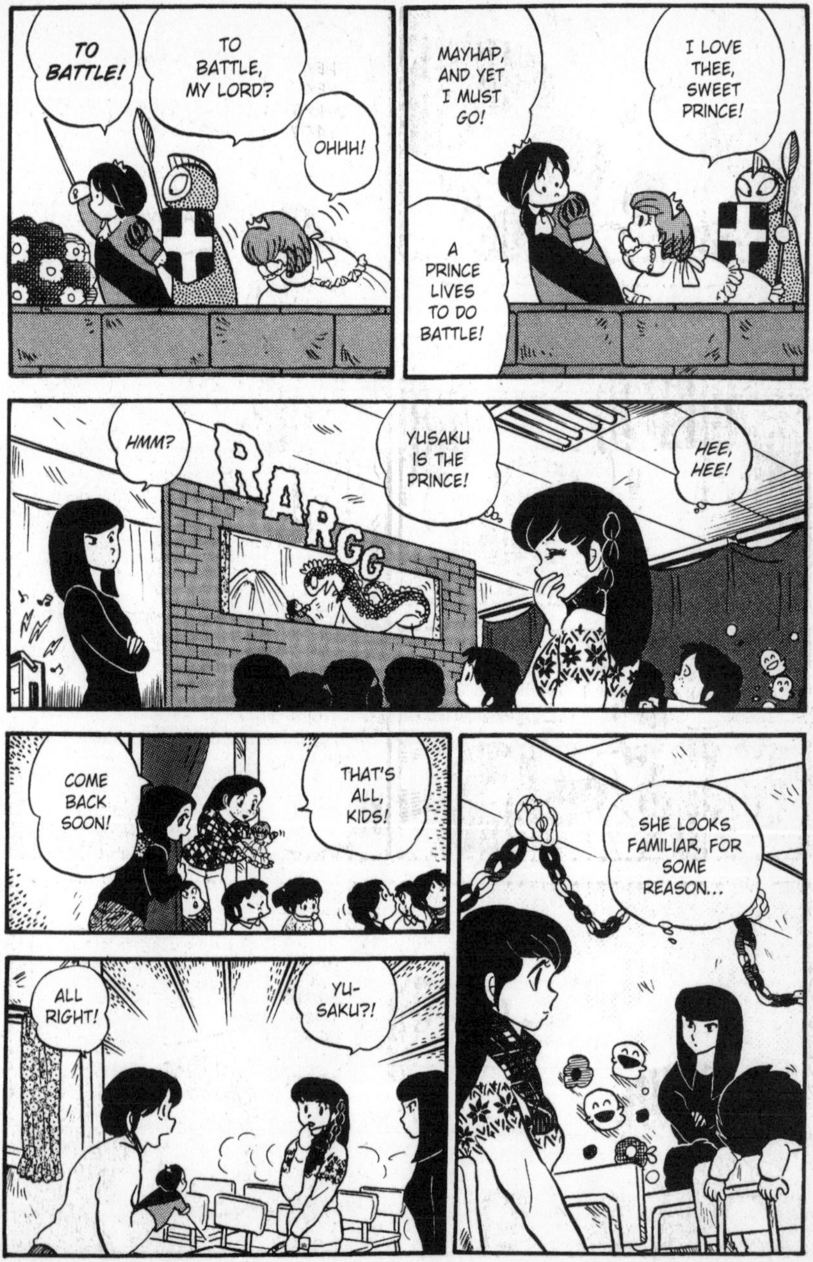
I LOVE THEE, SWEET PRINCE!
MAYHAP, AND YET I MUST GO!
A PRINCE LIVES TO DO BATTLE!
TO BATTLE, MY LORD?
OHHH!
TO BATTLE!
HEE, HEE!
YUSAKU IS THE PRINCE!
RARGG
HMM?
SHE LOOKS FAMILIAR, FOR SOME REASON...
THAT'S ALL, KIDS!
COME BACK SOON!
YU-SAKU?!
ALL RIGHT!

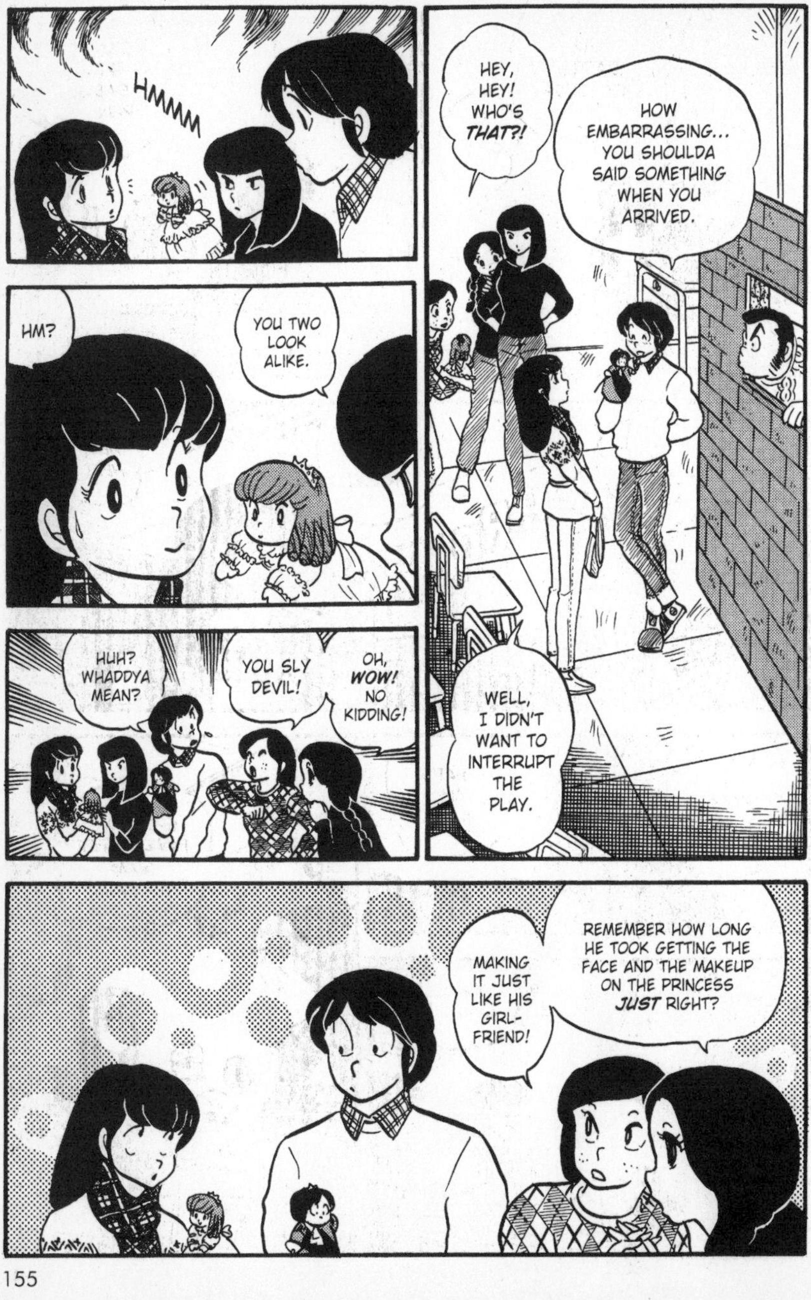
HOW EMBARRASSING... YOU SHOULDA SAID SOMETHING WHEN YOU ARRIVED.
HEY, HEY! WHO'S *THAT?!*
WELL, I DIDN'T WANT TO INTERRUPT THE PLAY.
HMMMM
YOU TWO LOOK ALIKE.
HM?
OH, *WOW!* NO KIDDING!
YOU SLY DEVIL!
HUH? WHADDYA MEAN?
REMEMBER HOW LONG HE TOOK GETTING THE FACE AND THE MAKEUP ON THE PRINCESS *JUST* RIGHT?
MAKING IT JUST LIKE HIS GIRL-FRIEND!

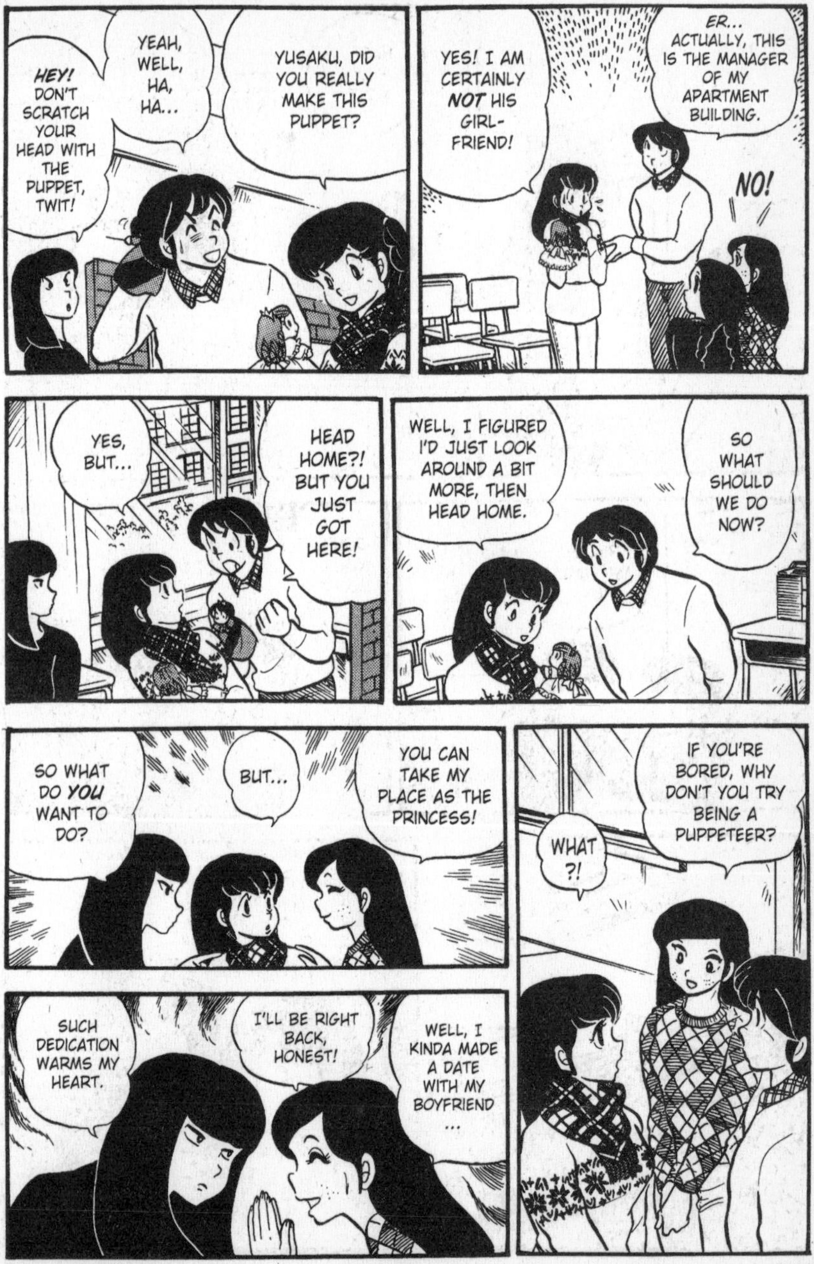
ER... ACTUALLY, THIS IS THE MANAGER OF MY APARTMENT BUILDING.
NO!
YES! I AM CERTAINLY **NOT** HIS GIRL-FRIEND!
YUSAKU, DID YOU REALLY MAKE THIS PUPPET?
YEAH, WELL, HA, HA...
HEY! DON'T SCRATCH YOUR HEAD WITH THE PUPPET, TWIT!
SO WHAT SHOULD WE DO NOW?
WELL, I FIGURED I'D JUST LOOK AROUND A BIT MORE, THEN HEAD HOME.
HEAD HOME?! BUT YOU JUST GOT HERE!
YES, BUT...
IF YOU'RE BORED, WHY DON'T YOU TRY BEING A PUPPETEER?
WHAT?!
YOU CAN TAKE MY PLACE AS THE PRINCESS!
BUT...
SO WHAT DO **YOU** WANT TO DO?
WELL, I KINDA MADE A DATE WITH MY BOYFRIEND ...
I'LL BE RIGHT BACK, HONEST!
SUCH DEDICATION WARMS MY HEART.

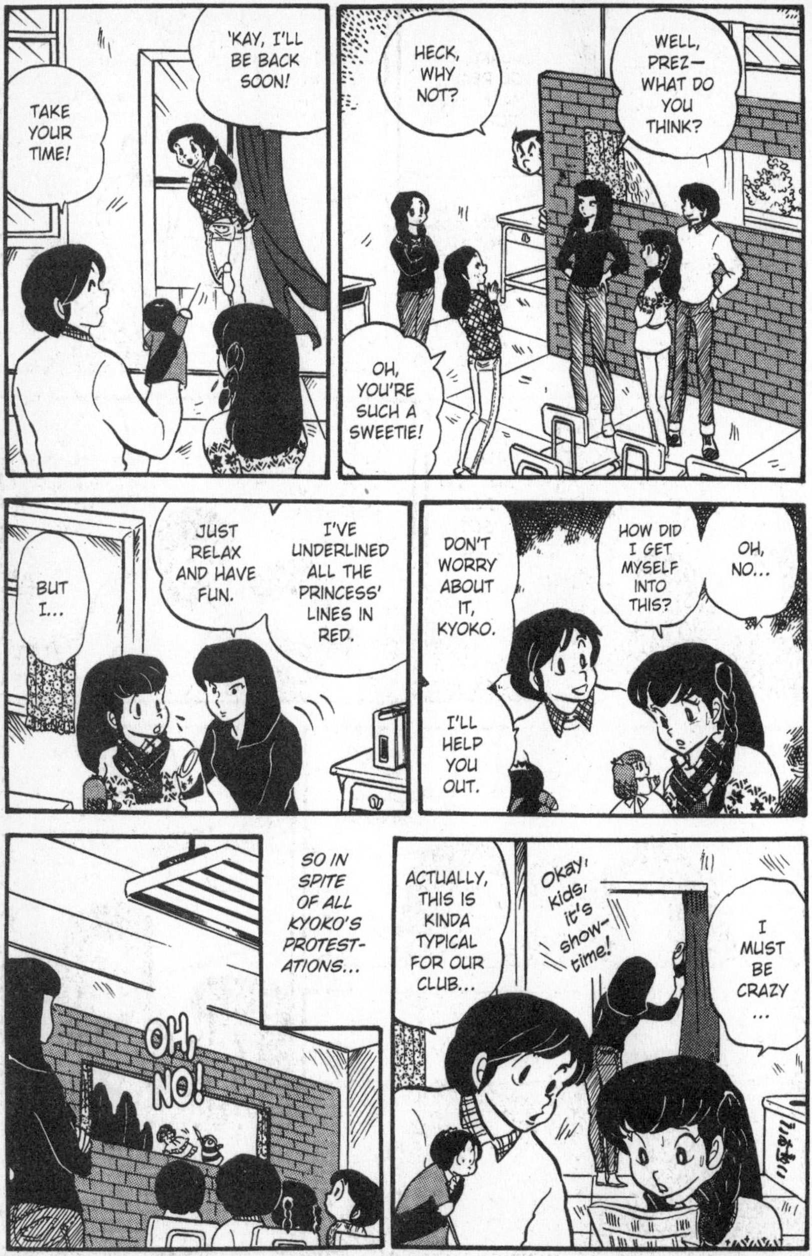
WELL, PREZ— WHAT DO YOU THINK?
HECK, WHY NOT?
OH, YOU'RE SUCH A SWEETIE!
'KAY, I'LL BE BACK SOON!
TAKE YOUR TIME!
OH, NO...
HOW DID I GET MYSELF INTO THIS?
DON'T WORRY ABOUT IT, KYOKO.
I'LL HELP YOU OUT.
I'VE UNDERLINED ALL THE PRINCESS' LINES IN RED.
JUST RELAX AND HAVE FUN.
BUT I...
I MUST BE CRAZY...
Okay, kids, it's show-time!
ACTUALLY, THIS IS KINDA TYPICAL FOR OUR CLUB...
SO IN SPITE OF ALL KYOKO'S PROTEST-ATIONS...
OH, NO!

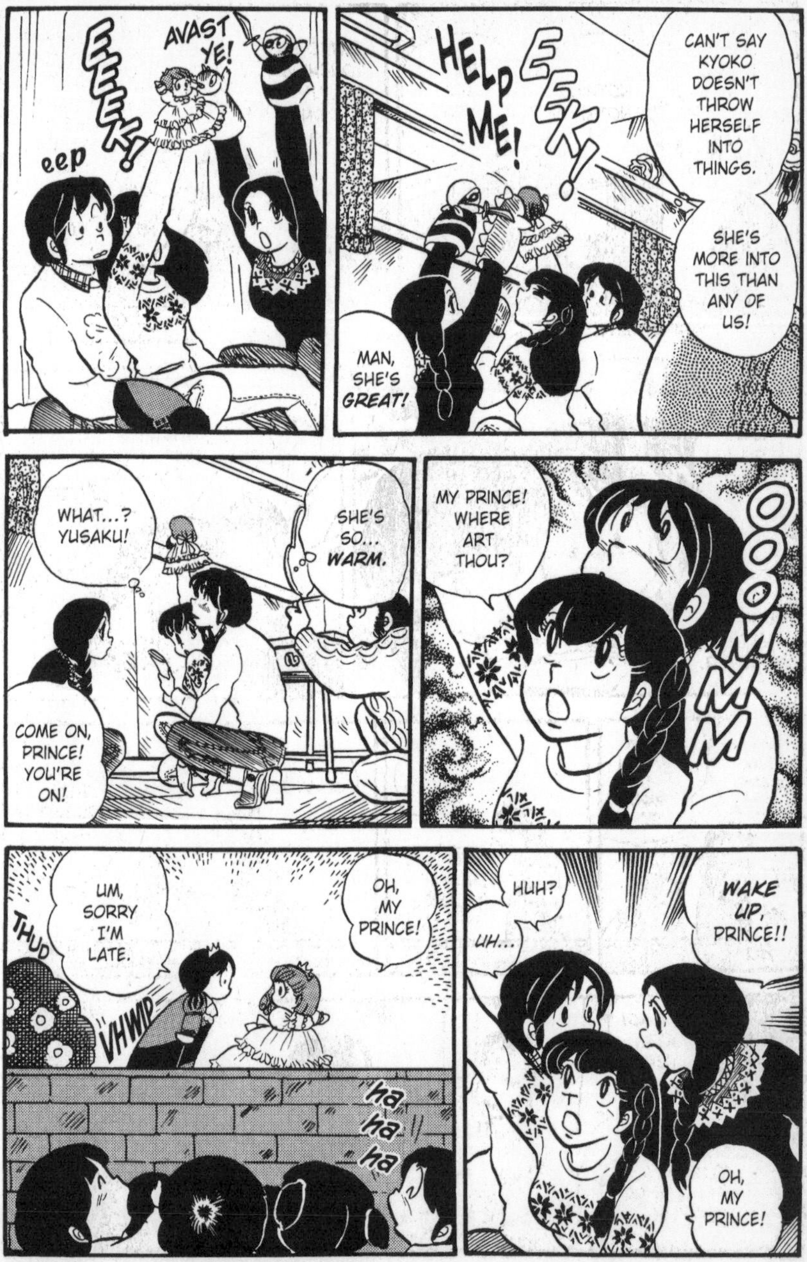
CAN'T SAY KYOKO DOESN'T THROW HERSELF INTO THINGS.
EEEK!
HELP ME!
SHE'S MORE INTO THIS THAN ANY OF US!
MAN, SHE'S **GREAT!**
AVAST YE!
EEEK!
eep
OOOMMMM
MY PRINCE! WHERE ART THOU?
SHE'S SO... **WARM.**
WHAT...? YUSAKU!
COME ON, PRINCE! YOU'RE ON!
WAKE UP, PRINCE!!
HUH?
UH...
OH, MY PRINCE!
OH, MY PRINCE!
UM, SORRY I'M LATE.
THUD
VHWIP
ha ha ha

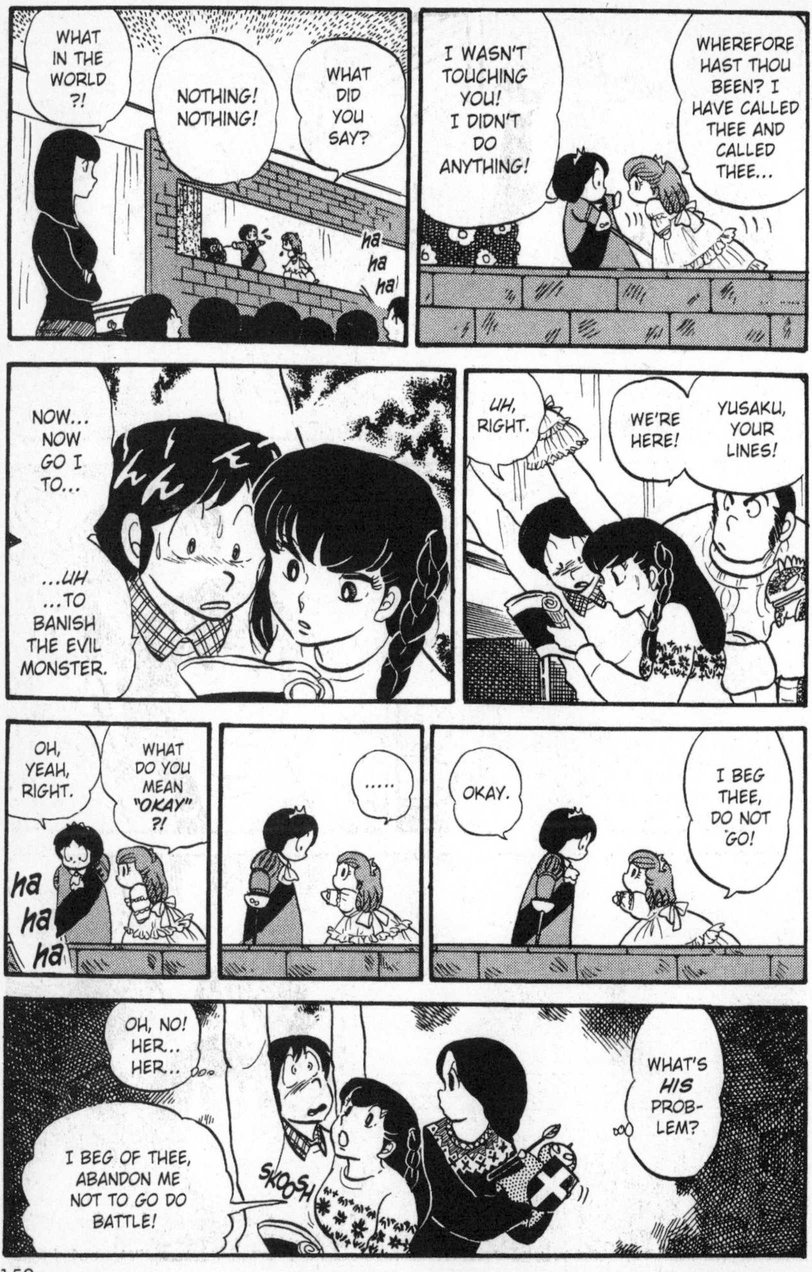
WHEREFORE HAST THOU BEEN? I HAVE CALLED THEE AND CALLED THEE...
I WASN'T TOUCHING YOU! I DIDN'T DO ANYTHING!
WHAT DID YOU SAY?
NOTHING! NOTHING!
WHAT IN THE WORLD ?!
ha ha ha
YUSAKU, YOUR LINES!
WE'RE HERE!
UH, RIGHT.
NOW... NOW GO I TO...
...UH ...TO BANISH THE EVIL MONSTER.
I BEG THEE, DO NOT GO!
OKAY.
.....
WHAT DO YOU MEAN "OKAY" ?!
OH, YEAH, RIGHT.
ha ha ha
WHAT'S HIS PROBLEM?
OH, NO! HER... HER...
I BEG OF THEE, ABANDON ME NOT TO GO DO BATTLE!
SKOOSH

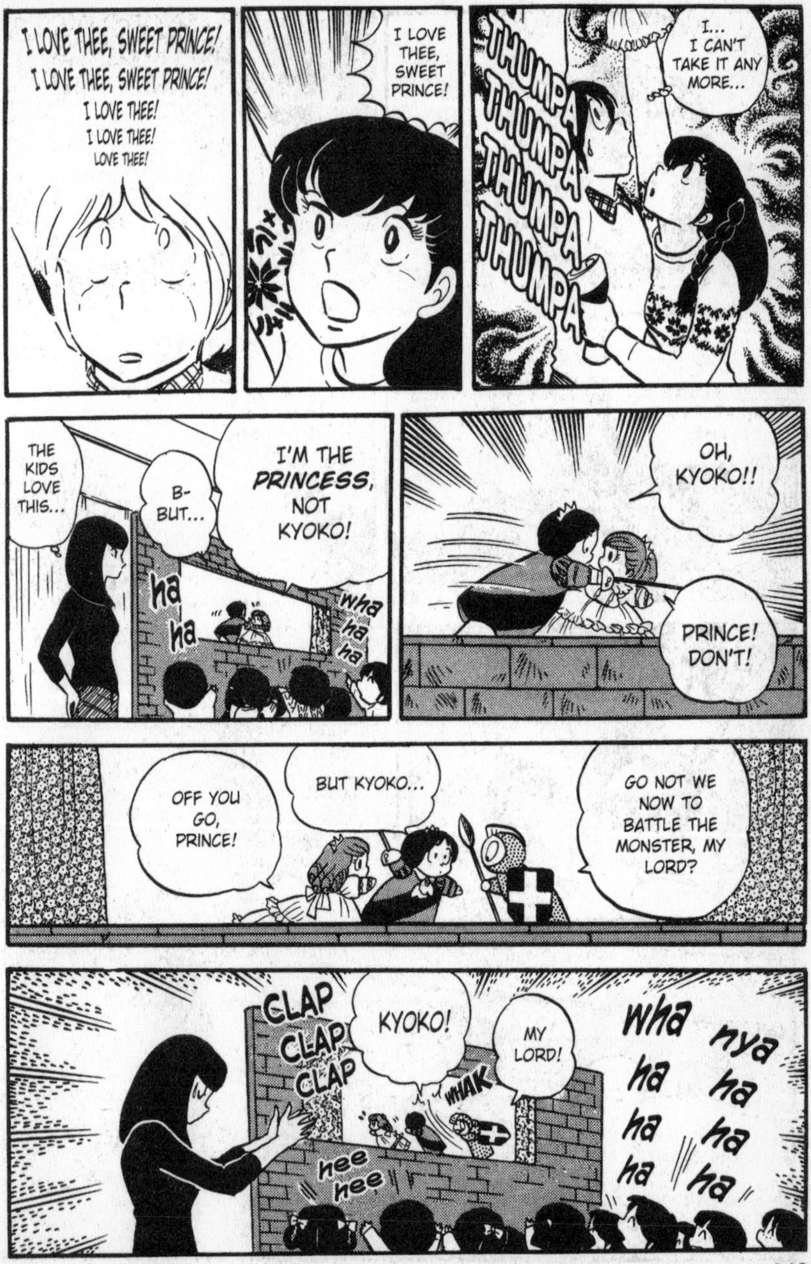
I... I CAN'T TAKE IT ANY MORE...
THUMPA THUMPA THUMPA THUMPA THUMPA
I LOVE THEE, SWEET PRINCE!
I LOVE THEE, SWEET PRINCE!
I LOVE THEE, SWEET PRINCE!
I LOVE THEE!
I LOVE THEE!
LOVE THEE!
OH, KYOKO!!
PRINCE! DON'T!
I'M THE *PRINCESS*, NOT KYOKO!
B- BUT...
THE KIDS LOVE THIS...
wha ha ha
ha ha
GO NOT WE NOW TO BATTLE THE MONSTER, MY LORD?
BUT KYOKO...
OFF YOU GO, PRINCE!
nya ha ha ha ha
wha ha ha ha
MY LORD!
WHAK
KYOKO!
CLAP CLAP CLAP
hee hee

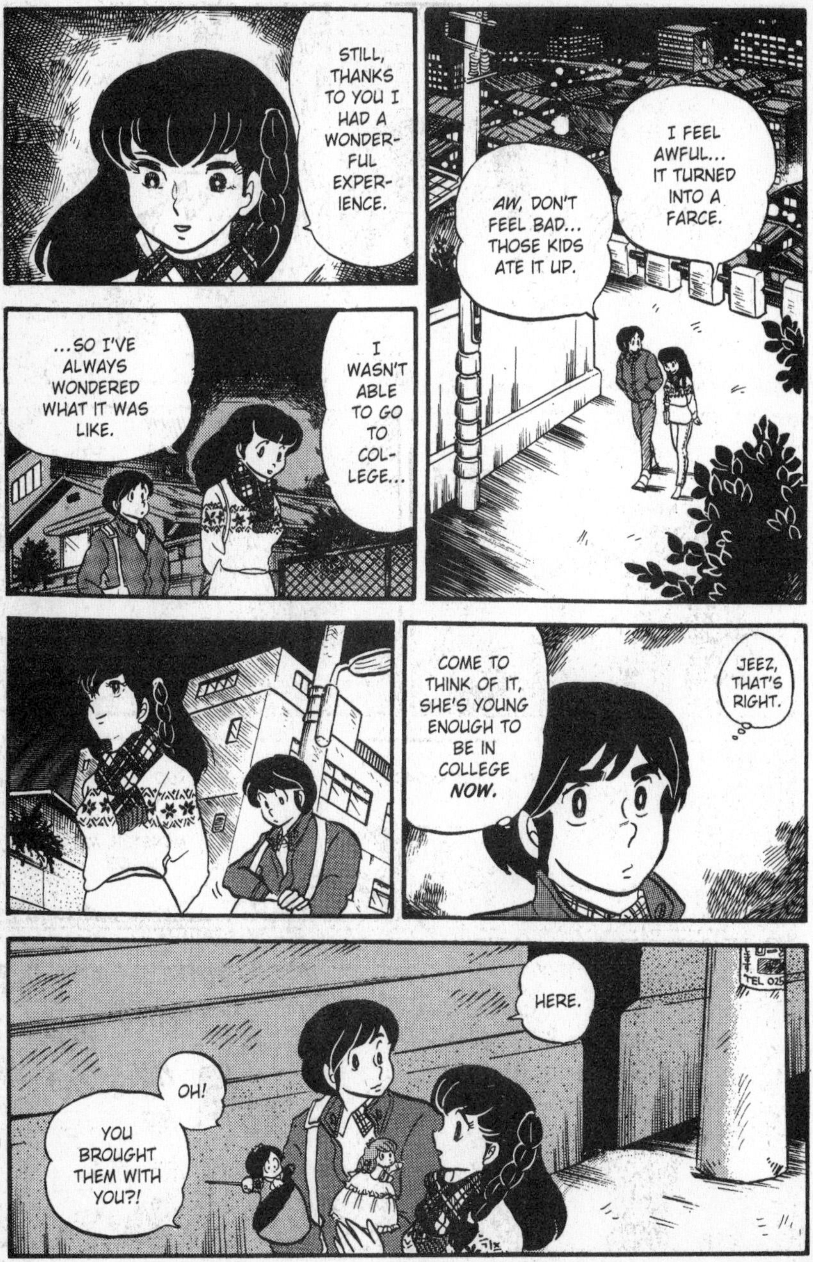

I FEEL AWFUL... IT TURNED INTO A FARCE.
AW, DON'T FEEL BAD... THOSE KIDS ATE IT UP.
STILL, THANKS TO YOU I HAD A WONDERFUL EXPERIENCE.
I WASN'T ABLE TO GO TO COLLEGE...
...SO I'VE ALWAYS WONDERED WHAT IT WAS LIKE.
COME TO THINK OF IT, SHE'S YOUNG ENOUGH TO BE IN COLLEGE *NOW.*
JEEZ, THAT'S RIGHT.
TEL 025
HERE.
OH!
YOU BROUGHT THEM WITH YOU?!

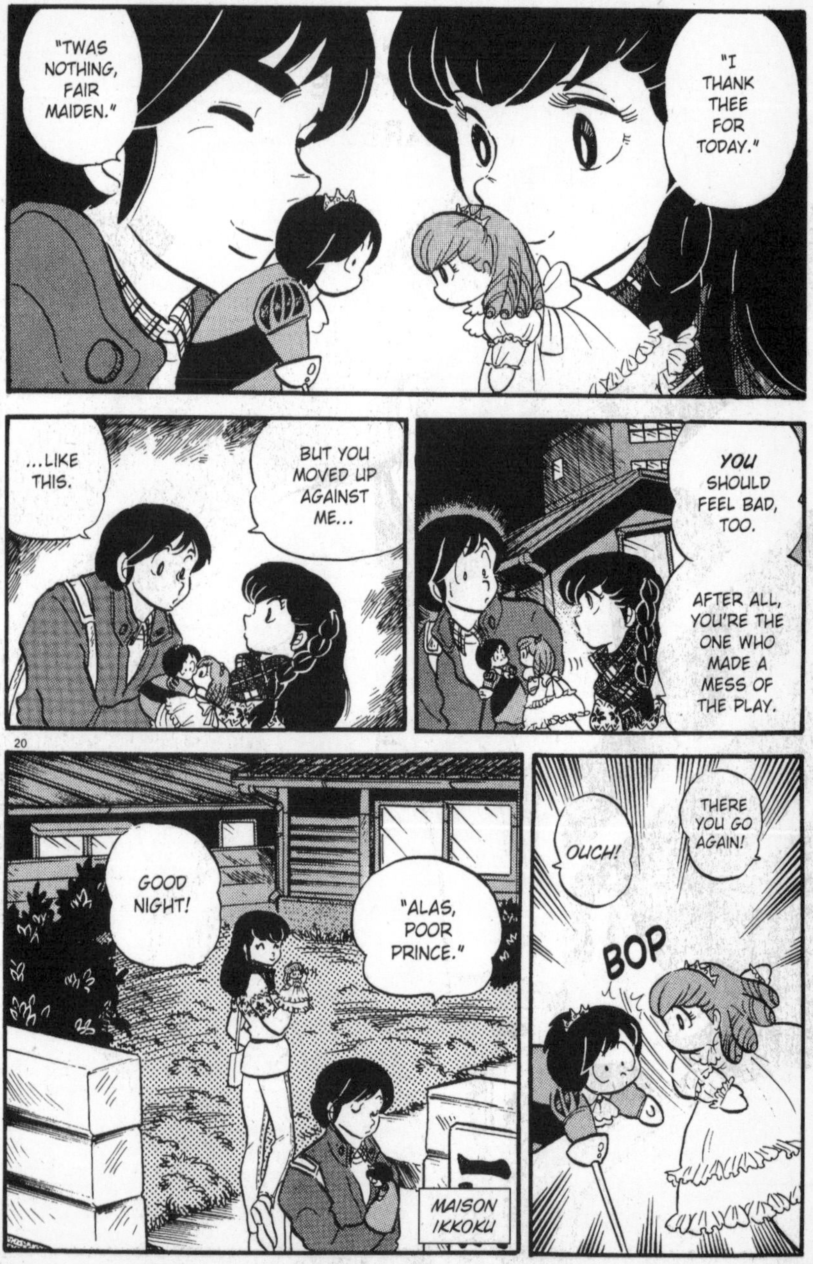
"I THANK THEE FOR TODAY."
"TWAS NOTHING, FAIR MAIDEN."
YOU SHOULD FEEL BAD, TOO.
AFTER ALL, YOU'RE THE ONE WHO MADE A MESS OF THE PLAY.
BUT YOU MOVED UP AGAINST ME...
...LIKE THIS.
THERE YOU GO AGAIN!
OUCH!
BOP
"ALAS, POOR PRINCE."
GOOD NIGHT!
MAISON IKKOKU

20

PART NINE

INTENSIVE CARE

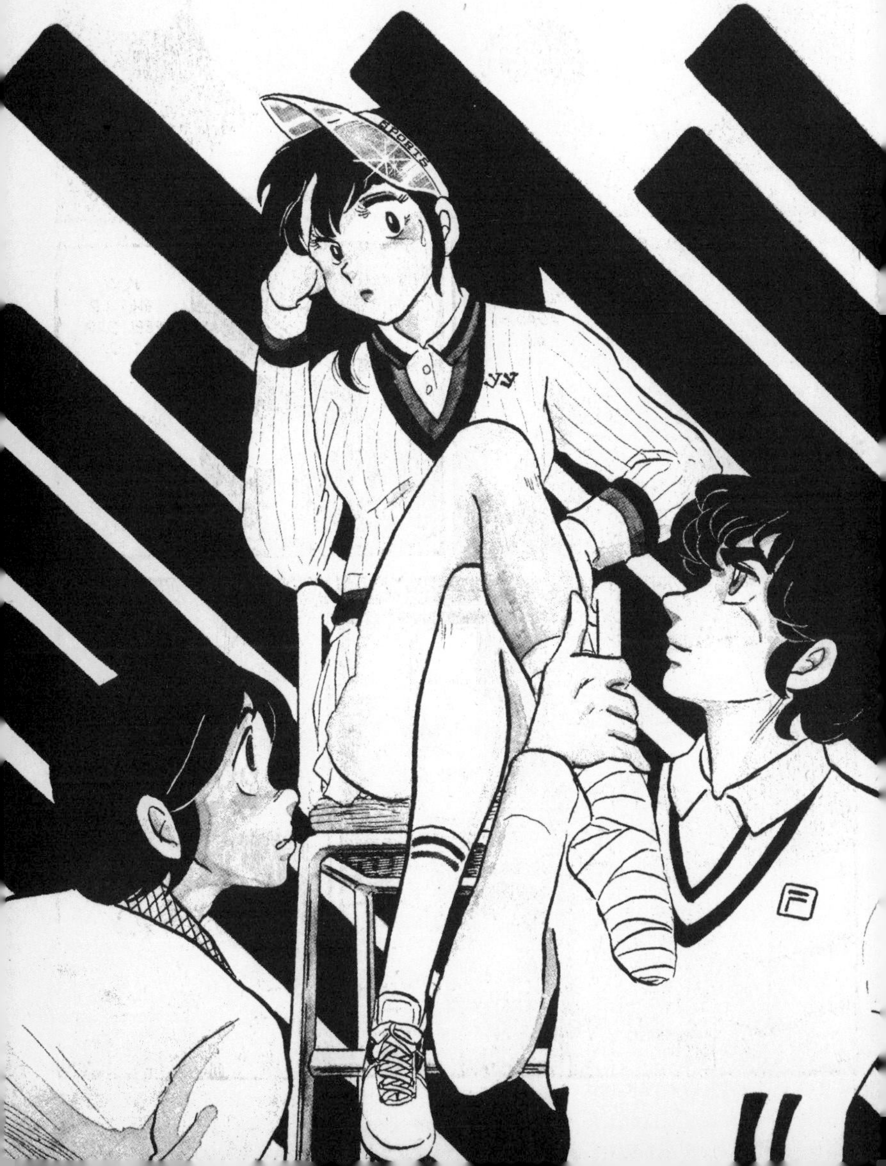
SPORTS

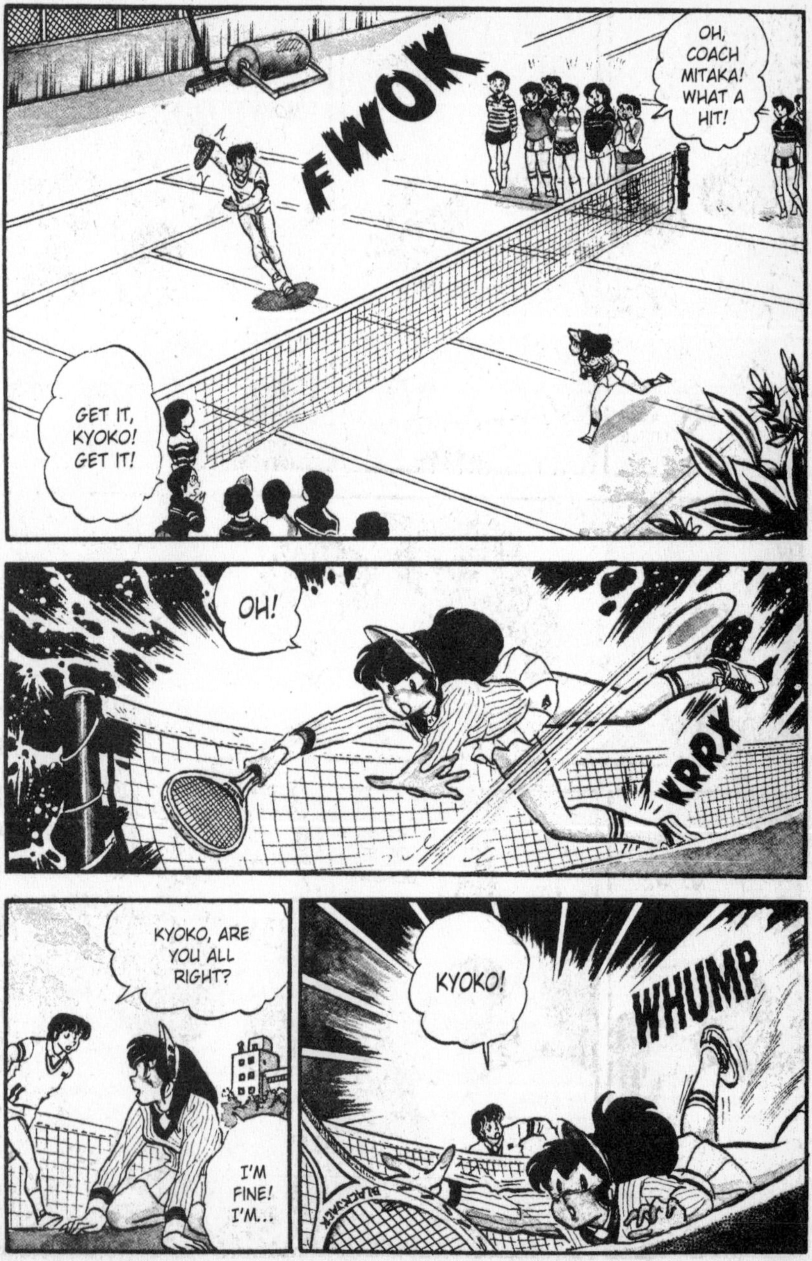
OH, COACH MITAKA! WHAT A HIT!
FWOK
GET IT, KYOKO! GET IT!
OH!
KRRX
KYOKO!
WHUMP
KYOKO, ARE YOU ALL RIGHT?
I'M FINE! I'M...

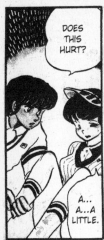

OW! OHHH...
DON'T TRY TO MOVE IT!
I SUPPOSE I DID TWIST IT...A BIT.
I'LL TAKE A LOOK.
DOES THIS HURT?
A... A...A LITTLE.
IT'S SPRAINED.
I SHOULDN'T HAVE HIT THE BALL SO HARD.
NO, PLEASE, IT ISN'T YOUR FAULT. I SHOULD HAVE...
BUT IT *IS* MY FAULT!
NO! REALLY!
LET GO OF IT, COACH!
HOW CAN I?!
SHE'S SUFFERING BECAUSE SHE PLAYED ME!
IT'S REALLY NOTHING TO...
DON'T STAND UP!

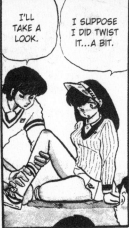

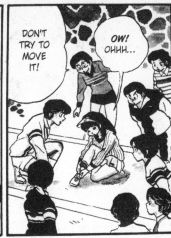

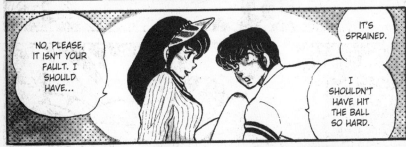

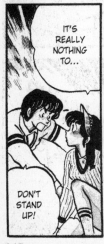

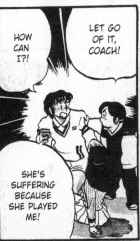

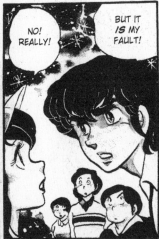

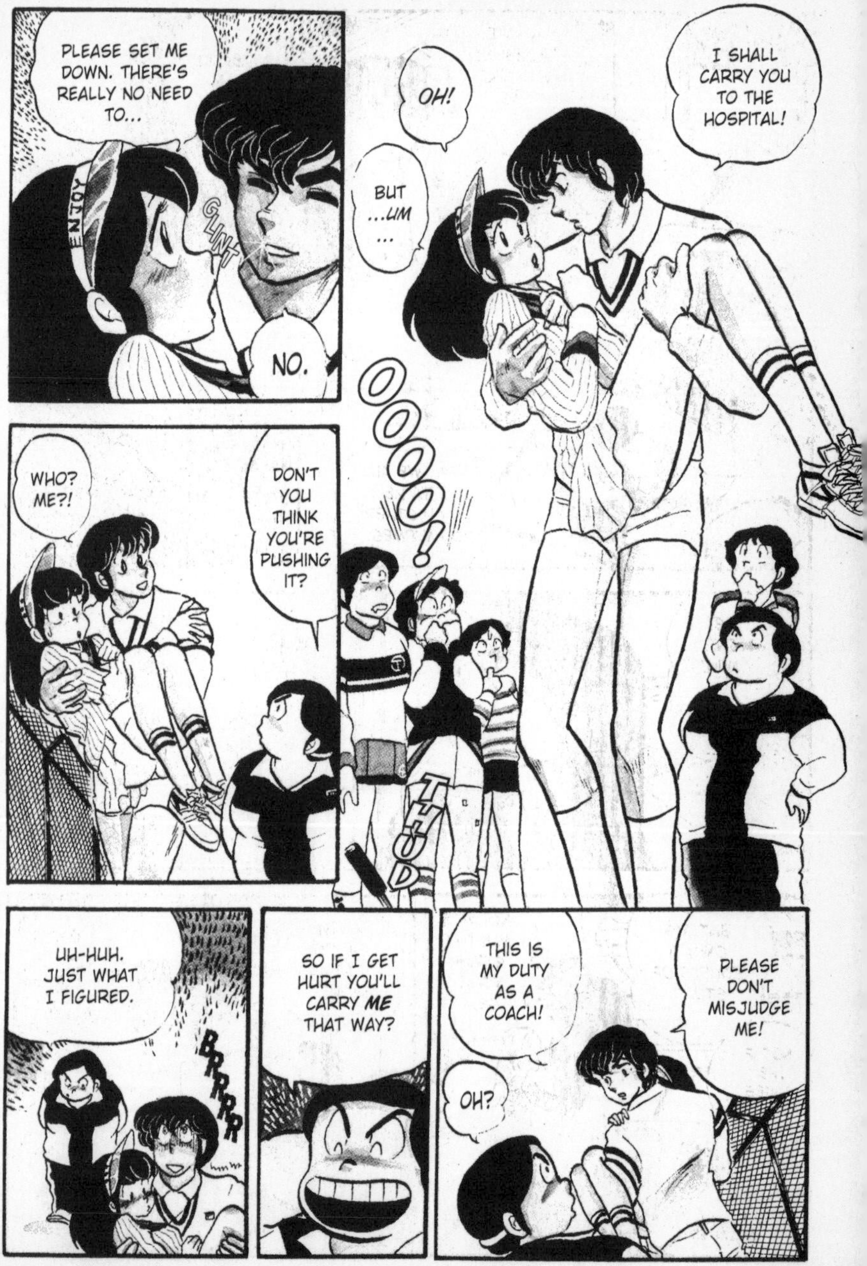
I SHALL CARRY YOU TO THE HOSPITAL!
OH!
BUT ...UM ...
OOOOO!
THUD
PLEASE SET ME DOWN. THERE'S REALLY NO NEED TO...
GLINT
NO.
DON'T YOU THINK YOU'RE PUSHING IT?
WHO? ME?!
PLEASE DON'T MISJUDGE ME!
THIS IS MY DUTY AS A COACH!
OH?
SO IF I GET HURT YOU'LL CARRY *ME* THAT WAY?
UH-HUH. JUST WHAT I FIGURED.
BRRRRR

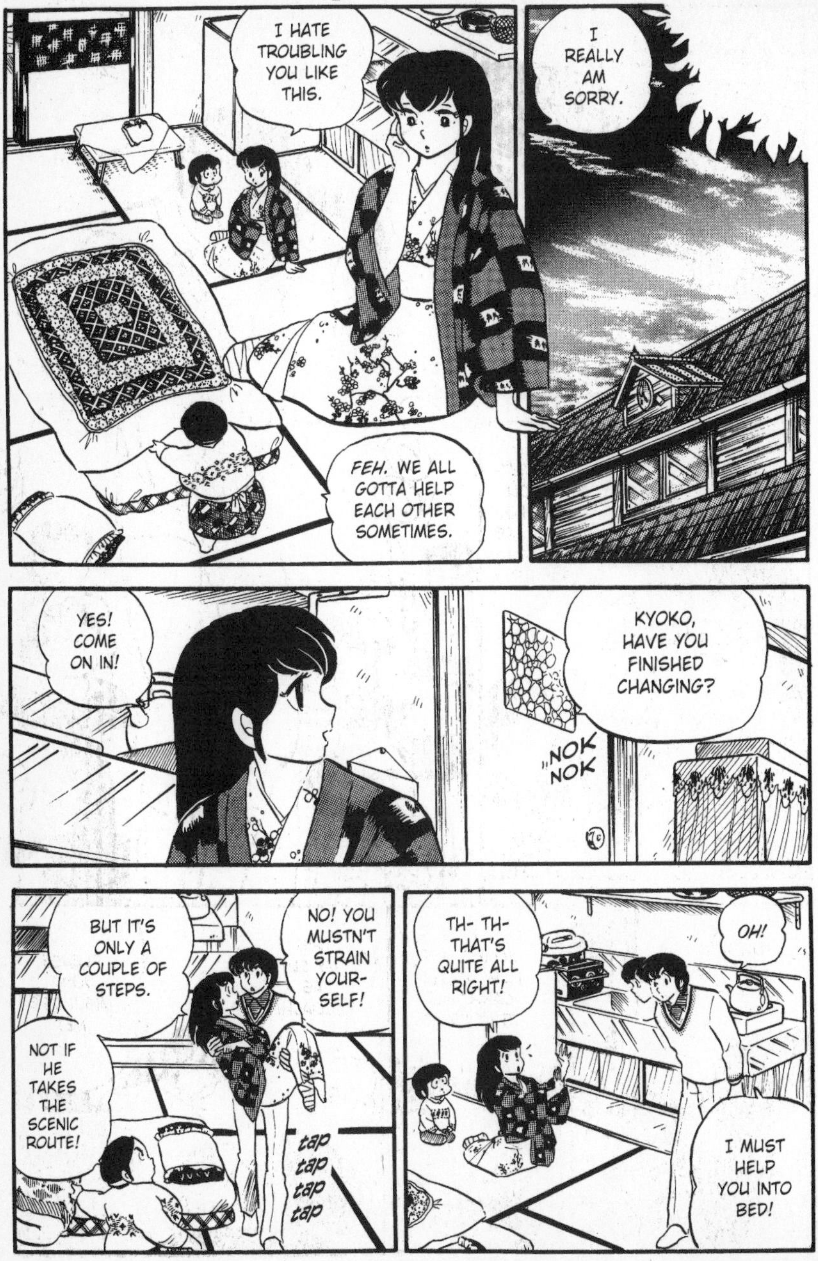

I REALLY AM SORRY.
I HATE TROUBLING YOU LIKE THIS.
FEH. WE ALL GOTTA HELP EACH OTHER SOMETIMES.
KYOKO, HAVE YOU FINISHED CHANGING?
NOK NOK
YES! COME ON IN!
OH!
I MUST HELP YOU INTO BED!
TH- TH- THAT'S QUITE ALL RIGHT!
NO! YOU MUSTN'T STRAIN YOUR-SELF!
BUT IT'S ONLY A COUPLE OF STEPS.
NOT IF HE TAKES THE SCENIC ROUTE!
tap tap tap tap

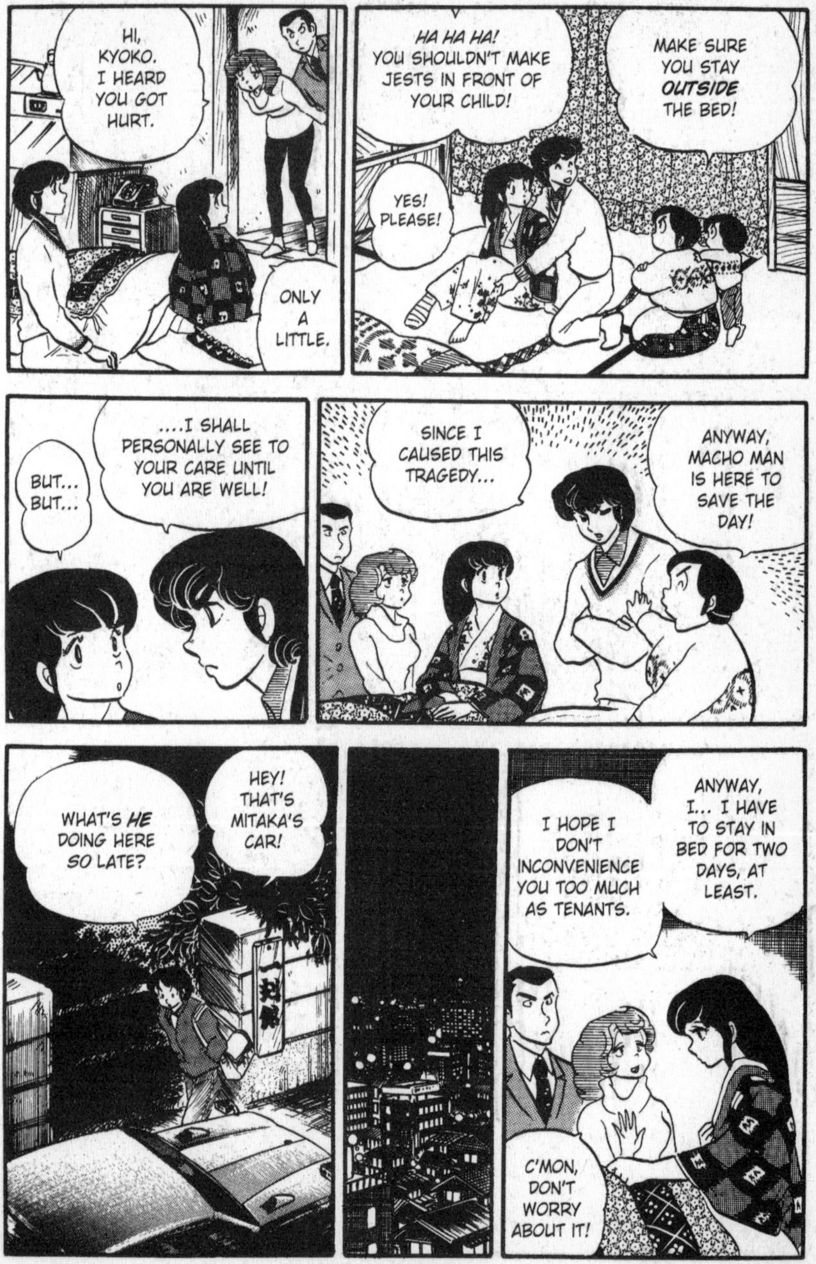
MAKE SURE YOU STAY **OUTSIDE** THE BED!
HA HA HA! YOU SHOULDN'T MAKE JESTS IN FRONT OF YOUR CHILD!
YES! PLEASE!
HI, KYOKO. I HEARD YOU GOT HURT.
ONLY A LITTLE.
ANYWAY, MACHO MAN IS HERE TO SAVE THE DAY!
SINCE I CAUSED THIS TRAGEDY...
....I SHALL PERSONALLY SEE TO YOUR CARE UNTIL YOU ARE WELL!
BUT... BUT...
ANYWAY, I... I HAVE TO STAY IN BED FOR TWO DAYS, AT LEAST.
I HOPE I DON'T INCONVENIENCE YOU TOO MUCH AS TENANTS.
C'MON, DON'T WORRY ABOUT IT!
HEY! THAT'S MITAKA'S CAR!
WHAT'S *HE* DOING HERE *SO LATE?*

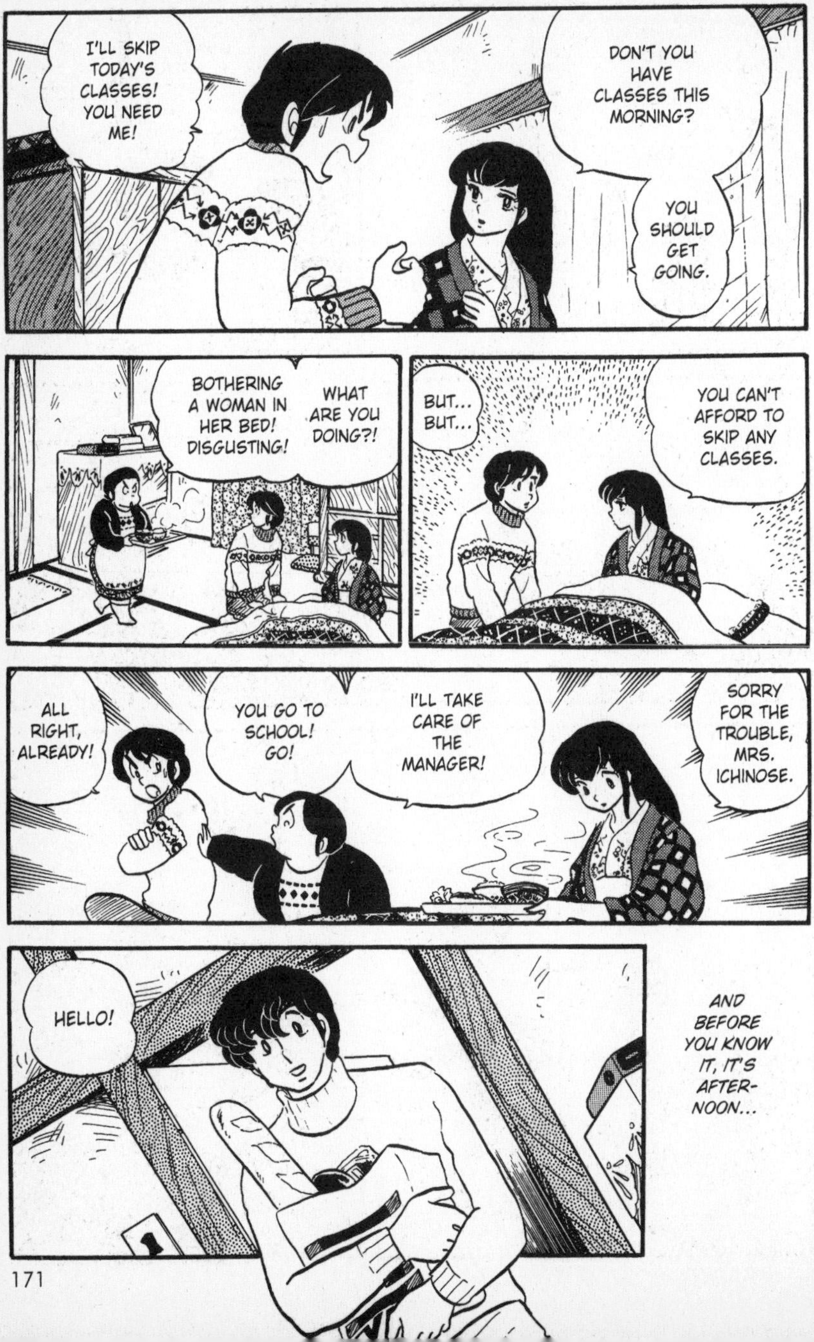
DON'T YOU HAVE CLASSES THIS MORNING?
YOU SHOULD GET GOING.
I'LL SKIP TODAY'S CLASSES! YOU NEED ME!
YOU CAN'T AFFORD TO SKIP ANY CLASSES.
BUT... BUT...
WHAT ARE YOU DOING?!
BOTHERING A WOMAN IN HER BED! DISGUSTING!
SORRY FOR THE TROUBLE, MRS. ICHINOSE.
I'LL TAKE CARE OF THE MANAGER!
YOU GO TO SCHOOL! GO!
ALL RIGHT, ALREADY!
AND BEFORE YOU KNOW IT, IT'S AFTER-NOON...
HELLO!

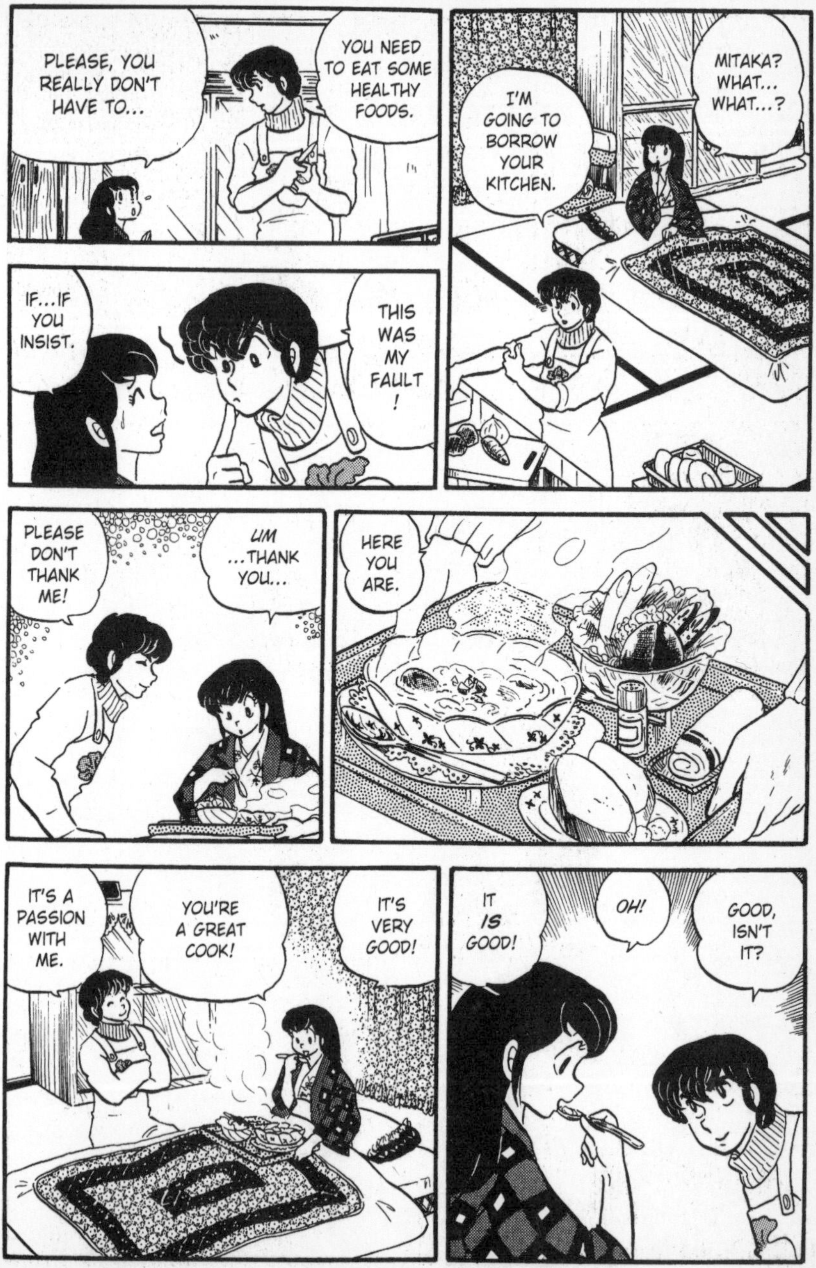
MITAKA? WHAT... WHAT...?
I'M GOING TO BORROW YOUR KITCHEN.
YOU NEED TO EAT SOME HEALTHY FOODS.
PLEASE, YOU REALLY DON'T HAVE TO...
THIS WAS MY FAULT!
IF...IF YOU INSIST.
HERE YOU ARE.
UM ...THANK YOU...
PLEASE DON'T THANK ME!
GOOD, ISN'T IT?
OH!
IT *IS* GOOD!
IT'S VERY GOOD!
YOU'RE A GREAT COOK!
IT'S A PASSION WITH ME.

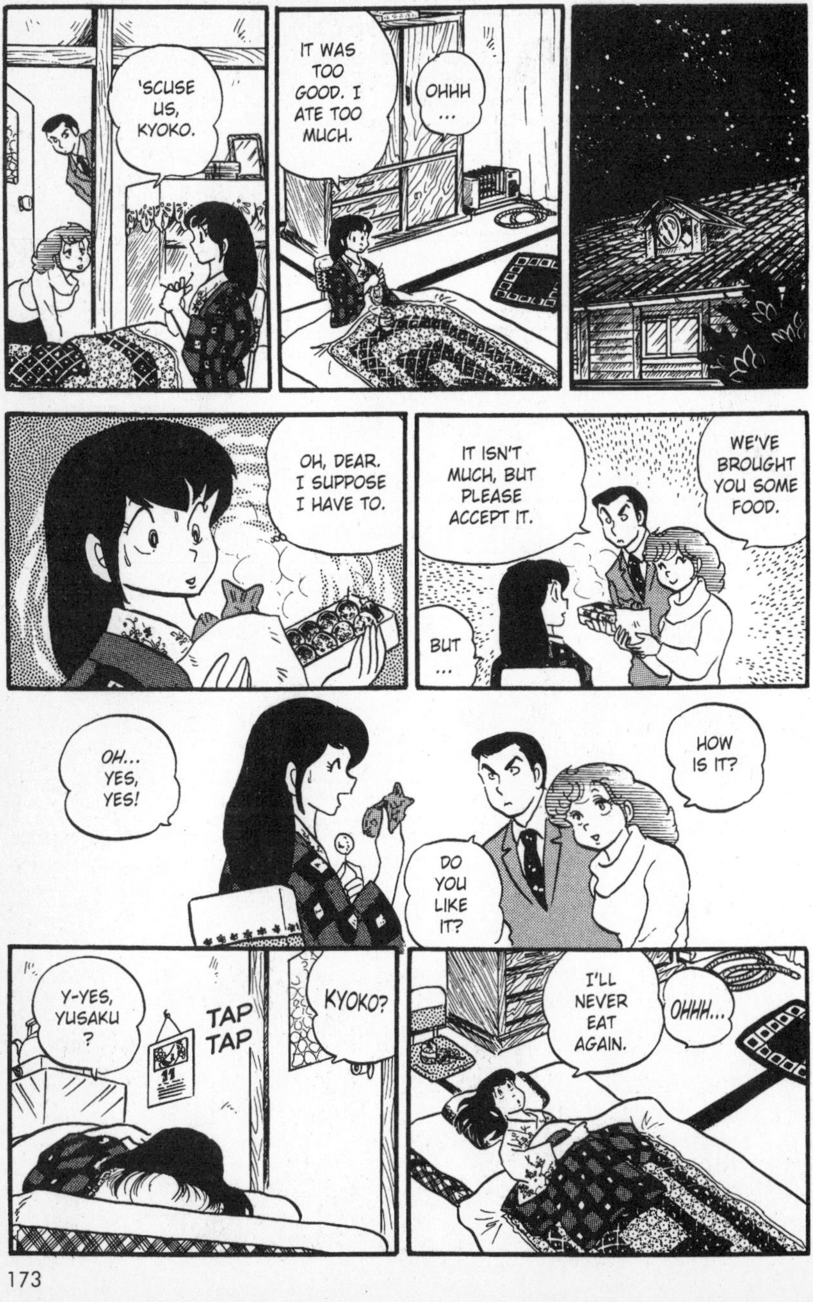
OHHH ...
IT WAS TOO GOOD. I ATE TOO MUCH.
'SCUSE US, KYOKO.
WE'VE BROUGHT YOU SOME FOOD.
IT ISN'T MUCH, BUT PLEASE ACCEPT IT.
BUT ...
OH, DEAR. I SUPPOSE I HAVE TO.
HOW IS IT?
DO YOU LIKE IT?
OH... YES, YES!
OHHH...
I'LL NEVER EAT AGAIN.
KYOKO?
TAP TAP
Y-YES, YUSAKU ?

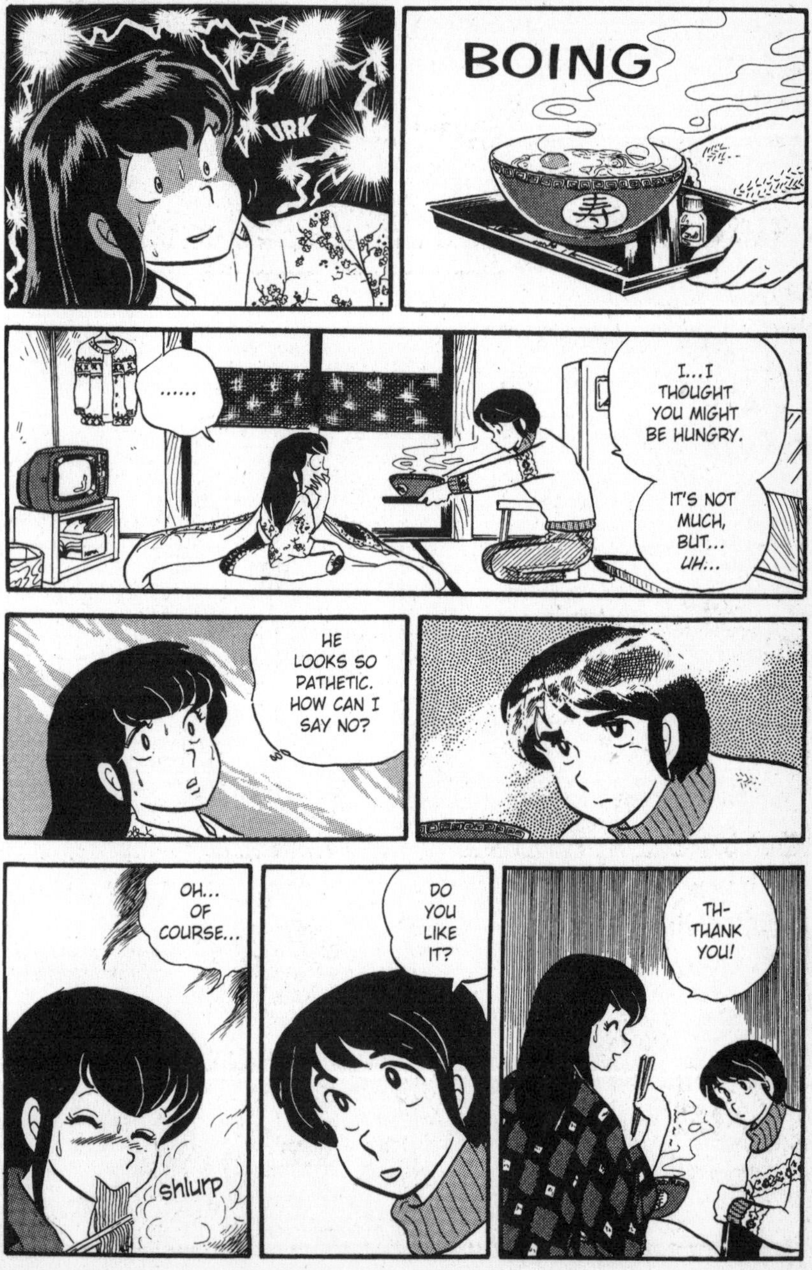
BOING
URK
I...I THOUGHT YOU MIGHT BE HUNGRY.
IT'S NOT MUCH, BUT... UH...
......
HE LOOKS SO PATHETIC. HOW CAN I SAY NO?
TH- THANK YOU!
DO YOU LIKE IT?
OH... OF COURSE...
shlurp

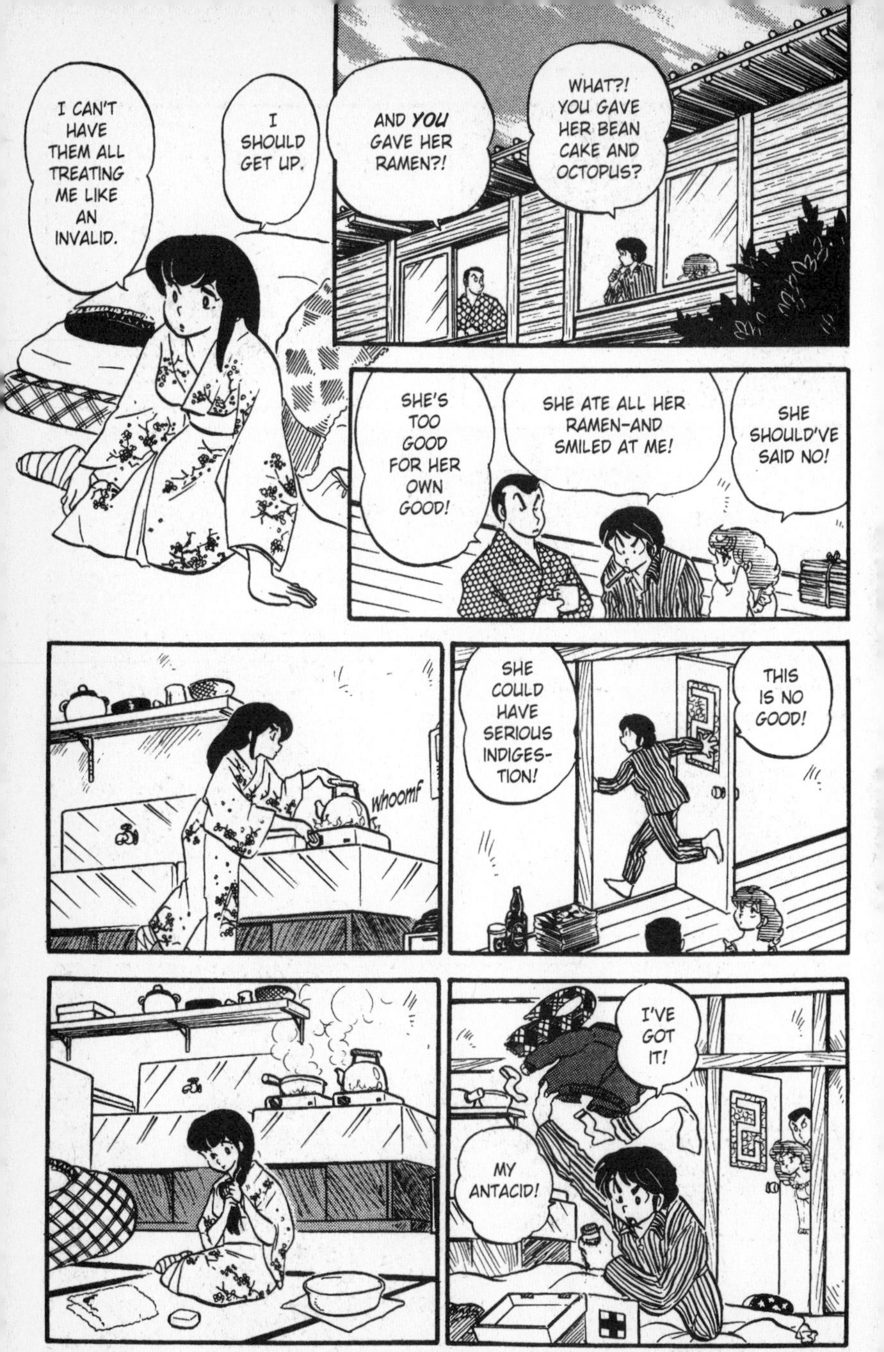
WHAT?! YOU GAVE HER BEAN CAKE AND OCTOPUS?
AND *YOU* GAVE HER RAMEN?!
SHE SHOULD'VE SAID NO!
SHE ATE ALL HER RAMEN–AND SMILED AT ME!
SHE'S TOO GOOD FOR HER OWN GOOD!
I SHOULD GET UP.
I CAN'T HAVE THEM ALL TREATING ME LIKE AN INVALID.
THIS IS NO GOOD!
SHE COULD HAVE SERIOUS INDIGES-TION!
whoomf
I'VE GOT IT!
MY ANTACID!

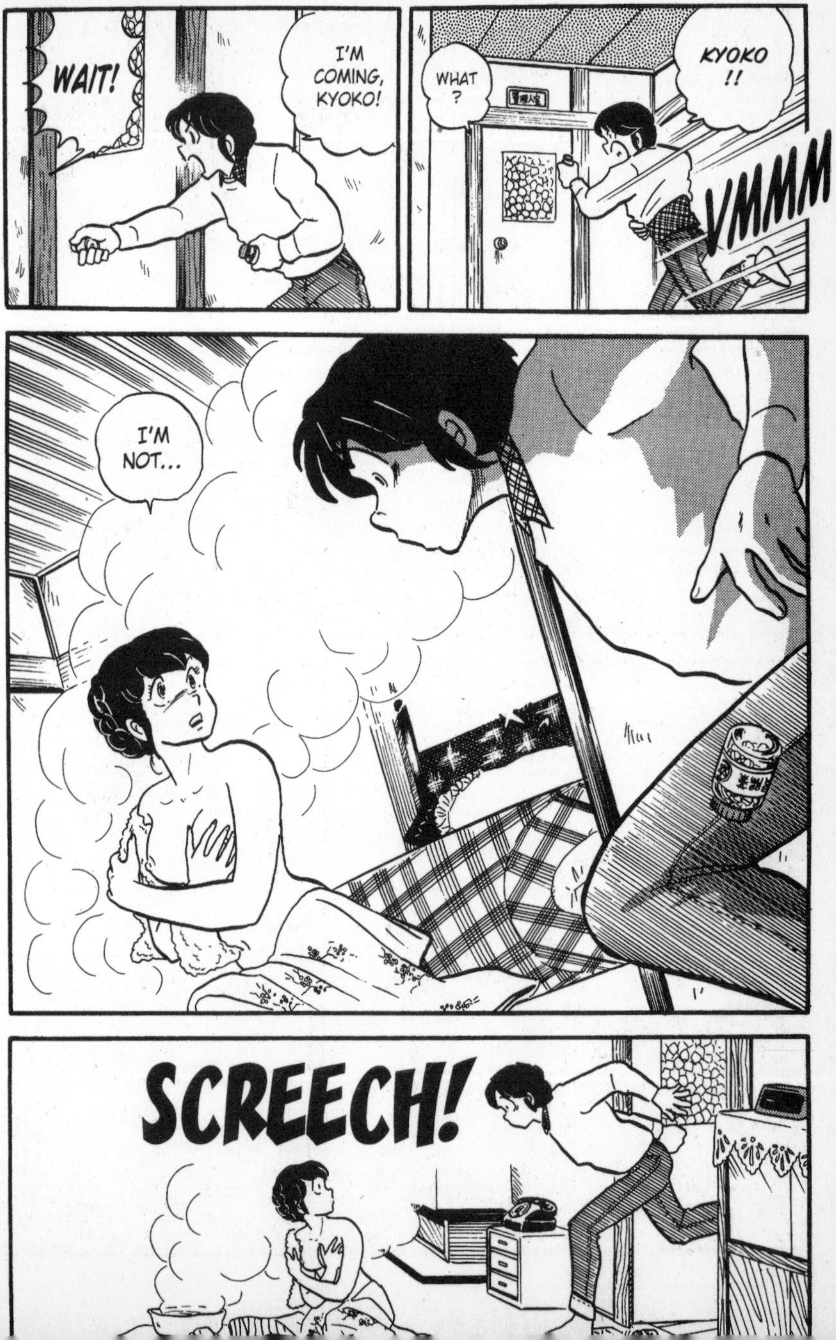
KYOKO !!
WHAT ?
VMMM
I'M COMING, KYOKO!
WAIT!
I'M NOT...
SCREECH!

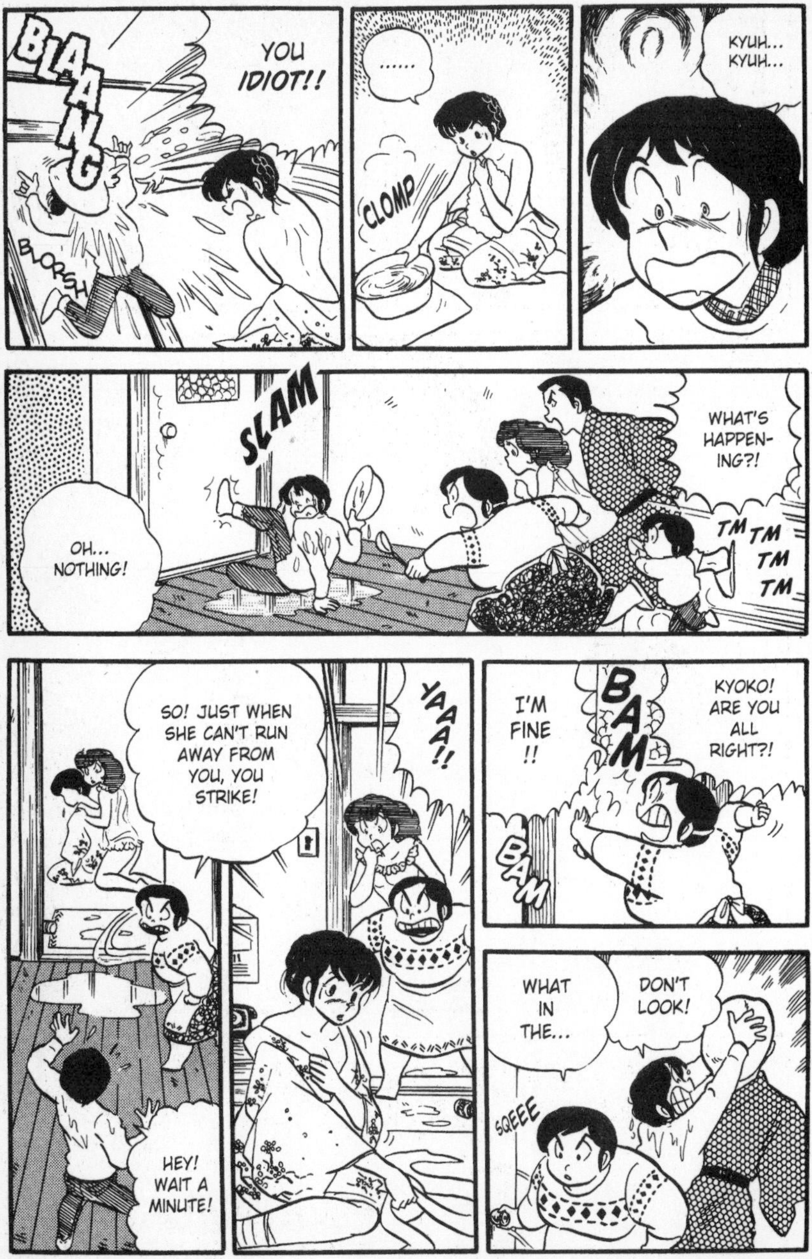

KYUH... KYUH...
......
CLOMP
YOU IDIOT!!
BLAANG
BLORSH
WHAT'S HAPPEN-ING?!
TM TM TM TM
SLAM
OH... NOTHING!
KYOKO! ARE YOU ALL RIGHT?!
BAM
I'M FINE!!
BAM
DON'T LOOK!
WHAT IN THE...
SQEEE
YAAAA!!
SO! JUST WHEN SHE CAN'T RUN AWAY FROM YOU, YOU STRIKE!
HEY! WAIT A MINUTE!

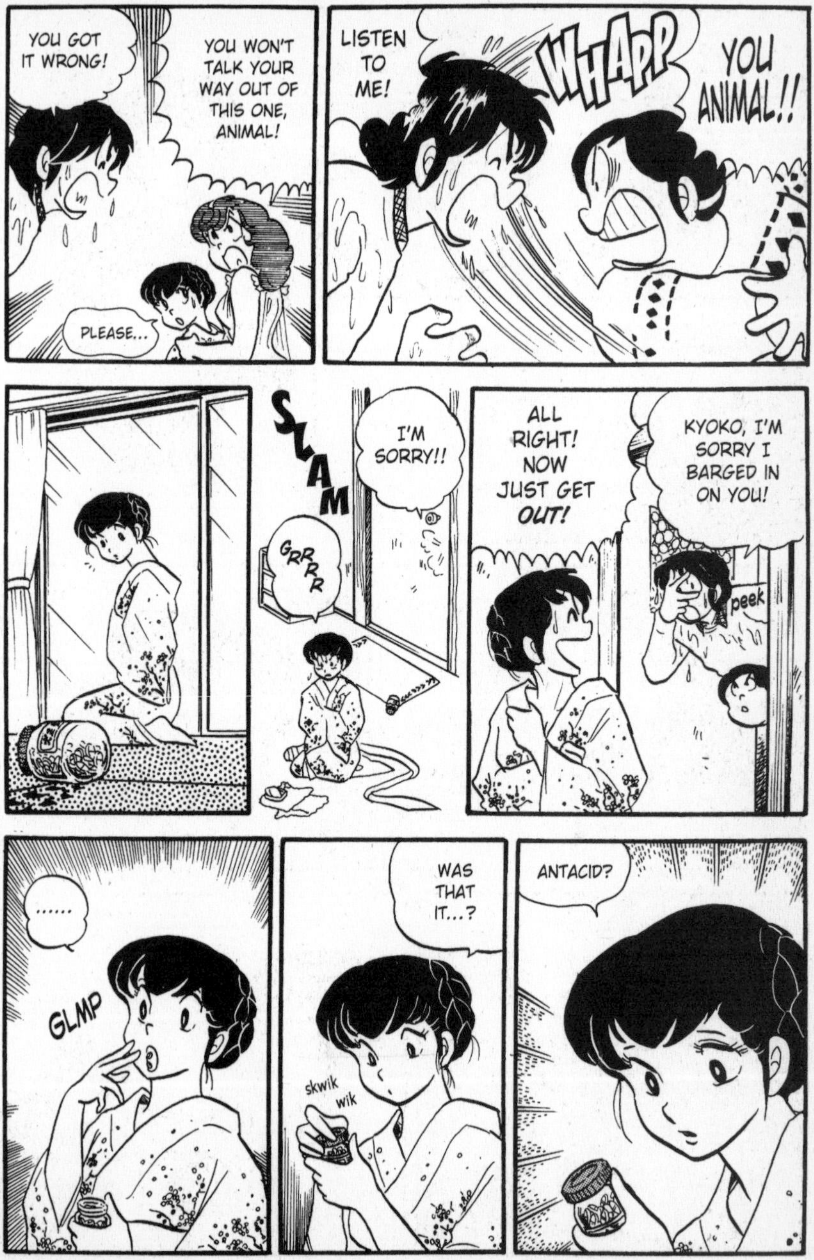
YOU ANIMAL!!
WHAPP
LISTEN TO ME!
YOU WON'T TALK YOUR WAY OUT OF THIS ONE, ANIMAL!
YOU GOT IT WRONG!
PLEASE...
KYOKO, I'M SORRY I BARGED IN ON YOU!
ALL RIGHT! NOW JUST GET OUT!
peek
I'M SORRY!!
SLAM
GRRRR
ANTACID?
WAS THAT IT...?
skwik wik
......
GLMP

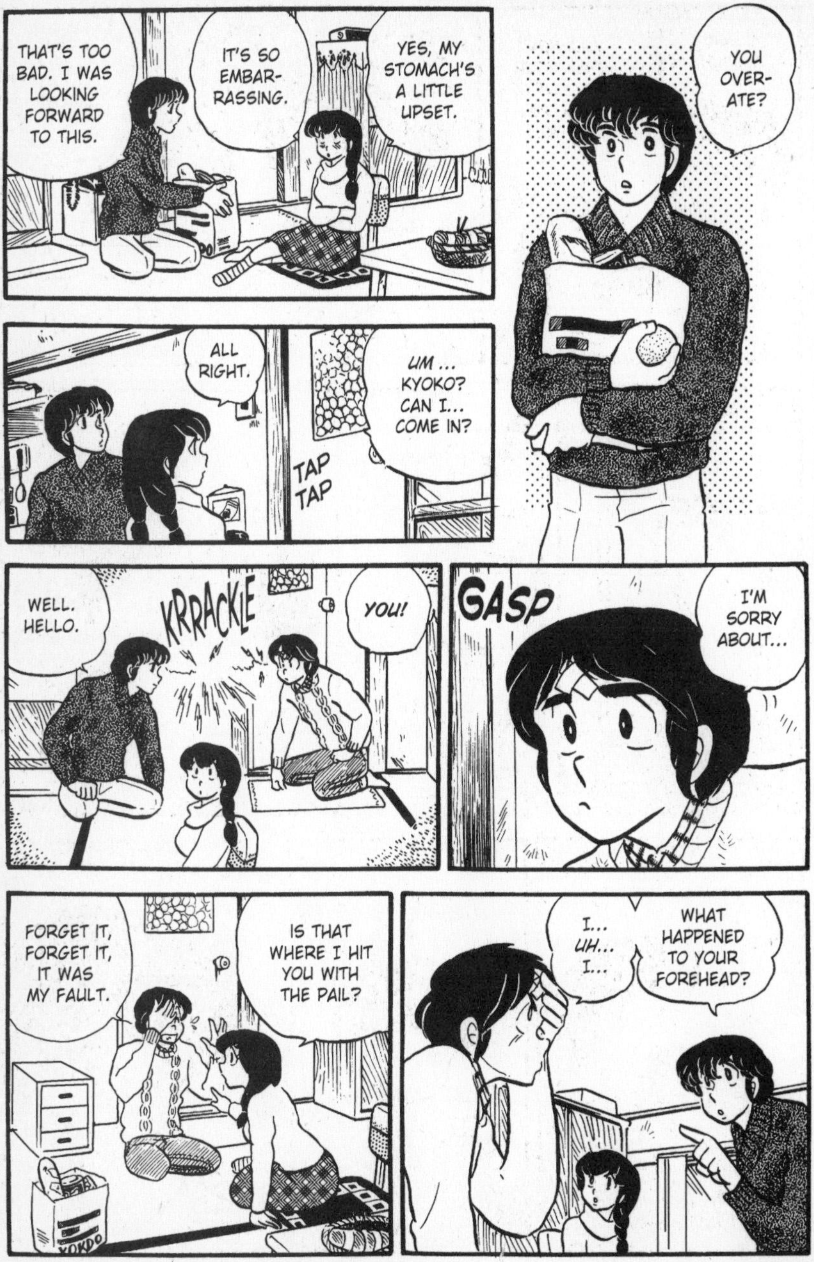
YOU OVER-ATE?
YES, MY STOMACH'S A LITTLE UPSET.
IT'S SO EMBAR-RASSING.
THAT'S TOO BAD. I WAS LOOKING FORWARD TO THIS.
UM ... KYOKO? CAN I... COME IN?
TAP TAP
ALL RIGHT.
GASP
I'M SORRY ABOUT...
YOU!
KRRACKLE
WELL. HELLO.
WHAT HAPPENED TO YOUR FOREHEAD?
I... UH... I...
IS THAT WHERE I HIT YOU WITH THE PAIL?
FORGET IT, FORGET IT, IT WAS MY FAULT.
YOKDO

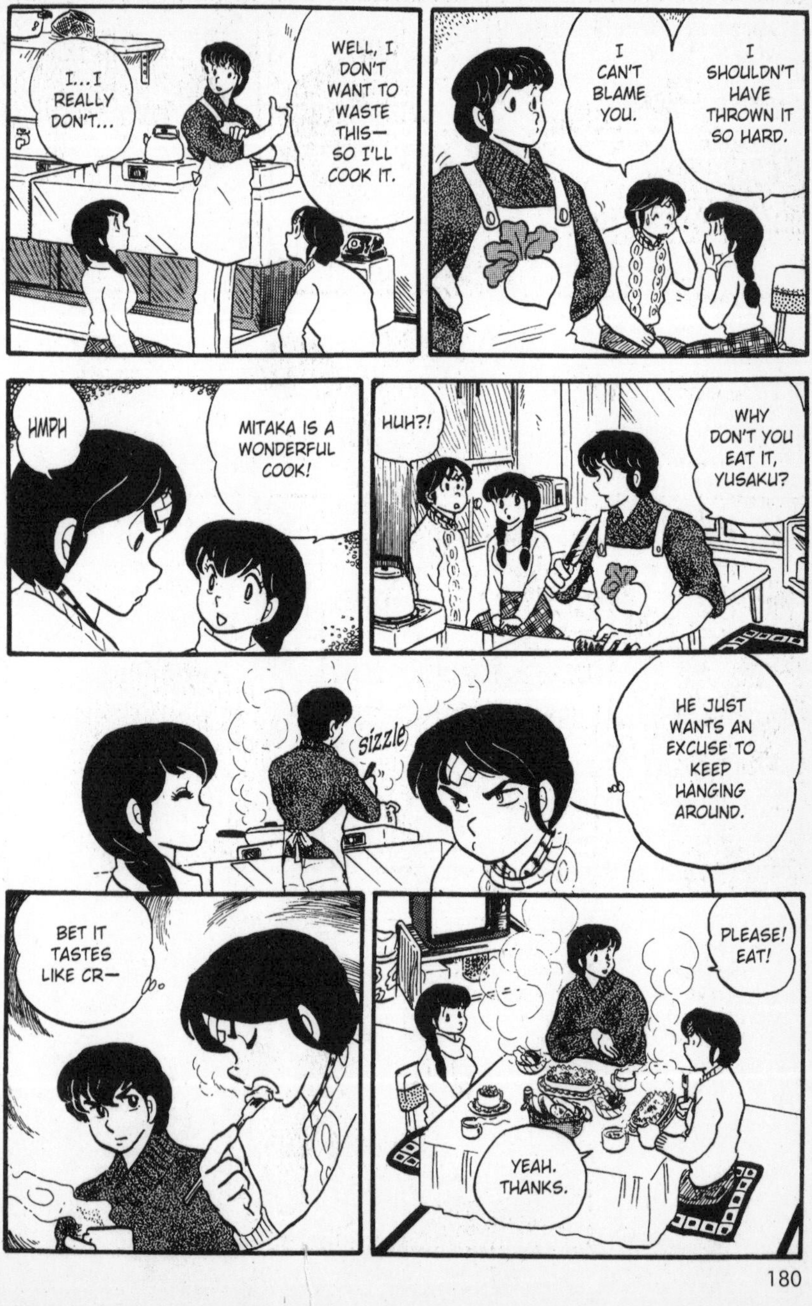
I SHOULDN'T HAVE THROWN IT SO HARD.
I CAN'T BLAME YOU.
WELL, I DON'T WANT TO WASTE THIS— SO I'LL COOK IT.
I...I REALLY DON'T...
WHY DON'T YOU EAT IT, YUSAKU?
HUH?!
MITAKA IS A WONDERFUL COOK!
HMPH
HE JUST WANTS AN EXCUSE TO KEEP HANGING AROUND.
sizzle
PLEASE! EAT!
YEAH. THANKS.
BET IT TASTES LIKE CR—

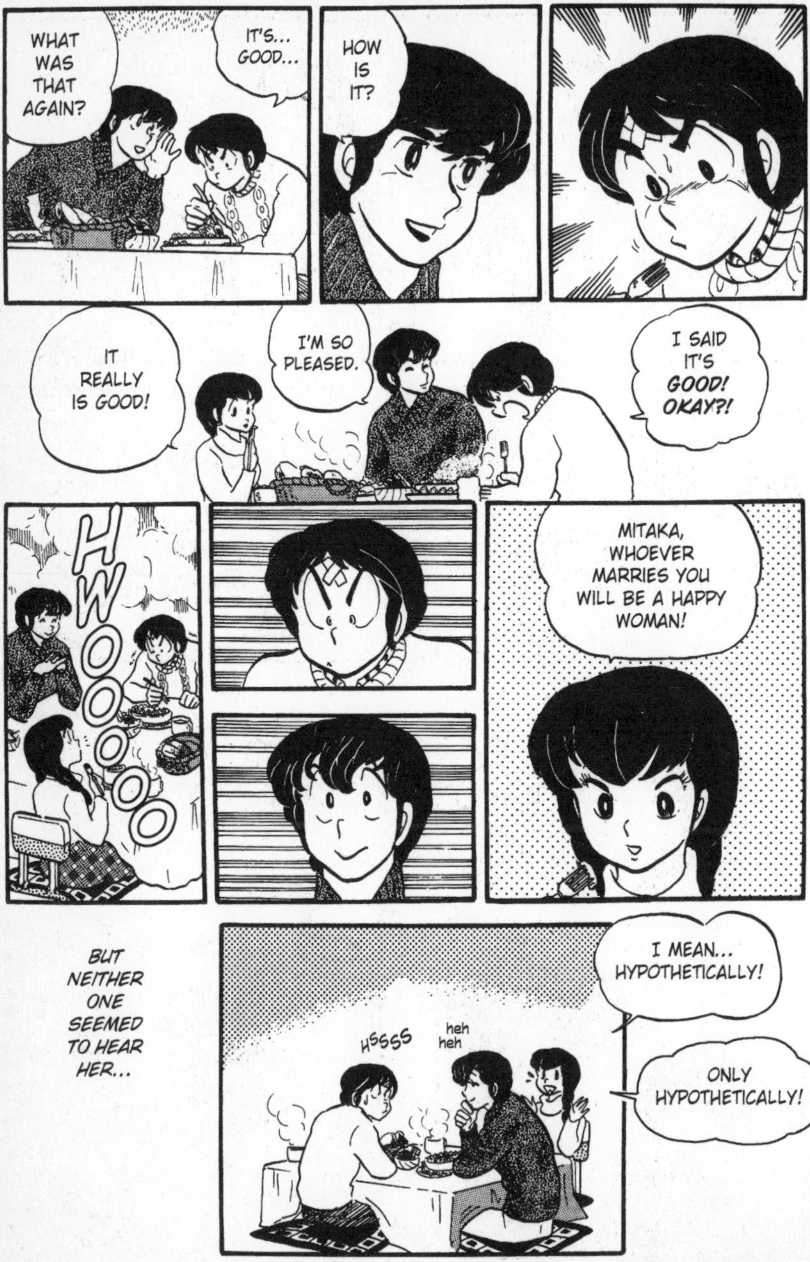
HOW IS IT?
IT'S... GOOD...
WHAT WAS THAT AGAIN?
I SAID IT'S GOOD! OKAY?!
I'M SO PLEASED.
IT REALLY IS GOOD!
MITAKA, WHOEVER MARRIES YOU WILL BE A HAPPY WOMAN!
HWOOOOOOO
I MEAN... HYPOTHETICALLY!
ONLY HYPOTHETICALLY!
heh heh
HSSSS
BUT NEITHER ONE SEEMED TO HEAR HER...

PART TEN

SHADOWS ON THE HEART

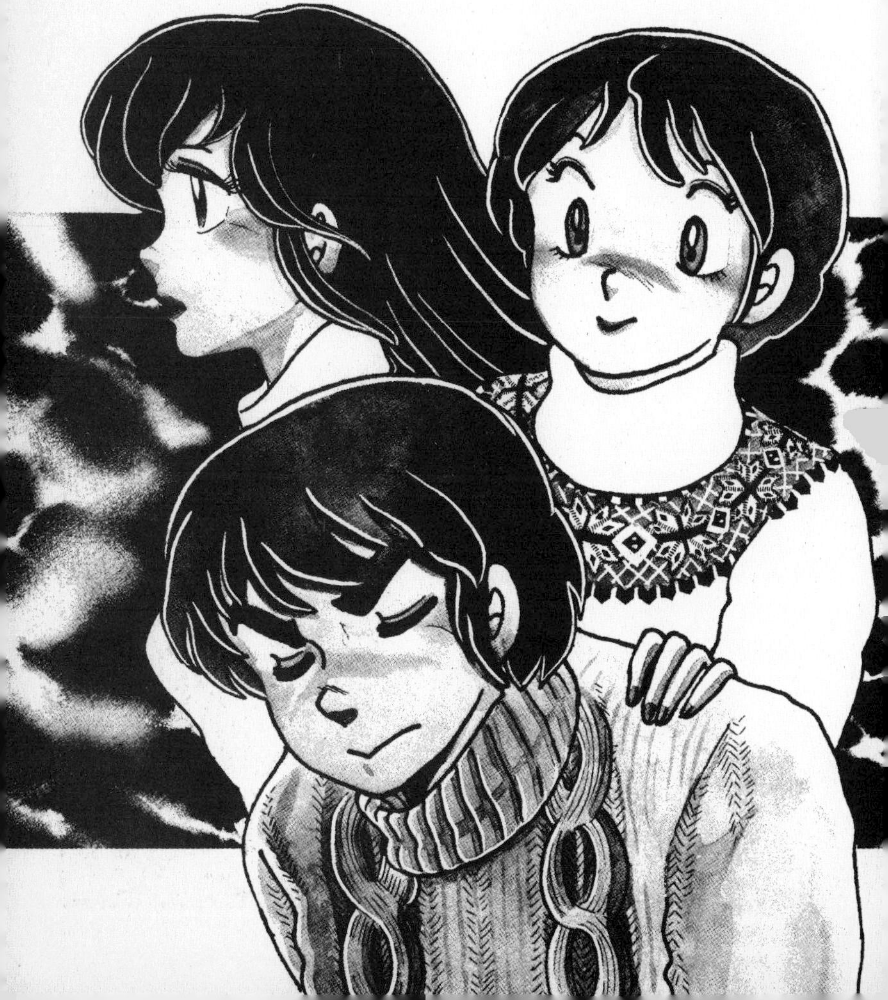

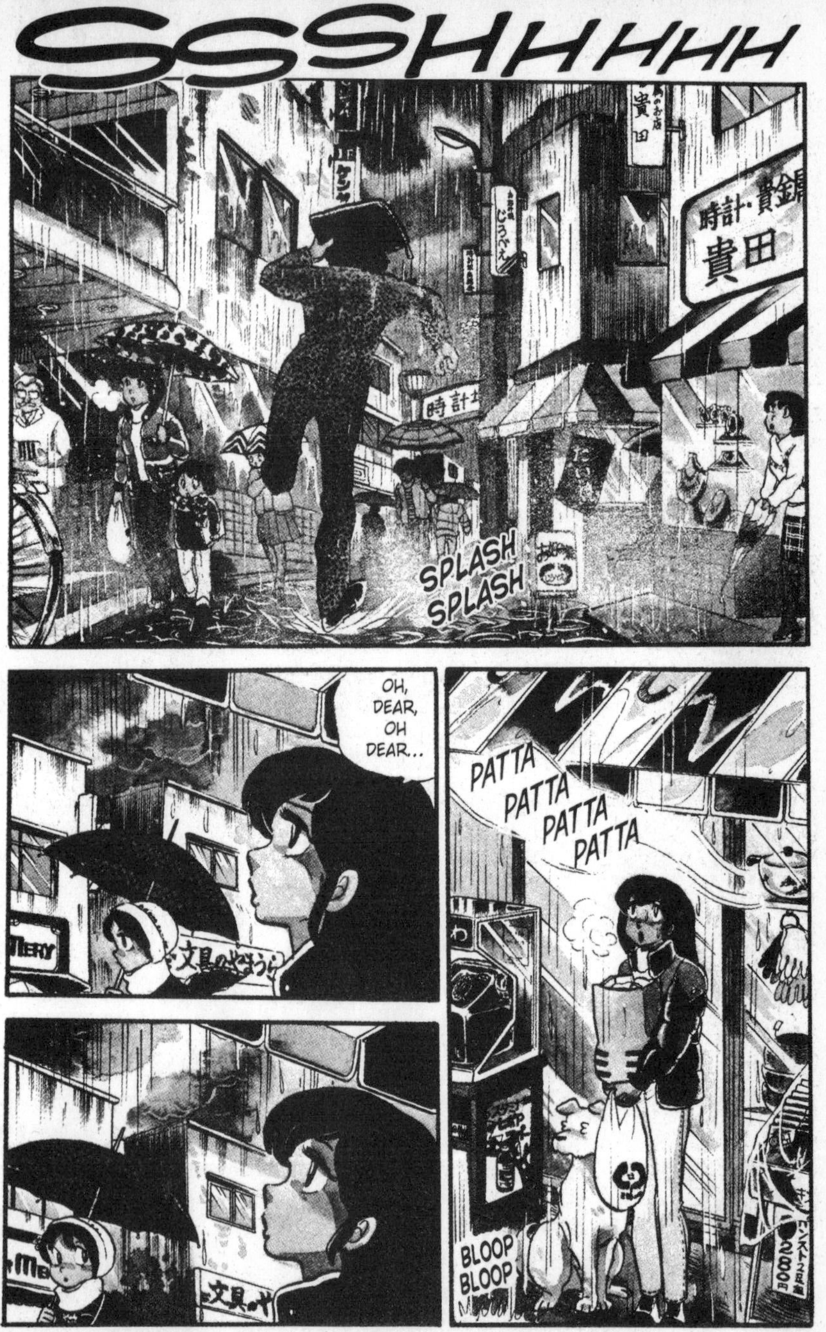
SSSHHHH
SPLASH SPLASH
PATTA PATTA PATTA PATTA
BLOOP BLOOP
OH, DEAR, OH DEAR...

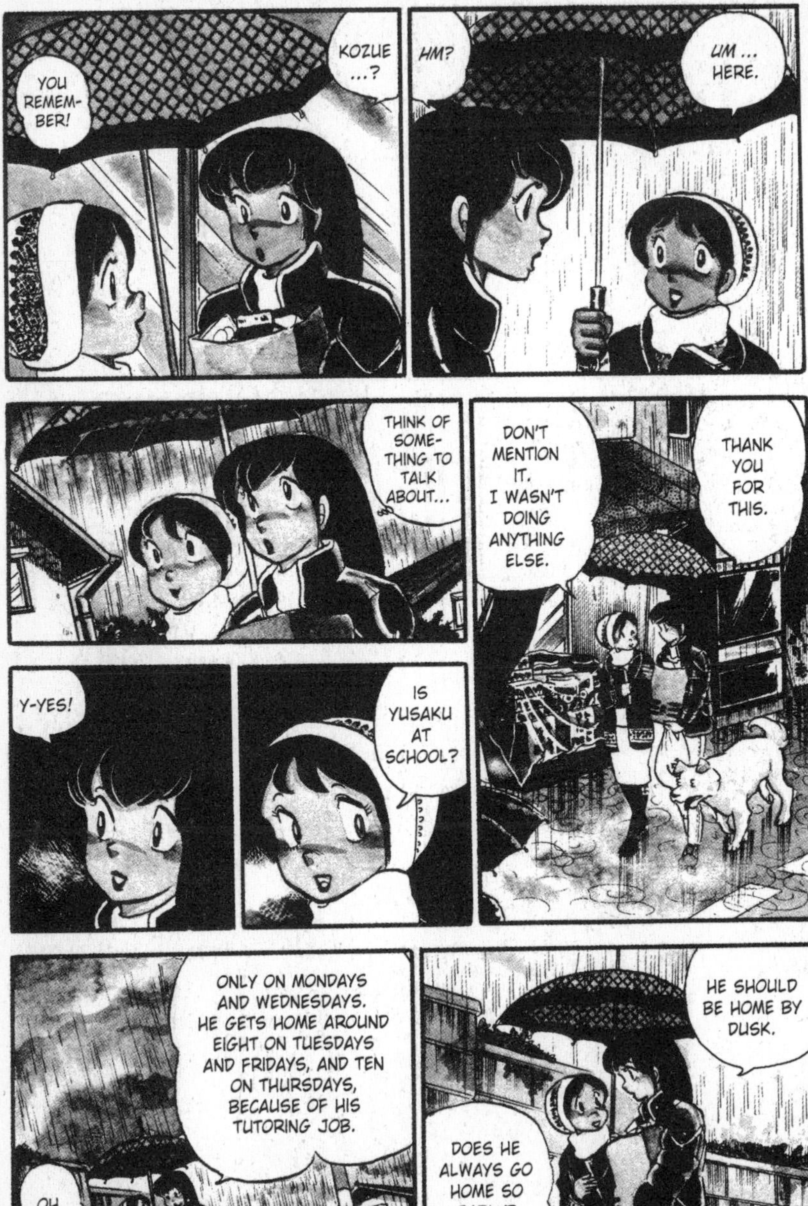
UM ... HERE.
HM?
KOZUE ...?
YOU REMEMBER!
THANK YOU FOR THIS.
DON'T MENTION IT. I WASN'T DOING ANYTHING ELSE.
THINK OF SOMETHING TO TALK ABOUT...
IS YUSAKU AT SCHOOL?
Y-YES!
HE SHOULD BE HOME BY DUSK.
DOES HE ALWAYS GO HOME SO EARLY?
ONLY ON MONDAYS AND WEDNESDAYS. HE GETS HOME AROUND EIGHT ON TUESDAYS AND FRIDAYS, AND TEN ON THURSDAYS, BECAUSE OF HIS TUTORING JOB.
OH.

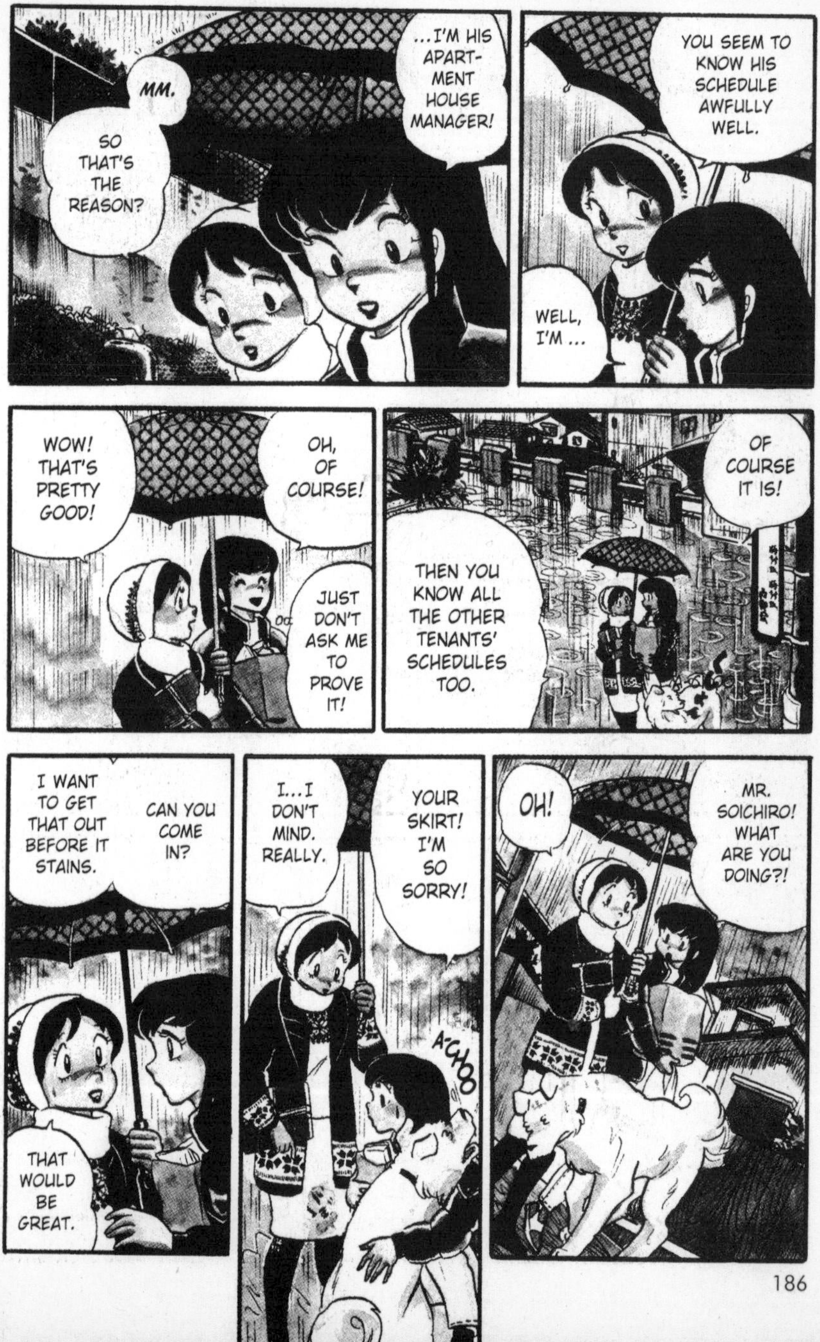
YOU SEEM TO KNOW HIS SCHEDULE AWFULLY WELL.
WELL, I'M ...
...I'M HIS APART-MENT HOUSE MANAGER!
MM.
SO THAT'S THE REASON?
OF COURSE IT IS!
THEN YOU KNOW ALL THE OTHER TENANTS' SCHEDULES TOO.
OH, OF COURSE!
WOW! THAT'S PRETTY GOOD!
JUST DON'T ASK ME TO PROVE IT!
MR. SOICHIRO! WHAT ARE YOU DOING?!
OH!
YOUR SKIRT! I'M SO SORRY!
I...I DON'T MIND. REALLY.
A-CHOO
CAN YOU COME IN?
I WANT TO GET THAT OUT BEFORE IT STAINS.
THAT WOULD BE GREAT.

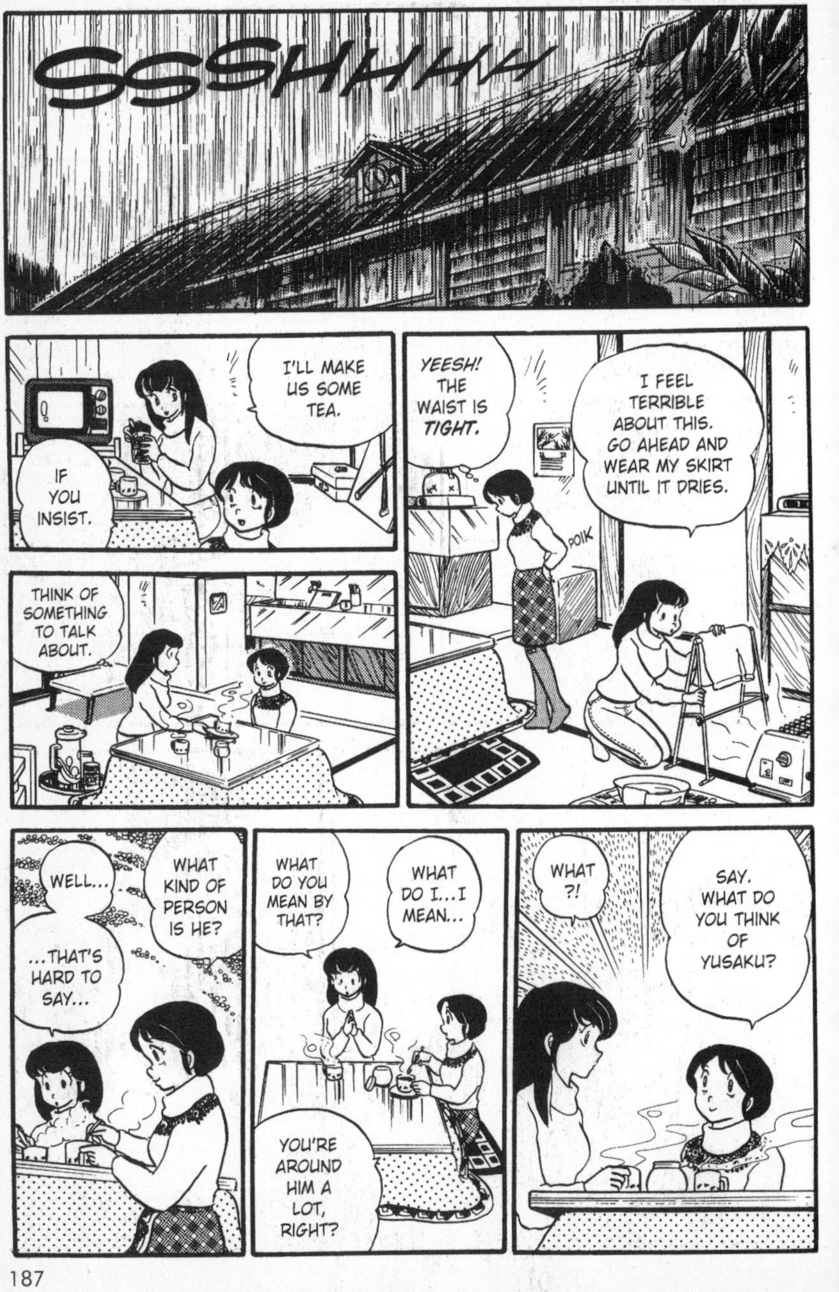
SSSHHHH
I FEEL TERRIBLE ABOUT THIS. GO AHEAD AND WEAR MY SKIRT UNTIL IT DRIES.
YEESH! THE WAIST IS *TIGHT.*
POIK
I'LL MAKE US SOME TEA.
IF YOU INSIST.
THINK OF SOMETHING TO TALK ABOUT.
SAY. WHAT DO YOU THINK OF YUSAKU?
WHAT ?!
WHAT DO I...I MEAN...
WHAT DO YOU MEAN BY THAT?
YOU'RE AROUND HIM A LOT, RIGHT?
WHAT KIND OF PERSON IS HE?
WELL...
...THAT'S HARD TO SAY...

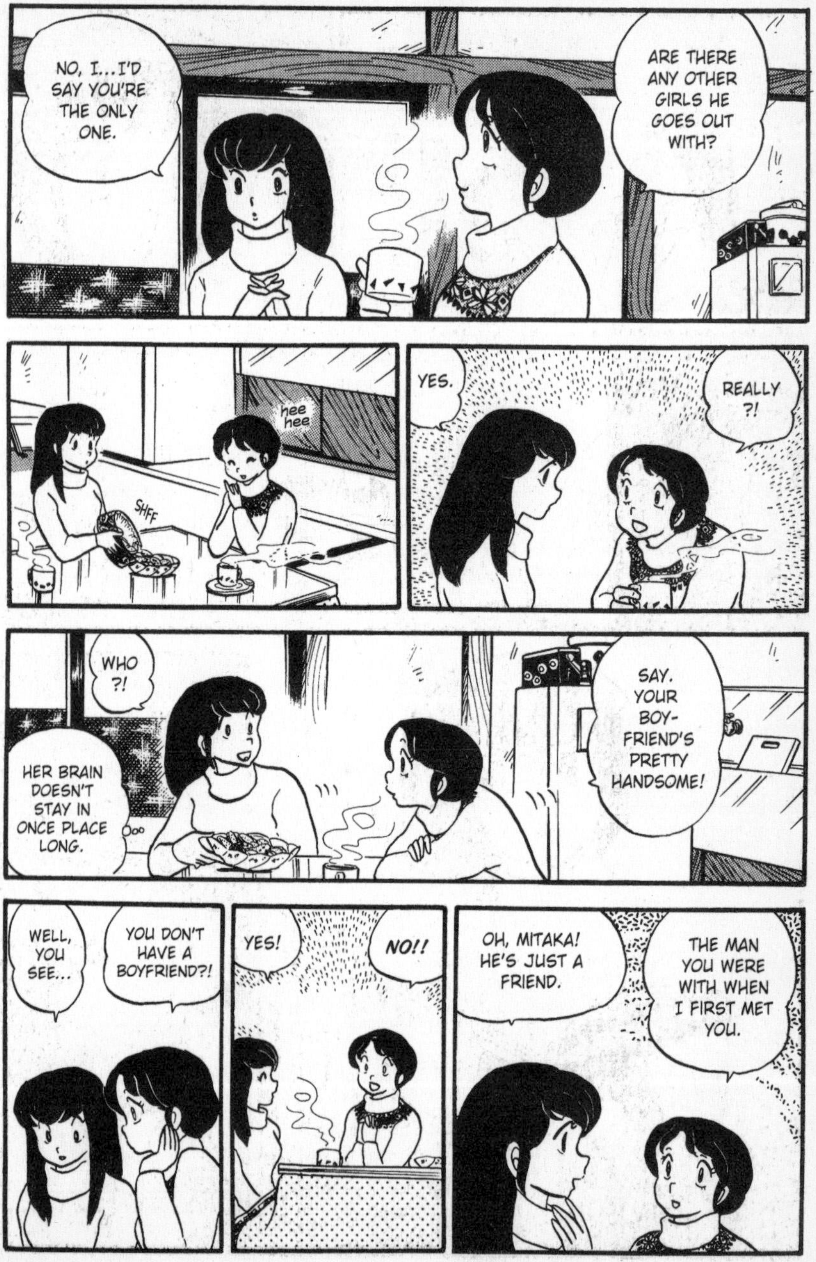
ARE THERE ANY OTHER GIRLS HE GOES OUT WITH?
NO, I...I'D SAY YOU'RE THE ONLY ONE.
REALLY ?!
YES.
hee hee
SHFF
SAY. YOUR BOY-FRIEND'S PRETTY HANDSOME!
WHO ?!
HER BRAIN DOESN'T STAY IN ONCE PLACE LONG.
Ooo
THE MAN YOU WERE WITH WHEN I FIRST MET YOU.
OH, MITAKA! HE'S JUST A FRIEND.
NO!!
YES!
YOU DON'T HAVE A BOYFRIEND?!
WELL, YOU SEE...

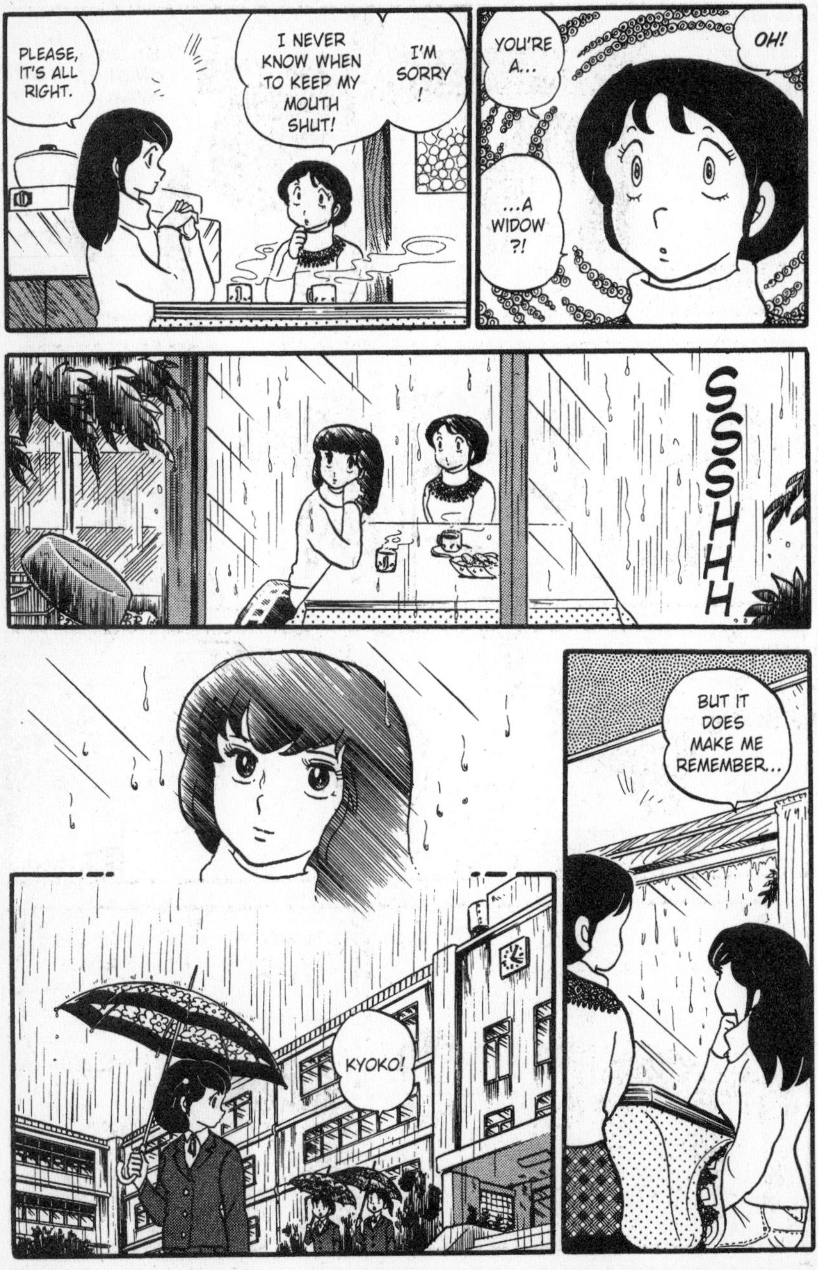
OH!
YOU'RE A...
...A WIDOW ?!
I'M SORRY!
I NEVER KNOW WHEN TO KEEP MY MOUTH SHUT!
PLEASE, IT'S ALL RIGHT.
SSSHHH
BUT IT DOES MAKE ME REMEMBER...
KYOKO!

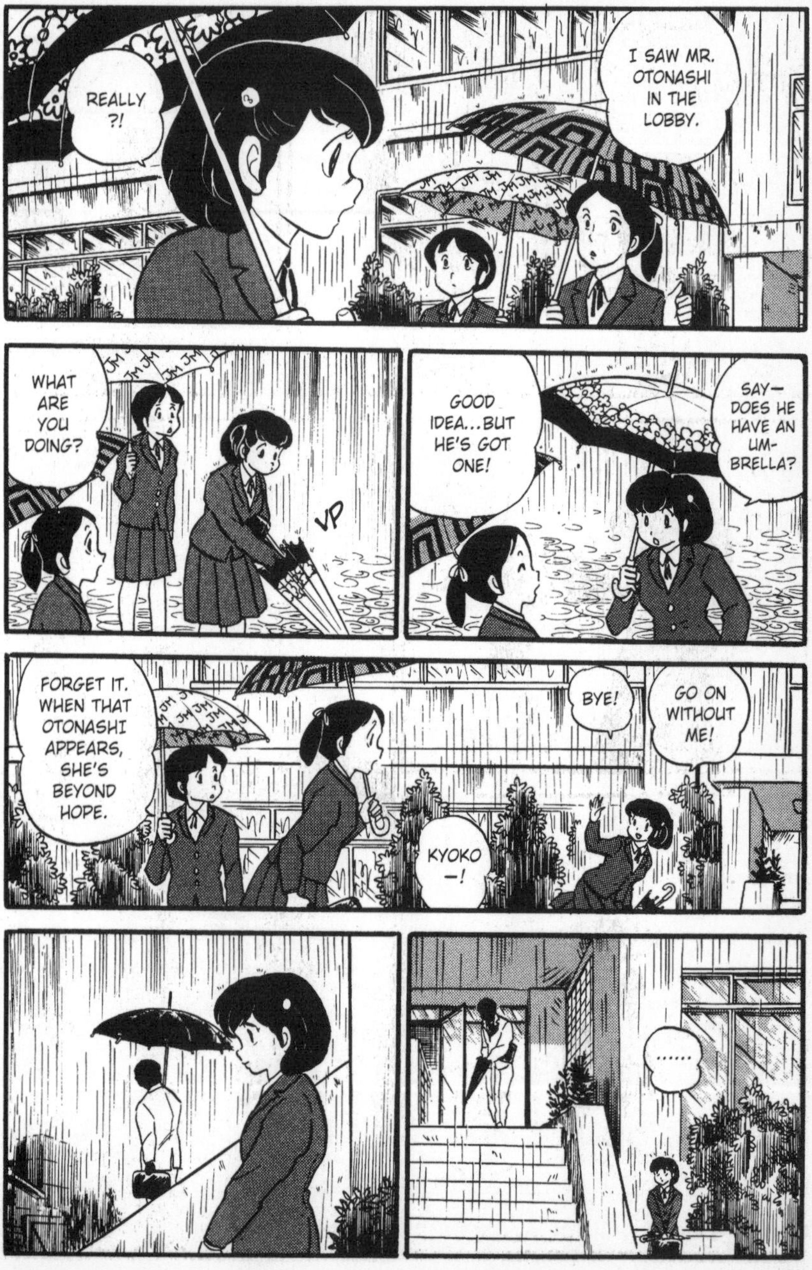

I SAW MR. OTONASHI IN THE LOBBY.
REALLY ?!
SAY— DOES HE HAVE AN UM- BRELLA?
GOOD IDEA...BUT HE'S GOT ONE!
WHAT ARE YOU DOING?
VP
GO ON WITHOUT ME!
BYE!
KYOKO —!
FORGET IT. WHEN THAT OTONASHI APPEARS, SHE'S BEYOND HOPE.
......

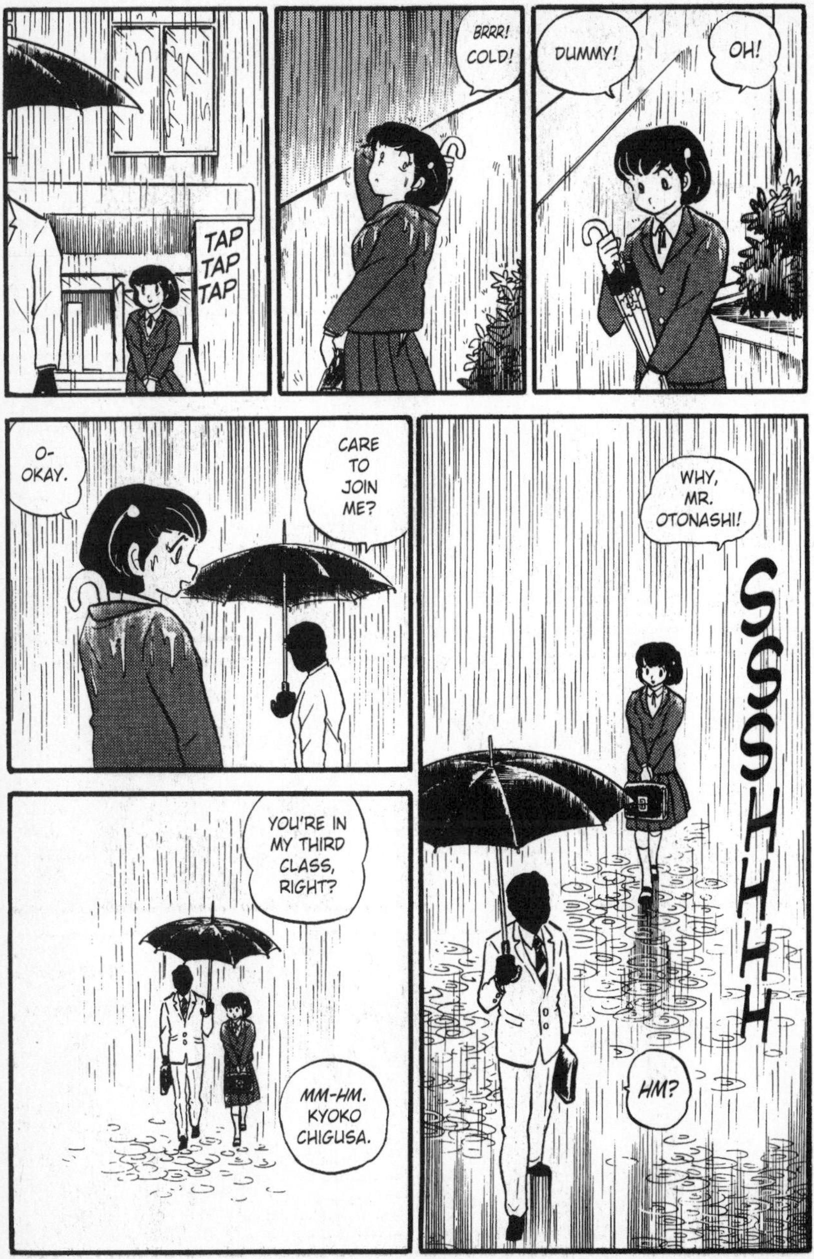
OH!
DUMMY!
BRRR! COLD!
TAP TAP TAP
WHY, MR. OTONASHI!
SSSHHHH
HM?
CARE TO JOIN ME?
O-OKAY.
YOU'RE IN MY THIRD CLASS, RIGHT?
MM-HM. KYOKO CHIGUSA.

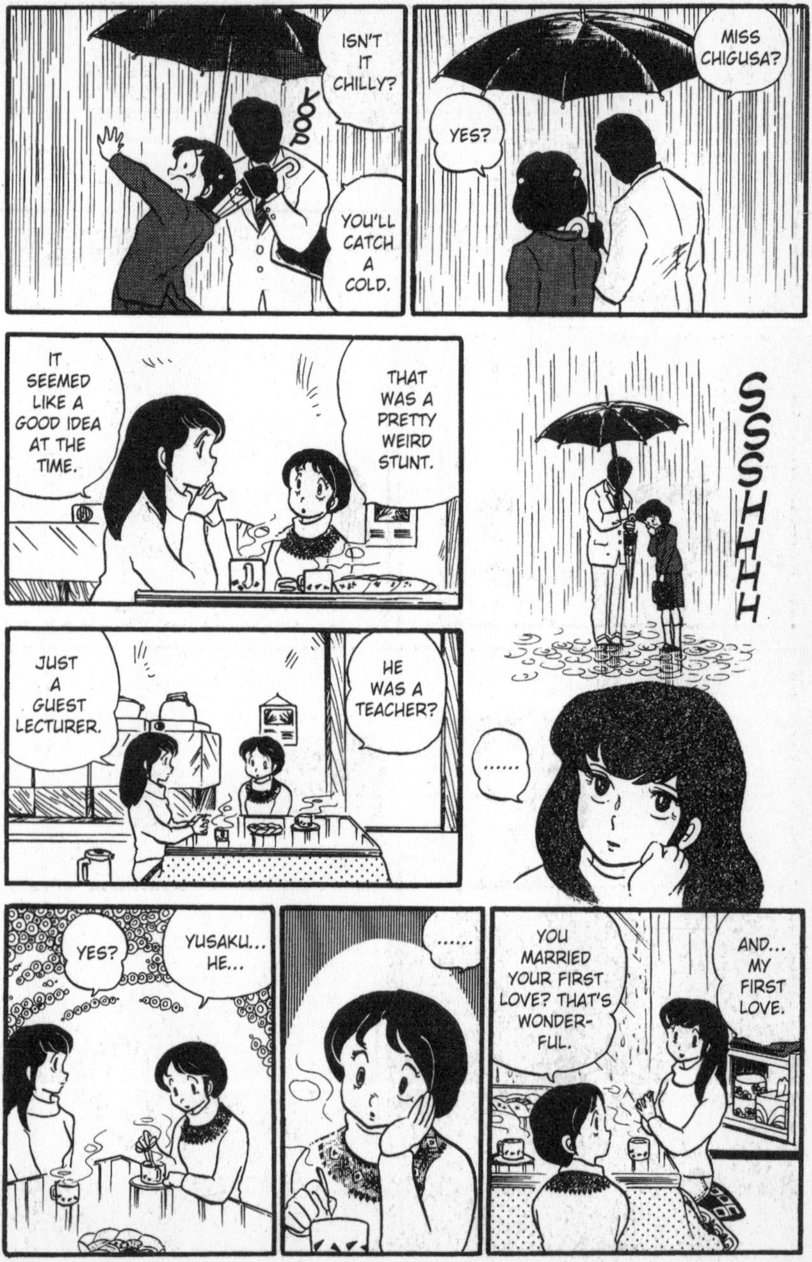
MISS CHIGUSA?
YES?
ISN'T IT CHILLY?
VOOP
YOU'LL CATCH A COLD.
SSSHHHH
......
THAT WAS A PRETTY WEIRD STUNT.
IT SEEMED LIKE A GOOD IDEA AT THE TIME.
HE WAS A TEACHER?
JUST A GUEST LECTURER.
AND... MY FIRST LOVE.
YOU MARRIED YOUR FIRST LOVE? THAT'S WONDERFUL.
......
YUSAKU... HE...
YES?

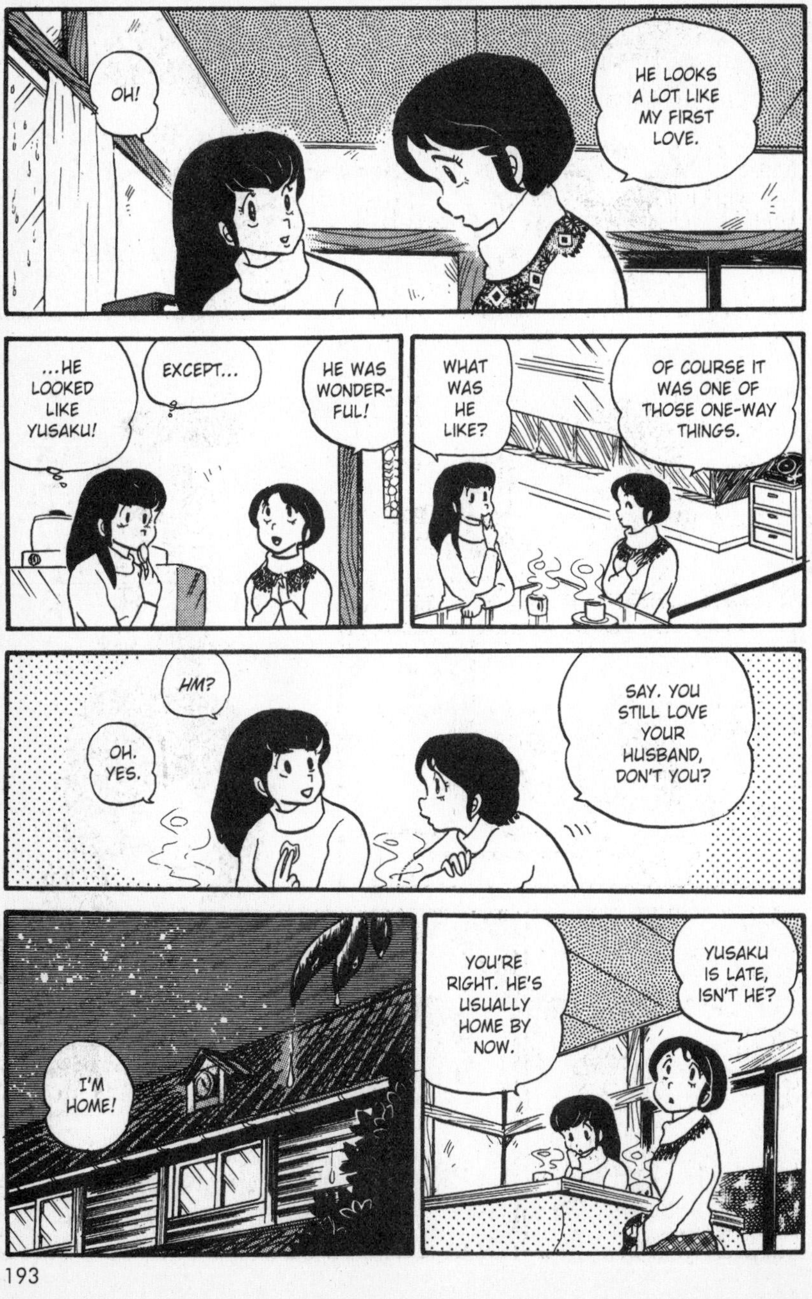
HE LOOKS A LOT LIKE MY FIRST LOVE.
OH!
OF COURSE IT WAS ONE OF THOSE ONE-WAY THINGS.
WHAT WAS HE LIKE?
HE WAS WONDER-FUL!
EXCEPT...
...HE LOOKED LIKE YUSAKU!
SAY. YOU STILL LOVE YOUR HUSBAND, DON'T YOU?
HM?
OH. YES.
YUSAKU IS LATE, ISN'T HE?
YOU'RE RIGHT. HE'S USUALLY HOME BY NOW.
I'M HOME!

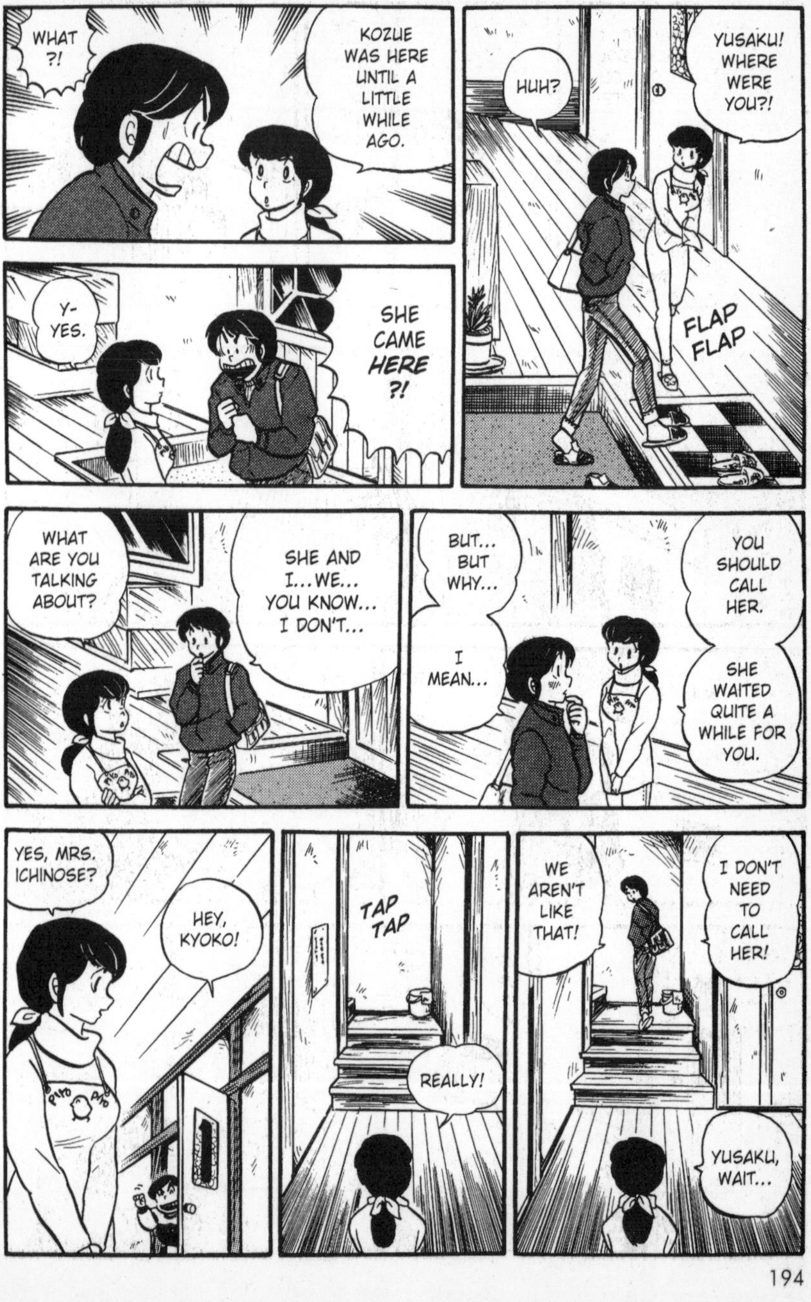
YUSAKU! WHERE WERE YOU?!
HUH?
FLAP FLAP
KOZUE WAS HERE UNTIL A LITTLE WHILE AGO.
WHAT ?!
SHE CAME HERE ?!
Y- YES.
YOU SHOULD CALL HER.
SHE WAITED QUITE A WHILE FOR YOU.
BUT... BUT WHY...
I MEAN...
SHE AND I...WE... YOU KNOW... I DON'T...
WHAT ARE YOU TALKING ABOUT?
I DON'T NEED TO CALL HER!
WE AREN'T LIKE THAT!
YUSAKU, WAIT...
TAP TAP
REALLY!
HEY, KYOKO!
YES, MRS. ICHINOSE?

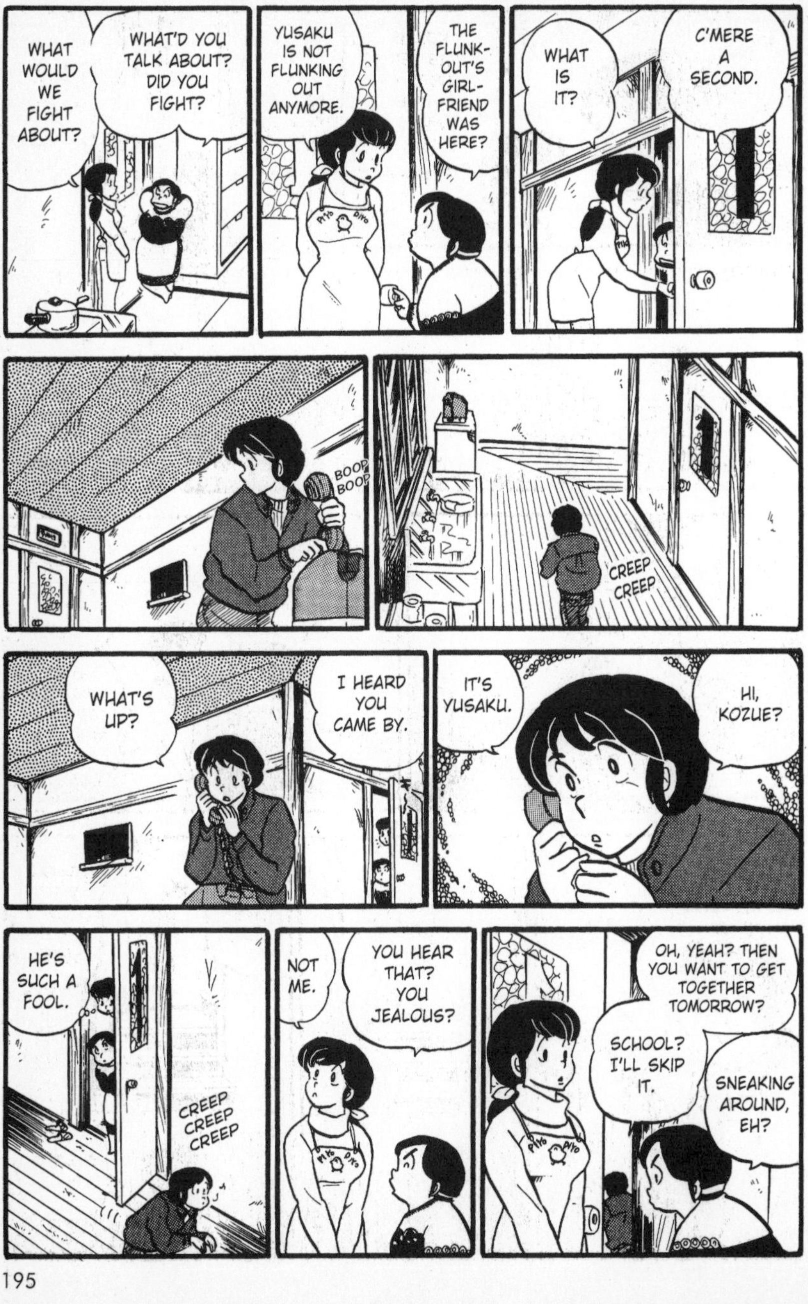
C'MERE A SECOND.
WHAT IS IT?
THE FLUNK-OUT'S GIRL-FRIEND WAS HERE?
YUSAKU IS NOT FLUNKING OUT ANYMORE.
WHAT'D YOU TALK ABOUT? DID YOU FIGHT?
WHAT WOULD WE FIGHT ABOUT?
CREEP CREEP
BOOP BOOP
HI, KOZUE?
IT'S YUSAKU.
I HEARD YOU CAME BY.
WHAT'S UP?
OH, YEAH? THEN YOU WANT TO GET TOGETHER TOMORROW?
SCHOOL? I'LL SKIP IT.
SNEAKING AROUND, EH?
YOU HEAR THAT? YOU JEALOUS?
NOT ME.
HE'S SUCH A FOOL.
CREEP CREEP CREEP

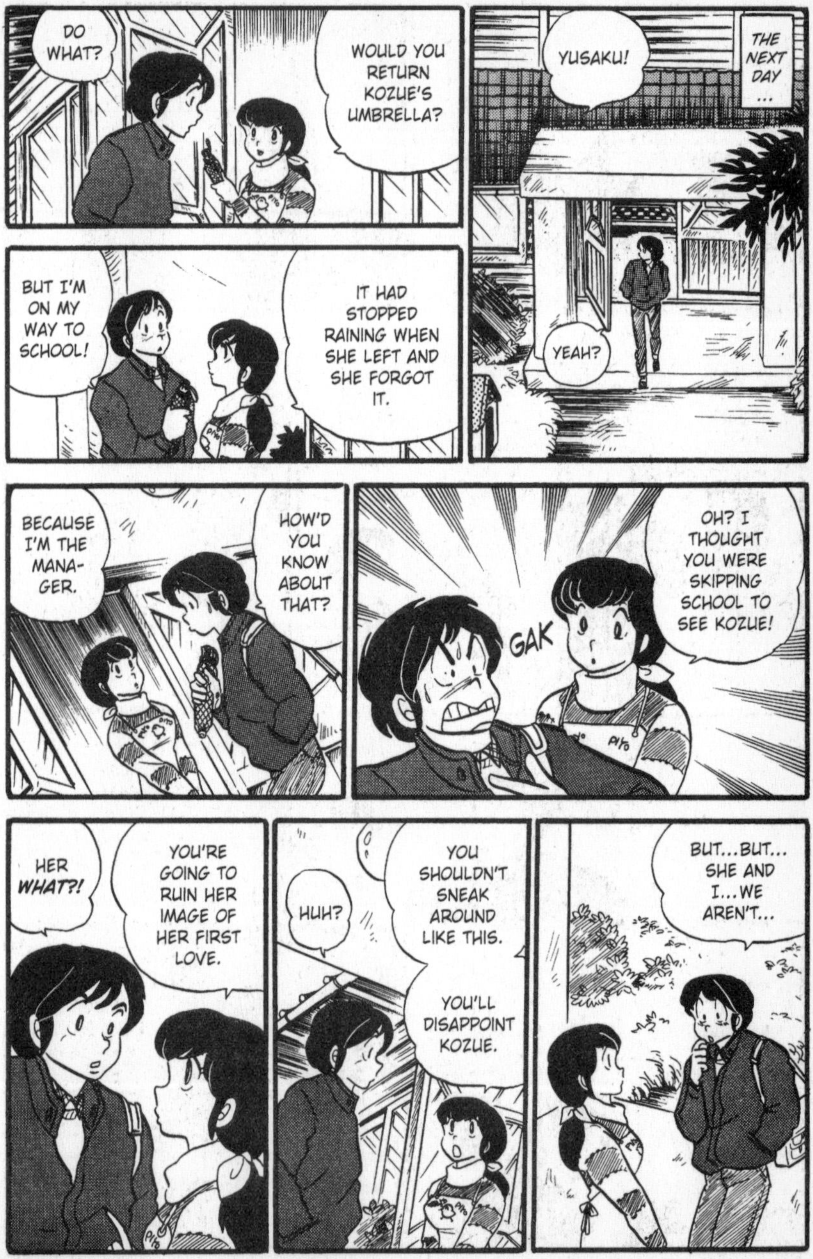
THE NEXT DAY ...
YUSAKU!
YEAH?
WOULD YOU RETURN KOZUE'S UMBRELLA?
DO WHAT?
IT HAD STOPPED RAINING WHEN SHE LEFT AND SHE FORGOT IT.
BUT I'M ON MY WAY TO SCHOOL!
OH? I THOUGHT YOU WERE SKIPPING SCHOOL TO SEE KOZUE!
GAK
HOW'D YOU KNOW ABOUT THAT?
BECAUSE I'M THE MANA-GER.
BUT...BUT... SHE AND I...WE AREN'T...
YOU SHOULDN'T SNEAK AROUND LIKE THIS.
HUH?
YOU'LL DISAPPOINT KOZUE.
YOU'RE GOING TO RUIN HER IMAGE OF HER FIRST LOVE.
HER *WHAT?!*

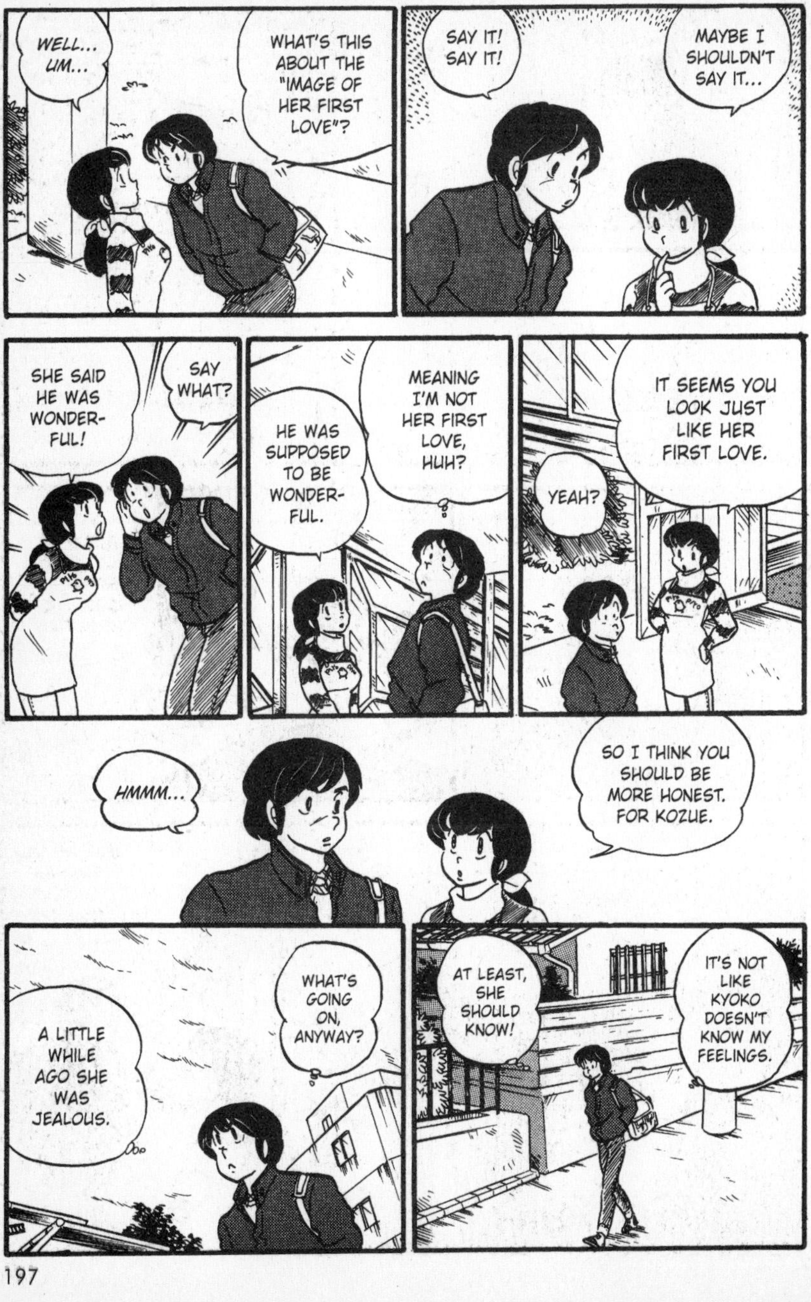
MAYBE I SHOULDN'T SAY IT...
SAY IT! SAY IT!
WHAT'S THIS ABOUT THE "IMAGE OF HER FIRST LOVE"?
WELL... UM...
IT SEEMS YOU LOOK JUST LIKE HER FIRST LOVE.
YEAH?
MEANING I'M NOT HER FIRST LOVE, HUH?
HE WAS SUPPOSED TO BE WONDERFUL.
SAY WHAT?
SHE SAID HE WAS WONDERFUL!
SO I THINK YOU SHOULD BE MORE HONEST. FOR KOZUE.
HMMM...
IT'S NOT LIKE KYOKO DOESN'T KNOW MY FEELINGS.
AT LEAST, SHE SHOULD KNOW!
WHAT'S GOING ON, ANYWAY?
A LITTLE WHILE AGO SHE WAS JEALOUS.

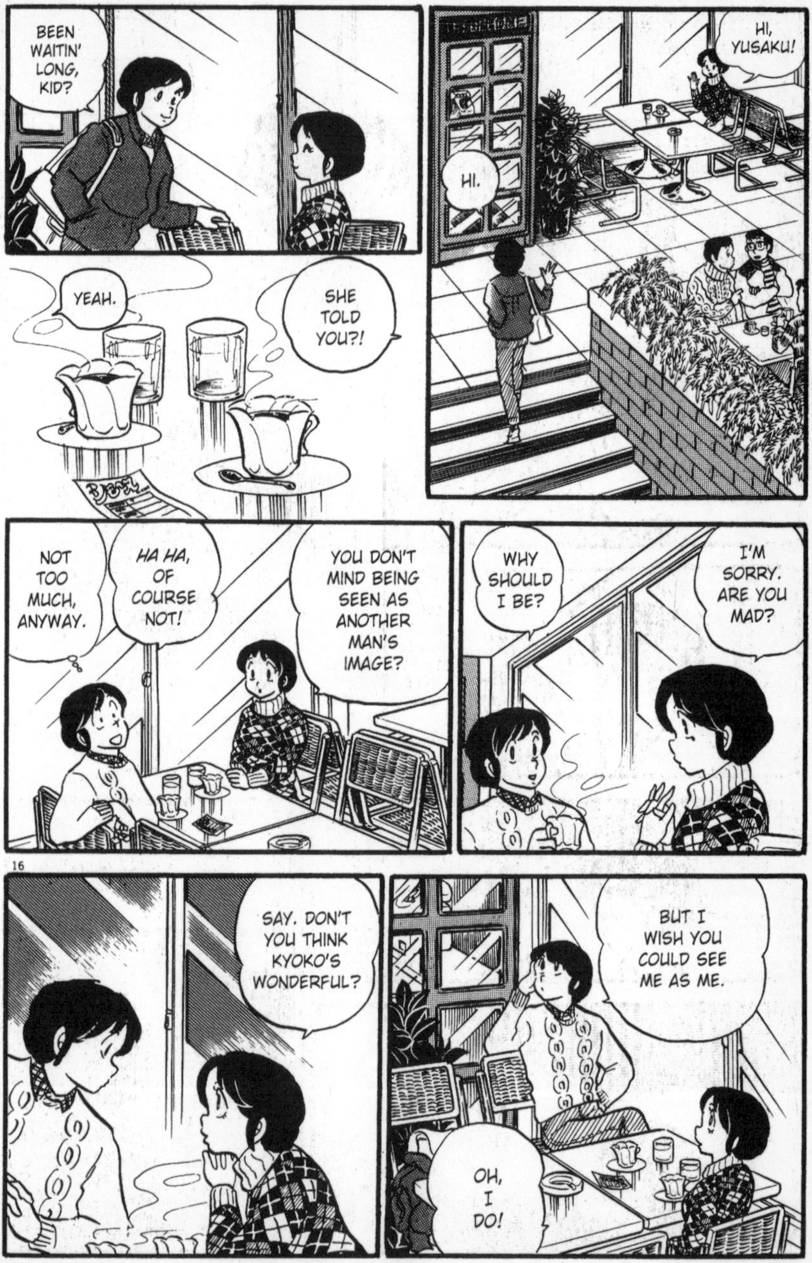
HI, YUSAKU!
HI.
BEEN WAITIN' LONG, KID?
SHE TOLD YOU?!
YEAH.
I'M SORRY. ARE YOU MAD?
WHY SHOULD I BE?
YOU DON'T MIND BEING SEEN AS ANOTHER MAN'S IMAGE?
HA HA, OF COURSE NOT!
NOT TOO MUCH, ANYWAY.
BUT I WISH YOU COULD SEE ME AS ME.
OH, I DO!
SAY. DON'T YOU THINK KYOKO'S WONDERFUL?
16

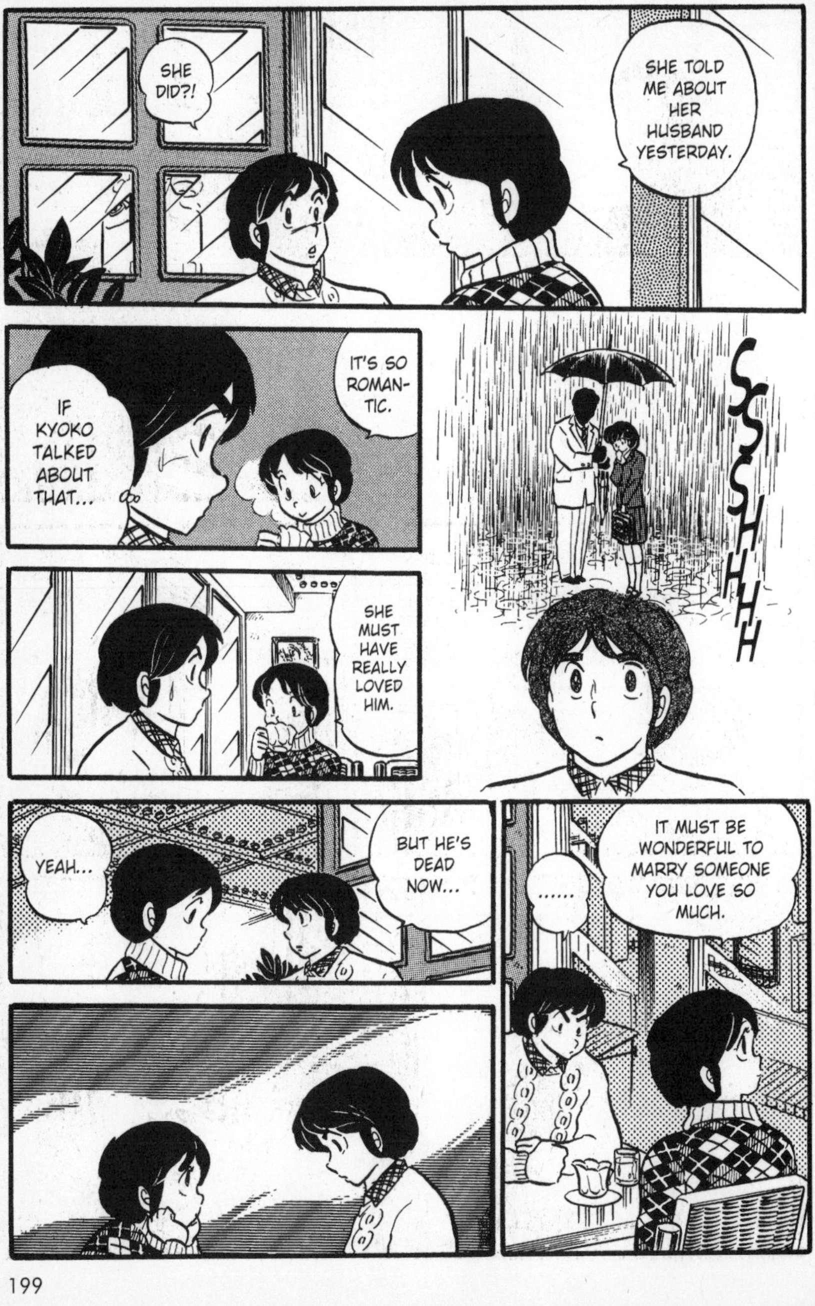
SHE TOLD ME ABOUT HER HUSBAND YESTERDAY.
SHE DID?!
SSSHHHHH
IT'S SO ROMAN-TIC.
IF KYOKO TALKED ABOUT THAT...
SHE MUST HAVE REALLY LOVED HIM.
IT MUST BE WONDERFUL TO MARRY SOMEONE YOU LOVE SO MUCH.
......
BUT HE'S DEAD NOW...
YEAH...

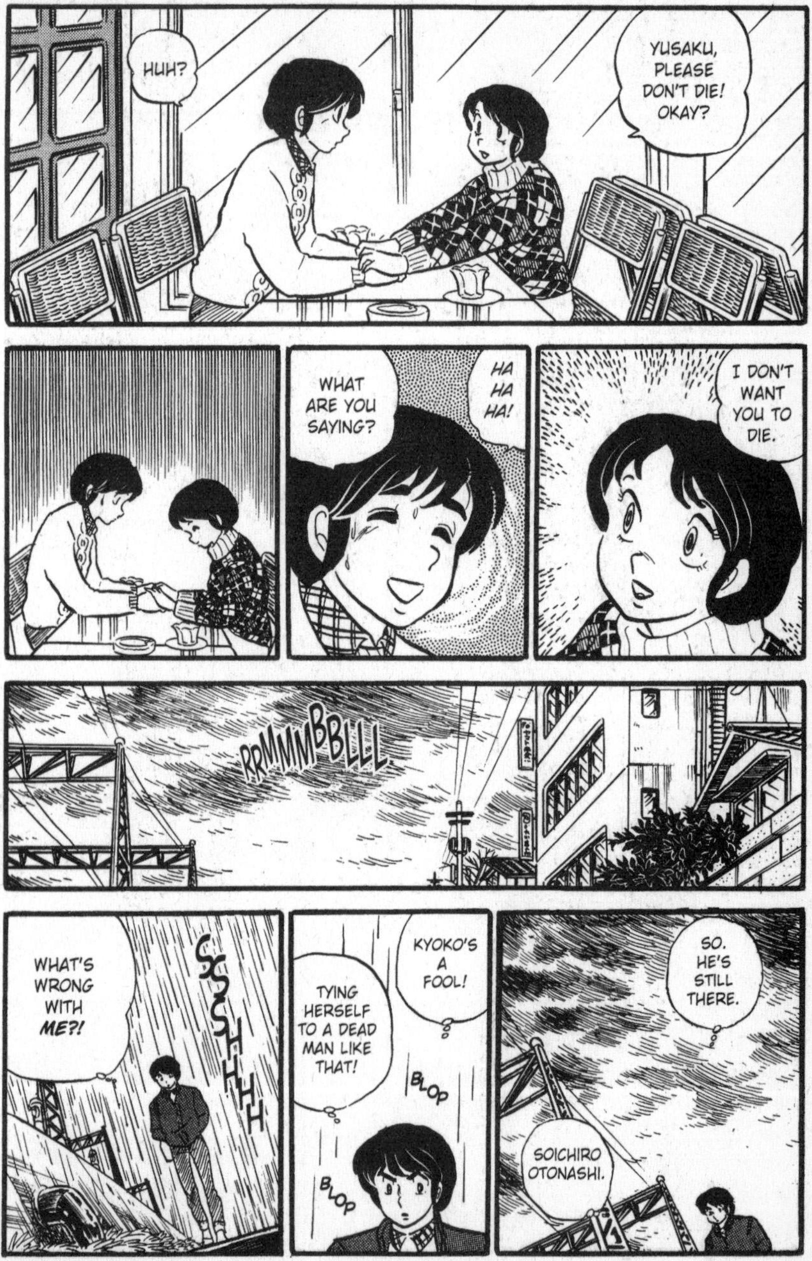
YUSAKU, PLEASE DON'T DIE! OKAY?
HUH?
I DON'T WANT YOU TO DIE.
HA HA HA!
WHAT ARE YOU SAYING?
RRMMMBBLLL
SO. HE'S STILL THERE.
SOICHIRO OTONASHI.
KYOKO'S A FOOL!
TYING HERSELF TO A DEAD MAN LIKE THAT!
BLOP
BLOP
SSSHHHHH
WHAT'S WRONG WITH *ME?!*

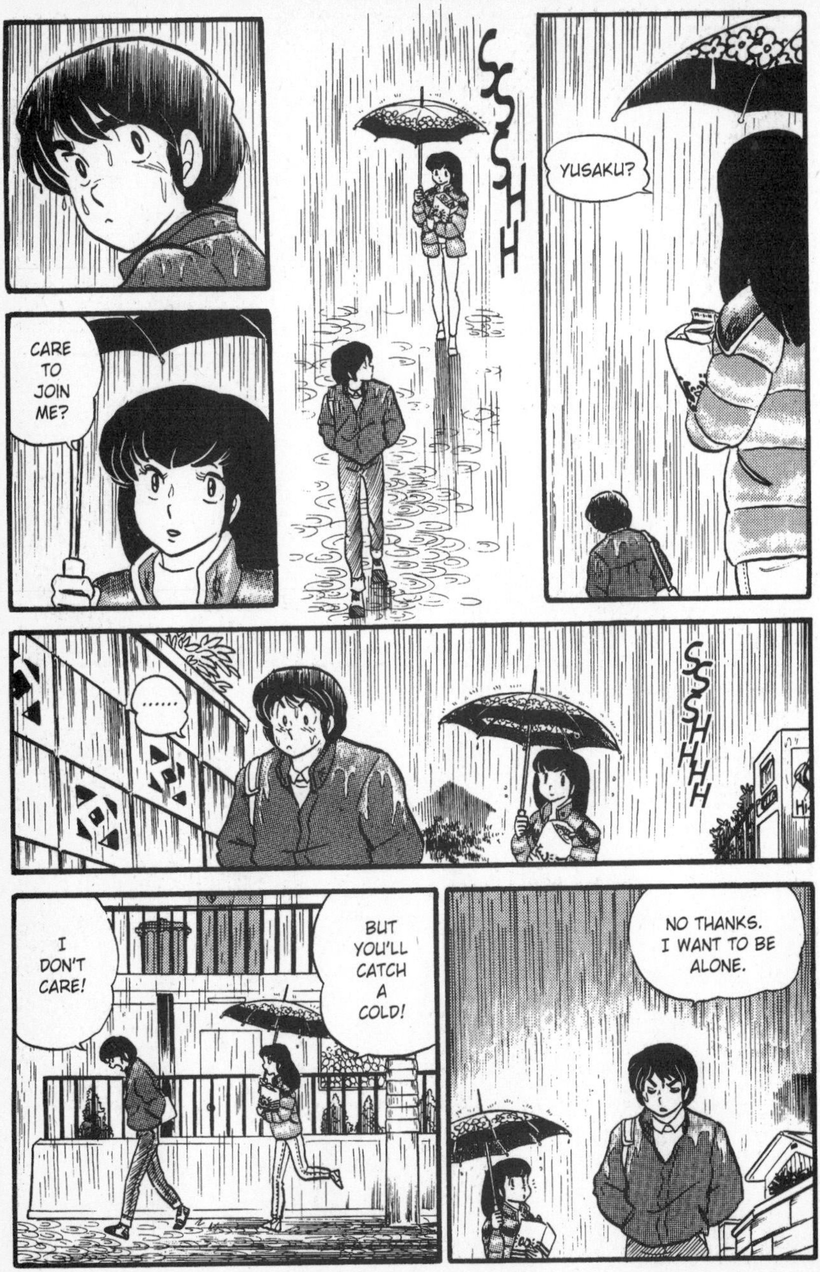
YUSAKU?
SSSHH
CARE TO JOIN ME?
SSSHHHH
......
NO THANKS. I WANT TO BE ALONE.
BUT YOU'LL CATCH A COLD!
I DON'T CARE!

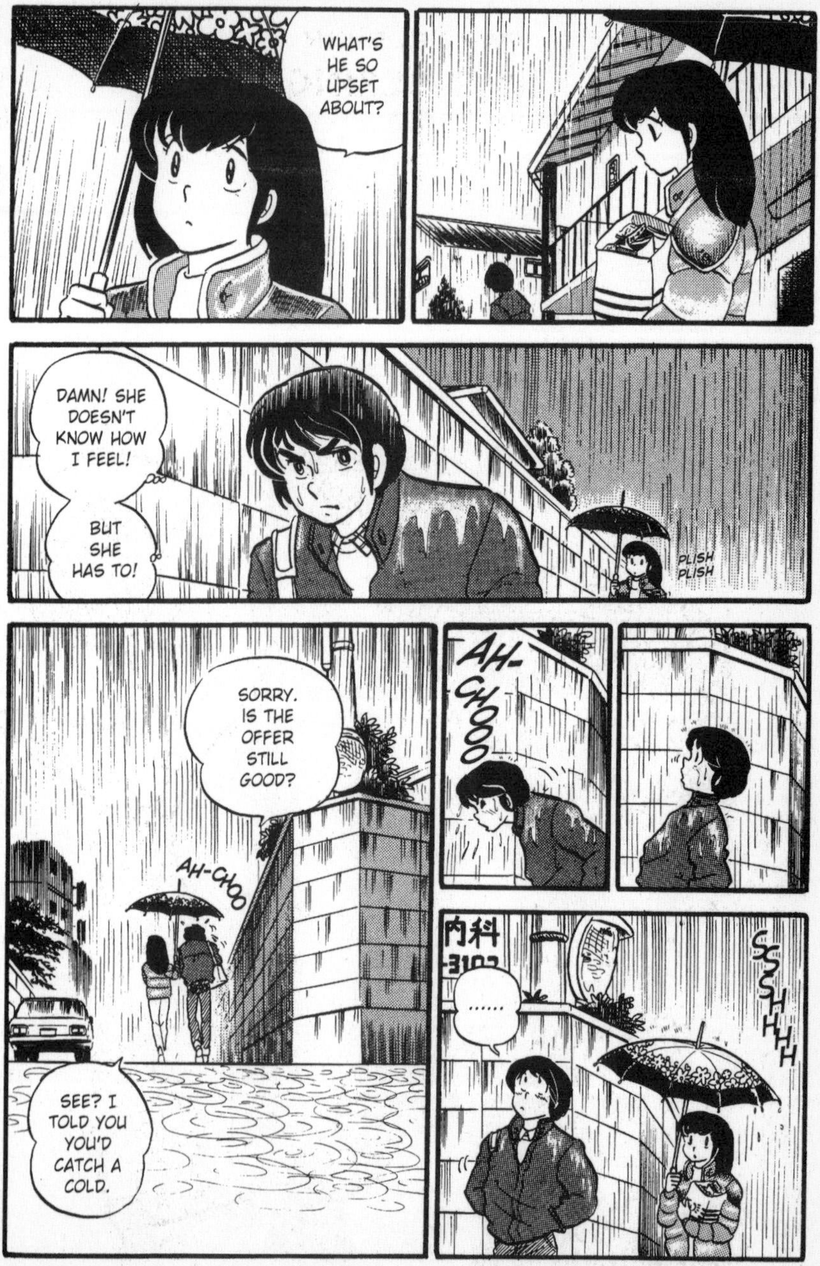
WHAT'S HE SO UPSET ABOUT?
PLISH PLISH
DAMN! SHE DOESN'T KNOW HOW I FEEL!
BUT SHE HAS TO!
AH-CHOOO
SSSHHHH
内科
-3102
......
SORRY. IS THE OFFER STILL GOOD?
AH-CHOO
SEE? I TOLD YOU YOU'D CATCH A COLD.

PART ELEVEN
KNIT-PICKING

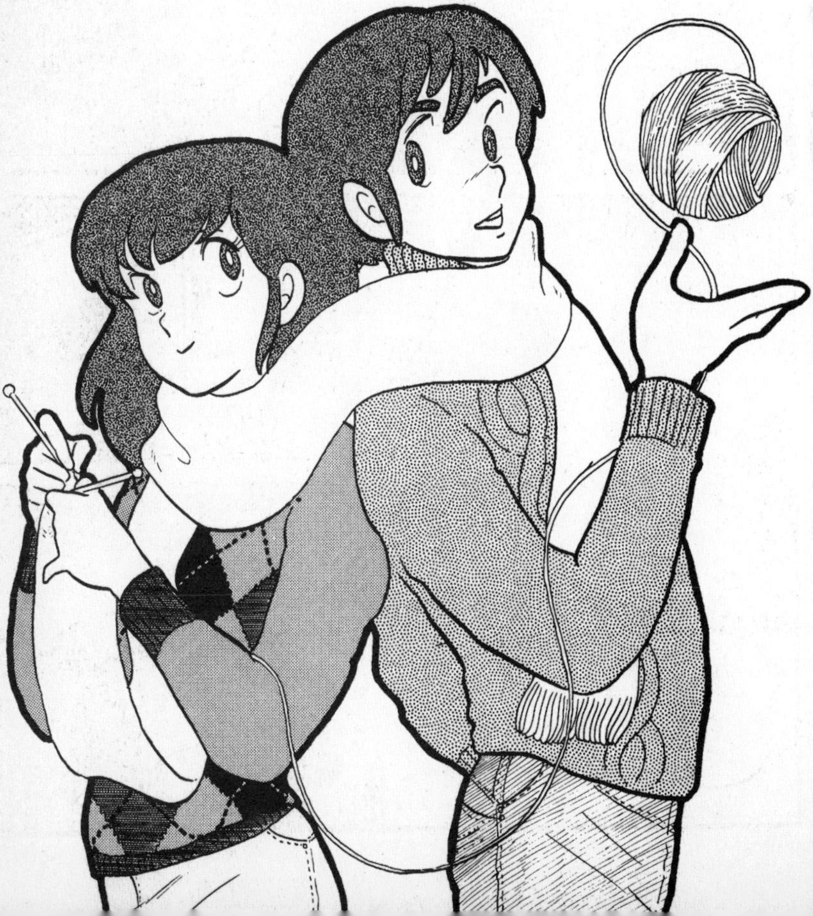

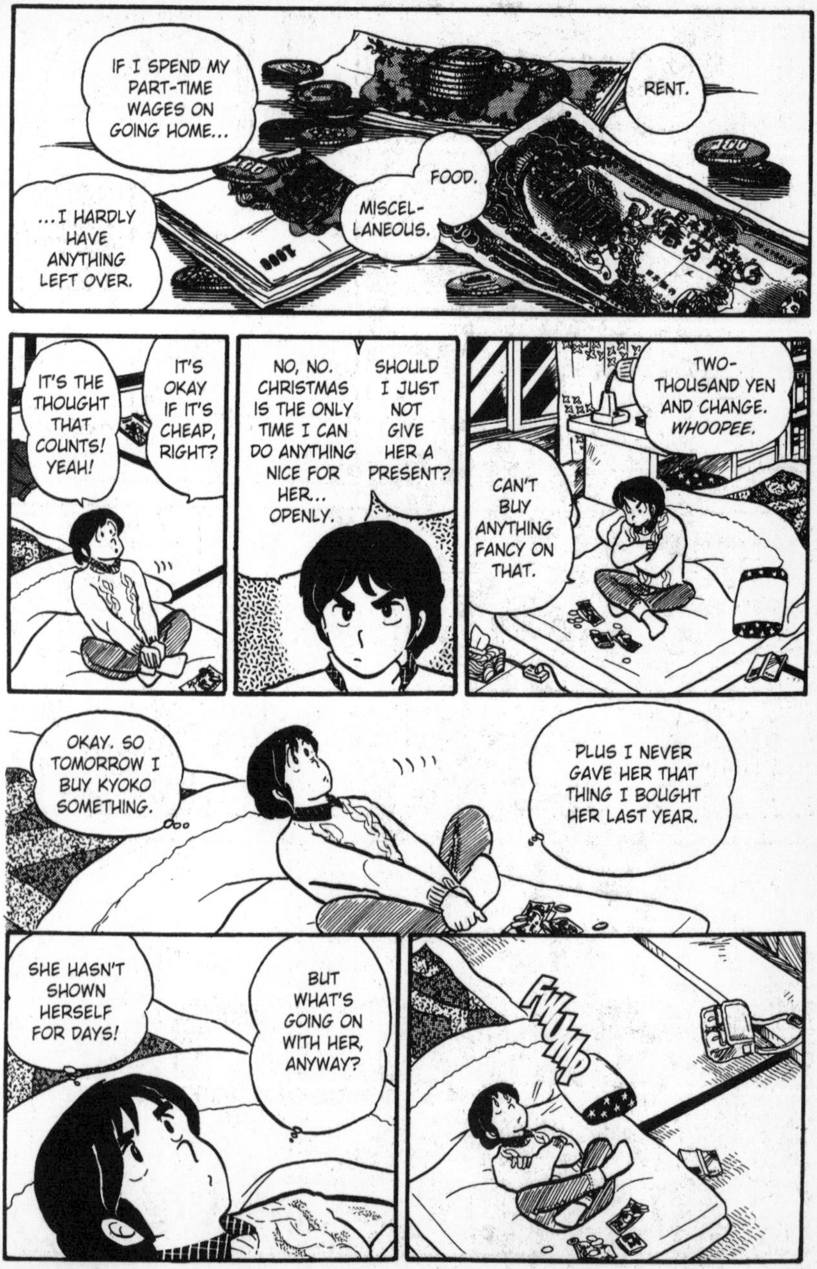
RENT.
FOOD.
MISCEL-LANEOUS.
IF I SPEND MY PART-TIME WAGES ON GOING HOME...
...I HARDLY HAVE ANYTHING LEFT OVER.
TWO-THOUSAND YEN AND CHANGE. *WHOOPEE.*
CAN'T BUY ANYTHING FANCY ON THAT.
SHOULD I JUST NOT GIVE HER A PRESENT?
NO, NO. CHRISTMAS IS THE ONLY TIME I CAN DO ANYTHING NICE FOR HER... OPENLY.
IT'S OKAY IF IT'S CHEAP, RIGHT?
IT'S THE THOUGHT THAT COUNTS! YEAH!
PLUS I NEVER GAVE HER THAT THING I BOUGHT HER LAST YEAR.
OKAY. SO TOMORROW I BUY KYOKO SOMETHING.
FWUMP
BUT WHAT'S GOING ON WITH HER, ANYWAY?
SHE HASN'T SHOWN HERSELF FOR DAYS!

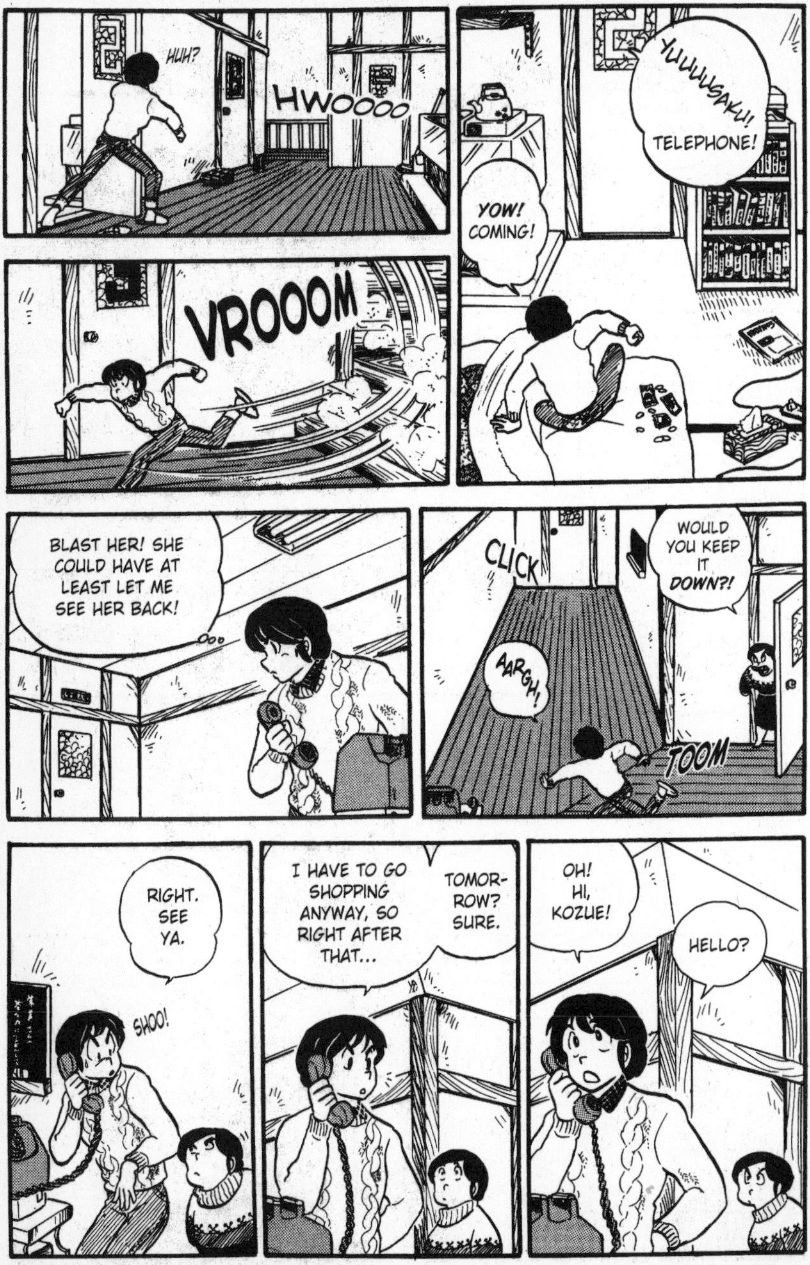
YUUUUSAKU! TELEPHONE!
YOW! COMING!
HUH?
HWOOOO
VROOOM
WOULD YOU KEEP IT DOWN?!
CLICK
AARGH!
TOOM
BLAST HER! SHE COULD HAVE AT LEAST LET ME SEE HER BACK!
HELLO?
OH! HI, KOZUE!
TOMOR-ROW? SURE.
I HAVE TO GO SHOPPING ANYWAY, SO RIGHT AFTER THAT...
RIGHT. SEE YA.
SHOO!

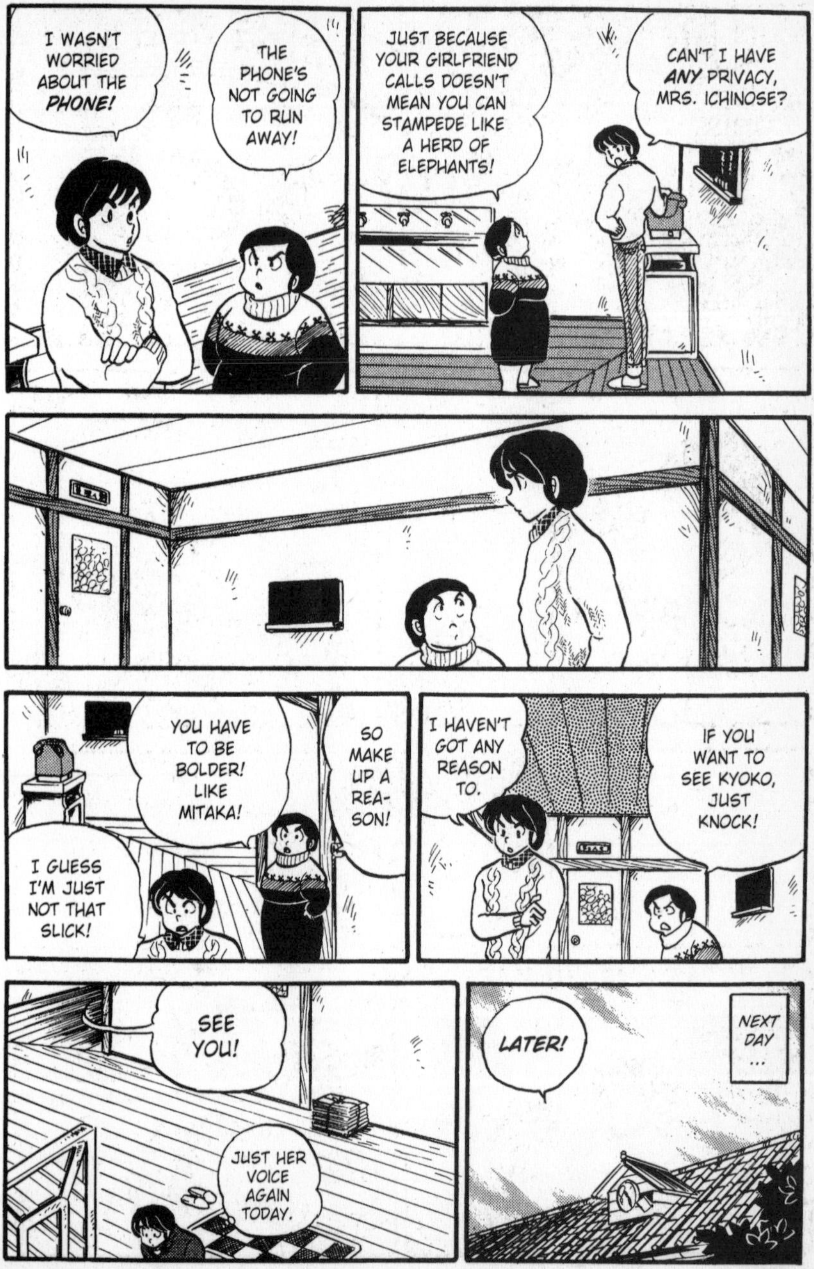
CAN'T I HAVE ANY PRIVACY, MRS. ICHINOSE?
JUST BECAUSE YOUR GIRLFRIEND CALLS DOESN'T MEAN YOU CAN STAMPEDE LIKE A HERD OF ELEPHANTS!
THE PHONE'S NOT GOING TO RUN AWAY!
I WASN'T WORRIED ABOUT THE PHONE!
IF YOU WANT TO SEE KYOKO, JUST KNOCK!
I HAVEN'T GOT ANY REASON TO.
SO MAKE UP A REA-SON!
YOU HAVE TO BE BOLDER! LIKE MITAKA!
I GUESS I'M JUST NOT THAT SLICK!
NEXT DAY ...
LATER!
SEE YOU!
JUST HER VOICE AGAIN TODAY.

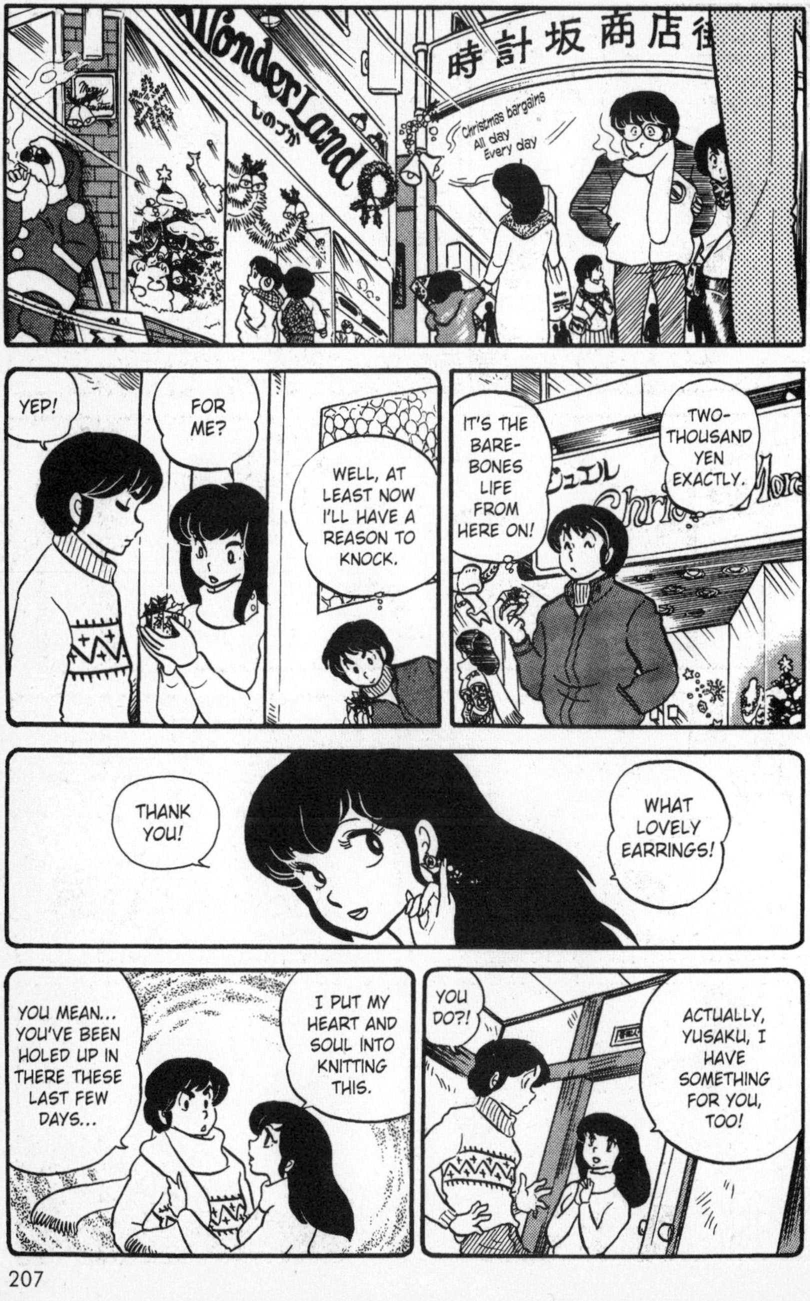
Wonder Land
しのづか
時計坂商店
Christmas bargains All day Every day
TWO-THOUSAND YEN EXACTLY.
IT'S THE BARE-BONES LIFE FROM HERE ON!
WELL, AT LEAST NOW I'LL HAVE A REASON TO KNOCK.
FOR ME?
YEP!
WHAT LOVELY EARRINGS!
THANK YOU!
ACTUALLY, YUSAKU, I HAVE SOMETHING FOR YOU, TOO!
YOU DO?!
I PUT MY HEART AND SOUL INTO KNITTING THIS.
YOU MEAN... YOU'VE BEEN HOLED UP IN THERE THESE LAST FEW DAYS...

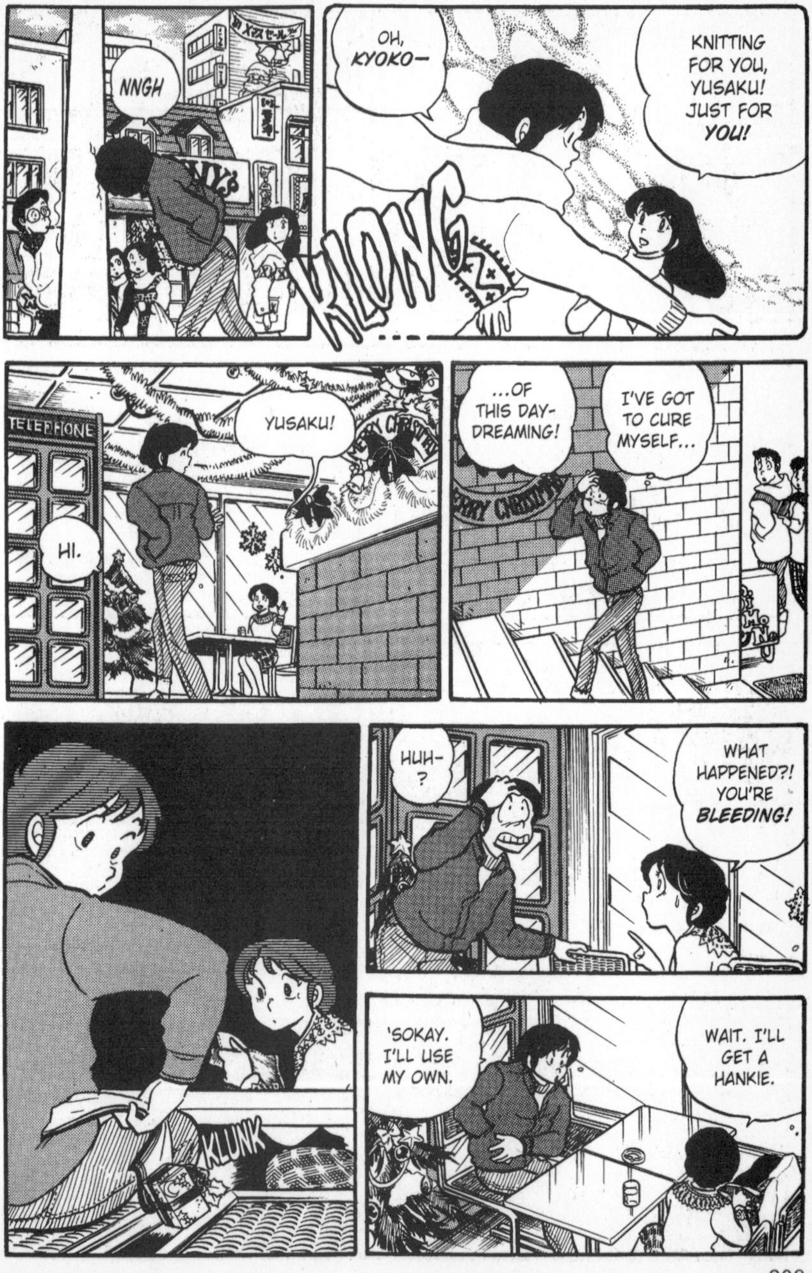
KNITTING FOR YOU, YUSAKU! JUST FOR *YOU!*
OH, *KYOKO—*
KLONG
NNGH
I'VE GOT TO CURE MYSELF...
...OF THIS DAY-DREAMING!
YUSAKU!
TELEPHONE
HI.
WHAT HAPPENED?! YOU'RE *BLEEDING!*
HUH-?
WAIT. I'LL GET A HANKIE.
'SOKAY. I'LL USE MY OWN.
KLUNK

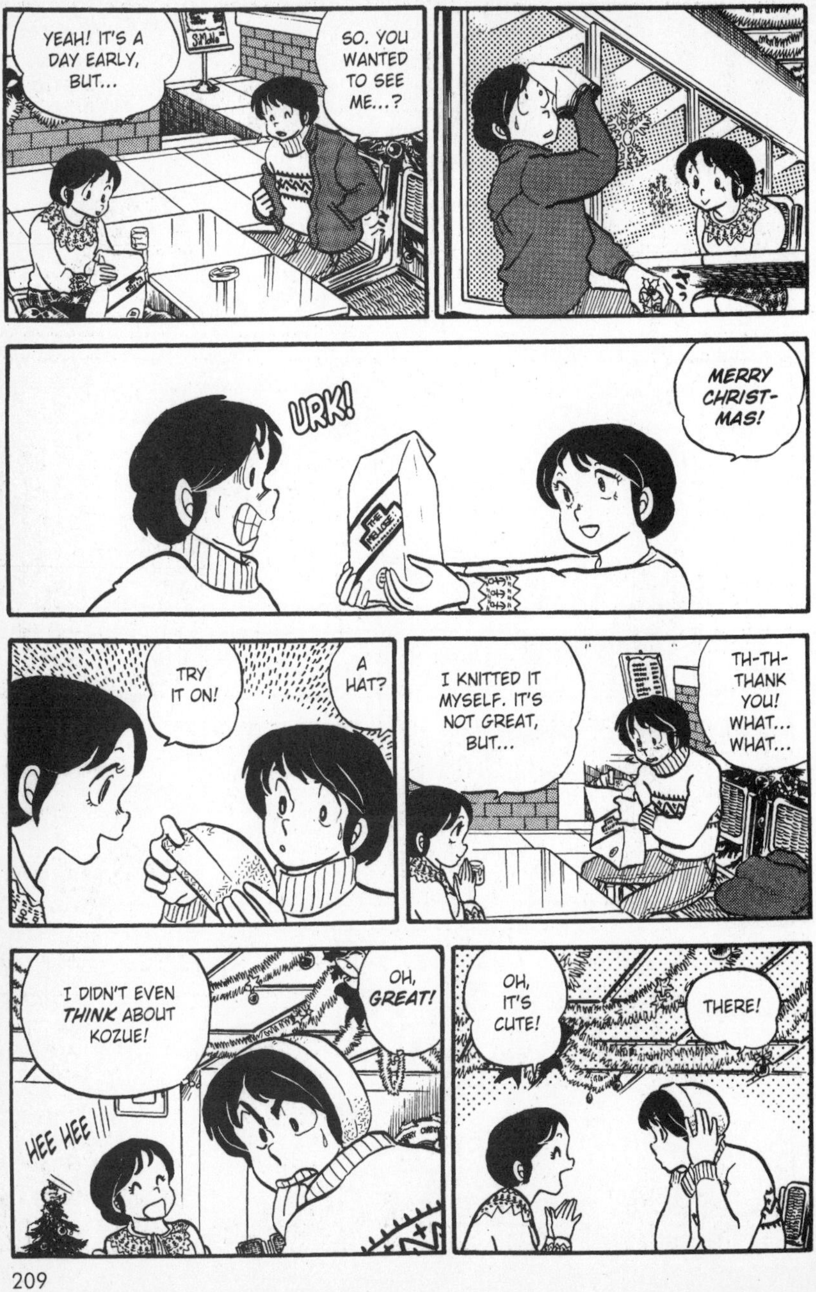
SO. YOU WANTED TO SEE ME...?
YEAH! IT'S A DAY EARLY, BUT...
MERRY CHRIST-MAS!
URK!
TH-TH-THANK YOU! WHAT... WHAT...
I KNITTED IT MYSELF. IT'S NOT GREAT, BUT...
A HAT?
TRY IT ON!
THERE!
OH, IT'S CUTE!
OH, GREAT!
I DIDN'T EVEN THINK ABOUT KOZUE!
HEE HEE

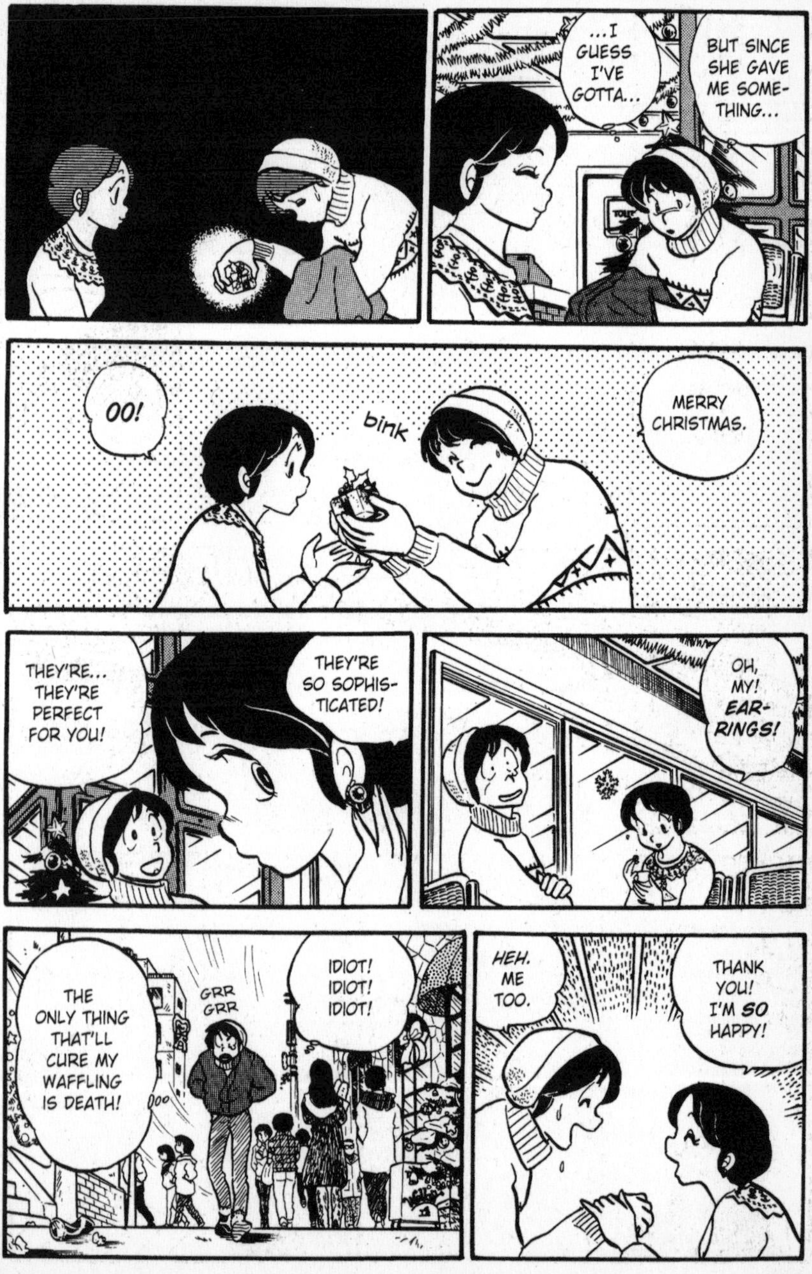
BUT SINCE SHE GAVE ME SOME-THING...
...I GUESS I'VE GOTTA...
MERRY CHRISTMAS.
bink
OO!
OH, MY! EAR-RINGS!
THEY'RE SO SOPHIS-TICATED!
THEY'RE... THEY'RE PERFECT FOR YOU!
THANK YOU! I'M SO HAPPY!
HEH. ME TOO.
IDIOT! IDIOT! IDIOT!
GRR GRR
THE ONLY THING THAT'LL CURE MY WAFFLING IS DEATH!

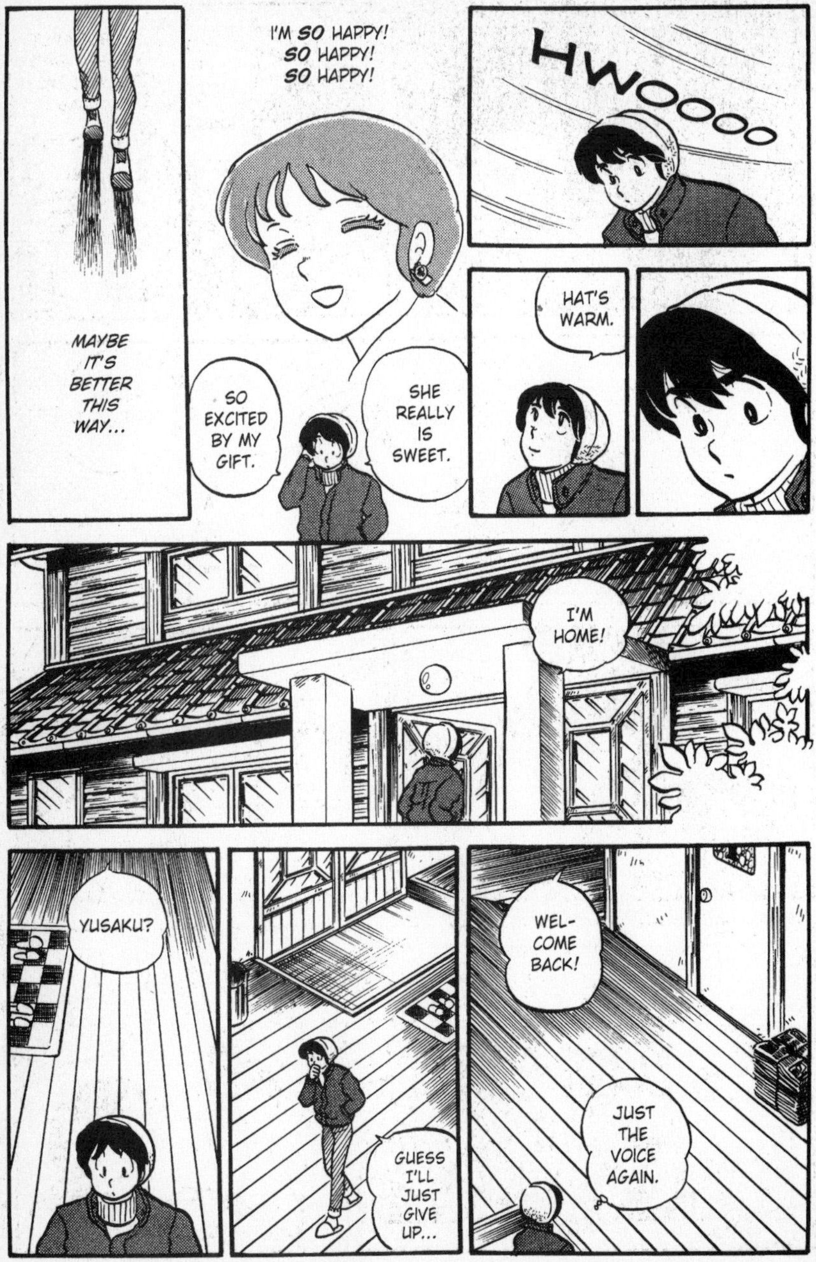
HWOOOO
HAT'S WARM.
I'M SO HAPPY! SO HAPPY! SO HAPPY!
SHE REALLY IS SWEET.
SO EXCITED BY MY GIFT.
MAYBE IT'S BETTER THIS WAY...
I'M HOME!
WEL-COME BACK!
JUST THE VOICE AGAIN.
GUESS I'LL JUST GIVE UP...
YUSAKU?

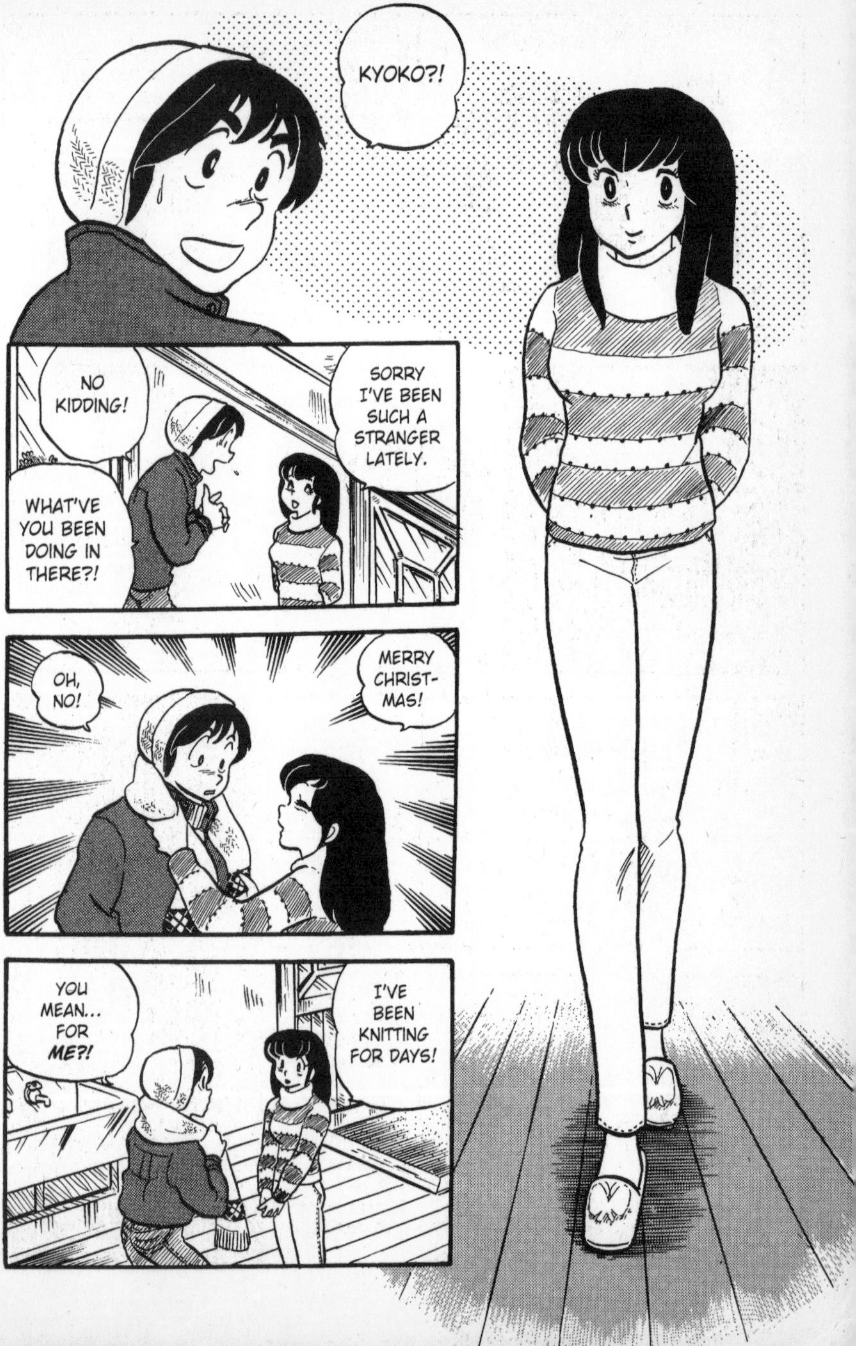
KYOKO?!
SORRY I'VE BEEN SUCH A STRANGER LATELY.
NO KIDDING!
WHAT'VE YOU BEEN DOING IN THERE?!
MERRY CHRIST-MAS!
OH, NO!
I'VE BEEN KNITTING FOR DAYS!
YOU MEAN... FOR *ME?!*

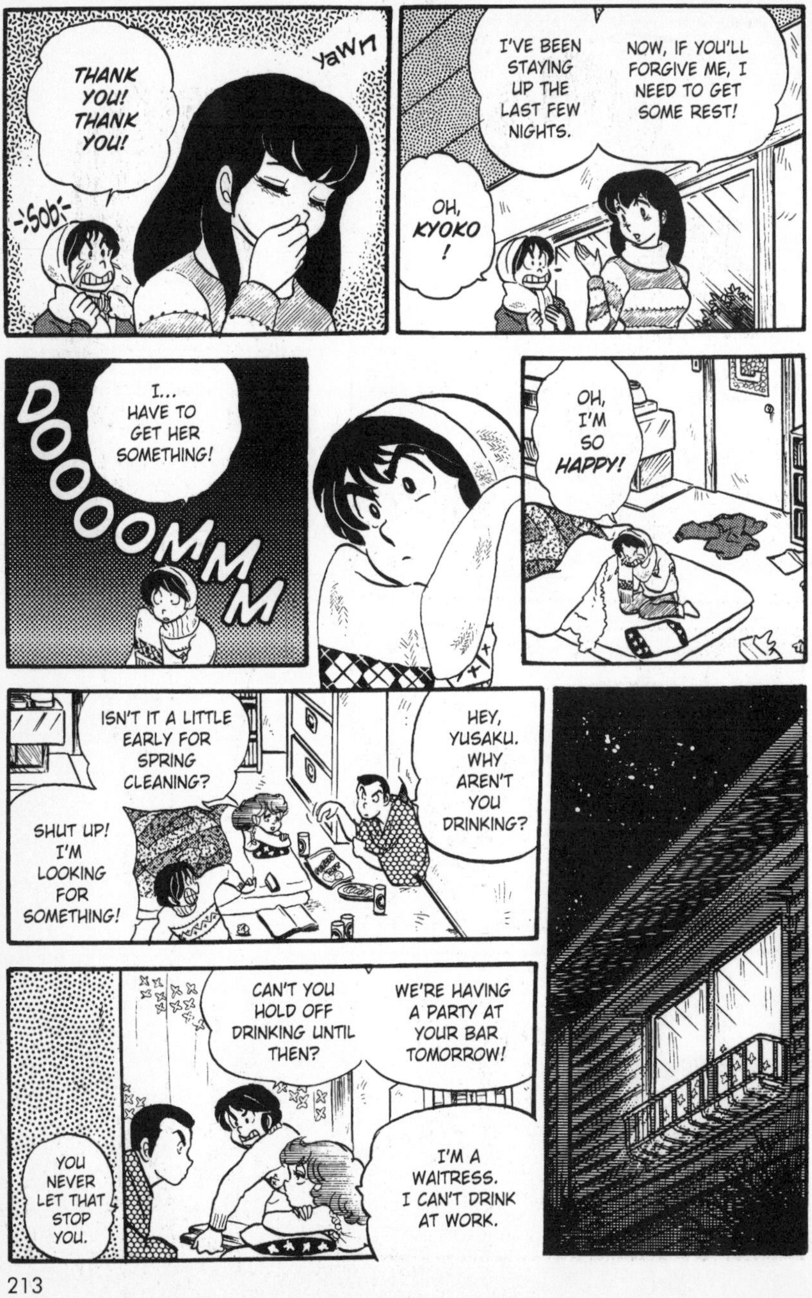
I'VE BEEN STAYING UP THE LAST FEW NIGHTS.
NOW, IF YOU'LL FORGIVE ME, I NEED TO GET SOME REST!
OH, KYOKO!
yawn
THANK YOU! THANK YOU!
Sob
OH, I'M SO HAPPY!
I... HAVE TO GET HER SOMETHING!
DOOOOOMMMM
HEY, YUSAKU. WHY AREN'T YOU DRINKING?
ISN'T IT A LITTLE EARLY FOR SPRING CLEANING?
SHUT UP! I'M LOOKING FOR SOMETHING!
WE'RE HAVING A PARTY AT YOUR BAR TOMORROW!
CAN'T YOU HOLD OFF DRINKING UNTIL THEN?
I'M A WAITRESS. I CAN'T DRINK AT WORK.
YOU NEVER LET THAT STOP YOU.

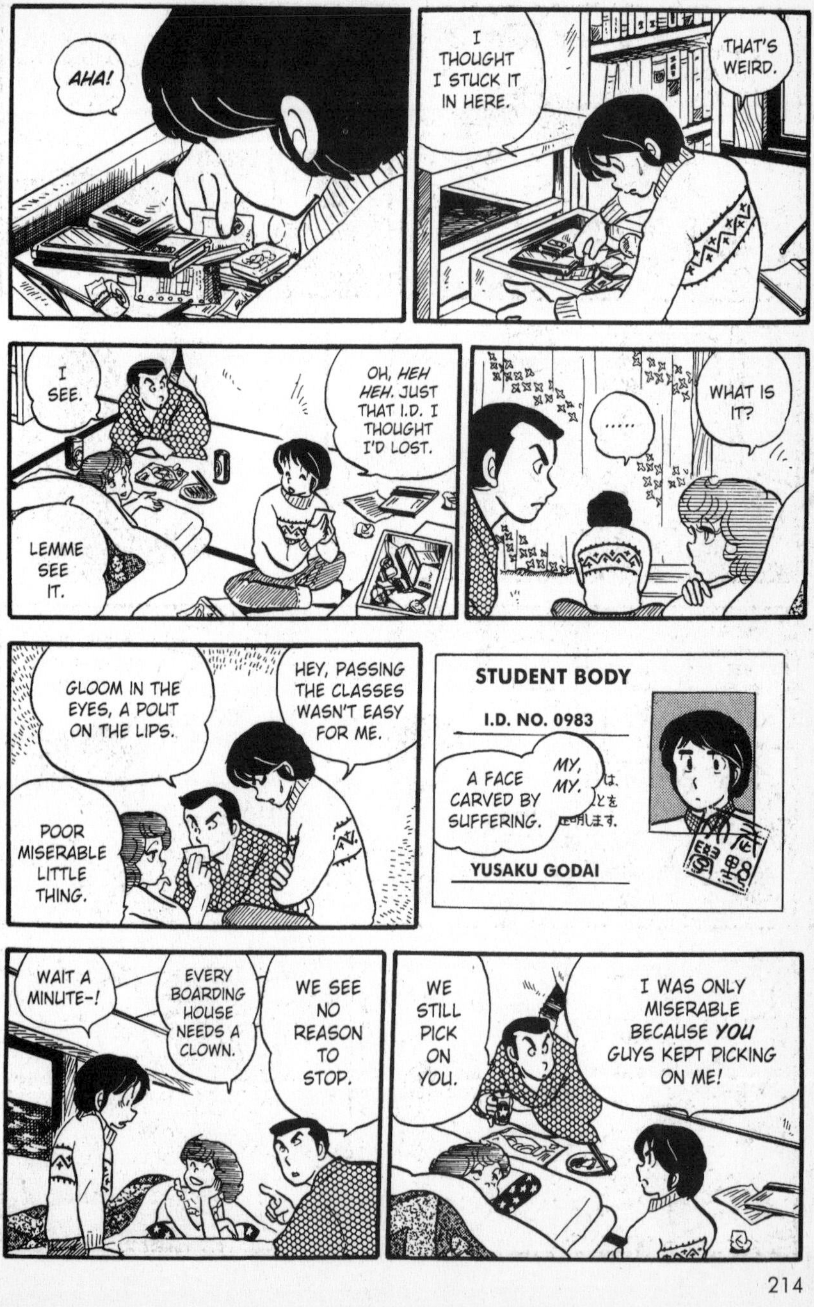
THAT'S WEIRD.
I THOUGHT I STUCK IT IN HERE.
AHA!
WHAT IS IT?
......
OH, *HEH HEH.* JUST THAT I.D. I THOUGHT I'D LOST.
I SEE.
LEMME SEE IT.
STUDENT BODY
I.D. NO. 0983
MY, MY.
A FACE CARVED BY SUFFERING.
YUSAKU GODAI
HEY, PASSING THE CLASSES WASN'T EASY FOR ME.
GLOOM IN THE EYES, A POUT ON THE LIPS.
POOR MISERABLE LITTLE THING.
I WAS ONLY MISERABLE BECAUSE *YOU* GUYS KEPT PICKING ON ME!
WE STILL PICK ON YOU.
WE SEE NO REASON TO STOP.
EVERY BOARDING HOUSE NEEDS A CLOWN.
WAIT A MINUTE-!

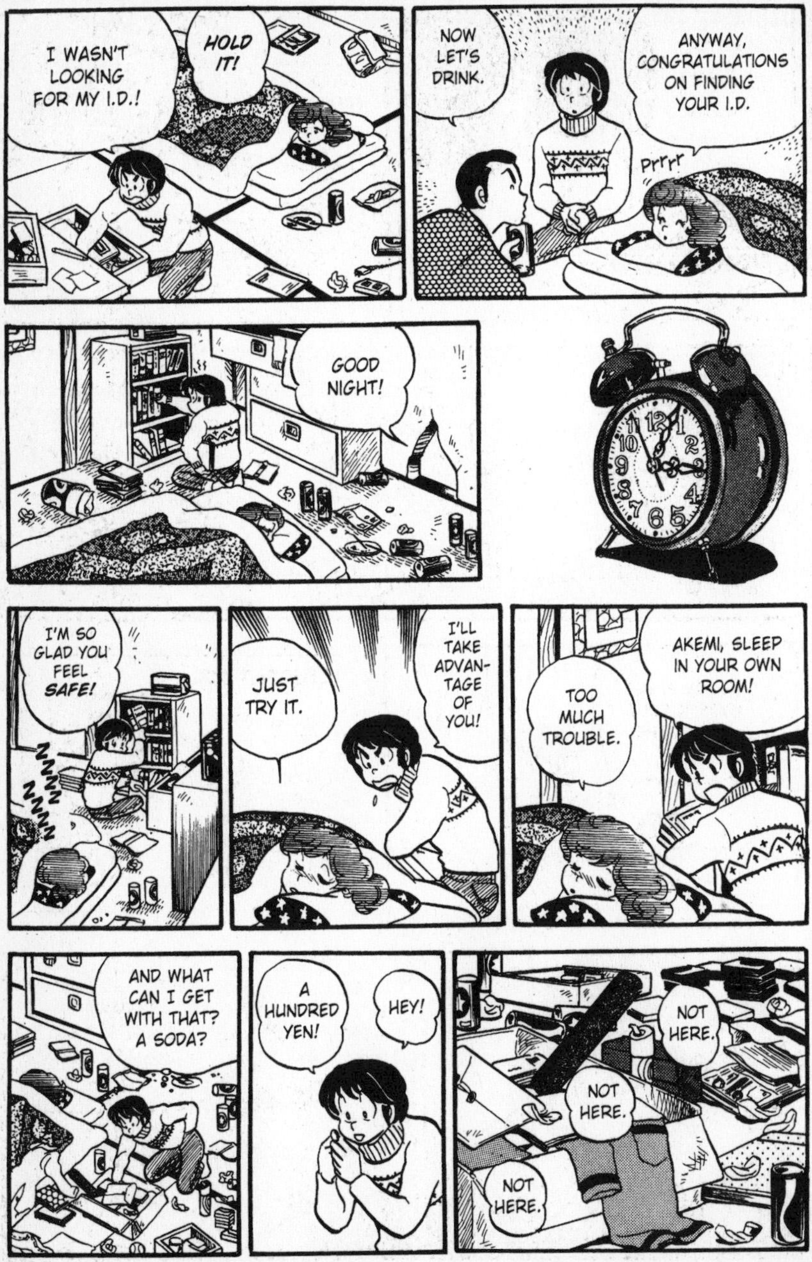
ANYWAY, CONGRATULATIONS ON FINDING YOUR I.D.
NOW LET'S DRINK.
Prrrr
HOLD IT!
I WASN'T LOOKING FOR MY I.D.!
GOOD NIGHT!
AKEMI, SLEEP IN YOUR OWN ROOM!
TOO MUCH TROUBLE.
I'LL TAKE ADVANTAGE OF YOU!
JUST TRY IT.
I'M SO GLAD YOU FEEL SAFE!
ZZZ ZZZZ
NOT HERE.
NOT HERE.
NOT HERE.
HEY!
A HUNDRED YEN!
AND WHAT CAN I GET WITH THAT? A SODA?

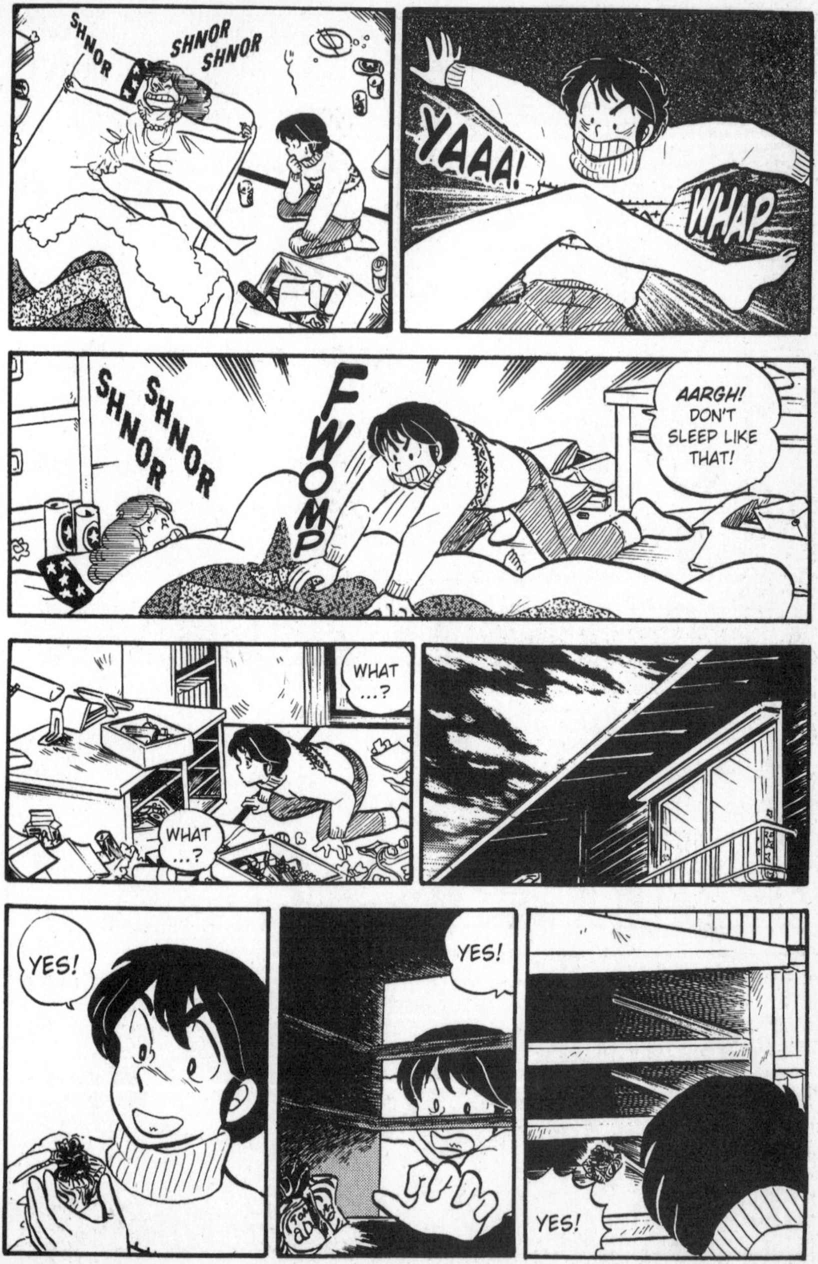
YAAA!
WHAP
SHNOR
SHNOR
SHNOR
AARGH! DON'T SLEEP LIKE THAT!
FWOMP
SHNOR
SHNOR
WHAT ...?
WHAT ...?
YES!
YES!
YES!

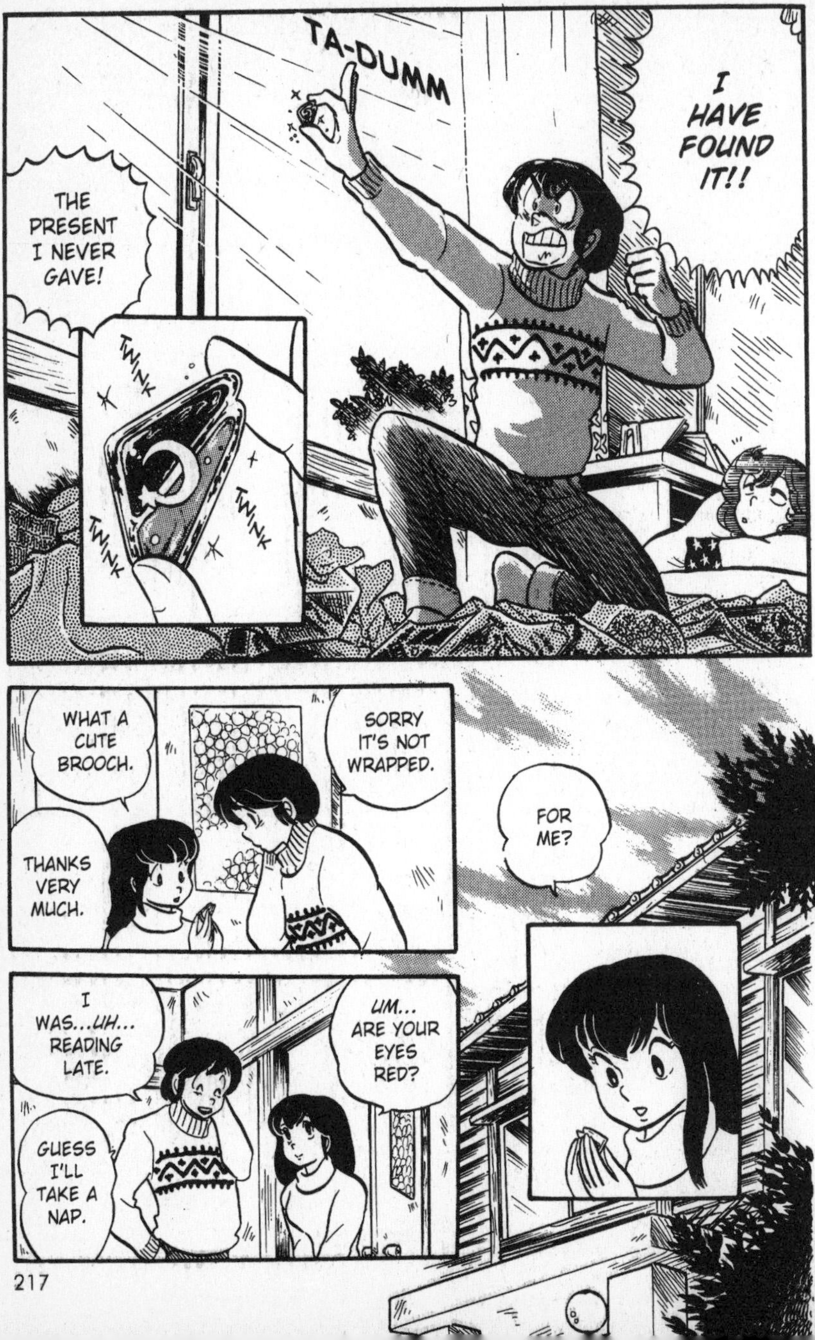
I HAVE FOUND IT!!
TA-DUMM
THE PRESENT I NEVER GAVE!
TWINK
TWINK
TWINK
FOR ME?
SORRY IT'S NOT WRAPPED.
WHAT A CUTE BROOCH.
THANKS VERY MUCH.
UM... ARE YOUR EYES RED?
I WAS...UH... READING LATE.
GUESS I'LL TAKE A NAP.

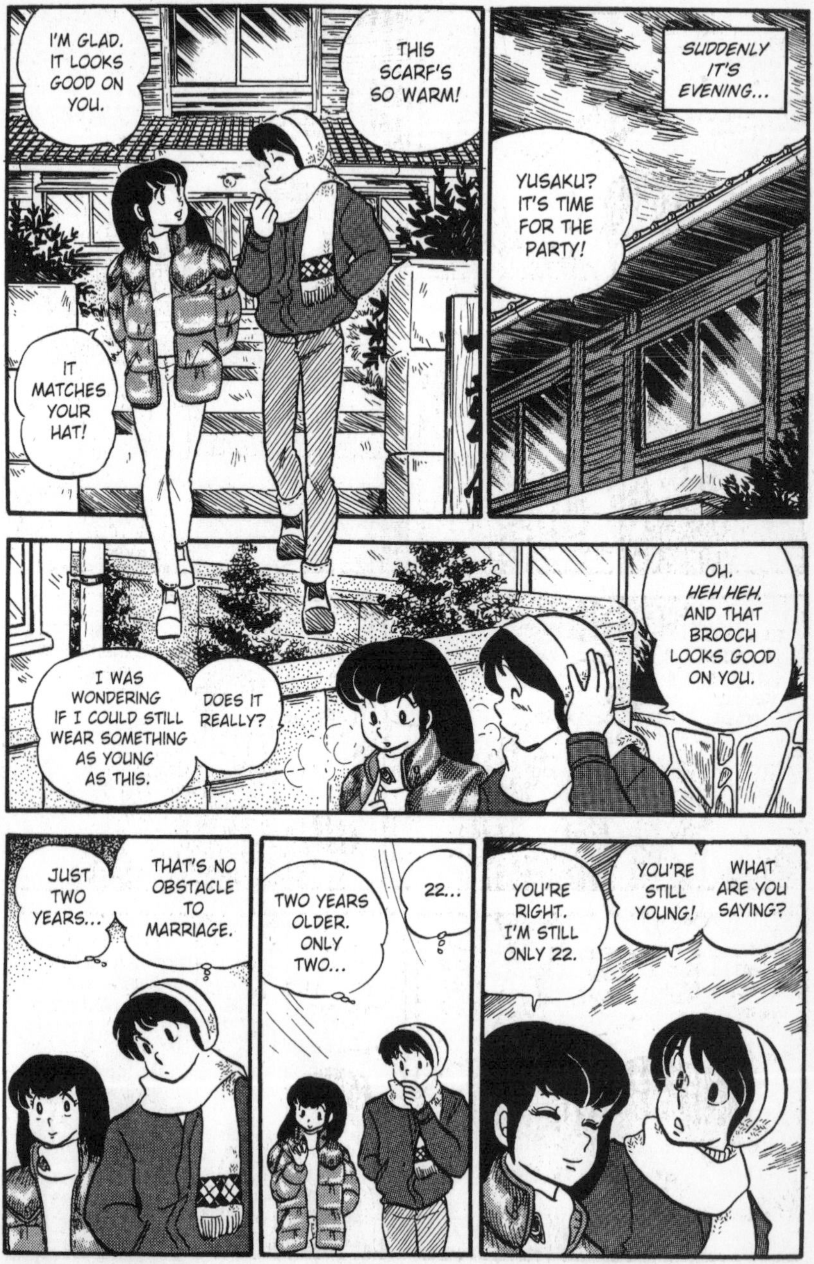
SUDDENLY IT'S EVENING...
YUSAKU? IT'S TIME FOR THE PARTY!
THIS SCARF'S SO WARM!
I'M GLAD. IT LOOKS GOOD ON YOU.
IT MATCHES YOUR HAT!
OH. *HEH HEH.* AND THAT BROOCH LOOKS GOOD ON YOU.
DOES IT REALLY?
I WAS WONDERING IF I COULD STILL WEAR SOMETHING AS YOUNG AS THIS.
WHAT ARE YOU SAYING?
YOU'RE STILL YOUNG!
YOU'RE RIGHT. I'M STILL ONLY 22.
22...
TWO YEARS OLDER. ONLY TWO...
THAT'S NO OBSTACLE TO MARRIAGE.
JUST TWO YEARS...

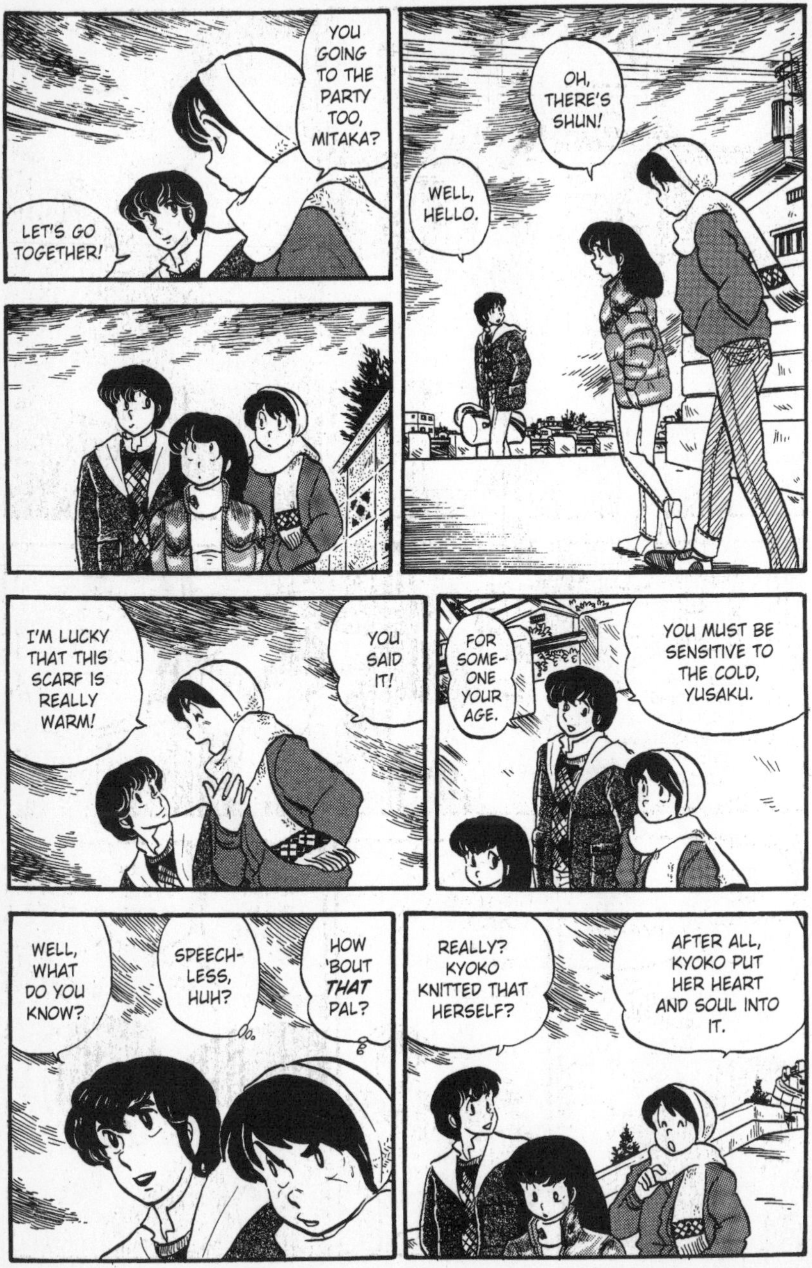
OH, THERE'S SHUN!
WELL, HELLO.
YOU GOING TO THE PARTY TOO, MITAKA?
LET'S GO TOGETHER!
YOU MUST BE SENSITIVE TO THE COLD, YUSAKU.
FOR SOMEONE YOUR AGE.
YOU SAID IT!
I'M LUCKY THAT THIS SCARF IS REALLY WARM!
AFTER ALL, KYOKO PUT HER HEART AND SOUL INTO IT.
REALLY? KYOKO KNITTED THAT HERSELF?
HOW 'BOUT *THAT* PAL?
SPEECHLESS, HUH?
WELL, WHAT DO YOU KNOW?

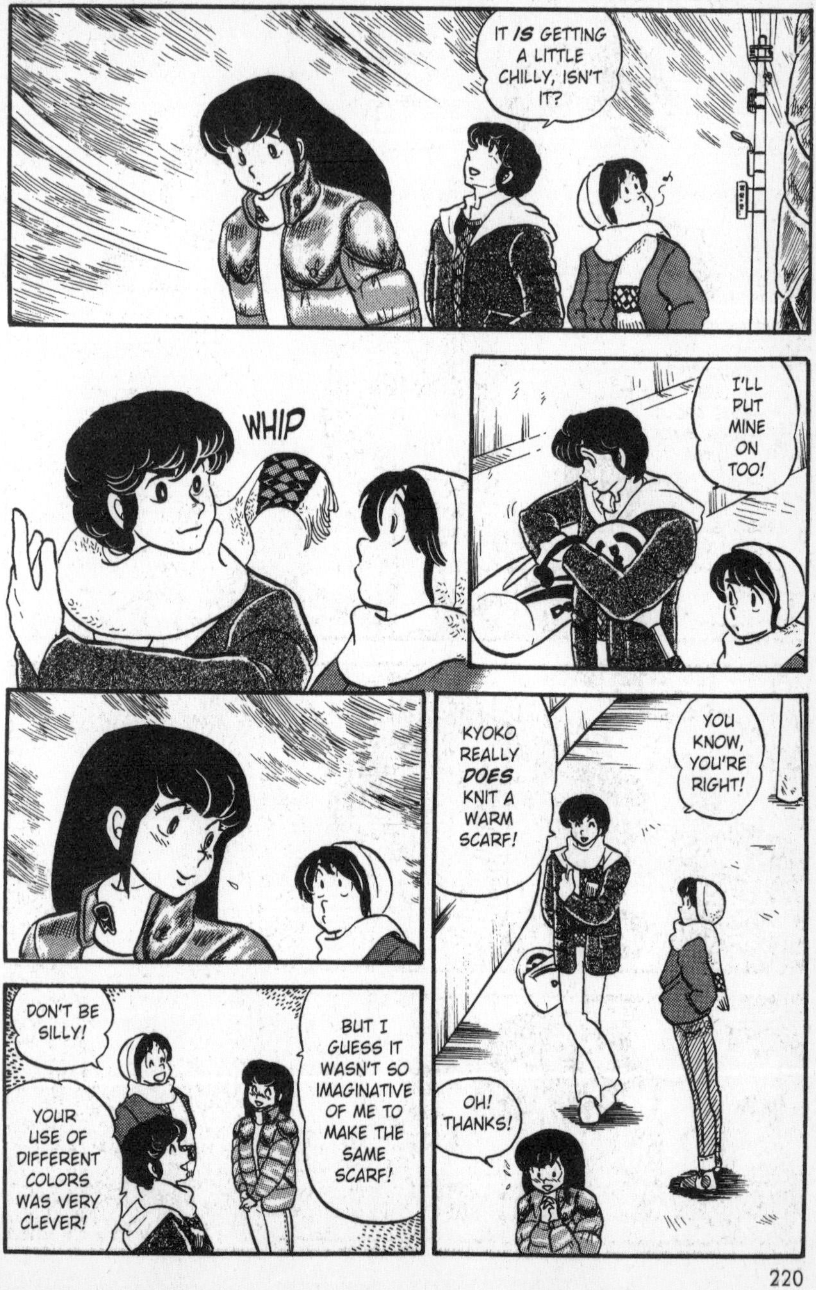
IT *IS* GETTING A LITTLE CHILLY, ISN'T IT?
I'LL PUT MINE ON TOO!
WHIP
YOU KNOW, YOU'RE RIGHT!
KYOKO REALLY **DOES** KNIT A WARM SCARF!
OH! THANKS!
BUT I GUESS IT WASN'T SO IMAGINATIVE OF ME TO MAKE THE SAME SCARF!
DON'T BE SILLY!
YOUR USE OF DIFFERENT COLORS WAS VERY CLEVER!

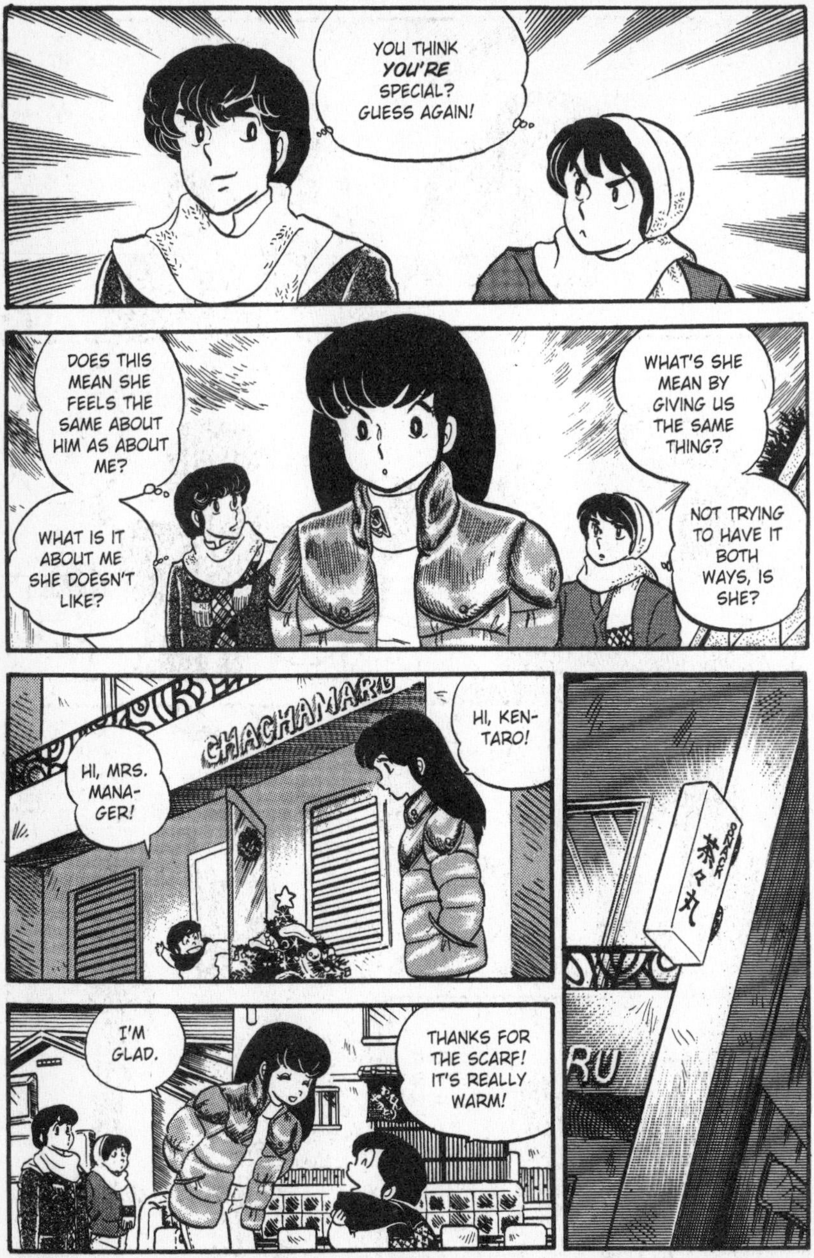
YOU THINK *YOU'RE* SPECIAL? GUESS AGAIN!
WHAT'S SHE MEAN BY GIVING US THE SAME THING?
NOT TRYING TO HAVE IT BOTH WAYS, IS SHE?
DOES THIS MEAN SHE FEELS THE SAME ABOUT HIM AS ABOUT ME?
WHAT IS IT ABOUT ME SHE DOESN'T LIKE?
SNACK
茶々丸
RU
CHACHAMARU
HI, KEN-TARO!
HI, MRS. MANA-GER!
THANKS FOR THE SCARF! IT'S REALLY WARM!
I'M GLAD.

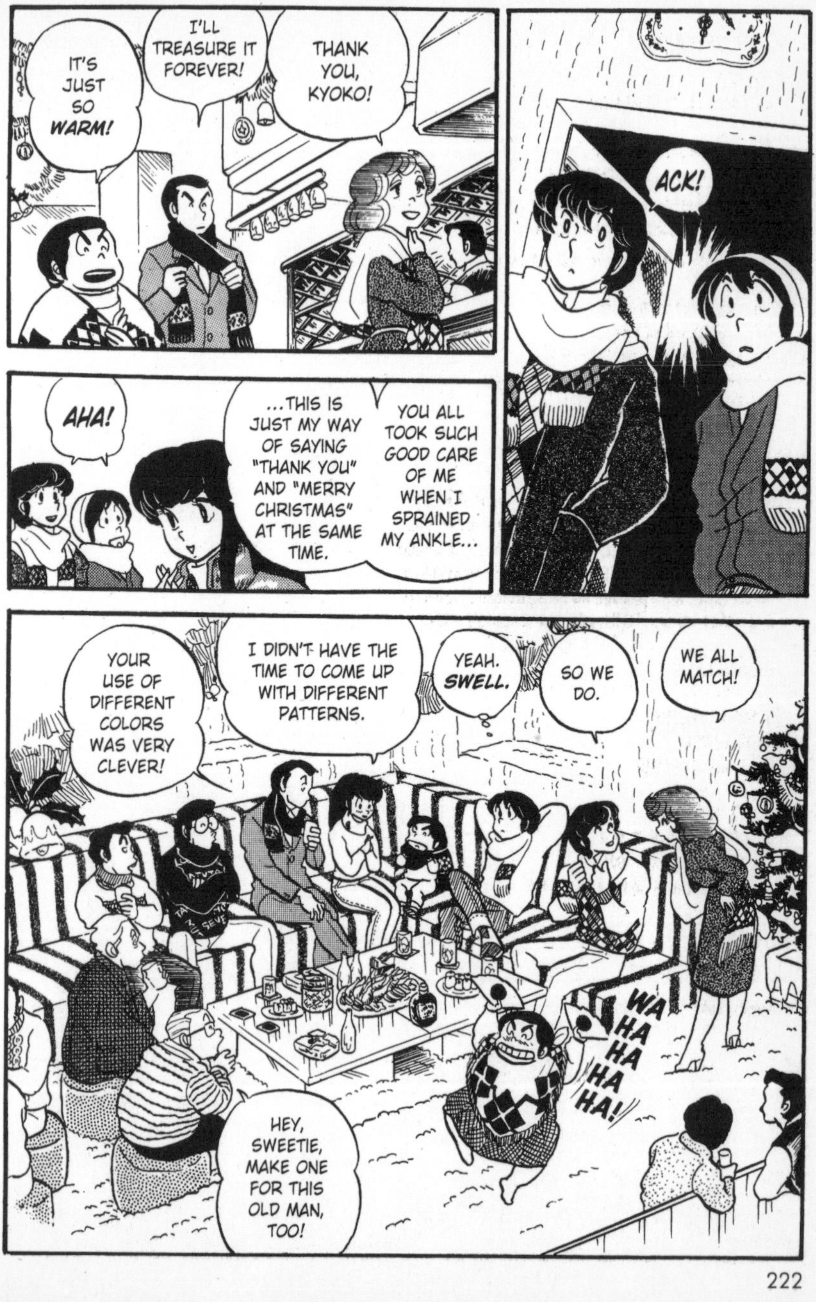
ACK!
THANK YOU, KYOKO!
I'LL TREASURE IT FOREVER!
IT'S JUST SO **WARM!**
YOU ALL TOOK SUCH GOOD CARE OF ME WHEN I SPRAINED MY ANKLE...
...THIS IS JUST MY WAY OF SAYING "THANK YOU" AND "MERRY CHRISTMAS" AT THE SAME TIME.
AHA!
WE ALL MATCH!
SO WE DO.
YEAH. **SWELL.**
I DIDN'T HAVE THE TIME TO COME UP WITH DIFFERENT PATTERNS.
YOUR USE OF DIFFERENT COLORS WAS VERY CLEVER!
WA HA HA HA HA HA!
HEY, SWEETIE, MAKE ONE FOR THIS OLD MAN, TOO!

MAISON IKKOKU

VOLUME 2

Story and Art by Rumiko Takahashi

Translation/Gerard Jones & Matt Thorn
Touch-up & Lettering/Susan Daigle-Leach
Design/Izumi Evers
Editors-1st Edition/Satoru Fujii & Trish Ledoux
Editors-2nd Edition/Elizabeth Kawasaki & Alvin Lu

Managing Editor/Annette Roman
Editor-in-Chief/William Flanagan
Production Manager/Noboru Watanabe
Sr. Director of Licensing & Acquisitions/Rika Inouye
V.P. of Sales & Marketing/Liza Coppola
Sr. V.P. of Editorial/Hyoe Narita
Publisher/Seiji Horibuchi

Printed in Canada

Published by VIZ, LLC
P.O. Box 77010
San Francisco, CA 94107

Editor's Choice Edition
10 9 8 7 6 5 4 3 2 1
First printing, November 2003
First English edition published 1994 & 1995

www.viz.com

ABOUT THE ARTIST

Rumiko Takahashi, born in 1957 in Niigata, Japan, is the acclaimed creator and artist of *Maison Ikkoku, InuYasha*, *Ranma 1/2* and *Lum * Urusei Yatsura*.

She lived in a small student's apartment in Nakano, Japan, which was the basis for the *Maison Ikkoku* series, while she attended the prestigious Nihon Joseidai (Japan Women's University). At the same time, Takahashi also began studying comics at Gekiga Sonjuku, a famous school for manga artists run by Kazuo Koike, author of *Crying Freeman* and *Lone Wolf and Cub*. In 1978, Takahashi won a prize in Shogakukan's annual New Comic Artist Contest and her boy-meets-alien comedy *Lum * Urusei Yatsura* began appearing in the weekly manga magazine *Shonen Sunday*.

Takahashi's success and critical acclaim continues to grow, with popular titles including *Ranma 1/2* and *InuYasha*. Many of her graphic novel series have also been animated, and are widely available in several languages.

EDITOR'S RECOMMENDATIONS

More manga!
More manga!

If you enjoyed this volume of

maison ikkoku

then here's some more manga you might be interested in.

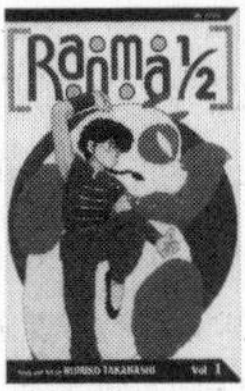
Ranma 1/2
©1988 Rumiko Takahashi/Shogakukan

RANMA 1/2

Rumiko Takahashi's gender-bending comedy series is the tale of a father and son who fall into cursed springs in China, and their lives are transformed, literally. When they get wet, the father turns into a panda and the son, Ranma, turns into a girl. Comic situations ensue as they try and keep their friends and family, especially Ranma's fiancé and her family, from finding out their secret.

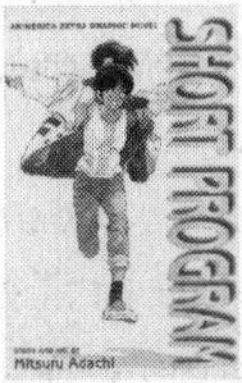
SHORT PROGRAM
©1996 Mitsuru Adachi/Shogakukan

SHORT PROGRAM

Writer/artist Mitsuru Adachi captures the drama, love and heartbreak of real life in his funny, whimsical collection of short stories. His perceptive storytelling and skillful artwork may even make some readers think their own lives have been captured on the pages of this manga.

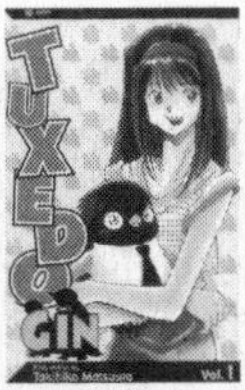
TUXEDO GIN
© 1997 Tokihiko Matsuura/Shogakukan

TUXEDO GIN

In Tokihiko Matsuura's romantic comedy, 17-year-old Ginji Kusanagi meets the girl of his dreams, Minako Sasebo, but is killed in an accident before they go on their first date. Ginji is reincarnated as a penguin, and Minako adopts him as her pet, but she has no idea that he's actually her dearly departed love.

"Takahashi's best gift might be that of characterization...it's no wonder these stories are so universally loved."

Your Favorite Rumiko Takahashi Titles...Now Available From VIZ!

Complete your collection with these Takahashi anime and manga classics!

www.viz.com

Get yours today!